SECOND EDITION

THE EUROPEAN UNION

Politics and Policies

John McCormick
*Indiana University—
Purdue University Indianapolis*

Westview Press
A Member of the Perseus Books Group

Copyright © 1999 by Westview Press, A Member of the Perseus Books Group

Published in 1999 in the United States of America by Westview Press, 5500 Central Avenue, Boulder, Colorado 80301-2877, and in the United Kingdom by Westview Press, 12 Hid's Copse Road, Cumnor Hill, Oxford OX2 9JJ

Library of Congress Cataloging-in-Publication Data
McCormick, John, 1954–
    The European Union : politics / John McCormick.—
2nd ed.
        (p. cm.)—(The new Europe)
    Includes bibliographical references.
    ISBN 0-8133-9032-X (paperback)
    1. European Union.   I. Title.   II. Series: New Europe (Boulder,
Colo.)
JN30.M37   1999
341.242'2—dc21   99-19924
                                                                                      CIP

The paper used in this publication meets the requirements of the American National Standard for Permanence of Paper for Printed Library Materials Z39.48-1984.

10   9   8   7   6   5

Contents

THE EUROPEAN UNION
SECOND EDITION

The New Europe: Interdisciplinary Perspectives

Stanley Hoffmann, Series Editor

The European Union: Politics and Policies,
Second Edition, *John McCormick*

An Imperfect Union: The Maastricht Treaty and
the New Politics of European Integration, *Michael J. Baun*

The European Sisyphus: Essays on Europe,
1964–1994, *Stanley Hoffmann*

France, Germany, and the Western Alliance,
Philip H. Gordon

FORTHCOMING

Integrating Social Europe: The International
Construction of a Democratic Policy, *Wolfgang Streeck*

New Perspectives on European Integration, *Marjorie Lister*

Tables and Illustrations

Figures

Boxes

Maps

Preface and Acknowledgments

The European Union (EU) is the world's newest superpower, a major actor in the global economic system, and the possible foundation of a European political union. Yet for most people it remains a mystery and an enigma. Even Europeans are perplexed: Most will tell pollsters they support the idea of integration yet admit that they don't know exactly how the EU works, or who makes all the decisions, or how the EU has changed their lives. There are several reasons for the confusion.

First, the EU is new and unusual. There has never been anything quite like it before, and it fits few of our conventional ideas about politics and government. Is it an international organization, or is it something more? Has it replaced the individual states of Europe? If it hasn't, how do its powers differ from those of its member states? Do the member states even matter anymore?

Second, much of its work is shrouded in secrecy. European leaders pay lip service to concepts such as "transparency" and "the citizens' Europe," but most of its decisions are still made behind closed doors by unelected officials, and the average European has little direct impact on those decisions.

Third, it keeps changing. Just as we think we've begun to understand it, a new treaty comes along that gives it new powers, or its leaders agree to a new set of goals that give it a different character and appearance. Learning about the governments of the United States and Canada is relatively easy, because their institutions don't change much. But trying to understand the EU means leafing your way through an increasingly messy set of treaties, making sure you have the latest set of amendments, and keeping up with all the latest news from Brussels.

Perhaps the most fundamental cause of the confusion is the dearth of books that provide a clear and accessible guide through the maze. There are shelves full of user-friendly guides to politics and government in the United States, Canada, Britain, and France, but most writing on the EU is mired in a swamp of treaty articles, Eurospeak, and conflicting definitions. Worst sin of all, far too much of it describes one of the most fascinating developments of the last fifty years in terms that make it sound dull, bureaucratic, and legalistic.

I have taught classes on European integration for several years, and I've heard concerns like these from students and colleagues alike; where are the books, they ask, that really *introduce* the politics and policies of the EU in a real, exciting, and approachable way? At a time when the EU is becoming a powerful new actor on the world stage, where can students look for help, for background they can use to understand the EU and better appreciate the points being made in all the more specialized studies of EU institutions and policies?

It was their concerns that prompted this book. It is aimed mainly at upper-division undergraduate students, but I hope it will also help researchers, people in business and government, and anyone who wants to learn more about the EU. Its goal is to help answer four fundamental questions: How and why did the EU evolve, what does it do, how does it work, and what difference does it make? I have not set out to be comprehensive or exhaustive; instead, I have tried to include all the basic factual material and to put that material in context by reviewing the motives and effects of European integration, the significance of the EU for both its member states and the rest of the world (particularly North America), the changes the EU has made in the lives of Europeans, and the long-term implications of the European experiment.

A Note on the Approach.   Unlike almost all the other books on the market, this one is written mainly (but not exclusively) for North Americans and addresses the kinds of questions readers on this side of the Atlantic are likely to have about the EU. For that reason, I have made comparisons between the EU and the structures of government in the United States and Canada. The book follows the same basic model of several other texts by covering the history, institutions, and policies of the EU, but it also includes a chapter on regional integration theory, a chapter that tries to come to grips with the character of the EU, and a chapter that assesses the EU policy process.

The text is broken up with boxes drawing attention to key events, concepts, processes, and institutions. Every chapter begins with an overview and ends with a brief set of conclusions and a brief list of recommended sources of further information that has a bias toward the most recent, readable, and enlightening Anglo-American sources. The book ends with a glossary of key terms, a chronology of events, short descriptions of key institutions, and recommended sources of further information.

A Note on Terminology.   The European Union began life as the European Coal and Steel Community (ECSC), became the European Economic Community in 1958, became more widely known as the "common market" or the "EEC," and by the 1980s was generally known simply as the "EC" or the "Community." The European Community still exists as one of three "pillars" of the European Union, so although it is still correct to use the term European Community in describing the Community itself, the broader process of European integration falls under the label European Union. I have used the latter everywhere except where I am writing about activities specific either to the ECSC or the EEC.

For convenience, figures in euros have also been converted into U.S. dollars at a rate of $1.20 to the euro.

Treaty article numbers do not reflect the changes made by the Treaty of Amsterdam, which had not yet gone into force as this book went to press.

A Note on the Second Edition. It was gratifying to see how widely the first edition was used both for graduate and undergraduate classes in North America and even in Europe, and I was delighted to agree to the suggestion from Westview for a second edition. It has the same basic structure, but the history in Part 1 has been fine-tuned, and Chapter 4 has been rewritten to incorporate developments since 1996. Part 2 has been thoroughly revised to account for developments since 1996, particularly in light of changes to the institutions brought by the Treaty of Amsterdam. In Part 3, all five chapters have been completely overhauled to include all the latest developments in the different policy areas. In addition, several of the boxes have been replaced, all the figures and tables have been updated, the glossary has been expanded, and new titles have been added to the lists of Further Reading.

The biggest influence on this book has come from the students in my European integration classes at Indiana University–Purdue University Indianapolis, so I want to thank them for being the unwitting test audience for the structure and content of the book; it was written—above all—for people like them. My thanks also to the anonymous reviewers drafted by Westview to comment on the first edition, and to Jeanie Bukowski, Eleanor Zeff, and Maria Chan Morgan, all of whom have used the book in their own classes and gave me valuable feedback as I was working on the second edition. And thanks to Stephen Heathorn for his help with the finer points of government and politics in Canada.

For the time they gave to help search for documents, my thanks to the staffs at the European Commission and the European Parliament in Brussels and Strasbourg, and the staff of the EU Depository Library at Indiana University in Bloomington. For their help and their suggestions on drafts of the first edition, I would like to thank Stanley Hoffmann, Andrew Moravcsik of Harvard University, and Andrew Appleton of Washington State University. The editing and production team at Westview Press—notably Rob Williams, Michelle Trader, Jon Taylor Howard, and Betty Taylor—did an excellent job on this second edition. Finally, and most importantly, my thanks and love to my wife, Leanne, who has been a help in every possible way.

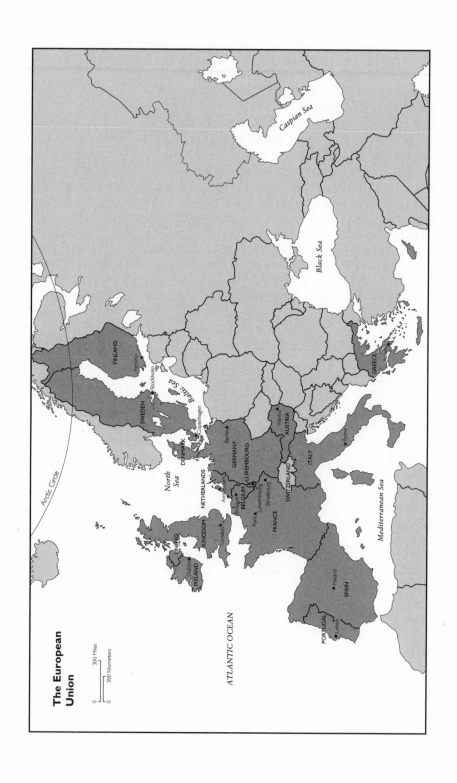

The European Union

300 Miles

300 Kilometers

ATLANTIC OCEAN

Arctic Circle

IRELAND
Dublin

UNITED
KINGDOM
London ★

PORTUGAL
Lisbon ★

SPAIN
★ Madrid

FINLAND
Helsinki

SWEDEN
Stockholm

DENMARK
Copenhagen

North
Sea

Baltic Sea

NETHERLANDS
Amsterdam ★

BELGIUM
Brussels ★

LUXEMBOURG
Luxembourg ★

GERMANY
Berlin ★

FRANCE
Paris ★

SWITZERLAND

Strasbourg

AUSTRIA
Vienna ★

ITALY
Rome ★

GREECE

Mediterranean Sea

Black Sea

Caspian Sea

Introduction

The sovereign nations of the past can no longer solve the problems of the present.

I am certain that the passing seasons will lead us inevitably towards greater unity; and if we fail to organize it for ourselves, democratically, it will be thrust upon us by blind force.

—*Jean Monnet*, Memoirs

The arrival of the European Union will go down in history as one of the defining events of the twentieth century. It has changed the political, economic, and social landscapes of Western Europe, changed the balance of power in the world by helping Europeans reassert themselves on the world stage, and helped to bring to the region the longest uninterrupted spell of peace in its recorded history. Western Europe begins the new millennium with a new identity, and though its governments and people still may not always agree with each other, they have set aside the kind of hostility that has led so often in the past to war.

The idea of European union is not new. Many have argued in favor of setting aside national differences in the collective interest over the centuries, sometimes in the interests of building peace and prosperity but sometimes for narrower reasons. The first serious thoughts about a peaceful and voluntary union came after the horrors of World War I, but the concept really matured following the devastation of World War II. The most serious Europeanists wanted a body that would replace national governments and become something like a European federation. They began talking about pulling down tariffs between states and eventually removing frontiers, driven by the desire to promote peace (especially between France and Germany) and to build a new market that could compete with the United States.

Despite the lingering doubts of the Euroskeptics, the idea of European unity has developed an irresistible momentum. The European Union now has its own institutions and body of laws, it has 15 member states and 373

1

million citizens, the national economies of Western Europe have grown and become more closely integrated, and it is now less realistic to think of Western European states in isolation but to think of them more as elements in a growing European Union. Many problems, obstacles, and doubts remain, but—if current trends continue—political union of some kind is inevitable, and Europe will play an entirely new role in the world.

This is a book about the European Union: about its history, its structure, its policies, and its changing relationship with the rest of the world. It is divided into three parts.

Part 1 looks at the history and the character of European integration. The process began in 1951 with the signing of the Treaty of Paris, which created the European Coal and Steel Community (ECSC) in 1952. This was a limited economic association involving France, West Germany, Italy, Belgium, the Netherlands, and Luxembourg. Its job was to coordinate the production and distribution of coal and steel, eliminate duplication of effort, and improve the efficiency of European industry.

The process went a step further in 1957 with the Treaty of Rome, which created the European Economic Community (EEC) and the European Atomic Energy Community (Euratom) in 1958. With the same six members as the ECSC, the EEC set out to build an integrated multinational economy among its members, achieve a customs union within twelve years, encourage free trade, and harmonize standards, laws, and prices among its members. Its member states witnessed greater productivity, channeled new investment into industry and agriculture, and became more competitive in the world market.

By the late 1960s, the European Community had all the trappings of a new level of government. It had its own executive and bureaucracy (the European Commission), its own protolegislature (the European Parliament), its own judiciary (the Court of Justice), and its own set of laws. Its successes drew new applicants, starting with Britain, Denmark, and Ireland, which joined in 1973. A second round of expansion came with the accession of Greece in 1981 and of Spain and Portugal in 1986. A third round came in 1990 with the integration of East Germany and in 1995 with the accession of Austria, Sweden, and Finland.

Further boosts to integration came with the first substantial changes to the founding treaties. In 1987, the Single European Act led to the elimination of all remaining barriers to the movement of people, goods, money, and services among the twelve member states. It was now possible for residents of the member states to travel and live almost anywhere in the Community. In 1993, the Maastricht Treaty on European Union committed the EC to the creation of a single currency, a common citizenship, and a common foreign and security policy and gave new powers over law and policy to the EC institutions. It also made the EC part of a broader new entity called the European Union. In 1998, the Treaty of Amsterdam built on these changes, fine-tuned the powers of the institutions, and helped prepare the EU for new members from Eastern Europe.

The EU now has its own flag, a circle of twelve gold stars on a blue background. It also has its own anthem, the "Ode to Joy" from Beethoven's Ninth Symphony. National passports have been replaced with a uniform EU passport, and in many ways Brussels has become the new capital of Europe. The European Union enters the opening years of the twenty-first century as the largest economic bloc in the world, accounting for 37 percent of global exports and 28 percent of global gross national product (GNP). It is also in the process of replacing most of its national currencies with a new common currency, the euro, which promises to take its place alongside the U.S. dollar and the Japanese yen as one of the world's most important currencies.

Part 2 looks at the institutions of the European Union and describes how they work and how they relate to each other. The development of the EU has some similarities to the evolution of the United States, which set out as a group of separate colonies that came together first under a confederation and then in 1789 became a federation. Skeptics doubted that the union would work, and the framing of the U.S. Constitution was surrounded by concerns over the balance of powers between the states and the federal government. The American experiment succeeded, though, and a workable balance was achieved between state and federal powers. The European Union is not yet a political federation or even a confederation, but it has created a set of institutions with powers and authority that have grown steadily since the 1950s, changing the balance of power in Western Europe.

There are five main institutions:

The European Commission.   Based in Brussels, this is the executive and administrative branch of the EU, responsible for initiating the development of new EU laws and policies and for overseeing their implementation.

The Council of Ministers.   Also based in Brussels, this is the major decisionmaking body of the EU and has been the real center of political power to date. Working with Parliament, the Council takes the votes that turn Commission proposals into law.

The European Parliament.   Split among Strasbourg, Luxembourg, and Brussels, the European Parliament represents the people of the EU; since 1979, it has been directly elected to five-year terms by the voters of the member states. Although it cannot introduce or pass new laws, it is slowly winning the powers of a conventional legislature.

The Court of Justice. Based in Luxembourg, the fifteen-member court interprets EU law and helps build a common body of law that is uniformly applied throughout the member states. It bases its decisions mainly on the treaties of Paris and Rome, the Single European Act, and the Maastricht and Amsterdam Treaties.

The European Council. This is less a physical institution than a forum, consisting of the individual heads of government of the EU member states. The Council meets at least once every six months and makes broad decisions on policy, the details of which are worked out by the European Commission and the Council of Ministers.

As the powers and reach of the EU have grown, new institutions have been created to deal with more specialized issues, such as monetary policy, regional development, environmental protection, and the control of international crime. These are described in Chapter 10.

Part 3 focuses on the policies pursued by the European Union, looking at what integration has meant for the member states and for Europeans themselves. Focusing on economic, agricultural, regional, environmental, social, foreign, and security policies, this section examines the EU policymaking process, identifies the key influences on that process, and looks at the consequences and implications of EU policy.

Because European integration is still a work in progress, the relative balance of power among national governments and EU institutions is still evolving. That balance will continue to change as more countries join the EU and as integration reaches further into the lives of Europeans. Why should North Americans care about all this, and what impact will these changes have on our lives?

The Changes Have Economic Implications. The EU and North America do about 25 percent of their trade with each other; the EU is the market for about 20 percent of U.S. and Canadian exports and is the source of about 19 percent of U.S. and Canadian imports. Foreign direct investment from the EU accounts for over one-third of all such investment in the United States, most of it coming from Britain, the Netherlands, and Germany. Subsidiaries of European companies employ over 3 million Americans— more than the affiliates of all other countries combined—and account for about 7 percent of all manufacturing jobs in the United States and Canada. U.S. corporations, meanwhile, have made their biggest overseas investments in the EU.

As barriers to internal trade in the EU have fallen, the number of cross-border corporate mergers in Europe has grown, and so have the European consumer market and European corporate power, all of which means more competition for U.S. and Canadian corporations. The new reach of corporate Europe is exemplified by the 1998 merger between Daimler-Benz and Chrysler, by the growth of Airbus Industrie, which has captured 30 percent of the world market for large commercial airliners, and by the success of Arianespace, which has won over half of the market for commercial satellite launches.

The Changes Have Security Implications.   The United States, long used to shaping its foreign policy more or less to its liking, is increasingly having to respond to the demands of a newly resurgent Europe (particularly on trade issues) and to amend its foreign policy to fit Europe's needs and priorities. As the balance of power in the world enters a new era of fluidity and uncertainty, the rise of the European Union as an economic superpower could mean its eventual emergence as a military superpower. The EU still relies on the United States for its defense, lacks a unified military, and is working on developing coordinated foreign policies, but the relative balance of power between the two sides is changing, something North American policymakers cannot afford to ignore.

There Is Much We Could Learn from the European Experiment.   As barriers to global trade come down under the auspices of the World Trade Organization (WTO), the idea of regional economic integration is winning more adherents (and more enemies). The global economy is already here, and the world may be moving toward a future in which economics and politics will revolve around several major economic blocs, rather than around the nearly two hundred separate nation-states we have today. Americans, Canadians, and Mexicans have much to learn from the European experience as they build a North American free trade area of their own.

In short, we cannot ignore the European Union, nor can we understand the world today without understanding how the EU has altered the balance of global power. The process of global political and economic change is accelerating, and the problems and possibilities of the European experiment could be a forerunner of the other regional blocs into which the world may be divided by the middle of the twenty-first century.

Part One

Evolution

1

Introduction to Regional Integration

The state has dominated modern studies of world politics. Usually defined as a community of individuals living under the jurisdiction of a common government within recognized frontiers and adhering to a common body of law, the state has long been the major actor in the global system. For decades, students of international relations have devoted their time and energy to the study of alliances, spheres of influence, changing patterns of cooperation and conflict, and fluctuations in the balance of power between and among states. However, the state is not the only kind of political community, or even necessarily the best. Many political scientists in fact argue that the modern state system is declining, undermined by challenges to its value and questions about its utility.

The most serious such challenges came during the first half of the twentieth century with two devastating world wars, each of which brought radical shifts in attitudes toward the relationship among states, and each of which led to renewed debate about the dangers of nationalism and the constant threat of war that seemed to hang over the state system. The growing pressures and desires to build peace through cooperation rather than competition among states reached a new level of intensity after World War II, but plans to build a new cooperative world order were disrupted first by the cold war and then by the emergence of an increasingly demanding and influential bloc of Asian, Latin American, and African states.

For many, the cold war exemplified all the doubts about the value of the modern state, which was forged out of conflict and seemed unable to guarantee the safety of its citizens except through a balance of terror with other states. Many theorists asked whether the modern state could ever promote the pursuit of happiness, given its emphasis on narrow nationalism and its potential for misunderstanding, conflict, and violence (prompted in part by the fact that states so rarely coincide with nations). These doubts encouraged widening support for the idea of peace and prosperity through international cooperation, collective security, and globalism. The search for these goals took many different forms, the most obvious of which was an explosion in the number of international organizations, spearheaded by the creation of the United Nations in 1945.

The search for peace has been expressed most dramatically in experiments in regional integration. The European Union is only one such experiment, but it has evolved the furthest and brought the greatest changes for its citizens and governments. Regional integration has also been attempted in Latin America, the Caribbean, Southeast Asia, western, eastern, and southern Africa, and—since 1989—in North America, but on a more modest scale (see Appendix II). The European Union could provide a model that might eventually lead to the breakdown of the state system as we know it and to its replacement with a new community of political and economic units and networks. However, we are still far from fully understanding its internal dynamics. In an attempt to provide some answers, this chapter surveys the major theories of integration and describes and assesses competing ideas about how the EU has evolved and what it has become.

International Organizations

The European Union is an international organization in the sense that its constituent members are nation-states, but it has moved well beyond conventional ideas about international cooperation. Most of the standard definitions of an international organization (IO) describe a body that promotes voluntary cooperation and coordination between or among its members but has neither autonomous powers nor the authority to impose its rulings on its members. The development of IOs has been mainly a twentieth-century phenomenon: In 1914, the world had just 220 IOs; today there are about 38,000.[1] Different kinds of IOs have developed for different reasons, and they have different structures, methods, and goals. Most fit broadly into one of two main categories:

Intergovernmental organizations (IGOs) consist of representatives of national governments and promote voluntary cooperation among those governments. IGOs have little or no autonomy in decisionmaking and little or no coercive power over their members. Examples include the United Nations, the Organization of American States, and NATO.

International nongovernmental organizations (INGOs) are made up of individuals or representatives of national nongovernmental organizations. They include multinational corporations, such as Coca-Cola and General

Motors, but most are interest groups that cooperate to pursue the collective goals of their members or to bring pressure on governments for policy change. Examples include the International Red Cross and Amnesty International.

In scope, IOs can be regional, universal, specialized, or multipurpose. In structural terms, they can involve cooperation (working together on policy without making major commitments or structural changes), association (reaching a formal agreement that might bring structural changes), or harmonization (making adjustments to policies to bring them into alignment). Their work rarely involves the surrender of significant sovereignty or independence by members (although no state has ever been truly independent because none has ever been wholly self-sufficient). However, if cooperation does lead to the surrender of sovereignty, we begin to move into the realm of supranationalism, a process of cooperation that results in a shift of authority (and perhaps of sovereignty) to a new level of organization that is autonomous, that is above the state, and that has powers of coercion that are independent of the state.

Structurally, supranationalism can take at least three different forms:

1. *Confederalism* is a structure in which the participants give up few powers to the "governing" body. Most INGOs, for example, work on a confederal basis, their members using the governing body to help them coordinate activities and to represent them in dealings with other bodies—but keeping a large measure of control over their own affairs. From 1776 to 1789 the United States was a confederal system, as was Switzerland until 1798 and Germany from 1815 to 1866. The European Union has many confederalist features, because the governments of the member states have worked hard to make sure they keep control over the key decisionmaking processes.
2. *Consociationalism* is a system sometimes proposed for societies with deep social, cultural, religious, racial, or linguistic divisions. It involves government by a coalition representing the different groups in that society. As much decisionmaking as possible is delegated to the groups, power and resources are divided in proportion to the size of each group, and minorities may be deliberately overrepresented and protected by the power of veto. Smaller European states such as Belgium, Switzerland, Austria, the Netherlands, and Luxembourg have used elements of consociationalism at some time during the twentieth century.
3. *Federalism* is a structure in which the participants give up overall sovereignty to a governing body but retain many independent powers. The United States, for example, is a federation, but it only became such in 1789, when the original thirteen colonies agreed to

move from a confederal relationship (based on the Articles of Confederation) to a federal union (based on the U.S. Constitution and the Bill of Rights), voluntarily giving up power over areas such as common security but retaining their own sets of laws and a large measure of autonomy over local government (raising their own taxes, for example, and keeping powers over education, the police, and roads).

The most enthusiastic European integrationists would like to see a federal United States of Europe in which the current national governments would become little more than local governments, with the same kinds of powers as state governments in the United States and provincial governments in Canada. Before this could happen, though, there would have to be—at the very least—a common European foreign and defense policy, a European military, European citizenship, and a single European currency, and there would have to be a European government with substantial powers over the making of domestic policy.

Theories of Integration

Standard theories of political integration argue that people and states create alliances and common political units for one of three reasons: They may be forced together by a Napoleon or a Hitler; they may share common values and goals and reach agreement on how to govern themselves as a whole; or they may come together out of a need for security in the face of a common external threat. A fourth possible reason is convenience or efficiency: People and states may decide that they can promote economic development and improve their quality of life more quickly and effectively by working together rather than separately.

Politics in Western Europe was long influenced and driven by the first three motives, but a shift to the fourth since 1945 has encouraged Europeans to develop the largest experiment in voluntary integration the world has ever seen. At least until the late 1970s, the focus was on integration in the interest of economic development: Barriers to trade were pulled down, national monetary and fiscal policies were harmonized, and the free movement of people, goods, money, and services was promoted—all in the hope of contributing to new levels of prosperity. The supporters of economic integration never saw such integration as an end in itself, however; as the EU member states built closer economic ties, some of their leaders flirted increasingly with ideas about political cooperation. Which came first is debatable; as Ernst Haas has argued, economic integration "may be based on political motives and frequently begets political consequences."[2]

In *The Uniting of Europe,* his groundbreaking 1958 study of the European Coal and Steel Community (ECSC), Haas defined political integration as "the process whereby political actors in several distinct national settings are persuaded to shift their loyalties, expectations and political activities toward a new center, whose institutions possess or demand jurisdiction over the pre-existing national states."[3] In his 1963 study of the European Economic Community (EEC), Leon Lindberg defined political integration as the process by which (1) nations forego the desire and ability to conduct foreign and key domestic policies independently of each other, instead making joint decisions or delegating the decisionmaking process to new central organs, and (2) political actors such as policymakers, bureaucrats, legislators, and interest groups shift their political activities to a new center.[4]

The evolution of the European Union has been characterized by at least two major sets of conflicting views about the nature of integration.

The first is *realism* versus *functionalism.* Attempts to explain the mechanics of European integration usually fall into one of two major schools of thought (see Table 1.1). Realists argue that states are the most important actors in international relations, that domestic policy can be clearly separated from foreign policy, and that rational self-interest and conflicting national objectives lead states to protect their interests relative to other states. Realists talk about an anarchic global system in which states use both conflict and cooperation to ensure their security through a balance of power among states. They see the EU as a gathering of sovereign states in which powers have been given to the EU institutions only as it suits the member states, which retain the right to take back those powers at any time. In short, the EU exists only because the member states have decided that it serves their best interests. Realism dominated the study of international relations from the 1940s to the 1960s and was taken a stage further in the 1970s and 1980s by neorealists who argued that the structure of institutions mattered more than their intentions. For example, neorealists have studied the changing power of states and the effect of such change on international relations.

A contrasting approach is offered by functionalists. While realists talk about competition and conflict, functionalists move from self-interest toward the common interests of states in cooperation. They argue that integration is a process that has its own internal dynamic and that if states cooperate in certain limited areas and create new bodies to oversee that cooperation, then they will cooperate in other areas through a kind of "invisible hand" of integration. In short, functionalists argue that European integration has its own logic, which the EU member states find hard to resist; although membership involves contracts that could theoretically be broken, in reality they have an almost irresistible authority, and integration

TABLE 1.1   Realism and Functionalism Compared

	Realism	*Functionalism*
Dominant goals of actors	Military security	Peace and prosperity
Instruments of state policy	Military force and economic instruments	Economic instruments and political acts of will
Forces behind agenda formation	Potential shifts in the balance of power and security threats	Mutual convenience and the expansive logic of sector integration
Policy issues	Emphasis on high politics, such as security and defense	Initial emphasis on low politics, such as economic and social issues
Role of international organizations	Minor; limited by state power and the importance of military force	Substantial; new, functional IOs will formulate policy and become increasingly responsible for implementation

Source: Adapted and expanded from a similar table in Robert O. Keohane and Joseph S. Nye, *Power and Interdependence: World Politics in Transition,* 2d ed. (Boston: Little, Brown, 1989).

has become so much a part of the fabric of Western European society that secession would cost a state far more than continued integration.

The second view about integration is *intergovernmentalism* versus *supranationalism*. Debates have long raged about whether the EU is an organization controlled by governments working with each other as partners or whether it has developed its own authority and autonomy. At the heart of this debate has been the issue of how much power and sovereignty can or should be transferred by national governments to bodies such as the European Commission and the European Parliament. Britons and Danes (and even the French at times) have balked at federalist or supranationalist tendencies, while Belgians and Luxembourgers have been more willing to transfer sovereignty.

Some political scientists have questioned the assumption that intergovernmentalism and supranationalism are the two extremes on a continuum,[5] that they are a zero-sum game (one balances or cancels out the other), that supranationalism involves the loss of sovereignty, or that the EU and its member states act autonomously of each other. David Mitrany, for example, argues that governments cooperate out of need and that this is "not a matter of surrendering sovereignty, but merely of pooling as much of it as may be needed for the joint performance of the particular task."[6] Robert Keohane and Stanley Hoffmann agree, arguing that the EU is "an experiment in pooling sovereignty, not in transferring it from states to supranational institutions."[7]

Leon Lindberg and Stuart Scheingold argue that it is wrong to assume that "each gain in capability at the European level necessarily implies a loss of capability at the national level"; they believe the relationship between the EU and its member states is more symbiotic than competitive.[8] Ernst Haas argues that supranationalism does not mean EU institutions exercise authority over national governments but that it is a process or a style of decisionmaking in which "the participants refrain from unconditionally vetoing proposals and instead seek to attain agreement by means of compromises upgrading common interests."[9]

Explaining European Integration

Functionalism has dominated the theoretical debates about how the EU has evolved since the 1950s. Jean Monnet and Robert Schuman (the two people most often described as the founders of the European Union) were functionalists in the sense that they opted for integrating a specific area—the coal and steel industry—with the hope that this would encourage integration in other areas. As Schuman put it, "Europe will not be made all at once or according to a single plan. It will be built through concrete achievements which first create a *de facto* solidarity."[10] Although some federalists have argued that "the worst way to cross a chasm is by little steps,"[11] functionalism is based on the idea of bridging the gaps between states incrementally by building functionally specific organizations. So instead of trying to coordinate major issues such as economic or defense policy, for example, functionalists believe they can "sneak up on peace"[12] by promoting integration in relatively noncontroversial areas such as postal services or a particular sector of industry or by harmonizing technical issues such as weights and measures.

Among the best-known exponents of this idea was David Mitrany, the Romanian-born British social scientist who defined the functional approach as an attempt to link "authority to a specific activity, to break away from the traditional link between authority and a definite territory."[13] Mitrany felt peace could not be achieved by regional unification, because this would replace international tensions with interregional tensions, or by world government, which would threaten human freedom. Writing in wartime London in 1943, he argued instead that separate international bodies should be organized, with authority in functionally specific fields, such as security, transport, and communication. They should be executive bodies with autonomous tasks and powers and should perform some of the same jobs as national governments, only at a different level. This focus on particular functions, he argued, would encourage international cooperation more quickly and effectively than grand gestures. The dimensions and structures of these international organizations would not have to be predetermined but instead would be self-determined.[14]

Once these functional organizations were created, Mitrany argued, they would find themselves having to work with each other. Rail, road, and air agencies would need technical coordination (on timetables, for example) and functional coordination (to deal with differences in densities of passenger and freight traffic, for example). Different groups of functional agencies might then have to work together, which would lead to coordinated international planning. This would result less in the creation of a new system than in the rationalization of existing systems through a process of natural selection and evolution. States could join or leave, drop out of some functions and stay in others, or try their own political and social experiments; in short, they would be allowed to share power only if they also shared responsibility. This could lead eventually to "a rounded political system . . . the functional arrangements might indeed be regarded as organic elements of federalism by installments."[15]

The study by Haas of the ECSC in 1958 and by Lindberg of the EEC in 1963 led to an amendment and a revival of Mitrany's theories as neofunctionalism. This theory argues that certain prerequisites are needed before integration can proceed, including public opinion that is less nationalistic and more supportive of cooperation, a desire by elites to promote integration for pragmatic rather than altruistic reasons, and the delegation of real power to a new supranational authority. Once these changes have occurred, there will be an expansion of integration caused by "spillover," described by Joseph Nye as a phenomenon in which "imbalances created by the functional interdependence or inherent linkages of tasks can press political actors to redefine their common tasks."[16] In other words, joint action in one area will create new needs, tensions, and problems that will increase the pressure to take joint action in another. For example, the free movement of people will only work if there is police cooperation, free movement of pensions, comparable working conditions, no restrictions on the movement of capital, mutual recognition of educational qualifications, and so on.

Neofunctionalist ideas include the notion of an "expansive logic of sector integration" that Haas saw as being inherent in the ECSC.[17] The ECSC was created partly to achieve short-term goals, such as a desire to encourage Franco-German cooperation, but EU "founders" Monnet and Schuman also saw it as the first step in a process that would lead to political integration.[18] Haas argued that the process of spillover was not automatic and found that initially very few people strongly supported the ECSC idea. Once it had been working for a few years, however, labor unions and political parties became more enthusiastic because they began to see its benefits, and the pressure grew for integration in other sectors. Derek Urwin noted that the sectoral approach of the ECSC was handicapped because it "was still trying to integrate only one part of complex industrial economies, and could not possibly pursue its aims in isolation from other economic segments."[19] This was part of the reason that only six years after the creation of the ECSC, agreement was reached among its members to achieve broader economic integration with the EEC.

Spillover is such an ambiguous term that it needs to be broken down into more specific subcategories, of which there are at least three:

Functional spillover implies that if states integrate one sector of their economies (for example), the impossibility of isolating one economic sector from another will lead to the integration of other sectors.[20] The logical conclusion is that so many functional IGOs would have to be created to oversee this process, and so many bridges would have to be built across the chasm between states, that the relative power of national government institutions would decline and the chasm would no longer exist. Eventually, complete economic and political union would be achieved (see Box 1.1).

Technical spillover implies that disparities in standards will lead different states to rise (or sink) to the level of the state with the tightest (or loosest) regulations. For example, although the poorer EU states (such as Greece and Portugal) may argue that environmental controls amount to a handicap on their economic development, making it more difficult for them to catch up to their wealthier partners, the EU decisionmaking process still encourages the states with the strongest environmental laws (such as Germany and Sweden) to accelerate the adoption of tighter controls by the poorer states.

Political spillover is based on the argument that once different functional sectors become integrated then interest groups (such as corporate lobbies and labor unions) will increasingly switch from trying to influence national governments to trying to influence the new regional institutions (which would encourage them in an attempt to win new powers for themselves). Those groups would appreciate the benefits of integration and would act as a barrier to a retreat from integration, and politics would increasingly be played out at the regional rather than the national level.[21]

Neofunctionalist ideas dominated studies of European integration during the 1950s and 1960s but briefly fell out of favor during the 1970s, which Haas explained by arguing that they lacked strong predictive capacities.[22] However, there were additional problems. First, the process of integrating Europe seemed to have ground to a halt in the mid-1970s, undermined in part by the failure of the Commission to provide the kind of leadership that was vital to the idea of neofunctionalism. The prevailing sense of despondency comes through clearly in a 1975 European Commission report on economic and monetary union, which complained that experience had done nothing to support the validity of the functional argument that unity would "come about in an almost imperceptible way" and that what was needed was "a radical and almost instantaneous transformation."[23]

BOX 1.1
Stages in the Process of Regional Integration

Economic integration can take several forms, representing varying degrees of integration, but if a logical progression could be outlined along functionalist lines, it might look something like this:

1. Two or more states create a free trade area by eliminating internal barriers to trade (such as tariffs and border restrictions) while keeping their own external tariffs against nonmember states.
2. The growth of internal free trade increases the pressure on the member states to agree to a common external tariff, otherwise all the goods coming in to the free trade area from abroad would come through the country with the lowest tariffs. Agreement on a common external tariff creates a customs union.
3. The removal of internal trading barriers expands the size of the market available to agriculture, industry, and services, so these sectors want to expand their operations to other members of the customs union. This increases investment in those countries and increases the demand for the reduction or removal of barriers to the movement of capital and labor, creating a common market (or a single market).
4. With citizens moving more freely among the member states of the common market, pressure grows for coordinated policies on education, retraining schemes, unemployment benefits, pensions, health care, and other services. This increases the demand for coordinated interest rates, stable exchange rates, common policies on inflation, and ultimately a single currency, thereby creating an economic union.
5. The demands of economic integration lead to growing political integration as the governments of the member states work more closely and more frequently together. The pressure grows for common policies in almost every other sector, including foreign and defense policy, possibly leading to political union.

While NAFTA is still in the first stage of this process, the EU has reached the fourth stage, and some of its leaders are already looking hopefully at the fifth stage.

The second problem was that the theory of spillover needed more elaboration. The most common criticisms of neofunctionalism were that it was too linear, that it needed to be expanded or modified to accommodate different pressures for integration, and that it needed to be seen in conjunction with other influences. Ten years after the original publication of *The Uniting of Europe*, for example, Ernst Haas was arguing in a new edition of the book that functional theory had paid too little attention to (1) changes in attitude following the creation of a body like the ECSC, (2) the impact of nationalism on integration, (3) the influence of external events, including changes in economic and military threats from outside, and (4) social and political changes taking place separately from the process of integration.[24] He later wrote about "fragmented issue linkage," which he felt took place "when older objectives are questioned, when new objectives clamor for satisfaction, and when the rationality accepted as adequate in the past ceases to be a legitimate guide to future action."[25]

Several new variations on the theme of spillover were described in 1971 by Philippe Schmitter:

Spillaround is an increase in the scope of the functions carried out by an IO without a corresponding increase in authority or power. For example, governments of the EU member states have allowed the European Commission to become involved in new policy areas but have tried to prevent it from winning too much power by limiting the size of the EU budget. Spillaround involves an increase in the breadth but not the depth of authority.

Buildup is an increase in the authority or power of an IO (depth) without a corresponding increase in the number of areas in which the IO is involved (breadth). Joseph Nye wrote about "rising transactions" (or a growing workload), which "need not lead to a significant widening of the scope (range of tasks) of integration, but to intensifying of the central institutional capacity to handle a particular task."[26] This, for example, would explain why the growing workload of the European Court of Justice led to the creation in 1989 of a subsidiary Court of First Instance to deal with less important cases (see Chapter 9).

Retrenchment is an increase in the level of joint arbitration between or among member states at the expense of the power and authority of the IO. This has happened at times of crisis in the EU, such as when member states pulled out of attempts to build exchange rate stability during the 1970s and the early 1990s as a prelude to establishing a single currency (see Chapter 4).

Spillback is a reduction in both the breadth and depth of the authority of an IO.[27] This has yet to happen in the case of the EU as a whole, although the powers of the European Commission over policy initiation have declined in relative terms as those of the European Parliament and the European Council have grown.

Joseph Nye added a new dimension to neofunctionalist ideas in 1971 by taking them out of the European context and looking at non-Western experiences as well. He concluded that experiments in regional integration involved an integrative potential that depended on several different conditions:

- The economic equality or compatibility of the states involved (which is partly why questions have long been raised about the wisdom of allowing poorer Southern and Eastern European states to join the EU). At the same time, differences in the size and wealth of the member states may be less important than the presence of a central motive force that helps bring them together. For the EU, that force has at times been the tension between France and Germany (see Chapter 3), at other times the economic dominance of Germany.

- The extent to which elite groups that control economic policy in the member states think alike and hold the same values. For example, the election of left-wing governments in Italy, France, Britain, and Germany during 1995–1998 was widely interpreted as a sign that there might be greater cooperation as eleven states prepared for the single currency.

- The extent of interest group activity, or pluralism. Such groups play a key role in promoting integration if they see it as being in their interests; the growth in interest group activity at the European level in recent years suggests that many corporate and public interest groups see Brussels as a new and important focus for lobbying.

- The capacity of the member states to adapt and respond to public demands (which depends in turn on the levels of domestic stability and the capacity—or desire—of decisionmakers to respond).[28]

On almost all of these counts, the EU has a relatively high integrative potential, in contrast to another key experiment in regional cooperation, the North American Free Trade Agreement (NAFTA) (see Box 1.2). The United States and Canada may be strong motive forces for integration, but they are much wealthier than Mexico in both per capita and absolute terms. Elite groups in Mexico are more strongly in favor of state intervention in the marketplace than are those in the United States and Canada, labor unions in the United States have been strongly critical of NAFTA, and public opinion in Mexico is heavily controlled and manipulated compared with that in the United States and Canada. NAFTA may help close some of the gaps, thereby leading to an improvement in integrative potential and removing some of the obstacles to a North American single market, but many obstacles remain.

New Developments in Integration Theory

Many theorists—notably Leon Lindberg—have emphasized that integration must be understood as a multidimensional phenomenon. They argue that it is impossible to separate economic and social pressures for integration from political pressures; that EU governments have given up powers over technical, social, and economic tasks but have been unwilling to give

BOX 1.2
NAFTA and the European Union Compared

Although the European Union has moved into the realms of economic and political union, one of the fundamental building blocks of economic integration is free trade. The reduction of barriers to trade has taken on a new significance for Americans, Canadians, and Mexicans, who are currently working on their own experiment in integration, the North American Free Trade Agreement.

The precursor to NAFTA was born on January 1, 1989, when the Canada-U.S. Free Trade Agreement signed in 1988 came into force, aimed at reducing (but not removing) barriers to trade between the two neighbors. Controversially, this was expanded to become NAFTA with the signing of a treaty in 1992 that expanded free trade to Mexico with effect from January 1, 1994. Negotiations began in 1995 to extend NAFTA to Chile.

The goals of NAFTA are to phase out all tariffs on textiles, apparel, cars, trucks, vehicle parts, and telecommunications equipment over ten years; phase out all barriers to agricultural trade over a period of fifteen years; open up the North American advertising market; allow truck drivers to cross borders freely; allow banks, securities firms, and insurance companies total access to all three markets; and loosen rules on the movement of corporate executives and some professionals. Energy and transportation industries are still heavily protected under NAFTA, there is nothing approaching the free movement of people, and all three member states can apply their own environmental standards. No institutions have been created beyond two commissions that can arbitrate disagreements over environmental standards and working conditions; special judges can also be impaneled to resolve disagreements on issues such as fishing rights and trade laws.

For some, NAFTA's real significance lies less in the content of the agreement than in the symbolism of its passage, representing as it does a shift in U.S. economic policy and in the structure of a U.S. economy gearing up for unparalleled levels of competition from abroad. Certainly it is a much looser arrangement than the European Union or even the European Economic Community in its early years. It is strictly intergovernmental, and although it has resulted in the reduction of trade restrictions, it involves the surrender of negligible levels of authority and sovereignty.

Whether NAFTA will become anything like the EU remains to be seen. Neofunctional logic suggests it might, but many obstacles will need to be removed. These include limited democracy and centralist-corporatist ideas of government in Mexico that run counter to traditions north of the Rio Grande; huge disparities in wealth, education, and per capita production; Canadian concerns about the cultural dominance of the United States; significant gaps in mutual knowledge and understanding among the citizens of the three countries; and public concerns about the nature and implications of free trade.

up political powers (although neofunctionalists would argue that this will happen as the pressures for integration increase); and that the EU experience has shown that integration often evolves because of political "acts of will" rather than because of functional or technical pressures.[29] In the end, the debate comes down to three basic questions: To what extent is integration brought about by coercion, altruism, or pragmatic considerations; to what extent is it voluntary; and to what extent does it have its own internal motive pressures?

Keohane and Hoffmann argue that spillover is an important concept but that it cannot be seen in isolation from other broader influences and pressures. They make at least three key arguments about the nature of integration.

1. First, they argue that spillover is not automatic but that its success depends on prior intergovernmental bargaining. Once a bargain has been made, the work of the EU can expand in the way predicted by functionalist theory. They quote the 1986 Single European Act as an example, arguing that national governments took the final steps that led to its agreement.[30]
2. Second, they argue that institutional change in the EU must be seen as a form of adaptation to pressures from the global economy, such as growing economic competition from Japan and the United States or Europe's response to the turbulence in global currency markets during the 1970s (see Chapter 4). They argue that the Single European Act was driven more strongly by events in the global economy outside Europe than by the internal logic of spillover. [31] The underlying thrust of this "political economy hypothesis" is that the EU has had to change to keep its businesses and economies competitive in the world economy.
3. Finally, Keohane and Hoffmann describe a "preference-convergence hypothesis," based on the argument that social change on a large scale often comes as a result of the conjunction of unrelated events and that changes in EU policy and policymaking structures can come out of a convergence of national government preferences rather than from internal or external pressures.[32] It could be argued that the Single European Act and the Maastricht and Amsterdam Treaties all resulted from that kind of convergence (see Chapter 4), but it would be difficult to isolate the different pressures that brought them about.

The European Union is still far from the kind of entity that federalists such as Monnet and Schuman had hoped for, but it has come a long way in only two generations. The member states have not yet transferred as many powers as the federalists would have liked, EU institutions do not yet have the kind of autonomy federalists had hoped for, the EU has faced many crises and has many critics, and no theories have yet fully explained the timetable of integration. As Ernst Haas argued in 1958, the causes of integration cannot be pinned down unless we can be clear about whether the rise in the number of common tasks (or transactions) precedes, reinforces, results from, or causes integration.[33]

None of these problems needs to detract from the value of neofunctional-ist theory, which has yet to be replaced by theories that better explain why and how the EU has evolved. Through a combination of political will on the part of elites, encouragement from the United States (at least during the early years), the need Europeans felt to protect themselves from each other, pressures for protection from external threats, and the need to rebuild the European economy to respond to competition from the United States and Japan, Europeans have built a complex web of economic, political, and so-cial ties among themselves. How and why this has happened is examined in more detail in the next few chapters.

Summary and Conclusions

Theories of economic and political integration have a lineage that dates back at least to the early work of David Mitrany during the 1930s and probably before.[34] Yet our understanding of the process—and of its mo-tives and results—is still patchy at best. The European Union is an entirely new kind of organization for which most of the standard theories of inter-national relations provide only a partial explanation.

The motives behind the creation of the EU are relatively clear (peace through cooperation being at the core—see Chapters 2 and 3), but the driv-ing forces behind the development of the EU since the 1950s are still widely debated. Shared values have played a part, as have external threats, con-venience, and the self-interest of elites, but whether the process of European integration has had its own internal logic or has been forced is still open to debate. Most explanations hover somewhere between the in-ternal logic arguments of the neofunctionalists and the emphasis realists place on EU member states as rational actors.

Wherever the truth lies, the European Union has emerged as a new species of international organization that does not easily fit most of the conventional explanations about why states cooperate. Terms such as fed-eral, confederal, intergovernmental, and supranational have only limited value in describing and understanding the EU. Attempts to define its nature are complicated by the fact that its dimensions and identity have changed over time. To grasp what the EU is today, we must first understand where it has come from.

Further Reading

David Mitrany. *A Working Peace System* (Chicago: Quadrangle, 1966).
  Arguably the grandparent of them all; one of the first modern expositions of the idea of building peace through cooperation.
  Ernst B. Haas. *The Uniting of Europe: Political, Social, and Economic Forces, 1950–1957* (Stanford: Stanford University Press, 1968).

Still widely seen as the starting point for modern ideas about the mechanisms and motives of integration; essential reading for anyone trying to understand the roots of the EU.

John Eastby. *Functionalism and Interdependence* (Lanham, Md.: University Press of America, 1985).

A commentary on and guide to the work of functionalist theorists and the basic ideas underlying regional integration theory.

Laura Cram. *Policy-Making in the EU: Conceptual Lenses and the Integration Process* (New York: Routledge, 1997).

An attempt to place the contribution of the EU into the context of integration theories, which are surveyed in the opening chapter.

Brent F. Nelsen and Alexander C.G. Stubb (Eds.). *The European Union: Readings on the Theory and Practice of European Integration*, 2d ed. (Boulder: Lynne Rienner, 1998).

A series of readings on European integration in theory and practice, bringing together selections from the speeches and writings of Mitrany, Churchill, Monnet, Haas, Lindberg, Thatcher, and others.

Notes

1. "Union of International Associations," home page, 1998, URL: <http://www.uia.org/welcome.htm>.

2. Ernst B. Haas, *The Uniting of Europe: Political, Social, and Economic Forces, 1950–1957* (Stanford: Stanford University Press, 1958), 12.

3. Ibid., 16.

4. Leon N. Lindberg, *The Political Dynamics of European Economic Integration* (Stanford: Stanford University Press, 1963), 6–7.

5. Robert O. Keohane and Stanley Hoffmann, "Conclusions: Community Politics and Institutional Change," in William Wallace (Ed.), *The Dynamics of European Integration* (London: Royal Institute of International Affairs, 1990).

6. David Mitrany, "The Functional Approach to World Organisation," in Carol A. Cosgrove and Kenneth J. Twitchett (Eds.), *The New International Actors: The UN and the EEC* (London: Macmillan, 1970).

7. Keohane and Hoffmann, "Conclusions," 277.

8. Leon N. Lindberg and Stuart A. Scheingold, *Europe's Would-Be Polity: Patterns of Change in the European Community* (Englewood Cliffs, N.J.: Prentice-Hall, 1970), 94–95.

9. Ernst B. Haas, "Technocracy, Pluralism and the New Europe," in Stephen R. Graubard (Ed.), *A New Europe?* (Boston: Houghton Mifflin, 1964), 66.

10. Robert Schuman, "Declaration of 9 May 1950," in David Weigall and Peter Stirk (Eds.), *The Origins and Development of the European Community* (London: Pinter, 1992), 58–59.

11. Clarence Streit, *Freedom's Frontier—Atlantic Union Now* (Washington, D.C.: Freedom and Union Press, 1961), 23.

12. Leon N. Lindberg and Stuart A. Scheingold, *Regional Integration: Theory and Research* (Cambridge: Harvard University Press, 1971), 6.

13. David Mitrany, *A Working Peace System* (Chicago: Quadrangle, 1966), 27.

14. Ibid., 27–31, 72.

15. Ibid., 73–84.

16. Joseph S. Nye, "Comparing Common Markets: A Revised Neofunctionalist Model," in Lindberg and Scheingold, *Regional Integration,* 200.

17. Haas, *The Uniting of Europe,* 283ff.

18. Cited in Derek Urwin, *The Community of Europe,* 2d ed. (London: Longman, 1995), 44–46.

19. Ibid., 76.

20. Stephen George, *Politics and Policy in the European Community,* 3d ed. (Oxford: Oxford University Press, 1996), 24.

21. Ibid., 22–23.

22. Ernst B. Haas, *The Obsolescence of Regional Integration Theory* (Berkeley: Institute of International Studies, University of California, 1975).

23. Commission of the European Communities, *Economic and Monetary Union 1980* (the Marjolin Report) (Brussels: Commission of the European Communities, 1975), 5.

24. Haas, *The Uniting of Europe* (1968 edition), xiv–xv.

25. Ernst B. Haas, "Turbulent Fields and the Theory of Regional Integration," *International Organization* 30:2 (Spring 1976), 173–212.

26. Joseph S. Nye, *Peace in Parts: Integration and Conflict in Regional Organization* (Boston: Little, Brown, 1971), 67.

27. Philippe C. Schmitter, "A Revised Theory of Regional Integration," in Lindberg and Scheingold, *Regional Integration,* 242.

28. Nye, "Comparing Common Markets," 208–214.

29. James E. Dougherty and Robert L. Pfaltzgraff, *Contending Theories of International Relations,* 3d ed. (New York: Harper and Row, 1990), 459.

30. Keohane and Hoffmann, "Conclusions."

31. Robert O. Keohane and Stanley Hoffmann, "Institutional Change in Europe in the 1980s," in Keohane and Hoffmann (Eds.), *The New European Community: Decisionmaking and Institutional Change* (Boulder: Westview Press, 1991), 18–25.

32. Ibid., 24–25.

33. Ernst B. Haas, "The Challenge of Regionalism," in *International Organization* 12 (Autumn 1958), 445.

34. See, for example, Simeon E. Baldwin, "The International Congresses and Conferences of the Last Century As Forces Working Towards the Solidarity of the World," *American Journal of International Law* 1, Part 2 (July–October 1907), 565–578.

2

Context:
The Postwar World

The roots of the European Union lie in the soil created by hundreds of years of conflict among the peoples of the continent. It began to flower with World War II, the last and most destructive of those conflicts, which brought dramatic changes to the global balance of power. Before the war, Europe had dominated global trade, banking, and finance; its empires stretched around the world; its military advantage was unquestioned. By 1945, the reality was very different. The war dealt a severe blow to European power and influence, clearing the way for the emergence of the United States and the Soviet Union as superpowers and creating a nervous new order in the distribution of political influence in the world.

Before the war, the United States had been both pacifist and isolationist and preferred to limit its foreign influence largely to the Americas. So limited were its interests, in fact, that its defense forces ranked twentieth in the world in size, behind those of the Netherlands.[1] However, even though the Neutrality Acts were passed during the period 1935–1939, the Roosevelt administration was clearly alarmed about the rise of fascist power during the 1930s and argued that isolationism was not the answer. When war broke out in Europe in 1939, Roosevelt issued a proclamation of neutrality, but he also announced that he could not ask every American to "remain neutral in thought." France fell to the Germans in 1940, but Britain was able to stave off a German invasion thanks to the success of the Royal Air Force during the Battle of Britain. American neutrality finally ended in December 1941 with the Japanese attack on Pearl Harbor.

Once the United States became involved in the European theater, Roosevelt took the view that the postwar settlement should ensure the removal of the potential causes of future war and that the United States should be actively involved in making this so. Britain was initially the se-

26

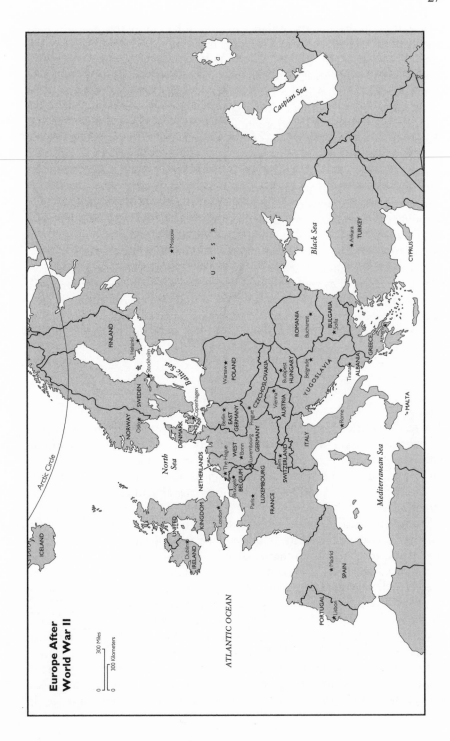

**Europe After
World War II**

0 — 300 Miles
0 — 300 Kilometers

ICELAND

Arctic Circle

ATLANTIC OCEAN

IRELAND
Dublin ★

UNITED
KINGDOM
London ★

NORWAY
Oslo ★

SWEDEN
Stockholm ★

FINLAND
Helsinki ★

Baltic Sea

North
Sea

DENMARK
Copenhagen ★

NETHERLANDS
The Hague ★

BELGIUM
Brussels ★

LUXEMBOURG
Luxembourg ★

FRANCE
Paris ★

WEST
GERMANY
Bonn ★

EAST
GERMANY
Berlin ★

POLAND
Warsaw ★

Prague ★
CZECHOSLOVAKIA

SWITZERLAND
Bern ★

AUSTRIA
Vienna ★

HUNGARY
Budapest ★

ITALY
Rome ★

YUGOSLAVIA
Belgrade ★

ROMANIA
Bucharest ★

BULGARIA
Sofia ★

ALBANIA
Tirana ★

GREECE
Athens ★

U S S R

Moscow ★

Caspian Sea

Black Sea

TURKEY
Ankara ★

CYPRUS

SPAIN
Madrid ★

PORTUGAL
Lisbon ★

Mediterranean Sea

" MALTA

nior partner in the Atlantic Alliance because it had more troops in the field, but as the war evolved, a gradual shift took place in the balance between the two countries. By the time of the D-Day landings in June 1944, U.S. troops outnumbered British troops, and the United States had assumed the dominant role in the Allied war effort. At the summit meetings between the three major Allied leaders (Roosevelt, British Prime Minister Winston Churchill, and Soviet leader Joseph Stalin), it was clear that Roosevelt was the senior partner in discussions with Stalin.

The changing balance of power was further symbolized by Allied research on the atom bomb. During 1940–1941, the British and the Americans were cooperating, but as U.S. research pulled ahead, the flow of information to Britain dried up, ending in 1946 with the McMahon Act, forbidding the exchange of nuclear secrets: The United States did not want to give up the secrets of a technology that would determine its role in the postwar world. The United States was now a military superpower, and the wartime devastation of Europe had paved the way for it to become an economic superpower as well. Its strategic interests after the war encouraged it to play a central role in European affairs—the first phase in that process was dominated by U.S. interests in economic reconstruction, by French interests in containing Germany, and by British resistance to any proposals that went beyond simple cooperation.

Building the Peace

The end of World War II found Western European states in varying degrees of political turmoil. The immediate priority was to create the conditions necessary for peacetime reconstruction. For some, this meant a fundamental reappraisal of their systems of government; for others it meant a new focus on social welfare; and for all it meant taking an entirely new view of international cooperation.

France emerged from the war in a state of confusion that was to persist for over a decade. The effects of wartime collaboration had been traumatic, and the only group that emerged with its credibility intact was the Resistance, whose spirit was embodied in Charles de Gaulle, leader of the Free French wartime government in exile. In 1946, the new constitution of the Fourth Republic went into force, but its prospects were compromised by the weakness of the executive and the existence of many different political parties.[2] The new government launched a plan for economic modernization and an extended welfare system and oversaw French participation in the earliest steps toward European integration, but its plans were undermined by a lack of strong leadership and by three external crises: Indochina in 1954, Suez in 1956 (see Box 2.1), and the mounting prob-

BOX 2.1
Two Crises That Changed Europe

Two major events in the mid-1950s exemplified the changes in the balance of power between Western Europe, the United States, and the USSR: the French defeat in Indochina, and the Suez crisis.

Indochina 1954.   Vietnam had been under French colonial control since the late nineteenth century. It was occupied by Japan during World War II, and was taken back by the French in 1945, by which time a nationalist movement had emerged that demanded independence. Communist groups under the leadership of Ho Chi Minh launched an uprising in 1946 in the north of the country, enmeshing the French in an increasingly bitter war. The end of the war came in April 1954 with the surrender of twelve thousand French troops surrounded by Vietminh guerrillas in the village of Dien Bien Phu. Vietnam was given its independence but was partitioned with a view to being reunited in 1956. The loss of Indochina was a severe blow to French national pride. It marked the beginning of the end of unilateral French influence outside Europe and Africa and the replacement of the French military presence in Southeast Asia by the United States.

Suez 1956.   If Dien Bien Phu had been the first critical blow to French aspirations to maintaining global influence, the fatal blow was struck at Suez[1], which also marked the beginning of the end of Britain's role as a major world power.

The Suez Canal had been built in the period 1856–1869 by the British and the French (using Egyptian labor), and had become a key conduit for British contacts and trade with India and the Pacific. Egypt became increasingly resentful over continued British control over the canal after World War II, especially after the 1952 coup that brought Gamal Abdel Nasser to power. Seeking a source of funds for his planned dam on the Nile at Aswan, Nasser nationalized the canal in July 1956. An outraged British government responded with sanctions, and then—with French and Israeli collusion—launched an attack on the canal zone in October 1956.

The United States led the opposition to the attack, underlining the fundamental differences that had emerged between it and Britain regarding the new world order. The United States was hostile to the idea of colonialism, and was eager to see Britain tie itself more closely to its European neighbors. The British, by contrast, refused to see themselves as European and saw their main interests lying outside Europe, notably in the white dominions: Canada, Australia, and New Zealand. Suez changed those perceptions, and the focus of British interests shifted from the empire to Europe[2]; within five years, Britain had applied to join the EEC.

Notes

1. Maurice Vaisse, "Post-Suez France," in William Roger Louis and Roger Owens (Eds.), *Suez 1956: The Crisis and Its Consequences* (Oxford: Clarendon Press, 1989).
2. Lord Beloff, "The Crisis and Its Consequences for the British Conservative Party," in ibid.

lems in Algeria, where the military refused to accept the idea of independence from France.

In 1958, de Gaulle was invited out of retirement to create the Fifth Republic, a new political system based around a strong executive and a relatively weak legislature—and over which he was to preside until 1969. De Gaulle's appeal came from his credibility, the strength of his leadership, and his nationalism, which expressed itself most notably in his plans for a new Europe dominated by France and Germany and his opposition to U.S. influence in Europe. De Gaulle went on to promote economic modernization, to withdraw France from most of its colonies in 1960–1962, and to redefine France's place in the world.

Britain, it is often said, won the war but lost the peace. Britain's sense of national identity had been strengthened by its successful resistance to Nazi invasion; it was politically stable, its economy grew rapidly after the war, and it was wealthier and more powerful than France and Germany. However, its role in the world was changing. The change began when Churchill was turned out of office in 1945 by voters looking for a new start. The new socialist Labour government embarked on a popular program of nationalization and welfare provision and signaled the beginning of the end of Britain's imperial status by granting independence to India and Pakistan in 1947.

Many Britons still believed their country was a major world power and agreed with Churchill's analysis that Britain's three spheres of interest were its special relationship with the United States, the empire and the Commonwealth, and—last and definitely least—the rest of Europe. The British position was that the security of Western Europe had to be based on the unchallenged leadership of the United States;[3] cooperation with the rest of Europe was far from British minds, and few Britons even thought of themselves as European. Although Labour and Conservative governments alike were skeptical about European integration, the Suez crisis forced a reappraisal because it revealed the fault lines in the transatlantic alliance and showed that Britain was no longer a great power. It also marked the beginning of a new (if halting) interest among Britons in forming alliances with the rest of Europe.

Ireland, meanwhile, had remained neutral during the war but was economically tied to Britain, so its economic development and attitudes toward European cooperation were heavily subject to the British lead. The two countries signed a free trade agreement in 1966, and Irish citizens living in Britain had equal rights and privileges with British citizens.

Germany, for its part, had become introverted, not only because of the scale of the destruction it had suffered in the war and the immediate challenges Germans now faced simply to survive from day to day but also because of shame over both its part in starting the war and the actions it had taken during the war. The four postwar occupying powers were divided on their plans for the new Germany, with the result that by 1948 the country had effectively been split in two: a socialist eastern sector and three capitalist western sectors. Few Germans were happy with this arrangement, but few felt they had much say in the decision.

The policy goals of the Western Allies were denazification (all vestiges of the Nazi system were removed), demilitarization (any West German capability to wage war was removed, and limits were placed on German military activities), democratization (a new constitution was drawn up and imposed on West Germany in 1949), and decentralization (a new federal administrative system was created that deliberately fragmented political power).[4] The conservative Christian Democrats won the 1949 elections, and the popular chancellor Konrad Adenauer set about siding West Germany firmly with the Western Alliance and rebuilding West German respectability; economic integration with its neighbors (especially France) accorded well with these goals.

Austria had been made a province of Germany with the 1938 *Anschluss* and was also divided into separate zones of occupation after the war, but the country was relatively undamaged by the war and was able to return to its 1920 constitution and quickly to hold democratic elections. Although it declared itself neutral in 1955, its economic interests pulled it increasingly toward integration with its Western European neighbors,[5] and the European Community was eventually to account for about half of Austria's trade.

Italy, like Germany, emerged from the war both introverted and devastated. Its main hope lay in rebuilding some of its lost respectability, a process that had begun when the government of the aging King Victor Emmanuel sided with the Allies against Hitler in 1943. The resistance came to be associated with the political left, but Christian Democrats consistently won the biggest share of the vote following the creation of the Italian republic in 1946. Italy's membership in the European Coal and Steel Community was negotiated by the administration of pro-European Prime Minister Alcide de Gasperi, who saw European integration as a way of fostering peace and of helping Italy deal with its internal economic problems, notably unemployment and the underdevelopment of the south.[6]

Italy was less successful than Germany in creating political stability, although its regular changes of government gave the impression of greater instability than actually existed. The country developed an extensive public sector and a multitude of political parties, suffered the consequences of political corruption and organized crime, and endured the persistence of major economic differences between the industrial north and the agrarian south. Membership in the European Economic Community (EEC) was eventually to contribute centrally to Italy's "economic miracle" of the 1960s and 1970s by providing new markets for Italian industry.[7]

Belgium, the Netherlands, and Luxembourg had all been occupied by the Germans, and agreement was reached in 1944 among the three governments-in-exile to promote trilateral economic cooperation after the war. This plan was made easier by the fact that Belgium and Luxembourg had formed an economic union as early as 1921, and all three states had a tradition of trade liberalism. The Benelux customs union was created in 1948 with the abolition of internal customs duties among the three countries and agreement on a joint external tariff. Tripartite cooperation was taken a step further in February 1958 with the signature in The Hague of a treaty creating the Benelux Economic Union (BEU), which came into force in November 1960. All three countries retained many protectionist measures, they were still building the customs union well into the 1960s, and the BEU was intergovernmental rather than supranational, leaving all true power in the trilateral Committee of Ministers. Even so, the BEU represented the first significant postwar experiment in European regional integration.

The Nordic states (Denmark, Finland, Iceland, Norway, and Sweden) had varied wartime experiences. Denmark had tried to ensure its neutrality in 1939 by signing a pact with Hitler, but the Nazis invaded in 1940, and Denmark was occupied until 1945; so, too, was Norway. Iceland declared its independence from Denmark in 1944 and emerged from the war newly confident as a state and doubtful about international cooperation.[8] Finland briefly went to war with the USSR in 1939, but it lost and had to cede territory. Hoping to regain that territory, it joined Germany in attacking Russia in 1941, then signed a separate peace in 1944. Finland followed a policy of neutrality after the war, but its decision in 1948 to sign another peace treaty with the USSR helped encourage Norway, Denmark, and Iceland to join NATO in 1949. Sweden alone had successfully retained its neutrality and did not join NATO.

These five countries enjoyed political stability after the war and firmly established their independence, so intra-Nordic economic cooperation had its own logic. The Committee on Legislative Cooperation was set up in 1946 to bring new national laws into line with one another and to encourage a common Nordic position at international conferences. The five countries also developed joint ventures, such as the airline SAS, founded in August 1946. In 1948, Denmark, Iceland, Norway, and Sweden began to explore possibilities for a Nordic customs union but opted instead for more modest sectoral cooperation. They formed the Nordic Council in 1952 as a consultative body to promote the abolition of passport controls, the free movement of workers, and the development of more joint ventures. The Council had its own governing institutions, and its development was helped by the facts that its members all had small populations, were relatively wealthy and homogeneous, had few major internal social problems, and were governed by socialist or social democratic governments. Finland joined the Council in 1956.

Spain, Portugal, and Greece were exceptions to the prevailing rule of democratic stability in Western Europe after the war. Spain languished from 1939 under the rule of Francisco Franco, who declared Spain neutral in 1943. Between 1910 and 1928 Portugal experienced twenty-five revolutions and military coups, the last of which launched Antonio Salazar on a term in office that was to last until 1968. Greece was occupied during 1941–1944, and a conservative government was elected in 1946. With U.S. financial and military assistance driven by the Truman Doctrine, Greece experienced economic growth, but political tensions ultimately led to a military dictatorship during the period 1967–1974.

Economic Reconstruction and the Marshall Plan

As Western Europeans worried about domestic reconstruction, changes were taking place at the global level that demanded new thinking. Economists on both sides of the Atlantic had given much thought during the war to the best means of achieving a stable and prosperous postwar world. In July 1944, representatives from the United States, Canada, and forty-two other countries met at Bretton Woods, New Hampshire, to plan for the postwar global economy. They agreed among them to an Anglo-American proposal to promote free trade, nondiscrimination, and stable rates of exchange, goals that were to be underpinned by the creation of the General Agreement on Tariffs and Trade (GATT), the International Monetary Fund (IMF), and the World Bank (see Box 2.2).[9] First, though, Europe's economies had to be rebuilt and placed on a more stable footing.

The war had covered most of Europe, resulting in as many as 40 million deaths and leaving behind numerous pockets of devastation. Major cities lay in ruins, agricultural production was halved, food was rationed, and communications were disrupted because bridges, railroads, and harbors had been prime targets. France, Denmark, and the Benelux countries had suffered heavily under the occupation. Many of Britain's major cities had been bombed, its exports had been cut by two-thirds, and its national wealth was cut by 75 percent. Before the war, Britain had been the world's second-largest creditor nation; by 1945 it was the world's biggest debtor nation. The USSR had sustained the heaviest losses on the Allied side, with severe fighting in the west (especially around Stalingrad) and an estimated 24 million deaths. Germany and Italy were left under Allied occupation and with their economies in ruins. In all of Europe, only Spain, Portugal, Ireland, Switzerland, Sweden, and Finland were relatively undamaged or unchanged.

Because the wartime resistance had been allied with left-wing political ideas, and because its leaders were among the few whose credibility was

BOX 2.2
The Bretton Woods System

The global economic system born out of Bretton Woods was underpinned by three new international organizations:

1. An International Trade Organization was designed to help bring down barriers to trade, such as tariffs and quotas. In the event, it was superseded by a looser arrangement, the General Agreement on Tariffs and Trade (GATT), signed by twenty-three states in Geneva in October 1947. GATT subsequently oversaw eight rounds of negotiations, during which barriers to trade were steadily removed through reciprocity (mutual agreement). Between 1948 and 1980 the average industrial tariff fell from 40 percent to just 4 percent,[1] the volume of world trade grew by 600 percent, its value in real terms grew by about 2,000 percent, and global production grew from $1.1 trillion in 1955 to $10.8 trillion in 1980.[2] (Despite concerns among some about a trend toward "world government," GATT was replaced in January 1995 by the World Trade Organization, and preparations are now under way for a Millennium Round of trade negotiations.)

2. The International Monetary Fund (IMF) was developed to work out a fixed pattern of exchange rates that would allow international trade to grow. It was hoped this would prevent the kind of turmoil in international currency markets that had caused so many problems in the 1930s, when the global economy had broken down into four blocs based around the pound, the dollar, the franc, and the mark. The IMF has gone on to make short-term loans, mainly to help countries deal with balance-of-payments problems (created when a country imports more than it exports, or sends more money abroad—as investments, loans, or grants, for example—than it receives).

3. The World Bank (the International Bank for Reconstruction and Development) was created to lend money to European countries affected by the war. When this role was taken over by the Marshall Plan, the Bank turned its attention to the rest of the world, lending money at commercial rates of interest, and mainly for the building of economic infrastructure.

The IMF and the World Bank between them have functioned as something like a global central bank, with a distinctly U.S. tilt to them. Not only are they both headquartered in Washington D.C., but the United States has provided most of their capital.

Under U.S. economic leadership, the Bretton Woods system promoted stable monetary relations, expanded trade and economic growth, and saw the emergence of the dollar as the new international reserve currency. This was made possible, argue Joan Edelman Spero and Jeffrey Hart, by the concentration of power in North America and Western Europe, a shared interest among North Americans and Europeans in capitalism and economic liberalism, and a U.S. willingness to assume leadership of the new system.[3]

Notes

1. Peter Calvocoressi, *World Politics Since 1945* (London: Longman, 1991), 153.

2. Gordon C. Schloming, *Power and Principle in International Affairs* (Orlando: Harcourt Brace Jovanovich, 1991), 25.

3. Joan Edelman Spero and Jeffrey A. Hart, *The Politics of International Economic Relations,* 5th ed. (New York: St. Martin's Press, 1996), 28.

still intact, there was a political shift to the left after the war, with socialist and social democratic parties winning power in several countries (West Germany and Italy were notable exceptions). Many of the new governments launched programs of social welfare and nationalization, emphasizing central planning and government involvement in the economy. At the heart of postwar economic policy were the theories of British economist John Maynard Keynes, who argued in favor of some government control over the economy in an attempt to control the cycle of booms and busts. West European governments expanded their control over their economies with the goals of controlling inflation and rebuilding industry and agriculture, but it soon became clear that substantial capital investment was badly needed, and the readiest source of such investment was the United States.

U.S. policy on Europe after 1945 had initially been driven by Pres. Harry S. Truman's desire to pull the military out as quickly as possible. Within two years, the U.S. military presence had been cut by 95 percent, encouraged by public opinion at home, which favored leaving future peacekeeping efforts to the new United Nations. However, it was becoming increasingly obvious to European leaders that Stalin had plans to spread Soviet influence and that the Nazi threat had simply been replaced by a Soviet threat. Churchill helped spark a change in U.S. public opinion with his March 1946 speech in Fulton, Missouri, in which he warned of the descent of an "iron curtain" across Europe.

When an economically exhausted Britain ended its financial aid to Greece and Turkey in 1947, President Truman argued that the United States needed to step into the vacuum to curb communist influence in the region. In an address to Congress in March 1947, he outlined what became known as the Truman Doctrine. Arguing that the world faced a choice between freedom and totalitarianism, Truman held that it must be U.S. policy "to support free peoples who are resisting attempted subjugation by armed minorities or by outside pressures." This confirmed a new U.S. interest in European reconstruction as a means of helping to contain the Soviets and discouraging the growth of communist parties in Western Europe.[10]

By now the U.S. State Department had begun to realize that it had underestimated the extent of the wartime economic destruction in Europe; despite an economic boom during the late 1940s, sustained growth was not forthcoming. Food rationing persisted (raising the specter of famine and starvation), and there were fears of the possible threat of communist influence spreading across a destabilized Europe. The United States had emerged from World War II in a strong economic position: Its industries were producing 40 percent of the world's armaments by 1944, there had been no direct attacks on its territory after Pearl Harbor, its exports had tripled during the war, and consumer spending was soaring. However, it needed new peacetime export markets.

Against this background, Secretary of State George Marshall argued that Europe should be given assistance. The United States had already provided over $10 billion in loans and aid to Europe during 1945–1947,[11] but something bigger and more structured was needed. Although motivated by political considerations as much as anything, Marshall made his argument more palatable to Congress by couching it in humanitarian terms: "Our policy is directed not against any country or doctrine," he announced in a speech at Harvard in June 1947, "but against hunger, poverty, desperation and chaos." Marshall argued that the initiative should come from Europe and that "the program should be a joint one, agreed to by a number, if not all European nations."[12] The original April 1947 State Department proposal for the plan made clear that one of its ultimate goals was the creation of a Western European federation.[13] Many in the State Department and elsewhere felt long-term stability demanded coordinated regional economic management that would prevent the breakdown of Europe into rival economic and political blocs.[14]

The British and the French took up the offer and approached the Soviets with the idea of developing a recovery plan. However, the Soviets suspected the United States of ulterior motives and bowed out. In July 1947, sixteen European countries met in Paris and established the Committee on European Economic Cooperation. They listed their needs and asked the United States for $29 billion in aid, much more than the United States had envisaged. With congressional approval, the European Recovery Program (otherwise known as the Marshall Plan) ultimately provided just over $12.5 billion in aid to Europe between 1948 and 1951.[15] In April 1948, the same sixteen states created a new body—the Organization for European Economic Cooperation (OEEC)—to coordinate the program. The OEEC was based in Paris and was governed by the Council of Ministers, made up of one representative from each member state.

The treaty creating the OEEC listed goals that included the reduction of restrictions on trade and payments, the reduction of tariffs and other barriers to trade, and an examination of the possibilities for a free trade area or customs union among its members.[16] The OEEC was created at U.S. insistence, Alan Milward notes, "as the first stage in the attempt to build a United States of Europe," but it ended up being "a clumsy, inadequate mixture of elements of forced international cooperation . . . and supranationality."[17] Opposition from several European governments (notably Britain, France, and Norway) ensured that the OEEC remained a forum for intergovernmental consultation rather than becoming a supranational body with powers of its own.[18] (In December 1960, the OEEC was reorganized as the Organization for Economic Cooperation and Development [OECD].)

Although the effects of the Marshall Plan are still being debated, there is little question that it helped underpin economic and political recovery in

Europe and helped tie the economic and political interests of the United States and Western Europe more closely together. It was a profitable investment for the United States, but it also had an important influence on the idea of European integration; as Western Europe's first permanent organization for economic cooperation, it encouraged Europeans to work together and played a key role in showing Europeans how much mutual dependence existed among their economies.[19] It also helped liberalize inter-European trade and helped ensure that economic integration would be focused on Western Europe. It ended up being based less on integration than on cooperation, however, and fell far short of promoting federalism or political unity.

Security and the Cold War

Derek Urwin has argued that U.S. policy in Europe after World War II was based on two misconceptions: first, that Europe had the people, resources, and wealth to recover, and second, that the Allies would continue to work together.[20] The United States wanted to share responsibility for security with the European powers and assumed that Britain would police the Mediterranean and the Middle East, that France would be dominant in continental Europe, and that the four Allies would share control of Germany. However, Western Europeans wondered how much the United States could be relied on to defend Europe, and doubts began to surface about U.S. motives, creating a split that pushed some Europeans (notably Britain) into the U.S. camp and others toward thinking of greater European cooperation.

Although the United States had quickly pulled most of its troops out of Europe, many were as quickly sucked back in as the extent of the Soviet threat became more obvious. The Allies were particularly undecided about what to do with Germany, which was left in a state of limbo. The Americans and the British had begun to think Germany would have to be made self-sufficient, but the Soviets first wanted massive reparations and a guarantee of security from further German aggression.

In June 1948, as a first step toward rebuilding German self-sufficiency, the Western Allies agreed to create a new West German state and a new currency for their three zones. In response, the Soviets set up a blockade around West Berlin. For the next year, a massive Western airlift was maintained to supply West Berlin. Concerns about the West German threat had encouraged Britain, France, and the Benelux states to sign the Brussels Treaty in March 1948, pledging the countries to provide "all the military and other aid and assistance in their power" in the event of attack. The Berlin crisis now shifted the emphasis to the Soviet threat and led to the arrival in Britain in 1948 of the first U.S. bombers suspected of carrying nuclear weapons.

The U.S. Congress was wary of any direct commitments or entanglements in Europe but saw the need to counterbalance the Soviets and to ensure the peaceful cooperation of West Germany. In 1949, the North Atlantic Treaty was signed, under which the United States (entering its first peacetime alliance outside the Western Hemisphere) agreed to help its European allies "restore and maintain the security of the North Atlantic area." Canada also signed, as did Britain, France, Italy, the Benelux countries, Denmark, Iceland, Norway, and Portugal. The pact was later given more substance with the creation of the North Atlantic Treaty Organization (NATO), headquartered in Paris until it was moved to Brussels in 1966. The United States was now committed to the security of Western Europe.

Although NATO gave Europe more security and more space in which to focus on reconstruction, it soon became obvious that it was an unbalanced alliance: Although only 10 percent of NATO forces were American, the United States exercised most of the political influence over NATO policy. NATO members agreed that an attack on one would be considered an attack on them all, but each agreed to respond only with "such actions as it deems necessary." This was an obviously loose arrangement designed to ensure that the United States would not immediately become involved in yet another European war. The Europeans attempted to take their own defense a step further in 1952 with proposals for the creation of a European Defence Community (EDC), but this faltered because of political opposition in Britain and France and the lack of a common European foreign policy (see Chapter 3).

Eager to encourage some kind of military cooperation, Britain invited its Brussels Treaty partners to join with West Germany and Italy to create the Western European Union (WEU).[21] The WEU was less supranationalist than the EDC, but it obliged each member to give all possible military and other aid to any member that was attacked. The WEU also went beyond purely defensive concerns, and agreements signed by the seven founding members in Paris in October 1954 included the aim "to promote the unity and to encourage the progressive integration of Europe." Within days of the launch of the WEU in May 1955, and the coincidental admission of West Germany into NATO, the Soviet bloc created the Warsaw Pact. The lines of the cold war were now defined, and its implications were illustrated only too clearly with events in Hungary in 1956.

In October 1956, the government of Imre Nagy announced the end of one-party rule, the evacuation of Russian troops from Hungary, and Hungary's withdrawal from the Warsaw Pact. As Britain and France were invading Egypt to retake the Suez Canal, the Soviets responded to the

Hungarian decision by sending in tanks. The United States wanted to criticize the Soviet use of force and boast to the emerging Third World about the moral superiority of the West,[22] but it obviously could not do so while British and French paratroopers were storming the Suez Canal. Britain and France were ostracized in the UN Security Council, British Prime Minister Anthony Eden resigned, and the Suez invasion was quickly abandoned.

The consequences of the combination of France's problems in Indochina, the Suez crisis, and the Hungarian uprising were tumultuous:[23] Britain and France began steady military reductions, finally recognizing that they were no longer world powers capable of acting independently in the Middle East or perhaps anywhere; both countries embarked on a concerted program of decolonization; Britain began looking increasingly to Europe for its economic and security interests; and it became obvious to Europeans that the United States was the major partner in the North Atlantic Alliance, a fact that particularly upset the French. Still not fully convinced about the extent of the U.S. commitment to the defense of Europe, Britain and France clung to their one remaining symbol of independence: their own nuclear forces.

Concerned over the way in which they had been marginalized by the Americans in the development of the atom bomb, and interpreting this as a sign of new U.S. isolationism, Britain developed its own bomb, carrying out its first test in 1952. The French were initially undecided about whether to develop the atom bomb, but their search for new respectability and distrust of the United States convinced them to do so. De Gaulle still harbored grudges because the Free French had not been sufficiently involved in wartime Allied planning, and he had been obsessed with the issue of French pride and independence since his return to power. He felt the world had been divided into two spheres—the Anglo-Saxon and the Soviet—and that France played an inferior role.[24] This was particularly clear in the halls of NATO, which was commanded by a U.S. general with a British deputy. De Gaulle's concerns led him to approve the first French atomic test in 1960, to rule that no nuclear weapons would be based on French soil unless they were under the total control of France, and to block British attempts to join the EEC (see Chapter 3). In 1966, he pulled France out of the NATO joint command, although he still supported the Atlantic Alliance.

Feelings about U.S. influence in European defense and the reliance on nuclear weapons also ran high in West Germany, which became alarmed during the 1950s at being used as a mock battlefield. Many West Germans preferred the development of conventional weapons and felt a strong West German army would reduce the need for a nuclear defense strategy. West German public opinion changed somewhat after events in Hungary in 1956 and the 1957 launch of Sputnik, the first Soviet satellite, at which time there was a massive buildup of U.S. nuclear warheads in Europe. Instead of guaranteeing European security, however, this buildup had the opposite effect of causing the Soviets to respond with their own buildup of nuclear weapons, thereby ushering in the era of mutually assured destruction (MAD).

Rising concerns over the nuclear threat sparked a vocal antinuclear movement in Britain during the late 1950s, orchestrated by the Campaign for Nuclear Disarmament (CND). A series of symbolic marches was held from London to the nuclear weapons research establishment in the village of Aldermaston. The CND view was that nuclear weapons were wrong and that Britain was a very junior partner in an Atlantic Alliance based on nuclear weapons. Although British public opinion largely favored the Alliance and CND represented the views of only a small minority, its activities were symbolic of a growing rift within the Alliance. It was becoming increasingly clear that Western Europe would have to build greater self-sufficiency.

Summary and Conclusions

World War II was a watershed in the evolution of the balance of global military, political, and economic power. During the 1920s and 1930s, Britain, France, and Germany were the major powers; their currencies were the most influential in the world; and their economic and military interests tended to be confined to their spheres of political interest: their colonies for Britain and France, and Central Europe for Germany. By contrast, the close of World War II saw the United States established as the dominant economic power in the world, and the new postwar international order was to be based largely on U.S. enthusiasm for free trade, stable exchange rates, and an Atlantic Alliance to contain the Soviets.

The West Europeans found themselves junior partners in this new system, were faced with the urgency of rebuilding internal political and economic stability, and saw the historical threat of Germany and the rising threat of the Soviet Union hanging over them. An urgent response was needed to urgent problems, but there was little agreement on the best way to proceed. Each of the European states still had its own set of national interests, but the political fallout from the war and the changing balance of military power symbolized by Suez had already begun to show very clearly that these interests could not be maintained without some form of inter-European cooperation. Tired of war, of nationalism, and of expensive competition for economic and political influence, Western Europe experienced a groundswell of opinion in favor of cooperation. The first opportunity had been missed with the OEEC, which the United States had initially seen as the foundation for a new era of European integration but that ended up as little more than an exercise in intergovernmental cooperation. The way was now cleared for something less ambitious and more specific.

Further Reading

Alan S. Milward. *The Reconstruction of Western Europe 1945–51* (Berkeley: University of California Press, 1984).

A detailed study of the Marshall Plan and its contribution to the first moves toward European integration.

Michael J. Hogan. *The Marshall Plan: America, Britain, and the Reconstruction of Western Europe, 1947–52* (New York: Cambridge University Press, 1987).

Complements Alan Milward by describing and assessing U.S. motives and the consequences of the Marshall Plan.

Cyril E. Black et al. *Rebirth: A History of Europe Since World War II* (Boulder: Westview Press, 1992).

A history of postwar Europe that combines overview chapters with separate chapters on each of the major states and regions of Europe.

David W. P. Lewis. *The Road to Europe* (New York: Peter Lang, 1993).

Combines a history of European integration with chapters on all of the major international organizations involved in Western European cooperation.

Clive Archer. *Organizing Western Europe*, 2d ed. (New York: Oxford University Press, 1994).

A guide to the history and structure of eight major European-dominated cooperative organizations, from the OEEC to the Western European Union.

Notes

1. Christopher Thorne, *The Far Eastern War: States and Societies, 1941–45* (London: Unwin, 1986), 211–212.

2. William Safran, *The French Polity,* 4th ed. (New York: Longman, 1995), 8–9.

3. Stephen George, *An Awkward Partner: Britain in the European Community*, 2d ed. (Oxford: Oxford University Press, 1997), 21.

4. David P. Conradt, *The German Polity,* 5th ed. (New York: Longman, 1993), 11.

5. D. Mark Schultz, "Austria in the International Arena: Neutrality, European Integration and Consociationalism," in Kurt Richard Luther and Wolfgang C. Muller (Eds.), *Politics in Austria: Still a Case of Consociationalism?* (London: Frank Cass, 1992).

6. Paul Ginsborg, *A History of Contemporary Italy: Society and Politics, 1943–1988* (London: Penguin, 1990), 16.

7. Ibid., 212–215.

8. Gunnar Helgi Kristinsson, "Iceland," in Helen Wallace (Ed.), *The Wider Western Europe: Reshaping the EC/EFTA Relationship* (London: Pinter, 1991).

9. Armand Van Dormael, *Bretton Woods: Birth of a Monetary System* (New York: Holmes and Meier, 1978).

10. Michael J. Hogan, *The Marshall Plan: America, Britain, and the Reconstruction of Western Europe, 1947–52* (New York: Cambridge University Press, 1987), 26–27.

11. Alan S. Milward, *The Reconstruction of Western Europe 1945–51* (Berkeley: University of California Press, 1984), 46–48.

12. Office of the Historian, *Foreign Relations of the United States,* vol. 3 (Washington, D.C.: U.S. Department of State, 1947), 230–232.

13. Quoted in John Gillingham, *Coal, Steel, and the Rebirth of Europe, 1945–1955* (Cambridge: Cambridge University Press, 1991), 118–119.

14. Hogan, *The Marshall Plan,* 36.

15. Milward, *Reconstruction of Western Europe,* 94.

16. Articles 4–6 of the Convention for European Economic Cooperation, quoted in Michael Palmer et al., *European Unity: A Survey of European Organizations* (London: George Allen & Unwin, 1968), 81.

17. Milward, *Reconstruction of Western Europe,* 208.

18. Immanual Wexler, *The Marshall Plan Revisited: The European Recovery Program in Economic Perspective* (Westport, Conn.: Greenwood Press, 1983), 209; Palmer et al., *European Unity,* 82; Milward, *Reconstruction of Western Europe,* 209–210.

19. Derek W. Urwin, *The Community of Europe* (London: Longman, 1995), 20–22.

20. Ibid., 13–14.

21. Clive Archer, *Organizing Western Europe,* 2d ed. (New York: Oxford University Press, 1994), 175.

22. Alan Sked and Chris Cook, *Post-War Britain: A Political History* (Harmondsworth: Penguin, 1984), 135–136.

23. See Albert Hourani, "Conclusions," in William Roger Louis and Roger Owen (Eds.), *Suez 1956: The Crisis and Its Consequences* (Oxford: Clarendon Press, 1989).

24. Don Cook, *Charles de Gaulle: A Biography* (New York: Putnam, 1983), 332–333.

3

Emergence:
The Road from Paris

The history of Europe prior to World War II was one of almost constant conflict and tension, and hardly a decade went by without war breaking out between two or more European states. For many, World War I, or the Great War, had been the war to end all wars, having brought to a head all of the tensions and political jealousies that plagued the European state system at the turn of the twentieth century. The League of Nations was created in 1919 to help prevent future conflict, but the peace treaty signed at Versailles contained the seeds of future conflict; it demanded drastic reparations from Germany, represented an attempt by Britain and France to stamp their authority on Europe, and was based on recriminations and inequality. For Jean Monnet, "a peace based on inequality could have no good results."[1]

The priorities after World War II were to avoid the mistakes of Versailles and to protect Europe both from itself and from external threats. The war had been physically and psychologically devastating, had discredited the old international order, had reminded Europeans that they were still capable of appalling violence, and had raised urgent questions about how future European conflict could be avoided and how Europe could best go about rebuilding. Different states had different ideas about how this should be done, but most of the suggestions pointed toward greater inter-European cooperation, with the goal of building both political and economic security.

For many, the major internal threats to Europe were nationalism and the nation-state, both of which had been glorified, abused, and discredited by the fascists. The development of a new European identity would reduce the role of nationalism, thereby removing one of the recurring causes of conflict. Because Germany had been at the root of three major wars in seventy

43

years, many now argued that peace was impossible unless Germany could be contained and its power diverted to constructive rather than destructive ends. It had to be allowed to rebuild its economic base and its political system in ways that would not threaten European security; France was particularly eager to make sure this happened.[2]

The external threats to Europe came from the growing hostility between the two superpowers, leading to concerns that Europeans were becoming pawns in that hostility. There was a determination to protect Western Europe from the spread of Soviet influence, but there were also worries about the extent to which Western Europe and the United States could find common ground and to which Western Europe could rely on the U.S. protective shield. Perhaps Europe would be better advised to take care of its own security. This, however, demanded a greater sense of unity and common purpose than Europe had ever been able to achieve before.

The Council of Europe

The rising groundswell of opinion in favor of European cooperation after the war was reflected in the emergence (or reemergence) of several groups of pro-Europeanists. Some groups traced their roots back to the interwar years and to movements such as Pan-Europa, founded in 1923 by Austro-Hungarian aristocrat Count Richard Coudenhove Kalergi. Others were born out of a concern to remove the causes of war and to respond to growing U.S. economic power. Among these were the United European Movement in Britain, the Europa-Bund in Germany, the Socialist Movement for the United States of Europe in France, and the European Union of Federalists.

The spotlight fell particularly on Britain, which had led the resistance to Nazism and was still the dominant European power. Winston Churchill became the focus of Europeanist sentiment, his credentials being based on his charisma, his last-minute proposal for an Anglo-French Union in 1940, and suggestions he had made during 1942–1943 for "a United States of Europe" operating under "a Council of Europe" with reduced trade barriers, free movement of people, a common military, and a High Court to adjudicate disputes.[3] He made the same suggestions in a speech at the University of Zurich in 1946, but it was clear that Churchill felt this new entity should be based around France and Germany and would not necessarily include Britain; before the war he had argued that Britain was "with Europe but not of it. We are interested and associated, but not absorbed."[4]

In an attempt to publicize the cause of European unity, the national pro-European groups organized the Congress of Europe in The Hague in May 1948, which was attended by delegates from sixteen states and observers

TABLE 3.1   Western European Membership of International Organizations

Year of foundation	1945	1948	1949	1949	1952	1955	1960
	UN	OEEC	Council of Europe	NATO	EU	WEU	EFTA[a]
Austria	1955	*	1956	—	1995	—	*
Belgium	*	*	*	*	*	*	—
Cyprus	1960	—	1961	—	—	—	—
Denmark	*	*	*	*	1973	—	*
Finland	1955	—	1988	—	1995	—	1986
France	*	*	*	*	*	*	—
Germany	1973	1949	1951	1955	*	*	—
Greece	*	*	1949	1952	1981	—	—
Iceland	1946	*	1950	*	—	—	1970
Ireland	1955	*	*	—	1973	—	—
Italy	1955	*	*	*	*	*	—
Luxembourg	*	*	*	*	*	*	—
Malta	1964	—	1965	—	—	—	—
Netherlands	*	*	*	*	*	*	—
Norway	*	*	*	*	—	—	*
Portugal	1955	*	1976	*	1986	1989	*
Spain	1955	1959	1977	1982	1986	1989	—
Sweden	1946	*	*	—	1995	—	*
Switzerland	—	*	1963	—	—	—	*
Turkey	*	*	1949	1952	—	—	—
United Kingdom	*	*	*	*	1973	*	*

*Founder members; other dates refer to year of accession.
[a]By 1995, only Iceland, Norway, Switzerland, and Liechtenstein remained in EFTA.
UN = United Nations, OEEC = Organization for European Economic Cooperation,
NATO = North Atlantic Treaty Organization, EU = European Union, WEU = Western
European Union, EFTA = European Free Trade Association.

from the United States and Canada. Calls were made for a European assembly, a European court, and a charter of human rights, but the only tangible outcome was the creation of the European Movement, with national groups in each country. The Movement took up the idea of a European assembly and urged influential Europeanists like Belgian Prime Minister Paul-Henri Spaak and Italian Prime Minister Alcide de Gasperi to promote the idea. After discussions among the governments of France, Britain, Italy, Belgium, the Netherlands, and Luxembourg, agreement was reached in January 1949 to create a ministerial council and a consultative assembly. The French and Italians wanted to use the name European Union, but the

British insisted on the more ambiguous and noncommittal title Council of Europe.[5]

The Council of Europe was founded in London in May 1949 with the signing of a statute by ten European states. The statute noted the need for "a closer unity between all the like-minded countries of Europe" and described the Council's aims as including "common action in economic, social, cultural, scientific, legal and administrative matters"; defense was explicitly excluded from the list. The Council was headquartered in Strasbourg, France, and had a governing Committee of Ministers, on which each state had one vote, and a 147-member Consultative Assembly made up of representatives nominated from national legislatures. The Committee of Ministers met once or twice annually; although it initially consisted of the foreign ministers of member states, deputy ministers were soon sent instead. The Assembly had few powers over the Committee, which promoted national interests at the expense of European interests. Although membership in the Council of Europe expanded, the Council never became anything more than a loose intergovernmental organization. It made progress on human rights, cultural issues, and even limited economic cooperation, but it was not the kind of organization European federalists wanted.

Opening Moves:
Coal and Steel (1950–1952)

The Organization for European Economic Cooperation (OEEC) and the Council of Europe encouraged Europeans to think and work together, but the opposition of antifederalists (notably those in Britain and Scandinavia) ensured that neither organization would promote significant regional integration. Among those who felt something bolder was needed were two Frenchmen: an entrepreneur named Jean Monnet (1888–1979) and Robert Schuman (1880–1963), foreign minister from 1948 to 1953. Both were enthusiastic Europeanists, both felt something practical needed to be done that went beyond the noble statements of organizations such as the Council of Europe, and both felt the logical point of departure should be the perennial problem of Franco-German relations.

By 1950, it was clear to many that West Germany had to be allowed to rebuild if it was to play a useful role in a Western alliance. One way of allowing industrial reconstruction in Germany without allowing it to become a threat to its neighbors (particularly France) was to let it rebuild under the auspices of a supranational organization, thereby tying Germany (particularly the resources of the Ruhr) into the wider process of European reconstruction. It was important not to be too ambitious and to start with something small but meaningful. The Congresses of the European

Movement in early 1949 had suggested that the coal and steel industries offered strong potential for common European organization, for several reasons:[6]

1. Coal and steel were the fundamental building blocks of industry, and the steel industry had a tendency to create cartels. Cooperation would eliminate waste and duplication, break down cartels, make coal and steel production more efficient and competitive, and boost industrial development.

2. The heavy industries of the Ruhr had been the traditional basis for Germany's power, and France and Germany had fought before over coal reserves in Alsace-Lorraine. Monnet argued that "coal and steel were at once the key to economic power and the raw materials for forging weapons of war."[7] Creating a supranational coal and steel industry would help contain German power.

3. Integrating coal and steel would ensure that Germany became reliant on trade with the rest of Europe, thereby underpinning its economic reconstruction and helping the French lose their fear of German industrial domination.[8]

Monnet felt that unless France acted immediately, the United States would become the focus of a new transatlantic alliance against the Soviet bloc, Britain would be pulled closer to the United States, Germany's economic and military growth would not be controlled, and France would be led to its "eclipse."[9] As head of the French national planning commission, Monnet could see that effective economic planning was beyond the ability of individual states working alone. He also knew from personal experience that intergovernmental organizations tended to be hamstrung by the governments of their member states and to become bogged down in ministerial meetings. To avoid these problems, he proposed a new institution independent of national governments that would have a life of its own, one that would be supranational rather than intergovernmental.

After discussions with Monnet and West German Chancellor Konrad Adenauer, Schuman took these ideas a step further at a press conference on May 9, 1950 (a date now widely seen as marking the birth of the idea of a united Europe). In what later became known as the Schuman Declaration, he argued that Europe would not be built at once or according to a single plan but only through concrete achievements:

> The coming together of the nations of Europe requires the elimination of the age-old opposition of France and Germany. . . . With this aim in view, the French Government proposes that action be taken immediately on one limited but decisive point. It proposes that Franco-German production of coal and

steel as a whole be placed under a common High Authority, within the framework of an organization open to the participation of the other countries of Europe.[10]

This, Schuman went on, would be "a first step in the federation of Europe" and would make war between France and Germany "not merely unthinkable, but materially impossible."[11] The proposal was revolutionary in the sense that France was offering to sacrifice a measure of national sovereignty in the interest of building a new supranational authority that could end an old rivalry and help build a new European peace.[12] Few other governments were enthusiastic, however, and only four took up the invitation to join: Italy, which wanted respectability and economic and political stability; and the Benelux countries, which were in favor because they were small and vulnerable, had twice been invaded by Germany, and felt the only way they could have a voice in world affairs and ensure their security was to be part of a bigger unit. They were also heavily reliant on exports and had already created their own customs union in 1948.

The other European states had different reasons for not taking part in the proposed High Authority: Spain and Portugal were dictatorships and had little interest in international cooperation. For Denmark and Norway, the memories of the German occupation were still too fresh, while Austria, Sweden, and Finland wanted to remain neutral. Ireland was predominantly agricultural (and thus had little to gain from the proposal) and was tied economically to Britain. Britain still had too many interests outside Europe and exported little of its steel to Western Europe (4–6 percent annually),[13] and the new Labour government had only recently nationalized its coal and steel industries and did not like the supranational character of the Schuman proposal; as British Prime Minister Clement Attlee told the House of Commons, his party was "not prepared to accept the principle that the most vital economic forces of this country should be handed over to an authority that is utterly undemocratic and is responsible to nobody."

Undeterred, the governments of the six founding member states (the Six) opened negotiations and on April 18, 1951, signed the Treaty of Paris creating the European Coal and Steel Community (ECSC). The new organization began work in August 1952 following ratification of the terms of the treaty in each of the member states (see Box 3.1). The ECSC was a small step in itself, but it represented the first time European governments had given significant powers to a supranational organization. It was allowed to pull down tariff barriers, abolish subsidies, fix prices, and raise money by imposing levies on steel and coal production. It faced national opposition, but its job was made easier by the fact that much of the groundwork had already been laid by the Benelux customs union.

BOX 3.1
The European Coal and Steel Community

The ECSC was governed by four institutions:

1. A High Authority of nine nominated members (at least one—and no more than two—from each member state). They served six-year terms and were expected to work toward removing all barriers to the free movement of coal and steel. They were given complete independence regarding decisions relating to the ECSC and had the power to issue binding decisions and recommendations, but they could not see themselves as representatives of their countries; they represented the joint interests of the ECSC. The Authority was a precursor to the European Commission but had much greater power in its own constituency; for example, it could give orders to national coal and steel industries without the approval of national governments. Jean Monnet became the first president.

2. A Special Council of Ministers consisting of the relevant minister from each member state. The Council was created as a result of Benelux concerns about the power of the three larger countries and was designed to allow the smaller member states to balance the power of the High Authority, to prevent the French and the Germans from having too much power, and to represent the interests of member states.

3. A Common Assembly consisting of seventy-eight members chosen by national legislatures, the numbers divided up roughly on the basis of population (eighteen each from the Big Three; ten each from Belgium and the Netherlands; and four from Luxembourg). The Assembly was the first international assembly in Europe with legally guaranteed powers. It became the forerunner of the European Parliament and helped Monnet circumvent the concerns of national governments about giving up powers; he argued that the High Authority would be responsible to the Assembly, which would eventually be directly elected. Although the Assembly was supposed to provide a democratic input into ECSC decisions, it had only advisory powers, and its members were not elected.

4. A Court of Justice consisting of seven judges (one from each country plus a seventh to make an odd number). The Court's tasks were to settle conflicts between states and rule on the legality of High Authority decisions on the basis of complaints from member states or national industries.

The Six were unable to agree on a single site for the ECSC, so the High Authority, the Council, and the Court were provisionally based in Luxembourg, and the Assembly in Strasbourg, France.

The ECSC showed that integration was feasible, and its very existence forced the Six to work together; even Britain was obliged to recognize its authority. John Gillingham has argued that it ensured that Germany did not become a threat to the new Europe but instead became its mainstay.[14]

Although the ECSC failed to achieve many of its goals (notably the creation of a single market for coal and steel),[15] it had ultimately been created to prove a point about the feasibility of integration, which it did. It continued to function independently until 1965, when the High Authority and the Special Council of Ministers were merged with their counterparts in the European Economic Community (EEC) and the European Atomic Energy Community (Euratom), as discussed later in this chapter.

Although the ECSC was at least a limited success, integrationists failed dismally with two much larger, more ambitious, and arguably premature experiments. The first of these was the European Defence Community (EDC), which was to promote Western European cooperation on defense while at the same time binding West Germany into a European defense system. Konrad Adenauer had first broached the idea in 1949, but it was given a decisive push with the announcement of U.S. plans to rearm West Germany in the wake of the outbreak of the Korean War in June 1950.[16] In an attempt to defuse concerns about German rearmament, a draft plan was outlined by Jean Monnet and was made public in October 1950 by French Prime Minister René Pleven. Echoing ideas outlined by Churchill in a speech to the Council of Europe in August of that year,[17] the plan argued the need for a common defense and "a European Army tied to the political institutions of a united Europe and a European Minister for Defense."[18] The six members of the ECSC moved ahead with the plan, assuming that the EDC would have the same structure as the ECSC, and in May 1952 they signed a draft EDC treaty.

When it came to national ratification, however, problems arose, particularly in Italy and France. The French were still nervous about German rearmament so soon after the war and did not want to give up control over their military. Additionally, any talk of a European defense system that did not include Britain—still the strongest European military power—was pointless. Furthermore, observed Konrad Adenauer, Europe could not have a workable common defense force without a common foreign policy.[19] French national prestige, meanwhile, was struck a blow with the surrender to Vietnamese communist forces at Dien Bien Phu in April 1954, further discouraging talk of giving up military sovereignty. Plans for the EDC were finally shelved in August 1954, when the French National Assembly voted it down on the basis that giving up the right to a national army was too much of a restriction on sovereignty. The EDC was replaced in 1955 by the Western European Union, a consultative organization that fell far short of being a common defense force (see Chapter 15).

The second failed experiment was the European Political Community (EPC), which was intended to be the first step toward the creation of a European federation. A draft plan was completed in 1953, based around a European Executive Council, a Council of Ministers, a Court of Justice, and a popularly elected Parliament. With ultimate power resting with the Executive Council, which would represent national interests, the EPC was more confederal than federal in nature.[20] With the collapse of the EDC, however, all hopes for a European Political Community died, at least temporarily. The failure of these two initiatives was a sobering blow to the integrationists and sent shock waves through the ECSC; Monnet left the presidency of the High Authority in 1955, disillusioned by the political resistance to its work and impatient to move on with the process of integration.[21]

From Paris to Rome (1955–1958)

Although the ECSC made modest but solid progress in its first four years, there were limits to its abilities, and Europeanists felt something more was needed to give integration real momentum. Schuman's original view was that political union would come about through economic integration, and although the six ECSC members agreed that coal and steel had been a useful testing ground, it was increasingly difficult to develop those two sectors in isolation. A meeting of the foreign ministers of the Six at Messina, Italy, in June 1955 resulted in a resolution that the time had come to "relaunch" the European idea. They agreed on a Benelux proposal "to work for the establishment of a united Europe by the development of common institutions, the progressive fusion of national economies, the creation of a common market, and the progressive harmonization of their social policies."[22]

A committee chaired by Belgian Foreign Minister Paul-Henri Spaak was set up to look into the options. Britain was briefly a member of the committee but withdrew when it became obvious that its hopes for a looser free trade agreement were at odds with the goals of the Six. As Spaak himself later admitted, the Treaty of Rome was motivated less by economic cooperation than by a desire to take another step toward political union.[23] The report of the Spaak committee led to a new round of negotiations, and the signing in March 1957 of the two Treaties of Rome, one creating the European Economic Community and one the European Atomic Energy Community (hereinafter EEC and Euratom). Following member state ratification, both came into force in January 1958 (see Box 3.2).

The EEC Treaty committed the Six to the creation of a common market and to the harmonization of their economic policies. Action would be taken in areas where there was agreement, and disagreements could be set aside for future discussion. The common market was to be created within twelve years through the removal of all restrictions on internal trade; agreement on a common external tariff; the reduction of barriers to the free movement of people, services, and capital among the Six; the development

---

BOX 3.2
The European Economic Community

Although the EEC and Euratom inherited the basic framework of the ECSC institutions, there were some changes:

1. Instead of a High Authority, the EEC had an appointed nine-member quasi-executive Commission, which had less power to impose decisions on member states and whose main job was to initiate policy and oversee implementation.
2. The EEC Council of Ministers was given greater power over decisionmaking yet still represented national interests. It had six members, but they shared seventeen votes (four each for France, Germany, and Italy; two each for Belgium and the Netherlands; and one for Luxembourg). Depending on their implications, some decisions had to be unanimous, while others could be taken by a simple majority, or—more often—by a qualified majority of twelve votes from at least four states. This system made it impossible for the larger states to outvote the smaller ones. Although the qualified majority system was seen as a temporary measure, it remains in place today.
3. A single Parliamentary Assembly was created to cover the EEC, ECSC, and Euratom; it had 142 members appointed by the member states. It could question or censure the Commission but had little legislative authority. The Assembly renamed itself the European Parliament in 1962.
4. A single Court of Justice was created with seven judges appointed for renewable six-year terms; it was responsible for interpreting the founding treaties and for ensuring that the three institutions and the member states fulfilled their treaty obligations.

---

of common agricultural and transport policies; and the creation of the European Social Fund and a European Investment Bank. The Euratom Treaty, meanwhile, was aimed at creating a common market for atomic energy. For Charles de Gaulle, Euratom came too close to interfering in his domestic nuclear weapons policy, so he made sure it focused primarily on research. When West Germany and Italy began developing their own nuclear programs, Euratom funding was cut, and it rapidly became a very junior actor in the process of integration.[24]

Integration Takes Root

Given the long history of inter-European hostilities and war, the integration of six Western European states under the auspices of the ECSC, the EEC, and Euratom was a remarkable achievement. By no means was it a trouble-free experience, however. Even Jean Monnet had warned that "Europe will be established through crises and ... the outcome will be the sum of the outcomes of those crises."[25] The most serious of the early crises came in 1965, with French objections to the growth of European Commission powers.

The roots of the problem went back to the collapse of de Gaulle's plans for political union, and the situation worsened because of the imperious manner in which de Gaulle rejected British membership in 1963 (discussed later in the chapter). At its heart were de Gaulle's attempts to discard the supranationalist elements of the Treaty of Rome and to build a Community dominated by France.[26] The final straw came with European Parliament demands for more power (especially over the budget), the fact that decision-making by majority vote on certain issues in the Council of Ministers was scheduled to come into force on January 1, 1966, and suggestions by the European Commission that it replace its reliance on national contributions from EEC members with an independent source of income and that more progress be made on a common agricultural policy.

This smacked of excessive supranationalism to the French, who insisted that EEC funding continue to come from national contributions, at least until 1970. The other five states disagreed, so in June 1965 France began boycotting meetings of the Council of Ministers, preventing any decisions from being taken on new laws and policies and setting off an "empty chair" crisis. The crisis was ended only with the January 1966 Luxembourg Compromise (actually an agreement to disagree), through which the voting procedure in the Council of Ministers was changed. Unanimity remained the ideal, but members would be allowed to veto matters they felt adversely affected their national interests. The effect was to curb the growth of Commission powers and put more power into the hands of the member states (in the form of the Council of Ministers). (The use of the veto had been virtually abandoned by the mid-1980s but still hovers over the EU as an option of last resort.)

Along with the problems, though, there were many achievements. First, the Treaty of Rome had set a twelve-year deadline for the removal in stages of all of the barriers to the creation of a common market among the Six (Article 8). Although this did not happen until the mid-1990s, internal tariffs fell quickly enough to allow the Six to agree on a common external tariff in July 1968 and to declare that an industrial customs union existed.

Second, decisionmaking was streamlined in April 1965 with the Treaty Establishing a Single Council and a Single Commission of the European Communities (the Merger Treaty); the three Communities already had a common Parliament and Court of Justice. The decisionmaking process was given further authority and direction by the formalization in 1975 of regular summits of Community leaders coming together as the European Council (see Chapter 10). The EEC was finally made more publicly accountable (and more democratic) with the introduction in 1979 of direct elections to the European Parliament.

Third, thanks to the removal of quota restrictions, instituted by members to protect their home industries from competition, intra-EEC trade between 1958 and 1965 grew three times faster than that with third-party countries.[27] Furthermore, an EEC report published in 1972 revealed an average annual growth of productivity in the Six of 5.7 percent, a 4.5 percent increase in per capita income and consumption, and a halving of the contribution of agriculture to economic output.[28]

Fourth, nontariff barriers to the free movement of goods across borders were reduced as standards and regulations on health, safety, and consumer protection were harmonized during the 1960s and 1970s. However, it was not until the 1986 Single European Act (see Chapter 4) that a concerted effort was made to finally bring all EEC members in line. Another priority was to lift restrictions on the free movement of workers; even though limits remained well into the 1990s, steady progress was made toward easing them during the 1960s and 1970s.

Fifth, a fundamental goal of the Treaty of Rome (Article 38) had been agreement on a Common Agricultural Policy (CAP), which was achieved in 1968 with the acceptance of a watered-down version of a plan drawn up by the agriculture commissioner, Sicco Mansholt.[29] Its goals were to create a single market for agricultural products and to assure EEC farmers of guaranteed prices for their produce. CAP initially encouraged both production and productivity, although it was also the largest single item in the budget and became enormously controversial (see Chapter 13).

Finally, the Six worked increasingly closer together on international trade negotiations and enjoyed a joint influence they would not have had negotiating individually. The EEC acted as one, for example, in the Kennedy Round of GATT negotiations during the mid-1960s and in reaching preferential trade agreements with eighteen former African colonies under the 1963 Yaoundé Conventions (see Chapter 15).[30]

Enlargement: Looking North and South

Winston Churchill had been an active proponent of European integration during both the war and his years in opposition (1945–1951), but neither the Labour government that ousted him in 1945 nor Churchill upon his return to office in 1951 took this philosophy any farther. Britain was uncomfortable with the federalist tendencies of the ECSC and the EEC. It was not fond of the European Defence Community because it would have limited Britain's defense options at a time when the British military was strung out across the Middle East, East Africa, and Southeast Asia. It did not support

Euratom because Britain was a nuclear power and did not want to give up its secrets to nonnuclear countries. Finally, the failure of the EDC had convinced many in the British government that the EEC had little potential; as Prime Minister Harold Macmillan recalled, the official view in the foreign policy establishment seemed to be "a confident expectation that nothing would come out of Messina."[31]

The Suez crisis finally put to rest Britain's nostalgic idea that it was still a great power and shook the foundations of the special relationship with the United States. It was also clear that global political and economic issues were being discussed and influenced bilaterally by the United States and the USSR. Britain decided to pursue the idea of a wider (but looser) free trade area based on the OEEC states, but preparations for the EEC had gone too far. Britain instead concentrated on the creation of the European Free Trade Association (EFTA), a loose intergovernmental body with the goal of free trade rather than economic and political integration. It was founded in January 1960 with the signing of the Stockholm Convention by Britain, Austria, Denmark, Norway, Portugal, Sweden, and Switzerland. Membership in EFTA was voluntary (unlike the contractual arrangements set up for the EEC by the Treaty of Rome), and EFTA had no political goals and no institutions beyond a Council of Ministers that met two or three times a year and a group of permanent representatives serviced by a small secretariat in Geneva.

EFTA helped cut tariffs but achieved relatively little over the long term. Several of its members did more trade with the EEC than with their EFTA partners, and questions were raised early about Britain's motives in pursuing the EFTA concept. EFTA was a marriage of convenience, created to prove a point about the relative merits of a looser free trade arrangement with low tariffs. It soon became clear to Britain that political influence in Europe lay not with EFTA but with the EEC, that Britain risked political isolation if it stayed out of the EEC, and that the EEC was actually working; the continent had made impressive economic and political progress, and British industry wanted access to the rich European market.[32] In August 1961, barely fifteen months after the creation of EFTA, Britain applied for EEC membership, at the same time as Ireland and Denmark. They were joined by Norway in 1962.

Denmark's motives for wanting EEC membership were agricultural; it was producing three times as much food as it needed, and much of that was being exported to Britain. Furthermore, the EEC itself was a big new market for Danish agricultural surpluses and would provide a boost for Danish industrial development. Ireland, for its part, saw the EEC as a potential boost for its industrial plans and its desire to reduce its reliance on agriculture and on Britain. Norway followed the British lead because of the importance of EEC markets. With four of its members apparently trying to

56

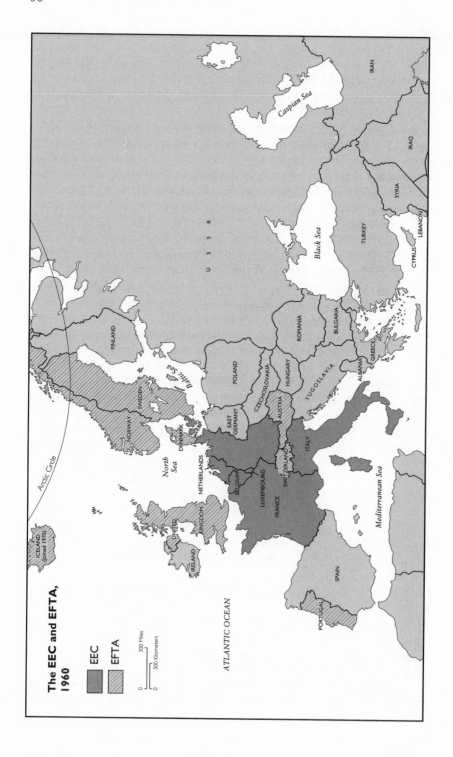

The EEC and EFTA, 1960

EEC

EFTA

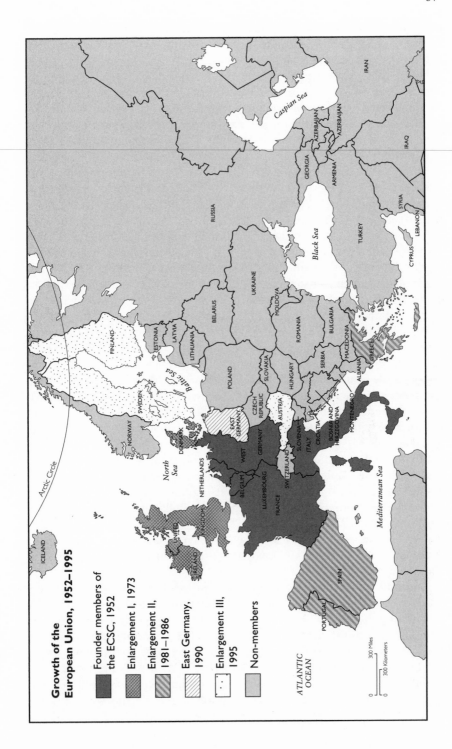

**Growth of the
European Union, 1952–1995**

Founder members of
the ECSC, 1952

Enlargement I, 1973

Enlargement II,
1981–1986

East Germany,
1990

Enlargement III,
1995

Non-members

ATLANTIC
OCEAN

0   300 Miles

0   300 Kilometers

ICELAND

Arctic Circle

NORWAY

SWEDEN

FINLAND

Baltic Sea

North
Sea

DENMARK

ESTONIA

LATVIA

LITHUANIA

RUSSIA

BELARUS

UKRAINE

MOLDOVA

POLAND

UNITED
KINGDOM

IRELAND

NETHERLANDS

EAST
GERMANY

WEST
GERMANY

CZECH
REPUBLIC

SLOVAKIA

AUSTRIA

HUNGARY

ROMANIA

BULGARIA

SERBIA

SLOVENIA

CROATIA

BOSNIA AND
HERZEGOVINA

MONTENEGRO

MACEDONIA

ALBANIA

GREECE

BELGIUM

LUXEMBOURG

FRANCE

SWITZERLAND

ITALY

SPAIN

PORTUGAL

Mediterranean Sea

Black Sea

Caspian Sea

GEORGIA

ARMENIA

AZERBAIJAN

AZERBAIJAN

TURKEY

CYPRUS

SYRIA

LEBANON

IRAQ

IRAN

defect, EFTA ceased to have much purpose, so Sweden, Austria, and Switzerland applied for associate membership in the EEC, followed in 1962 by Portugal, Spain, and Malta.

Negotiations between Britain and the Six opened in early 1962 and appeared to be on the verge of a successful conclusion when they fell foul of de Gaulle's Franco-German policy and his animosity toward Britain. De Gaulle had plans for an EEC built around a Franco-German axis, saw Britain as a rival to French influence in the EEC, and resented Britain's lack of enthusiasm toward the early integrationist moves of the 1950s. He also felt British membership would give the United States too much influence in Europe, a concern that seemed to be confirmed at the end of 1962 when Britain accepted the U.S. offer of Polaris missiles as delivery vehicles for Britain's nuclear warheads.

For his part, Monnet was eager for British membership and even tried to convince Adenauer of his point of view by suggesting that Adenauer refuse to sign the Franco-German treaty unless de Gaulle accepted the British application. But Adenauer shared de Gaulle's anglophobia and agreed that the development of the Franco-German axis was key. In the space of just ten days during January 1963, de Gaulle signed the Friendship Treaty with the Germans and vetoed the British application. He further upset Britain and some of his own EEC partners by reaching the veto decision unilaterally and making the announcement at a press conference in Paris. Paul-Henri Spaak felt de Gaulle "had acted with a lack of consideration unexampled in the history of the EEC, showing utter contempt for his negotiating partners, allies and opponents alike."[33] Since Britain's application was part of the package with those of Denmark and Ireland, their applications were rejected as well.

Britain applied again in 1967, and its application was vetoed for a second time by de Gaulle. Following de Gaulle's resignation in 1969, Britain applied for a third time, and this time its application was accepted, along with those of Denmark, Ireland, and Norway. Following membership negotiations during 1970–1971, Britain, Denmark, and Ireland finally joined the EEC in January 1973; Norway would have joined as well, but a public referendum in September 1972 narrowly went against its membership. The Six had now become the Nine.

A second round of enlargements came in the 1980s, which pushed the borders of the EEC farther south. Greece made its first overtures to the EEC during the late 1950s, but it was turned down on the grounds that its economy was too underdeveloped. It was given associate membership in 1961 as a prelude to full accession, which might have come sooner had it not been for the military coup in April 1967. With the return to civilian government in 1974, Greece applied almost immediately for full membership. The Commission felt Greece's economy was still too weak, but the

Greek government responded that EEC membership would help underpin its attempts to rebuild democracy. The Council of Ministers agreed, negotiations opened in 1976, and Greece joined in 1981.

Spain and Portugal had requested negotiations for associate membership in 1962, but both were dictatorships; although the EEC Treaty said that "any European State may apply to become a member of the Community," democracy has—in practice—been a basic precondition. Spain was given a preferential trade agreement in 1970 and Portugal in 1973, but only with the overthrow of the Caetano regime in Portugal in 1973 and the death of Franco in Spain in 1975 was EEC membership for the two states taken seriously. Despite the two states' relative poverty, problems over fishing rights, and concerns about Spanish and Portuguese workers moving north in search of work, the EEC felt membership would encourage democracy in the Iberian Peninsula and help link the two countries more closely to NATO and Western Europe. Negotiations opened during 1978–1979, and both states joined in 1986, bringing EEC membership to twelve.

The doubling of the membership of the EEC had several political and economic consequences: It increased the influence of the EEC (which was now the largest economic bloc in the world), it complicated the EEC's decisionmaking processes, it reduced the overall influence of France and Germany, and—by bringing in the poorer Mediterranean states—it altered the internal economic balance. Rather than enlarging any farther, it was time to deepen the relationships among the existing twelve members. Applications were made by Turkey (1987), Austria (1989), and Cyprus and Malta (1990), and although East Germany in a sense entered through the back door with the reunification of Germany in 1990, there was to be no further enlargement until 1995.

Summary and Conclusions

Concerns that Europe should be protected from itself were highlighted once again in the years following World War II, leading to a confluence of support among European and U.S. leaders for the idea of building bridges across the chasm of nationalism that had divided Europeans for so long. At the core of the debate was the need to end the long-standing Franco-German rivalry, but to do so in a way that would allow both societies to rebuild as partners rather than competitors and that would prevent German military and industrial power from again becoming a threat to European peace.

Attempts to build supranationalist or federalist bodies were scuttled by Britain and distrusted by some continental Europeans. The only alternative was to build narrower and less ambitious links among European states.

The ECSC was a disappointing compromise for European federalists, but despite its modest aims, it survived when other, more ambitious attempts at integration failed, and it provided the seed that would produce the EEC and Euratom and pull Western Europe slowly—if reluctantly—into pooling its resources and its interests.

Only six states chose to take part in the experiment at first, but its successes, combined with the failures of other experiments that were either too modest (EFTA) or too ambitious (EDC), encouraged other European states to consider EEC membership. The Six became the Nine in 1973 and had reached Twelve by 1986. There were problems along the way, though, bringing increased pressure to once again "relaunch" Europe by focusing on achieving the fundamental goals of the Treaty of Rome.

Further Reading

John Gillingham. *Coal, Steel, and the Rebirth of Europe, 1945–55* (New York: Cambridge University Press, 1991).

A detailed study of the background of the ECSC, its formation, and its early years of operation.

Derek W. Urwin. *The Community of Europe,* 2d ed. (London: Longman, 1995).

The best general history of European integration, tracing events from World War II to Maastricht.

David Weigall and Peter Stirk (Eds.). *The Origins and Development of the European Community* (Leicester: Leicester University Press, 1992).

A complement to Urwin: a history of European integration from 1918 to 1991 told through documents, speeches, treaties, white papers, and excerpts from key texts.

John Pinder. *European Community: The Building of a Union,* 2d ed. (Oxford: Oxford University Press, 1995).

A short and succinct survey of the origins and development of the European Union, assessing the underlying political and economic motives and describing the key steps in the construction of the EU.

Francois Duchene. *Jean Monnet: The First Statesman of Interdependence* (New York: W. W. Norton, 1995).

A combined biography of Jean Monnet and history of European integration, written by Monnet's former speechwriter and press liaison officer.

Notes

1. Jean Monnet, *Memoirs* (Garden City, N.Y.: Doubleday, 1978), 97.

2. John Gillingham, "Jean Monnet and the European Coal and Steel Community: A Preliminary Appraisal," in Douglas Brinkley and Clifford Hackett (Eds.), *Jean Monnet: The Path to European Unity* (New York: St Martin's Press, 1991), 131–137.

3. Quoted in Michael Palmer et al., *European Unity: A Survey of European Organizations* (London: George Allen and Unwin, 1968), 111.

4. Arnold J. Zurcher, *The Struggle to Unite Europe 1940–58* (New York: New York University Press, 1958), 6.

5. Derek W. Urwin, *The Community of Europe*, 2d ed. (Harlow, Essex: Longman, 1995), 34.

6. Alan S. Milward, *The Reconstruction of Western Europe 1945–51* (Berkeley: University of California Press, 1984), 394.

7. Monnet, *Memoirs*, 293.

8. Ibid., 292.

9. Ibid., 294.

10. Robert Schuman, "Declaration of 9 May 1950," in David Weigall and Peter Stirk (Eds.), *The Origins and Development of the European Community* (Leicester: Leicester University Press, 1992), 58–59.

11. Ibid., 58–59.

12. John Gillingham, *Coal, Steel, and the Rebirth of Europe, 1945–55* (New York: Cambridge University Press, 1991), 231.

13. Milward, *Reconstruction of Western Europe*, 402.

14. Gillingham, *Coal, Steel, and the Rebirth of Europe*, xi.

15. Ibid., 319.

16. Ibid., 262–263.

17. Sir Anthony Eden, *Memoirs: Full Circle* (London: Cassell, 1960), 32.

18. Pleven Plan, reproduced in Weigall and Stirk, *Origins and Development of the European Community*, 75–77.

19. Urwin, *Community of Europe*, 63.

20. Ibid., 64–65.

21. Monnet, *Memoirs*, 398–404.

22. Messina Resolution, reproduced in Weigall and Stirk, *Origins and Development of the European Community*, 94.

23. Urwin, *Community of Europe*, 76.

24. Ibid., 76–77.

25. Monnet, *Memoirs*, 518.

26. Don Cook, *Charles de Gaulle: A Biography* (New York: Putnam, 1983), 370–371.

27. Urwin, *Community of Europe*, 130.

28. Quoted in Ghita Ionescu, *Centripetal Politics: Government and the New Centres of Power* (London: Hart-Davis, McGibbon, 1975), 150–154.

29. See John Pinder, *European Community: The Building of a Union* (Oxford: Oxford University Press, 1991), 78–86; Urwin, *Community of Europe*, 132–135.

30. Urwin, ibid., 131.

31. Harold Macmillan, *Riding the Storm 1956–59* (New York: Harper and Row, 1971), 73.

32. Pinder, *European Community*, 46–47.

33. Paul-Henri Spaak, *The Continuing Battle: Memoirs of a European 1933–66* (Boston: Little, Brown, 1971), 375.

4

Consolidation:
The Road to Amsterdam

By 1986, membership in the European Economic Community (EEC) had grown to twelve, and the EEC had become known simply as the European Community (EC, or simply the Community). Its member states had a combined population of 322 million and accounted for just over one-fifth of all world trade. The Community had its own administrative structure and an independent body of law, and its citizens had direct (but limited) representation through the European Parliament (EP), which also gave them a more direct psychological and political stake in the evolution of the Community.

However, progress on integration remained uneven. The creation of a common market had been one of the fundamental goals of the Treaty of Rome, and yet during the early 1980s the EC still had far to go; the customs union was in place, but nontariff barriers remained to the free movement of people and capital—including different national technical, health, and quality standards and varying levels of indirect taxation (such as value-added tax, or VAT, a form of sales tax). Europe was also facing growing competition from Japan and the United States.

By the early 1970s, it had become common to hear the term "Euro-sclerosis" used to describe the economic stagnation, double-digit inflation, and high unemployment that afflicted Europe. European industry was not competing strongly on the global market, scientists and industrialists were failing to collaborate, and the remaining barriers to internal trade denied European businesses full access to a true single market. From the 1950s to the early 1970s, the EEC had focused on issues such as agriculture and building the common market. Changes in the balance of global power now combined with global exchange rate instability and disparities in the economic performance of European states to prompt a shift to issues such as foreign policy and economic union.

There could be no true single market without monetary union (uniform interest and inflation rates and complete financial integration).[1] In turn, it was a relatively short hop (in neofunctionalist terms) from monetary union to the creation of a single currency, which was a controversial idea because of its implications for national sovereignty; a state that gave up control over its currency would effectively give up control over its national economy. However, monetary union was also fundamental to the idea of true economic union and in turn would be a significant step on the road to political union. These issues now moved to the top of the European agenda; in the space of just ten years, three major new treaties were agreed upon that expanded the reach of integration, membership of the Community grew to fifteen, and agreement was reached on the development of a single European currency.

Toward Economic and Monetary Union

The EEC Treaty had mentioned the need to "coordinate" economic policies but had given the Community no specific powers to ensure this, and in practice coordination meant little more than "polite ritualistic consultation."[2] Monnet, Spaak, and others had long felt monetary union was essential, but the earliest proposals to move in that direction constantly met with concerns about loss of national sovereignty. A prerequisite for a single currency was a system of fixed exchange rates, but EEC leaders disagreed about whether economic union or monetary union should come first.[3] France thought monetary cooperation would lead to economic union, while West Germany thought economic union should come first. There was little question, though, that exchange rate stability was an essential foundation for both the common market and the Common Agricultural Policy.

The principle of economic and monetary union (EMU) was agreed at a 1969 summit of EEC leaders at The Hague, and an ad hoc committee was appointed under the leadership of Luxembourg Prime Minister Pierre Werner. It recommended movement on the economic and monetary fronts at the same time, as well as the achievement of fixed exchange rates in stages by 1980.[4] The Six accordingly agreed to control fluctuations in the value of their currencies by holding their exchange rates steady relative to each other while holding their value within ± 2.25 percent of the U.S. dollar in a structure known as the "snake in the tunnel." They would meanwhile make more effort to coordinate national economic policies, with their finance ministers meeting at least three times annually.

Unfortunately, the snake was launched in April 1972, just eight months after Richard Nixon's administration took the United States off the gold standard. Prompted by a growing U.S. defense budget, weakening productivity, falling exports, rising inflation, and a growing balance-of-payments deficit, Nixon had signaled the end of the Bretton Woods system by imposing domestic wage and price controls and placing a 10 percent surcharge on imports. The result was international monetary turbulence, which was deepened in 1973 with war between Egypt and Israel and the oil crisis sparked by the Organization of Petroleum Exporting Countries (OPEC). In their anxiety to control inflation and encourage economic growth, several EC member states left the snake: Britain and Denmark left within weeks of joining; France refused to join, then joined, then left in 1974, then rejoined in 1975, then left again. [5] The goal of achieving EMU by 1980 was quietly abandoned.

A new initiative was launched during 1977–1978, spearheaded by Commission President Roy Jenkins, West German Chancellor Helmut Schmidt, and French President Valéry Giscard d'Estaing. The result was the European Monetary System (EMS), which came into force in March 1979, replacing the snake with an Exchange Rate Mechanism (ERM) (operating on a similar basis) founded on a European Currency Unit (ecu). The goal of the EMS was to create a zone of monetary stability, with governments taking action to keep their currencies as stable as possible relative to the ecu, whose value was calculated on the basis of a basket of national currencies, weighted according to their relative strengths (the deutschmark made up nearly 33 percent of the ecu, the French franc nearly 20 percent, the Dutch guilder 10 percent, and so on). The hope was that the ecu would slowly become the normal means of settling international debts between EC members, psychologically preparing them for the idea of a single European currency.

EMU was taken a step further in 1989 with the elaboration by Commission President Jacques Delors of a three-stage plan: [6]

1. Stage one involved the establishment of free capital movement in the Community and greater monetary and macroeconomic cooperation between the member states and their central banks.
2. Stage two originally involved the creation of a European System of Central Banks that would coexist with national central banks and which would monitor and coordinate national monetary policies. The system was to have been in place by January 1994, but the European Monetary Institute (EMI) was created instead to pave the way for the final stage by promoting cooperation between national central banks, monitoring the EMS, and strengthening coordination of the monetary policies of the member states.
3. Stage three involved the fixing of exchange rates and the creation of a single currency.

The report was approved at the Madrid summit of the European Council in June 1989, when it was also agreed that an intergovernmental conference would meet to decide what changes would be made to the treaties. In the event, the Maastricht Treaty of 1993 (discussed later in this chapter) outlined several economic convergence criteria that the member states would have to meet before they could adopt the single currency (see Chapter 12). If at least seven EU states met these criteria, the European Council would set a date for stage three and create a European Central Bank, which would subsequently have sole authority for setting monetary policy and would pave the way for the development of a single currency.

The Commission argued that the benefits of full EMU included a more efficient European economy; a more effective platform from which to deal with inflation, unemployment, and regional economic disparities; and a way of enabling the EC to take a stronger role in the international economy and cushion the effects of external problems and crises. Some of the member states demurred, however, finding that the effort involved in controlling exchange rates caused their economies to overheat. For example, Britain initially stayed out of the ERM because of Margaret Thatcher's refusal to give up control over domestic fiscal policy, while Spain, Portugal, and Greece were concerned about the weaknesses of their currencies. Several exchange rate realignments were made to help member states build monetary stability, but this became more difficult as turbulence in world money markets worsened in the early 1990s and as the deutschmark came under pressure following German reunification.[7] By 1992–1993, the ERM appeared to have collapsed: Britain and Italy joined, then pulled out, and Spain, Portugal, and Ireland devalued their currencies.

Completing the Single Market

Economic integration was boosted by the early success of the EMS (or at least its survival against all the odds and its achievement of exchange rate "constraint")[8] and by a landmark 1978 decision by the European Court of Justice that goods meeting the standards of one EC member state could not be barred from sale in another member state (the *Cassis de Dijon* case; see Chapter 9). However, there were concerns that progress on economic integration was being handicapped by inflation and unemployment and by the temptation of member states to protect their home industries and to fragment the internal market with nontariff barriers such as subsidies.[9] Competition from the United States and Japan was also growing, and the EC was losing ground, especially in high-tech industries.

In response, a decision was reached at the 1983 European Council in Stuttgart to revive the original goal outlined in the Treaty of Rome to create a common (or single) market. The Commission was asked to draw up a concrete list of suggestions, which took the form of a white paper developed under the direction of internal market commissioner Lord Cockfield. Published in June 1985, the document listed nearly three hundred separate and specific pieces of legislation that would have to be agreed to and implemented in order to remove all remaining nontariff barriers and create a true single market.[10]

David Cameron has argued that several different economic and political factors came together to make the Single European Act (SEA) possible. The member states had become increasingly dependent on intra-EC trade, they were experiencing declining growth and worsening unemployment, the EMS was off the ground, and European business strongly favored the single market. At the same time, the Commission—especially under its new president, Jacques Delors—was building a strong case for the single market. The Court of Justice had helped clear the way with the *Cassis* decision, and both Parliament and the Council of Ministers were pushing for the kinds of institutional reforms in the EC that would coincidentally fit with the goals of the single market.[11] Even lukewarm Europeans could accept the idea of a single market.

The Single European Act was signed in Luxembourg in February 1986 and, after ratification by national legislatures, came into force in July 1987. It had several goals (see Box 4.1), the most important of which was to complete the single market by midnight December 31, 1992. This would be achieved by removing all remaining physical, fiscal, and technical barriers to trade, thereby creating "an area without internal frontiers in which the free movement of goods, persons, services and capital is assured" (SEA, Article 13). Even the Euroskeptical Margaret Thatcher was pleased: "At last, I felt, we were going to get the Community back on course, concentrating on its role as a huge market, with all the opportunities that would bring to our industries."[12]

The Single European Act was widely acclaimed as the single most important and successful step in the process of European integration since the Treaty of Rome. In practical terms, it meant that the Commission and the Council of Ministers had to agree on 282 new pieces of legislation, which then had to be applied at the national level. To give the member states at least two years to implement those laws, they all had to be agreed to by the end of 1990. In the event, the deadline came and went with only 92 percent of the proposals adopted by the Council of Ministers and only 79 percent adopted and transposed into national law.[13] (Ironically, Denmark and Britain had the best implementation rates.) Regardless, the single market went into force in January 1993 with the understanding that the backlog of legislation would be cleared as soon as possible.

The SEA created the single biggest market and trading unit in the world. Its effects included the following: Many internal passport and customs controls were eased or lifted; banks could do business throughout the Community; companies could do business and sell their products

BOX 4.1
The Single European Act

The Single European Act not only removed most of the remaining physical, fiscal, and technical barriers to the creation of a true common market but also had important political consequences:

- It gave the EC responsibility over new policy areas that had not been mentioned in the Treaty of Rome, such as the environment, research and development, and re gional policy.
- It gave new powers to the Court of Justice and eased its workload by creating a Court of First Instance to hear certain kinds of cases.
- It gave legal status to meetings of heads of government under the European Council and gave new powers to the Council of Ministers and the European Parliament (see Chapters 7 and 8).

    Under the new assent procedure, no new members could join the EC or be given associate membership without the approval of an absolute majority in Parliament.

    Under the cooperation procedure, decisionmaking was streamlined and Parliament was given more power over the Council of Ministers. The use of qualified majority voting in the Council was expanded; unanimity would be needed only for decisions on new members and on the general principles of new policies. For all other decisions, a qualified majority would be enough. At the same time, when the Council had made a decision on the basis of a qualified majority, Parliament had the right to amend or reject the proposal, and it could be overruled only by unanimity in the Council. This was a major step toward giving Parliament true legislative powers.

- It gave legal status to European Political Cooperation (foreign policy coordination) and said that member states should work toward a European foreign policy and work more closely together on defense and security issues.
- It made economic and monetary union an objective of the EC and promoted cohe sion (reductions in the gap between rich and poor parts of the EC, thereby avoiding a "two-speed Europe").

throughout the Community; there was little to prevent EC residents from living, working, opening bank accounts, and drawing pensions anywhere in the EC; protectionism became illegal; and monopolies on everything from the supply of electricity to telecommunications were broken down. In legal terms, it was now almost as easy for Europeans to move among the twelve member states as it was for Americans to move throughout the United States. In short, the dream of British Foreign Secretary Ernest Bevin in 1951—"to be able to take a ticket at Victoria Station in London and go anywhere I damn well please"—had finally (almost) come true.

Social and Regional Integration

Social policy was long a poor relation of economic and political integration. Among its elements were improved working conditions and standards of living for workers, equal pay for equal work among men and women, social security for migrant workers, and more geographical and occupational mobility for workers. Although the EEC Treaty made provision for the development of a European social policy, the issue was left in the hands of the member states and was very narrowly defined. The result was that social issues received little attention until the mid-1970s, when pressure began to grow to mitigate negative changes in the workplace brought on by increased competition and the opening of markets.

Even during the mid-1960s (before the poorer Mediterranean states and Ireland had joined), per capita gross domestic product (GDP) in the EEC's ten richest regions was nearly four times greater than that in its ten poorest regions. The gap closed during the early 1970s, but with the accession of Britain, Ireland, and Greece, it grew to the point at which the richest regions were five times richer than the poorest.[14] Social and regional policy has since focused on trying to close the gap and promoting economic and social "cohesion" by helping poorer regions, revitalizing those affected by serious industrial decline, working to combat long-term unemployment, providing youth job training, and helping to develop rural areas. Economic assistance is given by the Commission in the form of grants from four separate funds known collectively as structural funds: the European Social Fund (ESF), the European Regional Development Fund (ERDF), the Cohesion Fund, and part of the European Agricultural Guidance and Guarantee Fund (see Chapter 13).

The first real attempts to improve the quality of life and social security came only with the creation of the European Social Fund in 1974. Its initial focus was employment and retraining, but in 1983 the Council of Ministers decided it should focus on youth unemployment and job creation in the poorest parts of the EC. The Single European Act made cohesion a central part of economic integration, and a further boost for social policy came in 1989 with the Charter of Fundamental Social Rights for Workers (the Social Charter), which promoted free movement of workers, fair pay, better living and working conditions, freedom of association, and protection of children and adolescents. The Social Charter was adopted by eleven EC states at the December 1989 European Council, with Britain's Conservative government opting out because it did not want to give up control over employment law and policies. (One of the first actions of the new Blair government in 1997 was to adopt the Social Charter.)

The second major element in social policy was the European Regional Development Fund. The Commission had given relatively little attention to regional disparities until Britain and Ireland joined the EEC in 1973, changing the economic balance of the Community because of their relatively low levels of prosperity. The Commission sponsored the 1973 Thomson Report on the regional implications of enlargement, which concluded that these disparities were an obstacle to a "balanced expansion" in economic activity and to EMU.[15] Although some development funds had been channeled through the European Investment Bank during the 1960s, it was clear that something much more was needed.

France and West Germany became interested in regional policy as a means of helping Britain integrate with its new partners, and the government of Prime Minister Edward Heath promoted the creation of a regional fund as a way of making EEC membership more palatable to Britons concerned about the potential costs of membership.[16] Agreement was reached among the Six to launch the ERDF in 1973, but plans were disrupted by the fiscal and economic crises of 1973. The Fund was finally launched in 1975. It was made clear that ERDF funds would not replace national spending on the development of poorer regions but instead would complement them (the concept of "additionality"). At most, ERDF funds would match existing spending, and they could be used only for projects that would create new jobs in industry or services or improve infrastructure. The identification of priority regions was left up to the member states.

While structural funds accounted for 18 percent of EC expenditures in 1984, they took up over one-third of the EU budget (nearly $36 billion) in 1998. Despite increases in the funds made available under ERDF, regional disparities in the EU remain; the gap between the highest and lowest income levels in the EU is twice that in the United States, and neither the EU nor the member states have been able to deal effectively with unemployment, which stood at just over 10 percent in the EU in late 1998, compared with 4.5 percent in the United States and 4.1 percent in Japan.

Toward Political Union

The highly controversial idea of political integration long received less attention because of a prevailing feeling that there was little hope of building political union without first achieving economic union. False starts had been made with the European Political Community and with an attempt in 1961 to draw up a political charter that would spell out the terms of political union (the Fouchet Plan, named for Christian Fouchet, French ambassador to Denmark).[17] During the 1960s the foreign ministers of the Six looked at ways of promoting political union and concluded that it would best be done outside the EC framework rather than by giving the EC itself more power.

A report drawn up by Belgian diplomat Etienne Davignon and published in 1970 argued that a first step should be taken by encouraging cooperation in an area in which an obvious common set of interests already existed; he felt that foreign policy coordination was the answer, especially given the growing divergence between U.S. and Western European policies. The Davignon Report recommended quarterly meetings of the six foreign ministers, liaison among EC ambassadors in foreign capitals, and common EC instructions on certain matters for those ambassadors.[18]

At Community summits in 1972 and 1974, proposals were tabled for reaching political union by 1980—a target that was wildly unrealistic, given prevailing ideas about the EC and about the work that needed to be done to achieve economic integration. Work developed instead on the coordination of foreign policies, in a process known as European Political Cooperation (EPC). EPC achieved some early successes, such as the 1970 joint EC policy declaration on the Middle East and the signing of the Yaoundé Conventions on aid to poorer countries. In 1975, the Final Act of the Conference on Security and Cooperation in Europe (held in Helsinki) was signed by Italian Prime Minister Aldo Moro "in the name of the European Community." By 1976, EC ambassadors to the UN were meeting weekly to coordinate their actions.

EPC was finally given legal status with the Single European Act. It worked well in some areas but was more reactive than proactive. This became clear during the 1990–1991 Gulf crisis when the EC issued common demands to the Iraqi regime and imposed an embargo on Iraqi oil imports, but the member states contributed at very different levels to the 1991 counterinvasion (see Chapter 15). Differences also became clear in December 1991 when Germany unilaterally recognized Croatia and Slovenia without conferring with its EC partners.

Political union remained on the agenda of European Councils during the 1970s and 1980s, with the focus for discussion coming from reports written by various worthies. In 1976, a committee headed by Belgian Prime Minister Leo Tindemans recommended continuing cooperation on foreign and economic policies but also suggested more powers for the European Council and a new and more powerful bicameral Parliament. In 1984, a group of Members of the European Parliament (MEPs) under the leadership of Italian Altiero Spinelli, motivated in part by a concern among MEPs to prove the worth of the now directly elected Parliament, also suggested more powers for the European Council and the European Parliament and proposed a draft treaty on European Union. These reports set off a discussion about reforming EC institutions in such a way as to allow the Community to respond more quickly and effectively to emergencies and to take real steps toward economic and political integration.

Determined to reassert French leadership in the EC, President François Mitterrand focused on the political union theme at the Fontainebleau European Council summit in 1984, with the result that a decision was taken at Milan in June 1985 to open an intergovernmental conference (IGC) on political union. The IGC finally opened in December 1990, alongside an IGC on economic and monetary union. The outcome was the Treaty on European Union, agreed at the Maastricht European Council summit in December 1991 and signed by the EC foreign and economics ministers in February 1992 (see Box 4.2). The original wording of the draft treaty mentioned the goal of federal union, but Britain balked at this, so it was changed to "an ever closer union among the peoples of Europe, in which decisions are taken as closely as possible to the citizen."

The Maastricht Treaty had to be ratified by the twelve member states before it came into force. A major setback came with its rejection in a Danish referendum in June 1992. Following agreement that Denmark could opt out of the single currency, common defense arrangements, European citizenship, and cooperation on justice and home affairs, a second referendum was held in May 1993, and the treaty was accepted. Following ratification in the other eleven states, the Maastricht Treaty came into force in November 1993, eleven months late. With its passage, the European Community became one of the three "pillars" that made up the European Union.

One of those pillars was the Common Foreign and Security Policy (CFSP), which replaced EPC. Its goals were only very loosely defined, with vague talk about the need to safeguard "common values" and "fundamental interests," to "preserve peace and strengthen international security," and to "promote international cooperation." The continuing weaknesses in European foreign policy continued to be emphasized by the lack of a European military and by the often halfhearted response to security problems, such as U.S.-led attempts to put pressure on the Iraqi regime in 1998 and the violent suppression by the Yugoslav government of the secession movement among ethnic Albanians in Kosovo the same year.

The ink had barely dried on the amended Maastricht Treaty before EU leaders agreed that a new IGC should be convened to take stock of the progress of European integration and to introduce the institutional and policy changes that many felt were needed in light of the projected growth of the EU to a membership of twenty countries or more. The deliberations of the conference resulted in the Treaty of Amsterdam, which was signed in October 1997 and came into force in May 1999. Much was expected of the treaty, but it fell far short of moving Europe closer to political union, and the fifteen leaders were unable to agree to substantial changes in the structure of EU institutions. However, more focus was given to policies on asylum, immigration, unemployment, social policy, health protection, consumer protection, the environment, and foreign affairs; enlargement of the

BOX 4.2
The Treaty on European Union

The Maastricht treaty had several elements:

The creation of the European Union, a new label meant to symbolize the next stage in the process of European integration, based on three "pillars": a reformed and strengthened European Community and two areas in which there was to be more regularized intergovernmental cooperation: a Common Foreign and Security Policy, and home affairs and justice. Responsibility for the CFSP was to remain with the individual governments rather than being given to the EU.

A timetable for the creation of a single European currency by January 1999 at the latest. For this to happen, a majority of member states would have to achieve inflation rates that were no more than 1.5 percent higher than the three lowest national rates in the EU, set long-term interest rates that were no more than 3 percent higher than the three lowest EU rates, reduce their budget deficits to less than 3 percent of GDP, and avoid devaluing their currencies against any of those in the ERM for at least two years.

    If these terms were not met by the end of 1996, the EU leaders would decide in mid-1998 which EC states were ready for EMU and could launch a limited currency union among those states in January 1999. The European Central Bank would need to have been operating for at least six months before exchange rates were fixed.

Extension of EU responsibility to new areas such as consumer protection, public health policy, transportation, education, and (except in Britain) social policy.

More intergovernmental cooperation on immigration and asylum, the creation of a European police intelligence agency (Europol) to combat organized crime and drug trafficking, the creation of a new Committee of the Regions (see Chapter 10), and more regional funds for poorer EC states.

New rights for European citizens and the creation of an ambiguous European Union "citizenship," meaning, for example, the rights of citizens to live wherever they liked in the EU and to stand and vote in local and European elections.

More powers for the European Parliament, including the codecision procedure under which certain kinds of legislation were made subject to a third reading in Parliament before they could be adopted by the Council of Ministers (see Chapter 8).

EU to the east was given the green light, and the goal of launching the single currency in January 1999 was confirmed.

    A decision was taken in 1995 to call the new currency the euro, and leaders of the member states met in May 1998 to decide which qualified to become part of the single currency. It was decided that all but Greece had made sufficient progress, but Britain, Denmark, and Sweden opted not to join, at least initially. In June 1998, the new European Central Bank was created, and in January 1999, the eleven member states permanently fixed their exchange rates relative to each other and to the euro. If all goes to plan, euro coins and bank notes will become available on January 1, 2002, and national currencies will cease to be legal tender on July 1, 2002. Economic and monetary union will then be complete, at least among participating states.

More Enlargement: Looking North and East

Although any European state can apply to join the EU, in practice there are at least four basic requirements: In addition to being European, an applicant must also be democratic, must have a functioning free-market economy and the capacity to cope with the competitive pressures of capitalism, and must be able to take on the obligations of the *acquis communitaire* (the body of laws and regulations already adopted by the EU). Deciding which countries meet these criteria has been difficult, not least because of the problem of defining "Europe." There was little question about rejecting an application from Morocco in 1987, but the eastern borders of Europe are more debatable. Because these borders are usually demarked by the Ural Mountains, twenty-six countries theoretically qualified for membership in 1992: six in Western Europe, seven in Eastern Europe, the three Baltic states, three former Soviet republics, the five former Yugoslavian states, and two Mediterranean states.

The issue of future expansion was divided during the 1980s and early 1990s by a debate over deepening versus widening. Deepeners wanted the EU to develop closer ties before it took on new members, while wideners argued that membership should be opened to other states immediately. British Prime Minister John Major favored widening mainly because he wanted the process of integration to slow down, while German Chancellor Helmut Kohl wanted to bring in new Eastern European members to prevent them from breaking down into ethnic rivalries, as had occurred in Yugoslavia. In a sense, the admission of East Germany through the back door with the reunification of Germany in October 1990 was a dry run for the possibility of further eastward expansion.

Other Western European states were long the most obvious candidates for membership, if only because they would have to make the fewest adjustments. In 1990, negotiations began on the creation of the European Economic Area (EEA), under which the terms of the SEA would be extended to the seven EFTA members, in return for which they would accept the rules of the single market. The proposal made economic sense, given that 55 percent of EFTA exports went to the EC and 26 percent of EC exports went to EFTA.[19] The EFTA states were also stable and wealthy and would have to make relatively few adjustments to integrate themselves into the single market.

Negotiations on the EEA were completed in February 1992, but the Swiss turned down membership in a December 1992 referendum; thus, only six EFTA states joined when the EEA finally came into force on January 1, 1994. Almost before it was born, however, the EEA had begun to lose its relevance because Austria, Sweden, Norway, and Finland had already applied for EC membership. Negotiations were completed in early 1994, referenda were held in each country, and all but Norway (where once again the vote went against membership) joined the EU in January 1995. This increased the land area of the EU by one-third and gave it a common border with Russia.

The Swiss had considered applying for EC membership in 1992, but they rejected the EEA and are now completely surrounded by the EU. Demands on Switzerland to open its highways to EU trucks and intra-EU trade will undoubtedly increase the pressures for EU membership, although its neutrality and unique system of government remain major obstacles. Iceland, for its part, has a population of just 300,000, relies largely on exports of fish, and does over half its trade with the EU; it too will find the logic of joining the EU increasingly difficult to resist. With a population of just 30,000, Liechtenstein is little more than an enclave of Switzerland and will likely follow the Swiss lead.

Looking to the Mediterranean, Turkey, Cyprus, and Malta have long had associate membership of the EU and have applied for full membership, but each has problems:

- The EC agreed in 1963 that Turkish membership was possible, but Turkey is big, poor, and predominantly Islamic (which raises economic and social questions); its application is opposed by Greece; and there is a debate about whether it is really European (Europe ends at the Bosporus Strait, so only a small part of Turkey is actually in Europe). It has been an associate member since 1963 and applied for full membership in 1987, but Turkey has been told by the EU that it does not meet the political and economic criteria for membership. Perhaps as a first step to eventual accession, a customs union between the EU and Turkey came into force in December 1995.
- Cyprus has political problems, not the least of which is the division between Greek and Turkish sectors that has been in place since 1974. It has had associate membership since 1972 and applied for full membership in 1990.
- Malta has roughly the same population as Luxembourg and Iceland (about 350,000), but it is much poorer. There are also doubts about whether it should be granted the influence membership would give it

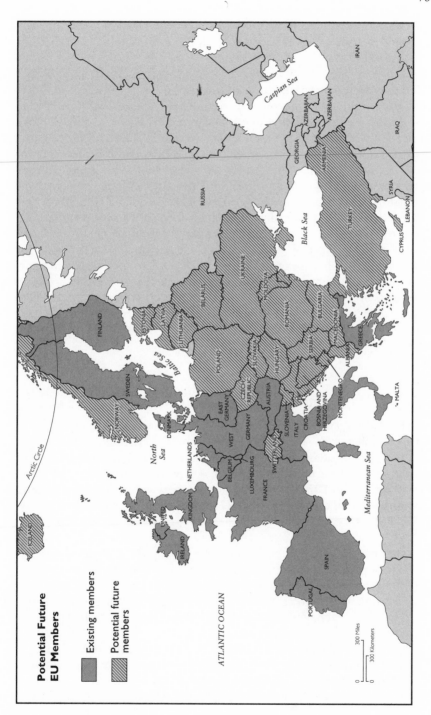

Potential Future EU Members

Existing members

Potential future members

over economic giants such as Germany. It has had associate membership since 1970 and applied for full membership in 1990, but it suspended its application in 1996.

For the medium term, the focus of interest lies in Eastern Europe. There are strong political and economic arguments in favor: EU membership would promote the transition to capitalism and democracy; it would open up new investment opportunities; and it would pull Eastern Europe into a strategic relationship with the West that could be useful if problems in (or with) Russia worsen. With some of these issues in mind, Europe Agreements were signed during 1994–1998 with Poland, Hungary, the Czech Republic, Slovakia, Romania, Bulgaria, and the three Baltic republics; these allow for gradual movement toward free trade and are designed to prepare the signatories for eventual EU membership. In 1997, the EU launched the Agenda 2000 program, which contained a list of all the measures that the European Commission felt needed to be agreed to in order to bring ten Eastern European states into the EU (see Chapter 15). In the spring of 1998, the EU decided to open negotiations with Hungary, Poland, the Czech Republic, Slovenia, Estonia, and Cyprus, but the expectation is that the first of these will not join until 2002 at the earliest, with 2004–2006 more realistic target dates for most.

Summary and Conclusions

The 1951 Treaty of Paris had barely been signed before the process of European integration was being dismissed by skeptics, and its demise has been predicted regularly ever since. Nonetheless, much has been achieved, and the voices of the doubters are much quieter than they once were. From a time during the 1970s, when the European experiment seemed to have become stuck in the doldrums, in the last decade the EU has picked up new speed and vitality, although by no means have all the problems gone.

- The single market has been all but been completed, opening up rich new opportunities for European business and industry.
- Monetary union appears to have survived many of its teething troubles, and as this book went to press, eleven EU member states had fixed their exchange rates with a view to replacing their national currencies with the euro in 2002.
- For all its problems, the Maastricht Treaty was a substantial step toward political union, even if much still remains to be done to develop an effective European foreign policy.

TABLE 4.1   Enlargement of the European Union

	Membership Application Lodged	Associate Membership	Europe Agreements	Full Membership
United Kingdom	1961, 1967, 1969	—	—	1973
Ireland	1961, 1967, 1969	—	—	1973
Denmark	1961, 1967, 1969	—	—	1973
Norway	1962, 1967, 1969, 1992	—	—	—
Greece	1975	1961	—	1981
Spain	1977	—	—	1986
Portugal	1977	—	—	1986
Finland	1992	—	—	1995
Austria	1989	—	—	1995
Sweden	1991	—	—	1995
Turkey	1987	1963	—	—
Cyprus	1990	1972	—	—
Malta	1990[a]	1970	—	—
Morocco	1987	—	—	—
Hungary	1994	1991	1994	—
Poland	1994	1991	1994	—
Estonia	1995	1995	1998	—
Latvia	1995	1995	1998	—
Lithuania	1995	1995	1998	—
Bulgaria	1995	1993	1995	—
Romania	1995	1993	1995	—
Slovakia	1995	1993	1995	—
Czech Republic	1996	1993	1995	—
Slovenia	1996	1996[b]	—	—

[a]Suspended 1996 by Malta
[b]Not ratified

- The member states have developed common positions in a wide range of policy areas—including social issues, internal security, and the environment—and have built a large body of common laws and regulations.
- Work still needs to be done to make the EU institutions more efficient and democratic; too much of what they do is shrouded in secrecy, and too few of their officials are publicly accountable.
- EU membership has grown to fifteen; it now reaches from the Arctic Circle to the Aegean Sea, from Berlin to the Strait of Gibraltar, and from Sicily to the North Atlantic coast of Ireland. It has a total population of 373 million and a gross national product of nearly $8 trillion, and it accounts for 42 percent of global exports. Meanwhile, several neighboring states hope to join the EU in the next few years.

Further Reading

Daniel Gros and Niels Thygesen. *European Monetary Integration: From the European Monetary System to European Monetary Union* (London: Longman, 1992).

A history of European monetary integration that discusses the evolution of the European Monetary System and prospects for EMU.

Gregory Treverton (Ed.). *The Shape of the New Europe* (New York: Council on Foreign Relations Press, 1992).

An edited collection of chapters written by scholars of European integration on Europe's prospects in the wake of the completion of the single market.

Andrew Duff, John Pinder, and Roy Pryce (Eds.). *Maastricht and Beyond: Building the European Union* (New York: Routledge, 1994).

A multiauthor collection that looks in detail at the content of Maastricht and assesses its likely effects on the policies and institutions of the EU.

Pierre-Henri Laurent and Marc Maresceau (Eds). *The State of the European Union, Vol. 4: Deepening and Widening* (Boulder: Lynne Rienner, 1998).

The most recent of this series of assessments of the EU, this one focusing on enlargement, the CFSP, social issues, monetary union, and external relations.

Laura Cram, Desmond Dinan, and Neill Nugent (Eds). *Developments in the European Union* (London: Macmillan, 1999).

An edited collection on recent developments in EU institutions and policies, including issues such as enlargement.

Notes

1. George Zis, "European Monetary Union: The Case for Complete Monetary Integration," in Frank McDonald and Stephen Dearden (Eds.), *European Economic Integration* (London: Longman, 1992).

2. Tommaso Paddoa-Schioppa, *Financial and Monetary Integration in Europe: 1990, 1992 and Beyond* (New York: Group of Thirty, 1990), 18.

3. Derek W. Urwin, *The Community of Europe,* 2d ed. (Harlow, Essex: Longman, 1995), 155.

4. Commission of the European Communities, "Economic and Monetary Union in the Community" (the Werner Report), *Bulletin of the European Communities,* Supplement 11 (1970).

5. Loukas Tsoukalis, *The New European Economy Revisited,* 3d ed. (New York: Oxford University Press, 1997), 190.

6. European Commission, *Report of the Committee for the Study of Economic and Monetary Union* (Luxembourg: Office of Official Publications, 1989).

7. Ian Barnes and Pamela M. Barnes, *The Enlarged European Union* (London and New York: Longman, 1995), 131–132.

8. Commission of the European Communities, *Report on Economic and Monetary Union in the European Community* (the Delors Report) (Luxembourg: Office for Official Publications of the European Communities, 1989).

9. For details on the development of the single market program, see Kenneth A. Armstrong and Simon J. Bulmer, *The Governance of the Single European Market* (Manchester and New York: Manchester University Press, 1998), chapter 1.

10. Commission of the European Communities, *Completing the Internal Market: The White Paper* (Luxembourg: Office for Official Publications of the European Communities, 1985).

11. David R. Cameron, "The 1992 Initiative: Causes and Consequences," in Alberta Sbragia (Ed.), *Euro-Politics: Institutions and Policymaking in the "New" European Community* (Washington, D.C.: Brookings Institution, 1992), 36–56.

12. Margaret Thatcher, *The Downing Street Years* (New York: HarperCollins, 1993), 556.

13. *Eurecom* 4:11 (December 1992).

14. Stephen George, *Politics and Policy in the European Community,* 3d ed. (Oxford: Oxford University Press, 1996), 196.

15. Commission of the European Communities, *Report on the Regional Problems of the Enlarged Community* (the Thomson Report), COM(73)550 (Brussels: Commission of the European Communities, 1973).

16. George, *Politics and Policy,* 175.

17. See Urwin, *Community of Europe,* 104–107.

18. Ibid., 148.

19. Rene Schwok, "EC-EFTA Relations," in Leon Hurwitz and Christian Lequesne, *The State of the European Community, Vol. 1: Policies, Institutions, and Debates in the Transition Years* (Boulder: Lynne Rienner, 1991).

5

Elaboration:
The European Union Today

The European Union has come a long way in just two generations, but its emergence has complicated discussions about the motives behind international cooperation and the nature of international relations. The EU only partly fits with conventional ideas about the ways societies organize and govern themselves, and its character is difficult to tie down.

Most scholars agree that the EU is not a "state" because it lacks many of the conventional features of a state, including a strong and separate legal identity, political unity and sovereignty, powers of coercion, and significant financial independence. There may be a European bureaucracy and a growing body of European law, but there is no European police force, there is no European army, and the EU cannot raise direct and universal taxes. At the same time, most scholars also agree that it has developed levels of power and influence over its members that go far beyond those enjoyed by conventional international organizations. This has led to the argument that the EU is not really an institution but is better approached as an ideal, a process, a regime, or even a network that has involved not so much as a transfer of powers as a pooling of sovereignty.[1]

Jean Monnet argued in 1975 that he saw no point in trying to imagine what political form the United States of Europe would take and that "the words about which people argue—federation or confederation—are inadequate and imprecise."[2] He and his contemporaries might have been able to avoid the issue then, but it is less easily avoided today. The powers of the EU have taken on new substance, making it essential that we understand its political form so that we better understand the implications of European integration for the lives of European citizens, for the future of the member states, and for the relationship between the member states and the rest of the world.

As discussed in the Preface, part of the reason why so many Europeans and Americans are still confused and unclear about the European Union is because it has changed its form so often. Chapter 1 looked at the different theories that have been proposed to explain how and why integration occurs, and Chapters 2–4 looked at how the EU has changed and at the forces that set off those changes. This chapter attempts to pin down the character and identity of the European Union today and to understand what the EU has become by looking at what it means to its citizens and to those outside Europe.

The European Polity

The key to understanding the EU as a polity (a politically organized system or regime) may be to see it as being caught in a complex network of competing tensions. At least five different sets of forces have been at work in Europe, pulling the EU in several different directions:

1. Intergovernmental versus supranational. One of the fundamental tensions in the process of European integration has been that between the governments of the member states, which are trying to preserve their sovereignty by relating to each other as equals, and the different forces and impulses that compel or encourage them to give up that sovereignty to a new supranational authority.
2. Independence versus dependence. Europe after World War II consisted of several legally independent polities, but they were linked more closely than some of them cared to admit by history, culture, and shared political and economic interests. The process of integration has caused those ties to be strengthened and redefined, so that the EU member states are moving from a high degree of independence to an increased degree of mutual dependence.
3. Competition versus cooperation. The history of Europe until 1945 was one of competition, conflict, and constantly changing alliances and balances of power. Some of those conflicts persist, and the balance of power continues to change, but it does so inclusively rather than exclusively and out of a sense of both cooperation and competition. The conflicting goals of separate states have been replaced by the common goal of addressing shared interests.
4. Autonomy versus unity. The process of integration has reduced the freedom of action of individual European states and has steadily encouraged them to work together by pulling down the structural,

political, technical, physical, fiscal, and attitudinal barriers that have divided them. As the autonomy of the states declines, so does their individual sovereignty, and the possibility of European political union becomes more real.

5. Elitism versus democracy. The citizens of Western Europe have had relatively little input into the development of the EU, because most of the initiatives have come from political, economic, and social elites. Only the European Parliament is directly elected, but it has less power over decisionmaking than other appointed or indirectly elected bodies. The balance is changing, though, as citizens become more interested and involved in influencing EU policy.

Wherever the EU now sits and wherever it is headed, its political form has always had some combination of objective features and characteristics at a given point in time. What are those features at the turn of the millennium?

First, the European Union has gone well beyond the powers of any international organization that has ever existed, and it has developed an unprecedented level of authority over its constituent members. However, even though it has several different "governing" institutions, it is not yet a "government" in the sense that it rules and has powers of control and coercion. It has executive, legislative, and judicial powers within its own sphere of authority but must share its authority with that of the individual governments of the member states. Although supranationalism may describe elements of the political process of the EU, it has been argued that the EU has always rested ultimately on a set of intergovernmental bargains.[3] Opinion is divided about the extent to which it has moved beyond those kinds of bargains; realists argue that the member states are still the key actors and that integration moves according to the decisions they take, while neofunctionalists argue that integration has its own expansive logic and has taken on an irresistible life and momentum of its own.

Second, although it has its own body of treaties and laws that amount to something like a constitution (see Box 5.1) and has a court that can interpret their meaning, the EU has limited institutional independence and limited powers of coercion. It lacks the powers to raise taxes and to implement laws, it relies almost entirely on the voluntary compliance of member states, and none of its institutions has either the power or the personnel directly to enforce EU law.

Third, the EU has its own executive (the European Commission) and a directly elected protolegislature (the European Parliament), but so much power has been kept in the hands of the intergovernmental Council of Ministers (where the key decisions are taken) that the Commission remains largely a servant of the national governments, and the Parliament has yet to

BOX 5.1
A Constitution for Europe

A constitution, by definition, is a contract between a government and its citizens that out-lines their relative powers, obligations, and responsibilities. Almost every modern state has a constitution, but they vary in the extent to which they are followed and respected and the extent to which they actually make sense; human society is so full of ambiguities and contradictions that constitutions (like old trucks) need constant tinkering and refine-ment to keep them roadworthy.

The European Union does not yet have a constitution in the sense that there is a single codified document, but it does have a set of treaties, a rapidly expanding body of laws, and a growing body of traditions and legal precedents that together amount to something like a constitution. There have been so many amendments to the founding treaties that the pow-ers and responsibilities of the EU are still ambiguous in many places, still open to different interpretations. The same is true of the constitution of the United States, which would be unintelligible in places were it not for over two hundred years' worth of amendments and judicial interpretation, and which in parts is anachronistic. For example, the "right" to bear arms and the ban on quartering troops in private homes grew out of particular historical circumstances, and the former idea is only kept alive today by opponents of gun control.

To have any meaning, a constitution must be respected, must have stability and perma-nence, must be capable of being enforced, and must be grounded in the reality of the pre-vailing political and social character of the state or body to which it applies; the bigger the gap between constitutional principles and political reality, the weaker the constitution. The extent to which the treaties and laws of the EU meet these conditions is debatable. Each new treaty that is agreed to and each new law that is passed makes the European "constitu-tion" increasingly messy. Its major guardian remains the European Court of Justice, which has helped "constitutionalize" the founding treaties by trying to remove the differences be-tween the Treaty of Rome and a conventional constitution, notably the lack of safeguards for individual rights and the absence of a constitutional right to European citizenship.[1]

Constitutions generally grow out of a crisis (such as a war or a revolution) or some watershed event (such as the independence of a former colony). No such crises or events have occurred in the European case; the EU has taken several decades to get to where it is today, and it still has much more evolving to do. If current trends continue, there will come a point when the EU has gained enough momentum and internal stability to make the need for a formal constitution irresistible. One of the agreements reached under the Treaty of Amsterdam was that at least one year before the membership of the EU grows to twenty, a new IGC will be convened to carry out a comprehensive review of the treaties and of the functioning of the EU institutions. Whether this will result in a more conventional European constitution remains to be seen.

Note

1. G. Federico Mancini, "The Making of a Constitution for Europe," in Robert O. Keohane and Stanley Hoffmann (Eds.), *The New European Community: Decisionmaking and Institutional Change* (Boulder: Westview Press, 1991).

win the kinds of powers to introduce, discuss, amend, reject, and accept laws that would make it a true legislature. Each of these institutions has undergone many changes since the Treaty of Paris, and we should expect many more changes before their powers are carved in stone.

Fourth, the EU is not very democratic. The European Coal and Steel Community was the brainchild of a few members of the elites of the six founding states, and almost every subsequent initiative in the process of European integration has been launched and adopted by political and economic elites, with little or no reference to Europe's voters. The balance is changing, though, and public opinion has played an increasingly important role since the institution of direct elections to the European Parliament in 1979. The Danish rejection of Maastricht in June 1992 also emphasized how dangerous it would be for the elites to overlook (and make assumptions about) the opinions of the people.

Finally, although the EU does not yet have exclusive responsibility for any single policy area, it has been given growing responsibility for making and implementing policy on issues such as external trade, agriculture, competition, financial services, interstate transportation, and the environment. Meanwhile, responsibility for issues such as education, policing, and criminal law still rests largely with the member states (much as they do with local government in the United States and Canada). The Single European Act, the Maastricht Treaty, and—to a much lesser extent—the Amsterdam Treaty represented steps in the process of the transfer (or pooling) of policy responsibility, and the conversion to a single currency will provide the final step in the integration of economic policy. Economic union will in turn provide greater pressures to complete the integration of other internal policy issues.

All of this begs the question of what kind of polity the European Union has become. Most people use labels to help them understand their environment, but there are no easy labels for the EU, or at least none on which most scholars can agree. Europeans know the dangers of the divisions they are leaving behind but are much less clear about the features of the unity toward which they are moving. As Benjamin Franklin argued after trying to find a model on which the new U.S. republic could be based, history consists only of beacon lights "which give warning of the course to be shunned, without pointing out that which ought to be pursued."[4] The EU today has some of the elements of a state but lacks others; it has some of the elements of a federation but lacks others; it is intergovernmental in some ways but supranational in others. To help pin down its character, we need to look in more detail at three core sets of ideas outlined briefly in Chapter 1, which together may hold the key to understanding what the European Union has become.

Confederalism

Confederalism is a system of government or administration in which two or more distinct political units keep their separate identity but transfer specified powers to a higher authority for reasons of convenience, mutual security, or efficiency. The local units are sovereign, and the higher authority is relatively weak; it exists solely at the discretion of the local units and can do only what they allow it to do. Federalism is different in the sense that it involves the local units surrendering some of their sovereignty and giving up power over joint interests to a new and permanent national level of government. Both, in turn, are distinct from the unitary system of government used in countries such as Britain, France, Japan, and Italy, where sovereignty rests almost entirely with the national government, which can abolish or amend local units at will.

Among the few examples of confederalism in practice are the United States in 1776–1789 and—to some extent—Switzerland today. In the case of the United States, the Founders were concerned in equal measure about anarchy (too little government) and tyranny (too much government), and until 1789 the original colonies related to each other as a loose confederation. The assumption was that they might cooperate sufficiently to eventually form a common system of government, but they did not do so; the 1781 Articles of Confederation created little more than a "league of friendship" that could not levy taxes or regulate commerce, and the army depended on state militias for its support. Only in 1787 did work begin on developing an entirely new federal system of government, redefining the idea of federalism in the process.

For its part, Switzerland was more purely confederal until 1798, and although it is now technically a federation, it has given up far fewer powers to the national government than has been the case in the United States. The Swiss encourage direct democracy by holding national referenda, have a Federal Assembly elected by proportional representation, and are governed by a Federal Council elected by the Assembly. One of the members of the Council is appointed to a one-year term as head of state and head of government.

The European Union is confederal in several ways. First, decisions taken by the leaders of the member states have resulted in a transfer of some authority from the parts to the whole, but the member states still have the upper hand, and the EU is governed as a whole through a process of negotiation and bargaining among national governments. Second, the member states are still distinct units with separate identities, have their own national defense forces and policies, can sign bilateral treaties with other states, and can still argue that the EU institutions exist at their discretion. A member state could theoretically leave the EU if it wished, and its action would not legally be defined as secession. Attempts to leave federations, by contrast, have almost always been defined as secession and have usually led to civil war (cf. the attempted secession of the Confederacy from the United States in 1861, of Chechnya from Russia during 1994–1995, and of Kosovo from Yugoslavia in 1998).

Finally, there is no European government in the sense that the EU has recognizable leaders, such as a president, a foreign minister, and a cabinet, and there exists only a variable sense of European identity among the inhabitants of the EU. The EU may have its own flag and anthem, but most citizens still hold a much higher sense of allegiance toward national flags, anthems, and other symbols, and progress toward building a sense of European citizenship has been mixed (as discussed later in this chapter).

Consociationalism

This concept is unfamiliar to most Americans and Canadians, and despite its value to helping us understand the EU, it is rarely mentioned in discussions of European integration. The idea of consociationalism grew out of attempts during the 1960s to shed light on how divided societies went about governing themselves. It was developed by political scientist Arend Lijphart in his 1968 study of politics in the Netherlands[5] and was later adopted by scholars in the field of comparative government as another means of understanding the different ways in which people can be governed. The term is usually applied to the structures and processes of parties and governments in small Western European states such as Austria and Belgium or is offered as a potential solution to the difficulty of governing divided communities such as Northern Ireland, Israel, and South Africa. However, it can also shed light on how regional integration has evolved and what it can become.[6]

Lijphart described four preconditions for consociationalism,[7] all of which are found in the EU. First, there must be several groups of people who are insulated from each other in the sense that their interests and associations are inwardly directed, but although they have a high degree of self-determination, they also come under a joint system of government. Second, the political elites of the different groups must decide to work and share power with each other in this joint system as something like a grand coalition or a cartel, reaching decisions on matters of common interest as a result of agreements and coalitions among themselves; it helps if they are encouraged to do this by external threats. Third, all the groups have the power of mutual veto, but government is based on the consensus of the elites of each group. Finally, the different groups are represented proportionally in all the major institutions of their common government, but at the same time the rights and interests of minorities are protected from a dictatorship of the majority, and decisionmaking authority is delegated as much as possible to the different groups.

Consociationalism applies to the EU in a number of ways. The member states could be described as the insulated groups about which Lijphart writes, and the leaders of the member states as the political elites. One of the most important of the EU institutions is the European Council, where the leaders of the member states meet as a cartel, and reach decisions through consensus, while enjoying the ability to veto those decisions, or at least to opt out of the commitments agreed to by the others. Finally, the different member states have voting powers in the Council of Ministers and the European Parliament that are roughly in proportion to their relative population sizes, while the blocking minority vote in the Council of Ministers allows smaller states to come together to prevent larger states from constantly outvoting them. Delegation is encapsulated in one of the defining mantras of the EU: "Subsidiarity" is a concept that encourages the leaders of Europe to give responsibility to the EU only in those policy areas that are best dealt with jointly rather than separately.

Paul Taylor suggests that the leaders in a consociational system "are faced continually with the dilemma of acting to preserve the general system whilst at the same time seeking to protect and further the interests of the groups which they represent."[8] An element of selfishness is also involved, because the leaders tend to pursue their own definitions of the common interest at the expense of (or at least overlooking) the views of citizens. Ian Lustick argues that the leaders must be able to rise above the divisions among the groups, work with the elites of the other groups in a common effort, and be able to accommodate the different interests involved. Those interests tend to be defined by the elites, which usually express them vaguely in terms of the common welfare of those groups. The elites work with each other in a system of political or material exchanges, bargains, and compromises; bureaucracies and legal agencies act as umpires in helping interpret the bargains that have been reached. A consociational system is like a set of delicately but securely balanced scales, but the stability of the entire system may occasionally oblige the leaders to use undemocratic methods to discipline the various segments.[9]

Federalism

A federal system is one in which national and local governments coexist with a system of shared and independent powers, but where neither has supreme authority over the other. Unlike confederalism, federalism usually involves an elected national government that has sole power over foreign and security policy. There is usually a single currency and a common defense force, a national system of law that coexists with local legal systems, a written constitution and a court that can arbitrate disputes among the different units of government, and at least two major levels of government, law, bureaucracy, and taxation. The national government has independent powers that can be expanded according to the interpretation of the federal constitution. The cumulative interests of the local units tend to define the joint interests of the whole, and the national government constantly couches its mission in terms of the importance of the citizens and describes itself as the servant of the people, functioning only for their convenience. This is the system found in the United States, Canada, Germany, India, and Australia.

According to the U.S. Constitution and the Bill of Rights, which comprises the first ten amendments, the U.S. model of federalism prohibits the states from making treaties with foreign nations, from having their own currencies, or—without the consent of Congress—from levying taxes on imports or exports, maintaining a military in peacetime, or making agreements with other states or foreign nations. The federal government, for its part, cannot unilaterally redraw the borders of a state, impose different levels of tax by state, give states different levels of representation in the U.S. Senate, or amend the Constitution without the support of two-thirds of the states. Meanwhile, the states reserve all of the powers not expressly delegated to the national government or prohibited to them by the national government. Another key feature of the U.S. model is the common sense of identity of its citizens, most of whom place their loyalty to the United States above their loyalty to the states in which they live.

The EU member states can do almost everything the states in the U.S. model (or provinces in the Canadian model) *cannot* do: They can make treaties, operate their own currencies, maintain an independent military, and the like. The EU institutions, meanwhile, have very few of the powers of the federal government in the United States or Canada: They cannot levy taxes, they have no common security policy or military, they have no written constitution, they do not yet enjoy the undivided loyalties of most Europeans, and they do not have the sole power to negotiate with the rest of the world on behalf of the member states. The EU is not yet the kind of federal institution Jean Monnet and his colleagues foresaw, but it *has* moved closer to a federal structure than any other international organization,[10] and it has some of the features of a federal polity:[11]

- A system of treaties and laws protected by the European Court of Justice;

- The directly elected European Parliament, whose powers are counterbalanced by a Council of Ministers representing the interests of the individual member states;
- The EU budget, which is the germ of a fiscally independent supranational level of government;
- An executive body (the European Commission) that has the authority to oversee external trade negotiations on behalf of all the member states.

One way of looking at the practice of federalism in the EU is to see the EU as a network in which individual member states are increasingly defined not by themselves but in relation to their EU partners and in which they prefer to interact with one another (rather than with third parties) because those interactions create incentives for self-interested cooperation.[12] Related to the neofunctionalist idea of the expansive logic of integration is the argument that the EU has become "co-optive," meaning that its participants have more to gain by being co-opted into the system than by going it alone.[13] Once the states are involved, they must take some of the responsibility for actions taken by the EU, and the governments of the member states find it increasingly difficult to get away with blaming Brussels.

We should try not to think of federalism solely according to the way it is practiced in the United States, Canada, and India. It is not an absolute or a static concept, and it has taken on different forms in different situations according to the relative strength and nature of local political, economic, social, historical, and cultural pressures. In the United States, federalism was in place long before Americans began their westward expansion, it explicitly includes a system of checks and balances and a separation of powers, and it was adopted more to avoid the dangers of chaos and tyranny than to account for social divisions. In India, by contrast, federalism was seen as a possible solution to the difficulty of governing a state that was already in place and that had deep ethnic and cultural divisions; the national government has a fused executive and legislature.

European federalism could eventually look very different from U.S., Indian, or even German federalism. For example, it already includes the peculiarly European idea of subsidiarity, while the U.S. federal model has seen power shift gradually toward the center. The presidency was much weaker than Congress, for example, until the administration of Franklin D. Roosevelt, when a combination of national emergencies and an entrepreneurial president caused the scales of power to tip in favor of Washington, D.C. A European federation could become one in which the European level of government does much less than is the case with national government in Canada and the United States.

The Idea of Europe

The concept of the West is synonymous with Europe, and the "world culture" that political scientist Lucien Pye described in 1966[14] is ultimately European culture (even if much of that culture has been exported and promoted by the United States, which is itself a product of European culture). Not only was nearly every part of the world colonized at some point by one European power or another (Japan and China are among the notable exceptions), but the spread of European ideas has meant that Western culture today is defined mainly in European terms. In short, we live in a European world.

This dominance has encouraged many North Americans to think of Europe as the Old World: a relatively stable and unchanging region with a strong identity and many venerable institutions and traditions. Nothing could be farther from the truth. Not only have Europeans constantly squabbled with each other and gone to war with tragic regularity and frequency, but the balance of power within Europe has often shifted, forcing mapmakers to constantly redraw the borders between different European tribes, nations, and states.

The changes continue, coming so fast that it is often difficult to keep up. In many ways, it is more accurate to think of Europe as new and dynamic rather than old and stable and to realize that many of its political institutions are relatively new. For example, no European country has a written constitution as old as that of the United States, a political party as old as the Democrats, or a judiciary as old as the U.S. Supreme Court. When the United States became independent in 1776, very few European countries existed in their modern form. England, France, Portugal, Spain, Sweden, and Switzerland were essentially in place, but almost all other European states are much younger—for example, Belgium (1830), Luxembourg (1848), Italy (1861), Poland and Hungary (1918), Yugoslavia (1918/1992), and Germany (1990). Other communities had a separate identity but (like Iceland, Ireland, Finland, and Norway) were provinces of bigger powers.

The prevailing situation in 1776 was only the latest chapter in the story of constant change that characterizes European politics. There were many more changes after 1776, culminating in two devastating world wars that began as little more than European civil wars and ended in 1945 with a final realization that Europeans needed to work more closely together to save themselves from the nationalism that had brought so much havoc, death, and destruction. This was by no means the first time the idea of integration or unity had surfaced. The Roman Empire (200 B.C.–A.D. 400), the Frankish Empire (which peaked in the ninth century under Emperor Charlemagne), the Holy Roman Empire (962–1250), the Napoleonic Empire (1804–1815), and Hitler's Third Reich (1933–1945) all stamped their own brands of unity on Europe, with different motives, ends, and consequences.

BOX 5.2
The Development of a European Identity

One of the identifying features of a state is a sense among its residents of a common identity or citizenship. Although the European Council agreed in 1984 to promote the idea of "a people's Europe," and Maastricht contained a chapter on European citizenship, the development of a European identity cannot be forced or built by law—it ultimately lies with Europeans themselves, with how they perceive the European Union, and with how quickly they can overcome the myths, biases, and misunderstandings that are the heritage of hundreds of years of war.

There are signs that the change of attitude is slowly taking hold. Eurobarometer polls since 1982 have found that about half of all EU citizens "sometimes" or "often" feel a sense of European identity. Europeans still see themselves primarily as citizens of one member state or another, but increased mobility is changing their perceptions. As the barriers to movement around the EU are taken down, Europeans have fewer reminders of the differences that divide them, and so they will tend to see other Europeans less as "foreigners" and more as partners in a joint venture. The gradual removal of border checks has been an important psychological step in that direction. Another step will come as Europeans see living in other parts of the EU less as emigration and more as a free choice based on factors such as employment, opportunity, and personal preference.

Other symbolic and functional changes are also important in the process. Europeans are still citizens of specific member states rather than the EU, but the EU flag is increasingly visible throughout the Union, the "Ode to Joy" from Beethoven's Ninth Symphony has been adopted as the anthem of the EU, national passports have been replaced with a common burgundy-colored EU passport (still bearing the name of the member state of which the holder is a citizen), Europeans can live and work wherever they like in the EU (with a few minor restrictions), and they can vote and even stand for certain offices in the member states in which they live. There are still nonlegal barriers to the free movement of people (such as language, customs, job opportunities, and personal preferences), but the walls are coming down throughout the EU and are slowly being replaced by attitudes less burdened by narrow nationalism.

One of the great ironies and unanticipated consequences of European integration has been its role in giving national minorities a greater sense of their separate identity. Long unable to wrest powers of self-determination from member-state governments, Basques, Catalans, Corsicans, Scots, and Walloons are reviving their separate identities as subgroups within the larger European Union. This injects an interesting new twist into discussions about the nature of citizenship in Europe.

The European Union has been the most successful of all of the attempts to bring peace to Europe, but the "idea" of Europe remains ambiguous (see Box 5.2). Europe lacks most of the conventional features of a sovereign nation-state, including fixed boundaries, a dominant common culture, a dominant common language, a common history, and shared values and ideals.

First, the physical and cultural boundaries of Europe are unclear. They are usually defined as the Mediterranean, the Atlantic, the Arctic, and the Ural Mountains in the east and the Caucasus Mountains and the Bosporus in the southeast. This means not only that Russians, Ukrainians, Georgians, and Turks could lay some claim to being European but also that over 270 million "Europeans" (and nearly 150 million Russians) live in Europe outside the EU.

Second, few of the EU's fifteen member states are culturally homogeneous. Many have national minorities, some of which have become integrated into the larger identity of the state, but others of which have not. One study identifies no less than sixty-seven separate national communities in the EU (including Frisians, Galicians, Walloons, Carinthians, Castilians, and Swabians) and an additional forty outside the EU.[15] Many EU states have also experienced major influxes of immigrants since 1955—including Algerians to France, Turks to Germany, and Indians to Britain. Not only is there no dominant culture but most Europeans shudder (not without reason) at the thought of their separate identities being subordinated in any way to some kind of sterile, homogeneous Euroculture. As the French say, *vive la différence.*

Third, citizens of the EU speak at least thirty-six different languages[16] and vigorously defend them as the symbol of their separate identities. The spread of English as the language of global commerce and diplomacy concerns the French in particular and other Europeans to some extent (see Chapter 14), but it is probably irresistible and will at least provide a way for Europeans to talk to each other. Nothing reminds them of their differences quite as strongly as traveling to a neighboring state and being unable to speak to many of the natives.

Finally, the histories of European states have overlapped for centuries as they have colonized, gone to war, or formed alliances with each other. However, those overlaps have served mainly to emphasize differences rather than to give the states a sense of a shared past, and European integration grew in part out of the essentially reactive idea of wanting to put an end to conflict. The differences have been further emphasized by the records of some European states as colonial powers, which made them emphasize external links at the expense of internal links.

The development of a European identity has been helped in some ways by the relative introversion of Western Europe since 1945. Helen Wallace has argued that in trying to improve the way they manage their own affairs, taking more responsibility for each other, and dealing with the uncertainties posed by change in the Soviet Union and then in Russia, Europeans have become more introverted, and their internal preoccupations have heavily shaped their attitudes toward the rest of the world.[17] These preoccupations have also influenced the way outsiders look at the EU. Many Americans and Japanese see the EU as both a threat and an opportunity, while most

Eastern Europeans view it as a new force for positive economic and political change and as a club many of them would very much like to join.

Wherever these trends lead, whatever Europeans can do to remind themselves of their similarities rather than their differences, and whatever political form the European Union finally takes, the process of European integration has ensured that Europeans will never see each other—or be seen by outsiders—in quite the same way again.

Summary and Conclusions

Coming to grips with the European Union is complicated by the facts that its character is constantly changing and that it fits none of the conventional ideas about the way modern societies govern themselves. It is distinctive and unique, but it cannot be neatly slotted into any of the usual ideas about government. "Boundaries are difficult to draw in a world of complex interdependence," argue Robert Keohane and Stanley Hoffmann; "because relationships cross boundaries and coalitional patterns vary from issue to issue, it is never possible to classify all actors neatly into mutually exclusive categories."[18]

The European Union at the turn of the millennium has many intergovernmental characteristics, but these have given way over time to a growing emphasis on supranationalism. The member states are steadily answering to a new level of higher authority with some of the features of confederalism and some of federalism. Both of these concepts take many different forms, and for Euroskeptics to talk about federalism as some kind of hell toward which Europe should not travel is too simplistic. The European brand of federalism already has several unique features, and once it achieves some kind of regularity, those features may look very different from most of the characteristics we usually associate with federalism. Commonly overlooked in the debates about European integration is the idea of consociationalism. This theory as it now stands is too elitist and undemocratic; revived in a new form, it may be one of the most illuminating ways of trying to understand the political form of the European Union

Further Reading

Simon Sefarty. *The Identity and Definition of Europe* (London: Pinter, 1992).
   Examines the emerging idea of "Europe" and discusses its position in post–cold war global politics.

Elizabeth Meehan. *Citizenship and the European Community* (Newbury Park, Calif.: Sage, 1993).
   An analysis of the meaning of European "citizenship," comparing it to national citizenship and looking at the possible emergence of a new European identity.

William Wallace. *Regional Integration: The West European Experience* (Washington, D.C.: Brookings Institution, 1994).
A study of the mechanics of European integration that draws conclusions about some of the lessons to be learned from the experience of the EU.

Most of the ideas about consociationalism have been published in journal articles or in chapters in books rather than as book-length studies. Among the key sources are the following:
Arend Lijphart. "Consociational Democracy." In Kenneth McRae (Ed.), *Consociational Democracy: Political Accommodation in Segmented Societies* (Toronto: McClelland and Stewart, 1974).
Arend Lijphart. "Consociation and Federation: Conceptual and Empirical Links." In *Canadian Journal of Political Science* 12:3 (September 1979), 499–515.
Paul Taylor. "Consociationalism and Federalism as Approaches to International Integration." In A.J.R. Groom and Paul Taylor (Eds.), *Frameworks for International Cooperation* (New York: St. Martin's Press, 1990).

Notes

1. Robert O. Keohane and Stanley Hoffmann, *The New European Community: Decisionmaking and Institutional Change* (Boulder: Westview Press, 1991), 10.
2. Jean Monnet, *Memoirs* (Garden City, N.Y.: Doubleday, 1978), 523.
3. Keohane and Hoffmann, *The New European Community*, 10.
4. Benjamin Franklin, *Federalist*, no. 37.
5. Arend Lijphart, *The Politics of Accommodation: Pluralism and Democracy in the Netherlands* (Berkeley: University of California Press, 1968).
6. Paul Taylor, "Consociationalism and Federalism as Approaches to International Integration," in A.J.R. Groom and Paul Taylor (Eds.), *Frameworks for International Cooperation* (New York: St. Martin's Press, 1990).
7. Arend Lijphart, "Consociation and Federation: Conceptual and Empirical Links," *Canadian Journal of Political Science* 22:3 (1979), 499–515.
8. Taylor, "Consociationalism and Federalism," 174.
9. Ian Lustick, "Stability in Deeply Divided Societies: Consociationalism Versus Control," *World Politics* 31:3 (April 1979), 325–344.
10. Ernst B. Haas, *The Uniting of Europe: Political, Social, and Economic Forces, 1950–57* (Stanford: Stanford University Press, 1968), 59.
11. See William Wallace, *Regional Integration: The West European Experience* (Washington, D.C.: Brookings Institution, 1994), 38–40.
12. Keohane and Hoffmann, *The New European Community*, 13–14.
13. Martin O. Heisler, with Robert B. Kvavik, "Patterns of European Politics: The 'European Polity' Model," in Martin O. Heisler (Ed.), *Politics in Europe: Structures and Processes in Some Postindustrial Democracies* (New York: David McKay, 1973).
14. Lucien Pye, *Aspects of Political Development* (Boston: Little, Brown, 1966).

15. Felipe Fernández-Armesto (Ed.), *Guide to the Peoples of Europe* (London: Times Books, 1997).

16. Victor Keegan and Martin Kettle, *The New Europe* (London: Fourth Estate, 1993), 92.

17. Helen Wallace, "What Europe for Which Europeans?" in Gregory F. Treverton (Ed.), *The Shape of the New Europe* (New York: Council on Foreign Relations Press, 1992), 16.

18. Keohane and Hoffmann, *The New European Community,* 12.

Part Two

Institutions

6

The European Commission

The most visible of the five major institutions of the EU is the European Commission, which is both the executive arm of the European Union and its bureaucracy. It is responsible for generating new laws and policies, for overseeing their implementation, for representing the EU in international negotiations, and for promoting the interests of the EU as a whole. As the most supranational of the EU institutions, it has long been at the heart of the process of European integration.

It has no direct equivalent in the United States (or anywhere else for that matter), being a unique amalgam of legislative and executive functions. Its legislative role comes from its responsibility for proposing and developing new laws and policies, jobs that would normally be done at the national level by an elected legislature. Its executive function comes from its responsibility for overseeing the implementation of those laws and policies by the member states. It can investigate suspected infringements or lack of compliance and if necessary can take a member state to the Court of Justice. The executive function is driven by a college of twenty commissioners, which functions much like a cabinet in that each member is responsible for particular policy areas and for overseeing one or more directorates-general (DGs), which are the functional equivalent of government departments.

The Commission is regularly the target of disdain and criticism, but its role is widely misunderstood. Euroskeptics grumble about waste and meddling by Eurocrats and complain that the leaders of the Commission are not elected and that its staff has little public accountability. For some, "Brussels" is synonymous with the Commission and has become a code word for some vague and threatening notion of government by bureaucracy, or so-called creeping federalism. But this is unfair. The Commission has much less power than its detractors often suggest, and the final decision on new laws and policies rests with the intergovernmental Council of

Ministers. It is also very small given the size of its task; it had just over 21,000 staff in 1998 (a ratio of about 1:18,000 EU citizens), compared with over 3 million civilian federal bureaucrats in the United States (1:87 U.S. citizens).

At the same time, the Commission deserves credit for the critical role it has played in the process of European integration. It has not only encouraged member states to harmonize their laws, regulations, and standards in the interest of bringing down the barriers to trade but has also been the source of some of the defining policy initiatives in the process of that integration, including the single market and efforts to create a single currency. As John Fitzmaurice has put it, the Commission's role is that of "animator, impresario, and manager," faced with the challenges of making the EU system work and of turning political principles into real and effective policies.[1] Unfortunately, the Commission still appears to many Europeans to be remote and intrusive.

The case for reforming its structure—and its relationship with other EU institutions—was given new urgency by a crisis in March 1999 that resulted in the resignation of the entire twenty-member College of Commissioners. Stories about fraud, nepotism, and cronyism had been circulating since 1995 and came to a head with an attempt by the European Parliament to fire the College in January 1999. The attempt failed, but a committee was appointed to investigate the allegations, resulting in the shock resignation of the College just hours after the committee report was published on March 16. Although the crisis was only partly a consequence of structural problems, it emphasized the need for a thorough review of the powers and operating procedures of the Commission.

Evolution

The European Commission grew out of the separate administrative arms of the European Coal and Steel Community (ECSC), the European Economic Community (EEC), and the European Atomic Energy Community (Euratom). The ECSC had a nine-member High Authority based in Luxembourg, whose members were nominated for six-year terms by the six national governments. Its job was to oversee the removal of barriers to the free movement of coal and steel, and its powers were checked by a Special Council of Ministers and a Common Assembly (the forerunners, respectively, of the Council of Ministers and the European Parliament).

The Treaties of Rome created separate nine-member Commissions for the EEC and Euratom, whose members were nominated by national governments for four-year terms. Under the terms of the 1965 Merger Treaty, the three separate Commissions were merged in 1967 into a new

Commission of the European Communities, known as the European Commission. As the Community expanded, the number of commissioners grew. At first there were nine (two each from France, West Germany, and Italy and one each from the Benelux states). The number increased to thirteen in 1973 with the accession of Britain, Denmark, and Ireland; to fourteen in 1981 with the accession of Greece; to seventeen in 1986 with the accession of Spain and Portugal; and then to twenty in 1995 with the accession of Austria, Sweden, and Finland.

The Commission has always been at the heart of the continuing debate over the balance of power between the EU and the member states. Concerns regularly surface about its supranationalist tendencies, and it has fought a constant tug-of-war with the intergovernmental tendencies of the Council of Ministers. European federalism was championed by the Commission's first president—Walter Hallstein of Germany—in the face of Charles de Gaulle's preference for limiting the powers of the EEC. The 1965 crisis broke when de Gaulle challenged the right of the Commission to initiate the policy process and it attempted to collect receipts from the EC's common external tariff.[2] This would have provided the Commission with an independent source of funds, thus loosening the grip of the member states. Although the Luxembourg compromise obliged the Commission to consult more closely with the Council of Ministers and de Gaulle was able to veto the reappointment of Hallstein in 1967, the crisis ironically confirmed the right of the Commission to initiate policies.

The Commission became less ambitious and aggressive and lost powers with the creation in 1965 of the Committee of Permanent Representatives (see Chapter 7), the creation in 1974 of the European Council (see Chapter 10), and the introduction in 1979 of direct elections to the European Parliament. After enjoying a newly assertive phase under President Jacques Delors during the late 1980s and early 1990s, and generating some of the EU's most important policy initiatives, the Commission found its powers declining in relation to those of the Council of Ministers and the European Parliament.

Structure

The European Commission is based in Brussels. Until 1992 it was headquartered in the Berlaymont Building near the city center, but it was then discovered that the Berlaymont had high levels of asbestos, so the building was emptied and renovated, and the Commission staff was relocated to various new and existing buildings around the city. It has five main elements: the College of Commissioners, the president of the Commission, the directorates-general, the Secretariat General, and the advisory committees.

The College of Commissioners

The European Commission is led by a group of twenty commissioners, who function as something like the cabinet of the EU system, taking collective responsibility for their decisions. Each has a portfolio for which he or she is responsible (see Table 6.1). The twenty posts are distributed among the EU member states, with the five largest countries (Germany, France, the United Kingdom, Italy, and Spain) each having two posts and the rest having one each. Commissioners served four-year renewable terms until the end of 1994; under Maastricht, the terms were lengthened to five years effective January 1995, to coincide with elections to the European Parliament. There are no limits on the number of terms they can serve.

Commissioners are appointed by their national governments, which—in practice—usually means the prime minister, or the president in France. The appointments are made in consultation with the president of the Commission, and appointees also usually must be acceptable to the other commissioners, other governments, the major political parties at home, and the European Parliament. Parliament does not have the right to hold confirmation hearings on individual commissioners, but it has the power to approve or reject the College as a whole at the beginning of its term and also to fire the College, which it tried to do following publication of the allegations of fraud and corruption in January 1999, but it failed when it fell short of the required two-thirds majority.

Despite the way they are appointed, commissioners are not supposed to be national representatives, and they must swear an oath of office before the European Court of Justice in Luxembourg saying they will renounce any defense of national interests. Under Article 157, they are expected to be "completely independent in the performance of their duties" and must not "seek nor take instructions from any Government or from any other body." Their independence from their home governments is underwritten by the inability of national leaders to remove commissioners in midterm. Many are reappointed, and some resign, but others are recalled at the end of their terms because of a change of political leadership at home or political disagreements with their national leaders.

One of the most famous examples of a fallout between a commissioner and a home government was that between Lord Cockfield and his sponsor, Margaret Thatcher. Cockfield was appointed in 1985 and was given responsibility to prepare for the single market. He began to pursue his job too enthusiastically for Thatcher's tastes, however, and she concluded that he had become "the prisoner as well as the master of his subject. It was all too easy for him, therefore, to go native and to move from deregulating the market to reregulating it under the rubric of harmonization."[3] She accordingly refused to reappoint him in 1989.

TABLE 6.1   The European Commissioners, January 1999

Name	Country	Key Portfolios
Jacques Santer	Luxembourg	President
Sir Leon Brittan	UK	External relations (North America, Southeast Asia, OECD, World Trade Organization), Trade Policy
Hans van den Broek	Netherlands	External relations (Eastern Europe and former USSR), Common Foreign and Security Policy
Manuel Marín	Spain	External relations (Southern Mediterranean, Middle East, Latin America)
Jao de deus Pinheiro	Portugal	External relations (ACP states)
Yves-Thibault de Silguy	France	Economic and financial affairs
Martin Bangemann	Germany	Industrial affairs, information and telecommunications
Karel van Miert	Belgium	Competition
Padraig Flynn	Ireland	Employment and social affairs
Franz Fischler	Austria	Agriculture
Neil Kinnock	UK	Transport
Erkii Liikanen	Finland	Budget, personnel and administration
Ritt Bjerregaard	Denmark	Environment, nuclear safety
Édith Cresson	France	Science, education, research and development, human resources
Emma Bonino	Italy	Consumer policy, fisheries
Mario Monti	Italy	Internal market, financial services, tax
Monika Wulf-Mathies	Germany	Regional policy, relations with the Committee of the Regions, Cohesion Fund
Christos Papoutsis	Greece	Energy
Marcelino Oreja	Spain	Relations with the European Parliament, culture, official pulications
Anita Gradin	Sweden	Justice, home affairs, immigration and financial control

There are no formal rules on appointments, but commissioners tend already to have national political reputations at home, albeit sometimes modest ones. They may be well-respected members of an opposition party or someone the governing party would like to remove from the national political scene for some reason. At one time, many were political lightweights whose usefulness at home had ended, so they were "kicked upstairs" to the Commission. As the powers of the Commission have increased and the EU has become a more significant force in European politics, postings to the Commission have become more desirable and important, and the pool of potential candidates has improved in quality. One indication of the change in emphasis came in 1994 when the former French Prime Minister Édith Cresson was appointed to one of the French posts and a former leader of the British Labour Party, Neil Kinnock, to one of the British posts.

At the beginning of each term, all twenty commissioners are given port-folios, which are distributed at the prerogative of the president. This has great political significance and is seen as an acid test of the president's abili-ties to lead.[4] The process is subject to lobbying by commissioners and na-tional governments, and portfolios are reshuffled to reward efficiency, abil-ity, and loyalty and to penalize incompetence. Despite regular claims of collegiality among commissioners, the College has its own internal hierar-chy of positions. While the senior positions in most national cabinets are those dealing with foreign affairs, the economy, and either internal affairs or defense, the key posts in the Commission are those concerned with the budget, agriculture, and external relations. The hierarchy is also based in part on the different abilities and political skills of individual commission-ers; some are respected and able, while others are not.

The reshuffling is usually done on the basis of seniority and political bal-ance, with the longest-serving commissioners receiving the best portfolios as a form of recognition or promotion. Commissioners with a strong repu-tation in a particular area will normally keep the same portfolio (industrial affairs Commissioner Martin Bangemann, for example, held that portfolio from 1989 until 1999). Member-state governments are obviously keen to see "their" commissioner win a good portfolio or one of particular interest to their country, so political influence is often brought to bear on the process. The Commission term that began in January 1989 was particularly important, given the imminent creation of the single market. Spain was ea-ger to be given the budget portfolio, and Prime Minister Felipe Gonzalez tried to use his influence to try to obtain the job for one of the two Spanish commissioners. In the event, the budget portfolio went to German Commissioner Peter Schmidhuber, but the senior Spanish commissioner, Manual Marín, was given two portfolios as consolation.

Little political direction is given to the College, mainly because commis-sioners must not seem to be promoting national interests or to be answer-ing to their home governments. This gives them a high level of freedom of movement, although their decisions are collegiate. Every commissioner has a personal staff of about half a dozen assistants and advisers, called a *cabi-net,* which is headed by a *chef* and provides advice and the basic informa-tion and services that help commissioners do their jobs; the quality of the *cabinet* staff can have a major bearing on the performance of a commis-sioner. The respective *chefs de cabinet* meet every Monday to prepare the weekly meeting of the College on Wednesday. *Cabinet* members usually come from the same country as the commissioner, although at least one commonly comes from another member state. Advisers are usually recruited from the same national political party as that of the commissioner, or from the national bureaucracy.

There are already concerns that the College has become too big, making more urgent the need to decide what to do when more states join the EU. At the time of the Maastricht negotiations, a suggestion was made that each member state be limited to one commissioner, and Germany proposed that membership be capped at ten. There were expectations that the issue of size—and of how the Commission is appointed—would have been addressed by the IGC that led up to the Treaty of Amsterdam, but it was not. The inevitable expansion of membership of the EU to twenty countries or more during the next few years will move the issue high up the agenda again.

The President

The dominating figure in the Commission hierarchy is undoubtedly the president, the person who comes closest to being able to claim to be the leader of the EU (although this is a debatable proposition, given the way power is divided and dissipated within the system). The president is technically no more than a first among equals and can be outvoted by other commissioners, but—as with prime ministers in parliamentary systems—the president's trump card is the power of appointment: The ability to distribute portfolios is a potent tool for patronage and political manipulation.

The new assertiveness of Jacques Delors during the period 1986–1994 may also have heralded the emergence of a more presidential system of government.[5] Delors personalized his position to an unprecedented degree, worked long hours, kept himself abreast of the work of all the other commissioners, and demanded high standards of them.[6] He also came to the job with firm ideas about a strong federal Europe asserting itself internationally,[7] and he used this vision to push the EU in many new directions. He was succeeded in January 1995 by Jacques Santer, former prime minister of Luxembourg, who entered office faced not only with having to follow a very tough act but also with having to guide the EU toward achieving economic and monetary union, preparing for further enlargement, developing a common foreign and security policy, and setting up the 1996 IGC. Santer proved much more low-key in his approach to the job, so much so that he was ultimately considered responsible by many for permitting the existence of a culture that led to the corruption scandal of 1999 (see Box 6.1).

The president of the Commission is comparable in some ways to the president of the United States. He or she oversees meetings of the College, decides on the distribution of portfolios, represents the Commission in dealings with other EU institutions, represents the EU at meetings with national governments and their leaders, and is generally responsible for ensur-

BOX 6.1
Jacques Santer at the Helm

The man who held the presidency of the Commission in the closing years of the twenti-eth century proved a notable contrast to his predecessor in almost every way. While Jacques Delors (1986–1994) was assertive and controversial and became one of the best known of all Commission presidents, Jacques Santer (1995–1999) was low-key and con-ciliatory, largely avoiding the spotlight. Delors was single-minded, hard working, demand-ing, and sometimes short-tempered, prompting a fellow Commissioner to describe his management method as a form of "intellectual terrorism." He was also well known for being a loner and a poor team player. Santer, by contrast, was collegial, congenial, pre-ferred quiet persuasion rather than confrontation, and promoted decisionmaking by com-promise and consensus.

Born in 1937, Santer served in several posts in Luxembourg government during the 1960s and 1970s, including a spell as secretary for social security. He was appointed to the European Parliament in 1974 and reelected for two more terms in 1979 and 1984. He became prime minister of Luxembourg in 1985 as head of the moderate right-wing Christian Social Union and was reelected twice before being chosen in 1995 as the presi-dent of the Commission. He came to the position by default, the front-runners for the position—including Dutch prime minister Ruud Lubbers and Belgian prime minister Jean-Luc Dehaene—having failed to win the support of all the leaders of the member states.

Many of those leaders made it clear that they expected Santer to pull back from the ambitious activism of the Delors years, which he did, going so far as to describe his ap-proach as "less, but better." His presidency was by no means quiet: It saw the final prepa-rations for the launch of the euro, the controversy over the ban on exports of British beef following outbreaks of mad cow disease, the development and signature of the Treaty of Amsterdam, and the development of a program aimed at preparing several Eastern European states for membership in the EU. However, Santer by all reports took a less ac-tive role in these issues than might his predecessor.

His presidency ended in ignominy in March 1999, following publication of a report by a committee set up to look into charges of mismanagement in the Commission. The report cataloged examples of mismanagement and nepotism, and while Santer claimed at a sub-sequent press conference to be "whiter than white," he and his nineteen colleagues on the Commission immediately resigned. EU leaders moved quickly to replace him with Romano Prodi, former prime minister of Italy. Born in 1940, Prodi served as prime minis-ter in 1996–1998, and made his name by pushing through political reforms designed to bring stability to Italian government and economic reforms designed to prepare Italy for the euro. His talents earned him the nickname "Il Professore" in the Italian press.[1]

Note

1. *Times* (London), March 25, 1999

ing that the Commission gives impetus to the process of European integration.

In other respects, the two presidencies are very different. Not only are Commission presidents appointed rather than elected but they are not accountable to Parliament in the way U.S. presidents are accountable to Congress, and they are clearly subservient to the leaders of the member states—to the point where they sometimes seem to be little more than glorified functionaries. In many ways the Commission president has the same status as early-nineteenth-century U.S. presidents, who had less of a role in government than either Congress or the states and were seen more as executives than as leaders. However, just as Franklin Roosevelt gave the job a newly powerful and assertive role in government in the 1930s, so the presidency of the Commission took on a new and more forceful character under Delors.

There are few formal rules regarding how the president is appointed. It has become normal for the leaders of the member states to decide on the appointment at the European Council held during the June before the term of the incumbent Commission ends, settling on someone acceptable to all of them and to the Commission itself. Maastricht made the appointment subject to confirmation by Parliament. The struggle to find a successor for Jacques Delors in 1994 gives some insight into the nature of the process. A successor was to have been appointed at the European Council meeting in Corfu in June. The favorite was Jean-Luc Dehaene, the incumbent prime minister of Belgium, who would have been the first conservative in many years to head the Commission and who had a reputation for engineering political compromises. His candidacy was strongly supported by Germany and France, but the Dutch were upset because outgoing Prime Minister Ruud Lubbers was not at the top of the list; and Italy, Spain, and Portugal all questioned the Franco-German assumption that Dehaene's candidacy was assured.[8]

Eight of the twelve leaders initially supported Dehaene, while Spain, Italy, and the Netherlands opted for Lubbers, and Britain favored Sir Leon Brittan, one of its commissioners. In the event, every leader ultimately fell in behind Dehaene except John Major, who vetoed Dehaene's appointment. Major argued that Dehaene was an interventionist who favored big government, but in truth he was probably trying to appease right-wing Euroskeptics in his own party at home. Although Major was painted as the sole voice of dissent, the tussle also revealed the resentment among smaller EU states about the assumptions by Germany and France that their favored candidate would win.[9] Having failed to reach agreement, the twelve leaders met at an emergency European Council in Brussels on July 15 and opted for Jacques Santer as a compromise. Santer was confirmed by only a narrow majority in the European Parliament, not because his choice was unpopular but because Parliament wanted to express its disapproval of the manner in which presidents are chosen.[10]

The president is usually someone with a strong political reputation, a strong character, and proven leadership abilities, but to date the incumbents have proved very different in their styles and abilities; Walter Hallstein, Roy Jenkins, and Jacques Delors are remembered as the most active and the remainder as relatively passive. To a large extent, the nature of the job depends on the character of the incumbents and the management style and agenda they bring to their task[11] (see Table 6.2).

Directorates-General

Below the College, the European Commission is divided into twenty-four directorates-general. Each DG is responsible for a specific area and ideally should be tied to a particular commissioner, but there are more DGs than commissioners, so some commissioners have more than one DG, and some DGs report to more than one commissioner. The DGs are usually known by their numbers rather than their areas, so the directorate-general dealing with external relations with North America is DGI, the directorate-general concerned with economic and financial affairs is DGII, and so on (see Table 6.3). Each DG has its own director-general who reports to the relevant commissioner.

The size of DGs varies roughly according to the size of their jobs; DGIX (personnel and administration) employs about 2,900 people and DGVI (agriculture) about 900, while the smallest DGs may employ fewer than 200 people. Employees consist of a mixture of full-time bureaucrats known as *fonctionnaires*, national experts seconded from the member states for short-term contracts, and supporting staff. The Commission is required to ensure balanced representation by nationality at every level, but nearly one in four Eurocrats is Belgian, mainly because of locally recruited secretarial and support staff. Although the people who eventually become directors-general theoretically work their way up through the ranks of the Commission, appointments at the higher levels are based less on merit than on nationality and political affiliation.

Member states exert pressure to ensure that they receive what they regard as a fair balance of senior positions and that they control departments close to their hearts; it is widely recognized, for example, that Germany will dominate the upper reaches of DGIV (competition), that France will dominate DGVI (agriculture), and that there will be a British lilt to the DGs dealing with external relations (DGs I, IA, and IB). About two-thirds of Commission staff members work on drawing up new laws and policies or on overseeing implementation, about 20 percent are involved in research, and the rest (about 2,500) are involved in translation and interpretation; although the Commission mainly uses English and French, each document must be translated into the eleven official EU languages. The vast majority of Commission staff members works in offices in and around Brussels, but

TABLE 6.2   Presidents of the European Commission

1958–1967	Walter Hallstein (West Germany) Christian Democrat; foreign minister 1951–1958. Federalist who provided dynamic and aggressive leadership, establishing the central role of the Commission in EU affairs. His attempts to expand the powers of the Commission and the European Parliament led to the crisis of 1965.
1968–1969	Jean Rey (Belgium) Centrist; economics minister in postwar governments. Appointed commissioner for external relations in 1958 and became first president of the newly merged European Commission. Subsequently served as an MEP and chaired the committee that produced the 1980 Rey Report on EC institutional reform.
1970–1972	Franco Maria Malfatti (Italy) Christian Democrat; minister for state industries. Reflecting the trough into which the EC had sunk, he resigned unexpectedly from his post as Commission president and returned to Italian politics.
1972	Sicco Mansholt (Netherlands) Centrist; agriculture minister. Appointed agriculture commissioner in 1958 and became principal architect of the Common Agricultural Policy. Author of 1968 Mansholt Plan on reform of agricultural policy. Served an interim term of nine months as president.
1973–1976	François-Xavier Ortoli (France) Gaullist; bureaucrat who headed the National Planning Commission before being elected to the French National Assembly in 1968. Became minister of economic affairs and finance. Following his term as president, served as commissioner for economic affairs.
1977–1980	Roy Jenkins (Britain) Socialist; home secretary and chancellor of the exchequer in Wilson governments. His term as president saw the creation of the EMS and establishment of the right of the Commission president to represent the EC at world economic summits, but the Commission lost power to the European Council and Parliament.
1981–1984	Gaston Thorn (Luxembourg) Socialist; elected to Luxembourg Parliament in 1959 and appointed to European Parliament, where he later became vice president of the Liberal Group. Minister of foreign affairs and foreign trade 1969–1980 and prime minister 1974–1979.
1985–1994	Jacques Delors (France) Socialist; economics and finance minister in first Mitterrand government (1981–1983). Longest-serving and most productive Commission president. His term saw the passage of the Single European Act, revival of economic and monetary union, the Maastricht Treaty, and the creation of the European Economic Area.
1995–1999	Jacques Santer (Luxembourg) Christian Democrat; prime minister from 1985 until his appointment. Santer chaired the negotiations leading to the SEA in 1986. More low-key than his predecessor, and more focused on deepening integration rather than broadening the powers and reach of the EU, he resigned in March 1999 as a result of a corruption scandal in the Commission.
1999–	Romano Prodi (Italy) Former Christian Democrat; prime minister from 1996 to 1998. Expected to focus on reforms to the Commission in the wake of the corruption scandal, and will have to deal with conversion to the euro, and eastern enlargement.

TABLE 6.3 Directorates-General of the European Commission

DGI	External Relations: Commercial policy, North America, Southeast Asia
DGIA/IB	External Relations: Rest of the world, CFSP
DGII	Economic and Financial Affairs
DGIII	Industry
DGIV	Competition
DGV`	Employment, Industrial Relations, and Social Affairs
DGVI	Agriculture
DGVII	Transport
DGVIII	Development
DGIX	Personnel and Administration
DGX	Information, Communication, and Culture
DGXI	Environment, Nuclear Safety, and Civil Protection
DGXII	Science, Research and Development
DGXIII	Telecommunications, Information Technologies, and Exploitation or Research
DGXIV	Fisheries
DGXV	Internal Market and Financial Services
DGXVI	Regional Policy and Cohesion
DGXVII	Energy
DGXVIII	*disbanded*
DGXIX	Budgets
DGXX	*disbanded*
DGXXI	Customs and Indirect Taxation
DGXXII	Education, Training and Youth
DGXXIII	Enterprise Policy, Distributive Trades, Tourism, and Cooperatives
DGXXIV	Consumer Policy and Consumer Health Protection

some work in Luxembourg, in other parts of the EU, or in the Commission's overseas offices.

Recruitment is both complex and competitive. About five hundred new positions become vacant each year, for which there are literally thousands of applicants. A university degree and fluency in at least two EU languages are minimum requirements, and specialist professional training (in law, business, finance, or science, for example) is increasingly required. Entrance exams are held in fifteen countries in eleven languages, and the process is so convoluted and detailed that applicants may have to wait as long as three years to learn whether they have been accepted. Once appointed, Commission staff members are well paid, and redundancies are rare. An affirmative action policy has ensured that women are well represented at the lower levels of the Commission and increasingly at the higher levels as well, although the College has been dominated by men. The first two women commissioners were Vasso Papandreou of Greece and Christiane Scrivener of France, appointed in 1989; the 1995–1999 College had a record five women among its twenty members.

The Secretariat General

Administration is overseen by a secretary general supported by a staff of about 350. The secretary general chairs the weekly meetings of the *chefs de cabinet,* sits in on the weekly meetings of the commissioners, directs Commission relations with other EU institutions, and generally makes sure the work of the Commission runs smoothly. The job of secretary general was held for nearly thirty years by Emile Noël of France and since 1997 has been held by Carlo Trojan of the Netherlands.

Advisory Committees

Most of the work of discussing and sorting out the details of proposed laws and policies is left to a series of expert and consultative committees. The expert committees consist of national officials and specialists appointed by national governments. Most are permanent and have fixed numbers of members, while others meet on an ad hoc basis to discuss Commission proposals. The consultative committees consist of people with sectional interests and are set up and funded directly by the Commission. Members are nominated by EU-wide organizations such as the European Trade Union Confederation and the Committee of Professional Agricultural Organizations. Committees are a good point of contact for lobbyists; any interest group or lobbyist who wants to influence EU policy would be well advised to give testimony before one of these committees.

How the Commission Works

The Commission—whose key powers are listed in Articles 155–163 of the treaties—is neither a full-blown "government" nor a "bureaucracy" in the literal sense of those terms, yet it has elements of both because its key task is to ensure that EU policies are advanced in light of the treaties. It does this in four ways.

Powers of Initiation

The Commission is legally obliged to "formulate recommendations or deliver opinions" on matters dealt with in the treaties (Article 155), which means, in effect, that it must ensure that the principles of the treaties are turned into practical laws and policies. In this respect it is sometimes described as a think tank and policy formulator and is expected to provide leadership for the EU.[12] It has the sole power to initiate new legislation

BOX 6.2
European Union Law

The foundations of the EU legal order is provided by the six major treaties: Paris, the two treaties of Rome, the Single European Act, Maastricht, and Amsterdam. These set out the basic goals and principles of European integration and describe—as well as place limits on—the powers of EU institutions and of member states in their relationship with the EU. They have also spawned thousands of individual laws, which come in five main forms:

Regulations. These are the most powerful of EU laws and play a central role in developing a uniform body of European law. Usually fairly narrow in their intent, they are often designed to amend or adjust an existing law. A regulation is binding in its entirety on all member states, directly applicable in the sense that it does not need to be turned into national law. Regulations usually go into immediate force on a specified date, upon—or soon after—publication in the *Official Journal of the European Communities.* The EU adopts between 250 to 300 new regulations each year.

Directives. These are binding on member states in terms of goals and objectives, but it is left up to the states to decide how best to achieve those goals. They can be directed at all or some member states; most focus on outlining general policy goals, while some are aimed at harmonization and set a date by which they must be implemented. The governments of the member states must tell the Commission what they plan to do to achieve the goals of a directive. The EU adopts about fifty to eighty directives each year.

Decisions. These are also binding and can be aimed at one or more member states, at institutions, even at individuals. They are usually fairly specific in intent and have administrative rather than legislative goals. Some are aimed at making changes in the powers of the EU, some at purely internal administrative issues (e.g., staff appointments and promotions), and others are issued where the Commission has to adjudicate disputes between member states or corporations. The EU adopts between 160 and 190 decisions each year.

Recommendations and Opinions. These have no binding force, so it is debatable whether or not they have the effect of law. They are sometimes used to test reaction to a new EU policy, but they are used mainly to persuade or to provide interpretation on the application of regulations, directives, and decisions.

They are not laws, but the Commission has relied increasingly for the development of policies on the publication of green and white papers; the former set out ideas for public discussion and debate, while the latter outline detailed policies for discussion and decision.

and can also draw up proposals for entire new policy areas (as it did with the Single European Act and the Delors package for Economic and Monetary Union) and pass them on to Parliament and the Council of Ministers for discussion and adoption.

Although neither Parliament nor the Council can initiate the lawmaking process and must wait for the Commission to generate proposals, pressure and influence are brought to bear on the Commission from many different quarters. Under Article 152, the Council of Ministers can ask the Commission to "undertake any studies the Council considers desirable for the attainment of the common objectives, and to submit to it any appropriate proposals"; Maastricht gave the same powers to Parliament, adding to a trend in which policy ideas come from outside the Commission. A proposal may also come from a commissioner or a staff member of one of the DGs, may come as a result of a ruling by the Court of Justice, or may flow out of one of the treaties. Member-state governments, interest groups, and even private corporations can exert direct or indirect pressure on the Commission. Since the mid-1970s, increasing numbers of policy suggestions have come from the European Council.

Typically, a piece of EU legislation will begin as a draft written by middle-ranking Eurocrats in one of the directorates-general. It will then be passed up through the ranks of the DG, referred to other interested DGs, and discussed by *cabinets* and advisory committees, being amended or revised along the way. The draft will finally reach the College of Commissioners, which meets every Wednesday to go through the different draft laws. Meetings take place in Brussels, or in Strasbourg if Parliament is in plenary session. By a majority vote (a quorum is eleven), the College can accept a law, reject it, send it back for redrafting, or defer making a decision. Once passed by the College, it will be sent to the European Parliament for an opinion and to the Council of Ministers for a decision. This process can take from months to years, and Commission staff members will be involved at every stage—consulting widely with national bureaucrats and interest groups, working with and making presentations to the Council of Ministers and the European Parliament, and carrying out their own research into the implications of the new law.

Powers of Implementation

The Commission must also ensure that the provisions of the treaties are applied, and once a law or policy has been accepted, it is responsible for ensuring that it is implemented by the member states. It has no power to do this directly but instead relies heavily on national bureaucracies.[13] The Commission has the powers to collect information from member states so it can monitor implementation; to take to the Court of Justice any member state, corporation, or individual that does not conform to the spirit of the treaties or follow subsequent EU law; and (if necessary) to impose sanctions or fines if a law is not being implemented. Detection can be difficult, especially because governments have sometimes worked with their industries to hide the fact that they are breaking the law or not implementing a law, so the Commission usually has to rely on two other methods:

1. Member-state reports. Every member state is legally obliged to report back to the Commission on the progress it is making in meeting deadlines and incorporating EU law into national law.
2. Whistle-blowing. The Commission relies to some extent on member states reporting on each other and on individuals, corporations, and interest groups drawing attention to laws being broken and failures to implement EU law. One example of this came in 1986, when Britain set out to privatize its water industry, which had been notorious among environmentalists for its secrecy. Interest groups noted that it was illegal under EU law for a private company to regulate itself, and the internal workings of the water supply industry were finally made public; the extent to which Britain was breaking EU laws on water quality was also revealed.[14]

The Commission adds to the pressure by publicizing progress on implementation, hoping to embarrass the slower states into action. Under the terms of the Single European Act, for example, 282 separate pieces of legislation had to be agreed to and implemented within a period of five years. In September 1989, halfway through that period, the Commission published a table of the leaders and the laggards, which showed that the wealthier countries had generally made the most progress and the poorer countries the least. Of the laws agreed to by that time, France, the Netherlands, Denmark, and Britain had implemented 50 percent or more, while Spain, Italy, and Portugal had implemented less than half.

If a member state falls behind schedule, the Commission can issue a warning (a Letter of Formal Notice) giving it time to comply (usually about two months). If the member still fails to comply, the Commission can issue a Reasoned Opinion explaining why it feels there may be a violation. If there is still noncompliance, the state can be taken to the European Court of Justice, although this only happens in 5–8 percent of cases (see Table 6.4). Until 1993, compliance was based on goodwill and an agreement to play the game, so to speak; Maastricht gave the Commission new powers to take a state back to the Court, which can then impose a fine. The Commission decides which cases should go to the Court and thus uses the Court to make rules on its behalf.

Italy, Greece, Belgium, and Germany have been the worst offenders; Italy has had the most proceedings started against it, and it has also been taken to Court more often than almost any other member state. Portugal

TABLE 6.4   Infringements of EU Law, 1994–1997

	Number of Times Taken to European Court of Justice				
	1994	*1995*	*1996*	*1997*	*Total*
Italy	12	17	9	20	58
Greece	17	12	17	10	56
Belgium	10	6	20	18	54
Germany	5	10	9	19	43
France	8	6	11	15	40
Spain	9	6	9	7	31
Portugal	5	4	6	14	29
Ireland	12	6	4	6	28
Luxembourg	6	3	4	8	21
Netherlands	4	0	2	3	9
United Kingdom	1	2	1	1	5
Austria	—	0	1	0	1
Denmark	0	0	0	0	0
Finland	—	0	0	0	0
Sweden	—	0	0	0	0
TOTAL	89	72	93	121	375

Source: Commission of the European Communities, *General Report of the Activities of the European Union* (Brussels/Luxembourg: various years).

has had many proceedings started against it (reflecting problems in reporting), but most problems have been resolved in time to prevent Court action. Ironically, Britain and Denmark—two of the most lukewarm members of the EU—have among the best records of compliance, a reflection of the seriousness with which both countries have traditionally taken their international treaty obligations. Most cases of noncompliance come less from a deliberate avoidance by a member state than from differences over interpretation or differences in the levels of efficiency of national bureaucracies; the latter accounts, for example, for many of Italy's infringements because its national bureaucracy is notorious for delay, inefficiency, and corruption.

Managing EU Finances

The Commission ensures that all EU revenues are collected, plays a key role in drafting and guiding the budget through the Council of Ministers and Parliament, and administers EU expenditures, especially under the Common Agricultural Policy and the structural funds.

External Relations

The Commission acts as the EU's main external representative in dealings with international organizations such as the United Nations, the World Trade Organization, and the Organization for Economic Cooperation and Development.[15] Discussions on global trade are overseen by the Commission acting on behalf of EU member states; thus the Commission has increasingly become the most common point of contact for U.S. and Japanese trade negotiators.

The Commission is also a key point of contact between the EU and the rest of the world. As the power and significance of the EU have grown, over 140 governments have opened diplomatic missions in Brussels accredited to the EU. The EU has also opened over 120 offices in other parts of the world, staffed by Commission employees. The growing significance of the EU and the Commission can be seen in the numbers of foreign leaders who visit Brussels (which is also the headquarters of NATO). Maastricht included the proviso that the Commission would be centrally involved in developing the EU's common foreign and security policy.

The Commission also oversees the process by which applications for full or associate membership are considered. Although the applications initially go to the Council of Ministers, the Commission looks into all of the implications and reports back to the Council. If the Council decides to open negotiations with an applicant, the Commission oversees the process.

Summary and Conclusions

The European Commission is the main executive and bureaucratic arm of the EU; it is responsible for ensuring that the underlying goals and principles of the treaties are turned into practical law and policies. As the power and reach of the EU have grown, so have the size and workload of the Commission, but it has much less power than most EU citizens probably think. The status of the Commission has been exaggerated in part because of traditional concerns and doubts about bureaucracies and in part because of the secrecy that surrounds the work of the much more powerful Council of Ministers.

The Commission has been behind much of the legal output of the EU as well as some of the most critical EU policy initiatives of the last ten to twenty years. Its powers have depended largely on a combination of its leadership—particularly the incumbent president—and the changing attitudes of the leaders of member states toward the work of the Commission. As time goes on, pressure is likely to grow for the Commission to become more accountable and for EU citizens to have more say through the European Parliament in the appointment of commissioners and the president. For example, pressure is growing for each commissioner to be subject to confirmation by the Parliament, and it is almost inevitable that there will eventually be a directly elected president, whose position and powers would be tied more closely to the balance of political party groups in the European Parliament. Although the true nexus of EU powers lies in the relationship between the Commission and the Council of Ministers, this is slowly changing as the Parliament becomes more powerful and assertive.

Further Reading

Michelle Cini. *The European Commission* (Manchester and New York: Manchester University Press, 1996), and Neill Nugent. *The European Commission* (London: Macmillan, 1999).

Despite its critical role in the EU, these are the only monographs that have been published on the Commission to date.

Geoffrey Edwards and David Spence (Eds.). *The European Commission*, 2d ed. (London: Cartermill, 1997), and Neill Nugent (Ed). *At the Heart of the Union: Studies of the European Commission* (New York: St. Martin's Press, 1997).

Two edited collections looking at the structure and workings of the Commission, and the ways in which it relates to the process of integration.

George Ross. *Jacques Delors and European Integration* (New York: Oxford University Press, 1995), and Ken Endo. *The Presidency of the European Commission Under Jacques Delors: The Politics of Shared Leadership* (New York: St. Martin's Press, 1998).

Two studies of the Commission under Delors, the first written by a scholar who was given unparalleled access to its meetings and documents.

Notes

1. John Fitzmaurice, "The European Commission," in Andrew Duff et al. (Eds.), *Maastricht and Beyond: Building the European Union* (London: Routledge, 1994), 181.

2. See Derek W. Urwin, *The Community of Europe*, 2d ed. (London: Longman, 1995), 107–113.

3. Margaret Thatcher, *The Downing Street Years* (New York: HarperCollins, 1993), 547.

4. Guy de Bassompierre, *Changing the Guard in Brussels: An Insider's View of the EC Presidency* (New York: Praeger, 1988), 8.

5. Helen Wallace, "The Council and the Commission After the Single European Act," in Leon Hurwitz and Christian Lequesne (Eds.), *The State of the European Community: Policies, Institutions, and Debates in the Transition Years* (Boulder: Lynne Rienner, 1991).

6. George Ross, *Jacques Delors and European Integration* (New York: Oxford University Press, 1995), 36.

7. Desmond Dinan, *Ever Closer Union? An Introduction to the European Community* (Boulder: Lynne Rienner, 1994), 203.

8. Lionel Barber, "Looking for the New Mr. Europe," *Europe* 338 (July–August 1994), 34–35.

9. *The Economist,* July 2, 1994, 45–46.

10. Martin Donnelley and Ella Ritchie, "The College of Commissioners and Their *Cabinets,*" in Geoffrey Edwards and David Spence (Eds.), *The European Commission,* 2d ed. (London: Cartermill, 1997), 34–35.

11. Michelle Cini, *The European Commission: Leadership, Organization and Culture in the EU Administration* (Manchester and New York: Manchester University Press, 1996), 109.

12. Ibid., 18–22.

13. Christopher Docksey and Karen Williams, "The European Commission and the Execution of Community Policy," in Edwards and Spence, *The European Commission,* 128.

14. John McCormick, *British Politics and the Environment* (London: Earthscan, 1991), 97–98.

15. See Michael Smith, "The Commission and External Relations," in Edwards and Spence, *The European Commission,* chapter 10.

7

The Council
of Ministers

The Council of Ministers is the forum in which national government ministers meet to discuss issues, build consensus, and take the final decisions on EU law and policy. It is the primary champion of national interests and, arguably, the most powerful of the EU institutions. Once the Commission has proposed a new law, the Council of Ministers—following a complex process of consultation with the European Parliament (EP)—is responsible for accepting or rejecting the proposal. Although it must work closely with the other institutions, it has the final say on what will and what will not become EU law.

Despite its powers, the Council is less well-known and more poorly understood than either the Commission or the Parliament. Its meetings are closed to the public, there has been surprisingly little scholarly study of its structure and processes, and most EU citizens tend to associate the work of the EU with the Commission, forgetting that their national government ministers—through the Council of Ministers—make the final decisions. In many ways, its lawmaking powers make the Council more like the legislature of the EU than is the European Parliament, although new powers for Parliament in recent years have made the two bodies into "colegislatures."

The term "Council of Ministers" is misleading, because the Council actually consists of several different councils, depending on the topic under discussion. For example, foreign ministers will meet to deal with foreign affairs, transport ministers to discuss new proposals for transport policy and law, and so on. To ensure that the Council does not become too parochial and nationalistic, the appropriate European commissioner sits in on Council meetings. Overall direction is provided by the presidency of the Council, which is held in rotation for six-month terms by each EU member state. Meanwhile, the day-to-day work of the Council is overseen—and most of its key decisions mapped out—by the Committee of Permanent Representatives (COREPER), a powerful body made up of the permanent representatives of the member states, and by a complex web of specialist working groups.

Opinion is divided on whether the Council is intergovernmental or supranational, with debate complicated by the Council's changing role, powers, and methods. Wolfgang Wessels argues that it is "the major control mechanism through which states give up autonomy in return for well-guaranteed access and influence" and feels the transfer of powers to the EU and their use by the Council have pushed the Council closer to having the same features of "cooperative federalism" as those found in the governments of the United States and Germany.[1] Changes in its voting procedures (discussed later in this chapter) have altered the Council's priorities over time, tending to push it more toward supranationalism. At the same time, however, there has been a tendency in recent years for the Council to develop greater influence at the expense of the Commission, strengthening the intergovernmental flavor of the EU.

Evolution

The Council of Ministers (officially the Council of the European Union) grew out of the Special Council of Ministers of the European Coal and Steel Community (ECSC), which was created at the insistence of the Benelux countries to defend their national interests in the face of the dominance of France, Germany, and Italy. Because its members consisted of national government ministers, the ECSC Council provided an intergovernmental balance to the supranationalist inclinations of the High Authority.

A separate Council of Ministers was created for the European Economic Community (EEC) in 1958, where the idea of defending national interests was taken a step farther with a weighted system of voting designed to prevent large countries from overwhelming small ones. The Council had only six members, but among them they had seventeen votes: four each for the three largest countries, two each for the Netherlands and Belgium, and one for Luxembourg. In the case of simple majority voting, the big three could easily outvote the small three, but some votes required a qualified majority, meaning a measure needed twelve votes from at least four states to pass. This protected small states and large states from each other, but it also encouraged them to work together. The Merger Treaty created a single Council of Ministers in 1967.

It was assumed that once Europe began to integrate and the member states learned to trust each other the Council would become less important and the Commission would be able to initiate, decide, *and* implement policy. In the event, the power and influence of the Council grew because member states were disinclined to give up powers to the Commission. The result was a perpetuation of the idea of the EEC as an intergovernmental rather than a supranational body, which displeased those who supported a federal Europe. The Luxembourg Compromise introduced the power of veto, but it was rarely used, and decisionmaking in the Council became increasingly consensual over time. It has recently shifted more toward qualified majority voting, thus forcing member states to put EU interests above national interests.

Several developments have added to the power and influence of the Council:[2]

1. It has increasingly adopted its own nonbinding agreements and recommendations, which are not legal texts, but which the Commission finds difficult to ignore
2. As the interests and reach of the EU have spread, both the Commission and the Council have become involved in new policy areas not covered by the founding treaties.
3. The presidency of the Council of Ministers has become an increasingly important part of the EU decisionmaking system and the source of many key initiatives on issues such as economic and monetary union (EMU) and foreign policy.

At the same time, however, both the European Council and the European Parliament have made inroads into the power of the Council of Ministers. The former has more power over deciding the broad goals of the EU, and the latter—particularly since direct elections began in 1979—has demanded and won a greater say in decisionmaking. Under changes introduced by the Single European Act (SEA), Maastricht, and Amsterdam, Parliament has had more power to comment on Council decisions and to force amendments (see Chapter 8).

Structure

The Council of Ministers (officially the Council of the European Union) is based in the Justus Lipsius building in downtown Brussels, across from the Berlaymont, the former headquarters of the European Commission. Named for a sixteenth-century Flemish humanist, the Justus Lipsius is a large, new, marble-clad building that was opened in 1995 and—much to the chagrin of the French—includes a meeting hall that could house the entire European Parliament should it ever move its plenary sessions from Strasbourg. The Council has four main elements: the various councils of ministers themselves, the Committee of Permanent Representatives, the presidency, and the Secretariat General.

The Councils

Nearly two dozen different technical councils come under the general heading of the Council of Ministers. Although supposedly equal in terms of their status and powers, some are—in Orwellian terms—more equal than others and have more well-defined identities. The most important and focused is the General Affairs Council (GAC), which brings the EU foreign ministers together at least once every month except for August (when much of Europe goes on vacation) to deal broadly with external relations and to discuss politically sensitive policies and proposals for new laws. Below the GAC, the two most powerful councils are Ecofin (consisting of economics and finance ministers) and the Agriculture Council. Below them are councils dealing with issues such as fisheries, transport, and the environment; these meet less often and are relatively junior members of the Council hierarchy. With the launch of the single currency, a new euro-11 council was formed in 1998, consisting of the finance ministers of the eleven participating member states.

Each council normally consists of the relevant government minister from the national governments and a representative from the Commission. Frequency of meetings depends on the importance of the council's area. The GAC and the Agriculture Council tend to meet monthly because of the sheer volume of work with which they have to deal, but the councils on education, transport, and energy meet perhaps only two to four times each year. Altogether, the technical councils now meet about eighty to ninety times each year (see Table 7.1). Most meetings are held in Brussels, but councils also occasionally convene in Luxembourg. Most meetings last no more than one or two days, depending on the agenda. Some are informal, but most are full negotiating and legislative sessions.[3]

In an ideal world, each of the councils would consist of the relevant and equivalent ministers from each member state, but this does not always happen. First, not all member states send their ministers but instead send deputy ministers or senior diplomats. The relevant minister may want to avoid political embarrassment on some issue; may have other, more urgent problems to deal with at home; or may not think the meeting is important enough to attend.

Second, not every member state has an identical set of ministers, and each divides policy portfolios in ways that are often different. For example, some member states have ministers of women's affairs, while others do not. France has a minister of culture, making it almost unique in the EU. The result is that council meetings are often attended by a mixed set of ministers with different responsibilities.

TABLE 7.1   The Council of Ministers: Frequency of Meetings

Council	1970	1975	1980	1985	1990	1996
General and foreign	12	16	13	14	13	13
Agriculture	15	15	15	14	14	13
Economy and finance	1	8	9	7	10	8
Internal market	—	—	—	—	7	5
Technology and industry	1	—	—	1	4	4
Environment	—	3	2	3	4	4
Fisheries	—	—	7	3	3	4
Research	—	2	—	2	4	4
Labor and social affairs	3	2	2	2	3	3
Transport	3	2	2	3	4	3
Development cooperation	—	2	1	2	3	3
Budget	—	3	5	5	2	3
Education	—	1	1	1	2	2
Energy	1	—	2	3	1	2
Consumer protection	—	—	—	1	2	2
Health	—	—	—	—	2	2
Euratom	2	—	—	—	—	—
Miscellaneous	3	2	4	8	8	12
Total	41	56	63	69	86	87

Source: Annual Reports of the Secretariat General of the Council of the European Union (various years).

Permanent Representatives

The ministers may be the most visible element of the Council hierarchy, but its heart and soul lies in the powerful and secretive Committee of Permanent Representatives (known by its French acronym, COREPER; see Box 7.1). Consisting of the permanent representatives, or the heads of the national delegations (or "embassies") of the member states in Brussels, COREPER undertakes the detailed work of the Council, working between meetings of the ministers to try and reach agreement on as many proposals as possible; it has been estimated that perhaps as much as 90 percent of the work of the Council is resolved before the ministers even meet.[4] Only the most politically sensitive and controversial proposals are normally sent to the ministers without a decision having been reached. One former British government minister, Alan Clark, perhaps overstated things when he noted in his diaries that "it makes not the slightest difference to the conclusions of a meeting what Ministers say at it. Everything is decided, and horse-traded off by officials at COREPER. . . . The ministers arrive on the scene at the last minute, hot, tired, ill, or drunk (sometimes all of these together), read out their piece and depart."[5]

BOX 7.1
The Democratic Deficit

The lack of institutional openness and accountability has been a recurring problem through-out the short history of the EU. The European Parliament is the only directly elected body in the EU system, but most of the power resides with the Commission and the Council of Ministers—neither of which is directly elected, and neither of which has much public ac-countability. As one MEP put it in 1991, if the EC were a state and applied for Community membership, it would be turned down on the grounds that it was not a democracy.[1] Descriptions of the way EU institutions work commonly include words such as "remote," "secretive," and "elitist."

The result has been persistent concerns about the democratic deficit, which is usually de-fined as the lack of accountability of the EU institutions[2] or the gap between the powers transferred to the EU and the ability of the European Parliament to oversee and control those powers.[3] Several problems create the deficit:

Meetings of the Council of Ministers, COREPER, and the College of Commissioners are closed to the public, despite the fact that many important decisions on law and policy are taken by all three.

Key decisions are taken by the European Council, COREPER, and the Council of Ministers without much reference to the people, either directly or through the European Parliament. A case in point was the Maastricht Treaty, negotiated largely be-hind closed doors, poorly explained to the European public, and put to the test of a referendum in just three member states.

The Commission is an unelected executive with considerable powers, but its work is subject to little direct or indirect public accountability. Most notably, the citizens of Europe have no direct input into the process by which the President of the Commission is chosen, and Parliament lacks the power of confirmation over Commissioners or judges in the Court of Justice.

The input of national legislatures into the work of the Commission is severely limited (although it grew under the terms of the Treaty of Amsterdam).

Few European citizens feel they can directly influence the EU policy process or even re-ally know how to go about exerting such influence.

The most serious effect of the democratic deficit is to make the EU seem distant and in-accessible to the citizens of the EU, doing little to promote public enthusiasm for European integration. Leaders of the member states occasionally pay lip service to the idea of "trans-parency," but their noble statements will remain devoid of substance until such time as fun-damental institutional reforms are made of the kind needed to close the democratic deficit.

Notes

1. David Martin, quoted in Vernon Bogdanor and Geoffrey Woodcock, "The European Community and Sovereignty," *Parliamentary Affairs* 44:4 (October 1991), 481–492.

2. Ibid.

3. Brigitte Boyce, "The Democratic Deficit of the European Community," *Parliamentary Affairs* 46:4 (October 1993), 458–477; Clive Archer and Fiona Butler, *The European Union: Structure and Process*, 2d ed. (London: Pinter, 1996), 58.

No mention of COREPER was made in the Treaty of Paris, but a Coordinating Committee helped to prepare ministerial meetings in the ECSC, and member states began to appoint permanent representatives to the EEC in 1958.[6] COREPER was finally recognized in the 1965 Merger Treaty, by which time the growing workload of the Council had led to a decision to create two committees: Permanent representatives meet in COREPER II, and their deputies in COREPER I. COREPER II deals with broad issues coming before the GAC and Ecofin, while COREPER I concentrates on the work of most of the other councils.[7]

The permanent representatives act as a valuable link between Brussels and the member states, ensuring that the views of the member states (or at least their governments) are represented and that the capitals are kept informed on what is happening in Brussels. Because they work with each other so much and come to know each other well, the representatives are occasionally torn between defending national positions and trying to ensure that their meetings lead to successful conclusions.[8] At the same time, they know each other better than do the ministers and so are better placed to reach compromises and to negotiate deals, often informally over lunch. They also play a key role in organizing Council meetings by preparing agendas, deciding which proposals go to which council, deciding which of the proposals can be automatically approved by the Council (A points) and which need discussion (B points). Meetings of COREPER II are prepared by senior members of the national delegations, known as the Antici Group (after Paolo Antici, the Italian diplomat who chaired its first meeting in 1975).

Much like a national legislature, the Council of Ministers also has a complex network of committees and working groups that does most of the preparatory work and tries to reach agreement on proposed legislation before it goes to the Council. There are eight standing committees (including those on energy, education, and agriculture), each made up mainly of national government officials but occasionally including representatives from interest groups (for example, the Committee on Employment includes representatives from industry). The working groups are organized along policy lines (so the environment group will look at environmental proposals) and bring together policy specialists, national experts, members of the Permanent Representations, and staff from the Commission. They usually meet several times each week to analyze Commission proposals and try to identify points of agreement and disagreement. The groups come and go according to the Council's workload, but as many as 150 to 180 may be functioning at any one time.

The Presidency

The presidency of the Council of Ministers (and of the European Council) is held not by a person but by a country (in effect, the prime minister—or president in the case of France—and the foreign minister of that country). Every EU member state takes turns holding the presidency for terms of six months, beginning in January and July each year. Six months is usually a long enough time to make an impression on the direction of the EU, but it is also a short enough period to ensure that every member state is periodically at the helm and to guarantee a balance between small and large countries. At one time, the cycle ran in alphabetical order by the name of the country in its national language, but because the workload of the presidency is not spread evenly (negotiations on farm prices take place during the spring, and most of the work on the EU budget is concentrated in the second half of the year), the cycle of presidencies beginning in January 1993 inverted each pair of states. Then, as foreign policy issues came to the fore, it was decided that—with effect from 1998—small countries would alternate with large ones (see Table 7.2).

As the breadth and depth of European integration have grown, so have the value, influence, and power of the presidency. The state holding the presidency today has several responsibilities.

1. First, it sets the agenda for Council meetings and also effectively for the EU as a whole. The presidency looks out for the broader goals of the EU but also gives the incumbent member state the chance to push issues of special interest farther up the EU agenda, although it must balance this with the task of brokering agreements among the member states as a whole.

2. Second, the presidency arranges and chairs meetings of the Council of Ministers and COREPER and represents the Council in relations with other EU institutions. An active presidency will lean heavily on COREPER to push its favorite proposals and to ensure that agreement is reached.[9]

3. Third, it mediates and bargains and is responsible for promoting cooperation among member states and for ensuring that policy development has consistency and continuity. The success of a presidency is measured according to the extent to which it is able to encourage compromise and build a consensus among the EU members. At the same time, it is evaluated as much by what it delays or opposes as by what it promotes.[10]

4. Finally, the presidency oversees EU foreign policy for six months, acts as the main voice of the EU on the global stage, coordinates member-state positions at international conferences and negotiations in which the EU is involved, and (along with the president of the Commission) represents the EU at meetings with the president of the United States and at the annual meetings of the Group of Seven (G7) industrialized countries. Finally, it hosts the biannual summit of the European Council (see Chapter 10).

TABLE 7.2   Schedule of Presidencies of the Council of Ministers

1991 first half	Luxembourg	1997 first half	Netherlands
1991 second half	Netherlands	1997 second half	Luxembourg
1992 first half	Portugal	1998 first half	United Kingdom
1992 second half	United Kingdom	1998 second half	Austria
1993 first half	Denmark	1999 first half	Germany
1993 second half	Belgium	1999 second half	Finland
1994 first half	Greece	2000 first half	Portugal
1994 second half	Germany	2000 second half	France
1995 first half	France	2001 first half	Sweden
1995 second half	Spain	2001 second half	Belgium
1996 first half	Italy	2002 first half	Spain
1996 second half	Ireland	2002 second half	Denmark

To ensure continuity from one presidency to the next, the Council uses a troika system in which ministers from the incumbent presidency work closely with their predecessors and their successors. When Germany took over the presidency in the first half of 1999, for example, German ministers worked particularly closely with their Austrian predecessors and their Finnish successors.

Holding the presidency allows a member state to convene meetings and launch strategic initiatives on issues of particular national interest, to try to bring those issues and initiatives to the top of the EU agenda, and to earn prestige and credibility (assuming it does a good job). The presidency allows the leaders of smaller states to negotiate directly with other world leaders—which they might otherwise rarely be able to do—and also helps the process of European integration by making the EU more real to the citizens of that country; it helps them to feel more involved and to see that they have a stake in the development of the EU.

The main disadvantage of the job is the huge amount of work involved, a burden that is especially onerous to member states with limited resources and small bureaucracies. A member state can pass up its turn as president, as Portugal did immediately after it joined the EC in 1986, on the grounds that it was not yet in a position to do a good job. A member state can also ask another state to help bear some of the workload. Ireland, for example, won widespread respect for its presidency during the first half of 1990 but had difficulty meeting its foreign policy obligations. Officially neutral, Ireland has full-time embassies in barely thirty countries, which means it lacks an intelligence-gathering system and a pool of foreign policy experts; the Irish Parliament does not even have a foreign affairs committee. Ireland's low-key approach led to the old joke that its most useful role in international relations lies in occupying the seat between Iraq and Israel at international gatherings.

Ireland dealt with its resource problem by asking Italy (which was next in line for the presidency) to help with information-gathering.

Different states have different approaches to the presidency, depending upon a combination of their national administrative and political cultures, their attitudes toward the EU, and their policy priorities. This was illustrated in colorful terms by *The European* when it likened the 1990 Italian presidency to "a bus trip with the Marx brothers in the driver's seat," while the subsequent Luxembourg presidency was more like "being driven by a sedate couple who only take to the road on Sundays and then infuriate other motorists by respecting the speed limit."[11] The records of some recent presidencies illustrate the often very different styles and priorities different member states bring to the job.

Spain. The Spanish presidency during the second half of 1995 was judged a success despite the fact that the government of Felipe Gonzalez was distracted by corruption scandals, economic problems, and the possibility of an election. Part of the explanation lies in its refusal to be too ambitious or to outline potentially divisive policy proposals; by contrast, the German presidency during the second half of 1994 had been undermined in part by an attempt by Germany to propose environmental taxes for the EU and to reach agreement on Europol and social policy. With its much smaller bureaucracy, Spain focused on less ambitious objectives, such as development in the Mediterranean and Latin America and paving the way for the intergovernmental conference that was to be launched in Italy in 1996.

Britain. The British presidency during the first half of 1998 saw the arrival on the international scene of the new Labour prime minister, Tony Blair, and other European leaders watched expectantly for Britain to take a more progressive position on European affairs than those taken by Margaret Thatcher and John Major during the previous eighteen years of Conservative government. The British presidency coincided with several key events: the launch of the euro, the Asia-Europe summit of April 1998, the outbreak of hostilities in Kosovo, and the decision on the next round of enlargement; its official agenda included an emphasis on dealing with unemployment and crime, promoting environmental protection, and "bringing Europe closer to the people." It achieved little on Kosovo, and the launch of the euro in May was marred by an absurd squabble between France and its EU partners regarding who would be the first president of the European Central Bank. The best that Blair was able to do was to broker an agreement whereby Wim Duisenberg of the Netherlands would serve the first half of the eight-year term of the president, then be replaced by Jean-Claude Trichet of France. Opinions were mixed on the overall performance of the first Blair presidency.

Austria. The second half of 1998 saw the mantle pass for the first time to Austria, which saw its priorities as creating jobs, paving the way for the creation of the single currency, preparing for enlargement, and taking up the discussion on transparency and democratic rights that had been begun at the Cardiff European Council in June 1998. These were all relatively unambitious and noncontroversial goals, befitting a country that was coming to the job for the first time, that is small, that is neutral, and that is not a major actor in international affairs. The Austrian presidency included an informal meeting among heads of government at Pörtschach in October to discuss the future development of the EU.

As the EU membership expands the pressure to rethink the presidency and the structure of the Council of Ministers will grow. As the EU becomes bigger and more powerful the smaller states will be less likely to be able to take on the responsibilities of the presidency, and as the number of member states grows each will have to wait longer for its turn (enlargement to fifteen members in 1995 put the presidency on a seven-and-a-half-year cycle). One solution may lie in regionalizing the presidency; for example, the Benelux countries might have a joint presidency, as might the Iberian states (Portugal and Spain) and the Scandinavian states. Regional groupings such as these could alternate with the bigger states holding the presidency alone.

The General Secretariat

This is the bureaucracy of the Council, consisting of about 2,400 staff members based in Brussels, most of whom are translators and service staff. The office is headed by a secretary general appointed for a five-year term. The Secretariat supports the presidency and the Council by preparing draft agendas, keeping records, and generally giving the work of the Council some continuity by working closely with the permanent representatives and briefing every Council meeting on the status of each of the agenda items.

How the Council Works

According to the treaties, the Council must ensure coordination of EU economic policies, has the "power to take decisions," and confers powers of implementation on the Commission (Article 145). Since the European Commission has a virtual monopoly on proposing new laws and policies, if it did not feed proposals to the Council, the Council—theoretically—would have nothing to do. However, the Council and Parliament can instruct the Commission to investigate an issue and to submit proposals for new policies or laws (Article 152), and the Council has exploited loopholes in the treaties to expand this power over the years. The struggle between the

Council and the Commission for power and influence has become one of the most important internal dynamics of EU decisionmaking.

What happens to a Commission proposal when it reaches the Council depends on its complexity and urgency and the extent to which problems have already been ironed out in discussions between Council and Commission staff. The more complex proposals usually go first to one or more of the working parties, which look over the proposal in detail and identify points of agreement and disagreement.[12]

The proposal then goes to COREPER, which considers the political implications and tries to clear up as many of the remaining problems as it can, ensuring that meetings of ministers are as quick and as painless as possible. The proposal then moves on to the relevant Council; if agreement has been reached by working parties or by COREPER, the proposal is listed as an A point, and the Council will approve it without debate. If agreement has not been reached, or if the item was left over from a previous meeting, it is listed as a B point. The Council has to discuss B points and try to reach a decision. A tendency toward trying to govern on the basis of consensus has meant that issues rarely come to a vote, but if they do, the founding treaties give the Council three options.

1. First, a *simple majority* is used if the Council is dealing with a procedural issue or working under treaty articles, with each minister having one vote. Exemplifying the secrecy by which the Council works, no reliable statistics are publicly available on the frequency of majority voting, although rumors suggest that such votes are relatively rare and painless.[13] In practice, the "vote" rarely (if ever) comes down to a show of hands but is often deduced by the chair simply by silence, the absence of opposition, or both.[14] Negotiations are occasionally allowed to run on until the opposition has been worn down and a consensus has emerged, which is part of the reason Council meetings often drag on until the small hours of the morning. If a single member state refuses to adopt the consensus, the presidency will occasionally resort to setting up a package deal whereby several proposals are carefully tied together in complex compromises and the dissenting state is encouraged to give in on the proposals it opposes in return for having its favored proposals go through.[15]

2. Second, *unanimity* was once needed if the Council was looking at a new law that would set off an entirely new policy area or substantially change an existing policy. Since the passage of the SEA, the use of unanimity has been heavily reduced, and it is now restricted mainly to votes on issues dealing with foreign policy, justice, and certain financial areas or to instances where the Council wants to change a Commission proposal against the wishes of the Commission. Each minister again has one vote and may abstain.

TABLE 7.3 Qualified Majority Voting in the Council of Ministers

Member State	Number of Votes Through December 1994	Number of Votes Since January 1995	Number of Citizens per Vote (millions)
Germany	10	10	8.22
France	10	10	5.85
United Kingdom	10	10	5.82
Italy	10	10	5.72
Spain	8	8	4.96
EU Total	—	—	4.29
Netherlands	5	5	3.14
Greece	5	5	2.10
Belgium	5	5	2.04
Portugal	5	5	1.96
Sweden	—	4	2.20
Austria	—	4	2.05
Denmark	3	3	1.73
Finland	—	3	1.70
Ireland	3	3	1.20
Luxembourg	2	2	0.20
Total	76	87	—
Qualified majority	54	62	—
Blocking minority	23	26	—

3. Third, a *qualified majority vote* (QMV) is needed for almost every other kind of decision on which ministers have failed to reach a consensus. Rather than each minister having one vote, each is given several votes very roughly in proportion to the population of his or her member state (see Table 7.3). Through December 1994, the Council had a total of seventy-six votes, with the Big Four states having ten each, Spain eight, and so on down the line to Luxembourg with two votes. To be successful, a proposal had to win fifty-four of the seventy-six votes (slightly over 71 percent of the total). To help the smaller states even more, there was also a *blocking minority* whereby twenty-three votes against a proposal would be enough to defeat it. This allowed three or more states to form a blocking minority, and it also prevented any pair of big states from defeating a proposal.

With the accession of three new members in January 1995, the total number of votes was increased to eighty-seven, the qualified majority to sixty-two (still 71 percent of the total), and the blocking minority to twenty-six. Concerned that the power of the bigger states would be reduced, Britain and

Spain had tried to keep the blocking minority at twenty-three but agreed to twenty-six on the condition that a delay would be built in to allow the Council to do "all within its power" to reach a compromise that would make such a minority unnecessary. The QMV system forces states to form coalitions, encourages cooperation, and reduces the tendency toward nationalism inherent in the way the Council of Ministers is structured.

Since the Luxembourg Compromise, each member state has also possessed the implied power to veto issues it believes affect its vital national interests. Although it is rarely used, the very existence of the veto can be employed as a threat, and governments can use it to convince their citizens that national sovereignty has not been compromised by EU membership.

Before the Council can adopt a proposal, it must refer it to the European Parliament, using one of several complex procedures (see Box 7.2). Under the consultation procedure, the EP has the right to a single reading of the proposal and can offer a nonbinding opinion. Changes under the Single European Act and Maastricht gave Parliament the right to a second reading (the cooperation procedure, now rarely used) and a third reading (the codecision procedure) for specified kinds of legislation (see Chapter 8). When everyone has had their say, a final decision is reached by the Council of Ministers, and the proposal is either rejected or becomes law.

The volume of the Council's work has grown rapidly. In 1970 the Council met just forty-one times; in 1998 it met 87 times. In 1970 the Council adopted 345 new pieces of legislation; by the late 1990s it was adopting 550–650 new laws each year (see Table 7.4). These figures reflect the growth of the EU and the movement of the Council into new areas of policy not covered by the founding treaties. The frequency of particular council meetings also reflects the changing priorities of the European Union; the councils that meet most frequently are those dealing with foreign affairs, agriculture, and economic issues, while those that meet least often deal with issues such as education and health.

When the membership of the European Community was small, the workload was lighter, and it was also easier to reach decisions. As both membership and workload increased, the number of technical councils grew, and more of the preparatory work was delegated to support staff. Much of this work is accomplished in meetings of Council and Commission staff, by Council working parties, and by COREPER. The informal meetings outside the technical councils are designed to clear up as many points of disagreement as possible so the final meeting of the councils can be short and straightforward.

Because the Council of Ministers is a meeting place for national interests, the keys to understanding how it works are found in terms such as compromise, bargaining, and diplomacy. The ministers are leading political figures at home, so they are motivated by national political interests.[16] They are

BOX 7.2
Meetings of the Council of Ministers

Meetings of the Council of Ministers can often seem chaotic and unwieldy, with national delegations of perhaps half a dozen members, delegations from the Commission and the Secretariat, and a phalanx of interpreters. There may be as many as 120–130 people in the meeting room at any one time (although that number can rise to 250–300 at key meetings of the General Affairs Council). If the meeting threatens to get out of hand, the president can call for a restricted session and clear the room of everyone but "ministers plus two," "ministers plus one," or ministers and the commissioner.

The delegations are seated at a table in order of the rotation of the presidency, with the Commission delegation at one end, the delegations from the presidency and the Secretariat at the other. The member state holding the presidency not only chairs the meeting but also has separate national representation. National delegations are normally headed by the relevant minister, backed up by national officials and experts. The performance of individual ministers is influenced by several factors, including national interests, the ideological leanings of the minister, public opinion at home (especially if an election is in the offing), and their own personalities and relationships with other ministers.

In addition to general discussions, there are regular postponements and adjournments, huddles of delegates during breaks, regular communication with national capitals, and a constant flow of ministers and officials coming and going. When negotiations are becoming bogged down, the president might use a device known as a *tour de table*, during which the heads of delegations are asked in turn to give a brief summary of their positions on an issue. This procedure gives every delegation the chance to take part in discussions and raises possible new points of agreement and compromise, but it can also be time consuming.

Council meetings are not the only forum in which discussions take place and decisions are made. In addition to the preparatory committee and working party meetings, Council meetings also break for lunches attended only by ministers and translators, and agreements are often reached over a meal.

The seating plan for Council meetings in the first half of 1999 was as follows:

President	Secretariat
(Deutschland)	

Suomi (Finland)		Deutschland
Portugal		Osterreich (Austria)
France		United Kingdom
Sverige (Sweden)		Luxembourg
Belgie/Belgique		Nederland
Denmark		Ireland
Ellas (Greece)		Italia
Espana (Spain)		

Commission

TABLE 7.4   Workload of the Council of Ministers

	Meetings Held	Permanent Staff	Regulations Adopted	Directives Adopted	Decisions Adopted	Total New Laws Adopted
1990	86	2,183	380	65	169	614
1991	83	2,097	335	72	174	581
1992	89	2,147	383	166	189	738[a]
1993	96	2,170	319	63	164	546
1994	95	2,289	274	46	148	468
1995	76	2,445	242	29	175	446
1996	88	2,404	247	58	179	484
1997	83	2,417	208	14	157	379

[a]Increased workload caused by completion of single market and reforms to agriculture, fisheries, and transport policies.

Source: Commission of the European Communities, General Report of the Activities of the European Communities (various years).

also ideologically driven; thus Council decisions will be influenced by the relative weight of left-wingers, right-wingers, and centrists. The authority of different ministers will also depend to some extent on the stability of the governing party or coalition in their home states. All of these factors combine to pull ministers in many different directions and to deny the Council the kind of consistency and regularity enjoyed by the Commission.

Summary and Conclusions

Speaking at the first session of the ECSC Council of Ministers in September 1952, West German Chancellor Konrad Adenauer argued that the Council stood "at the crossroads of two kinds of sovereignty, national and supranational. . . . While it must safeguard the national interests of the member states, it must not regard this as its paramount task . . . which is to promote the interests of the Community."[17]

The Council has been torn ever since between these two goals, which some see as compatible and others as contradictory. The Council is dominated by national government ministers with their own parochial concerns, so its work is ultimately the sum of those concerns. The search for compromise can encourage ministers to reach decisions that promote the broader EU interest, but the Council continues to tend toward being intergovernmental.

It is the most powerful of the EU institutions (except for the European Council, which is more a process than an institution), but its role will almost inevitably change as public demands for accountability and closure of the democratic deficit grow. This is particularly true of COREPER and the Council working groups, which are arguably the most powerful elements in the entire EU decisionmaking process, but which function almost entirely outside the public eye. The Council must at least become more open and less secretive, and it will likely be transformed at some point into a directly elected body, but one that still represents the national interests of EU member states.

Further Reading

Given its powers and significance, the Council of Ministers is surprisingly poorly covered in the literature. The first, and so far only, full-length study of the Council is Fiona Hayes-Renshaw and Helen Wallace, *The Council of Ministers* (New York: St. Martin's Press, 1997), which is useful, but very dense, and fails to convey the power and the color of the Council. Among the other useful sources of information are the following:

Guy de Bassompierre. *Changing the Guard in Brussels: An Insider's View of the EC Presidency* (New York: Praeger, 1988).

A look at the inside workings of the Council of Ministers and the European Council by a Belgian diplomat with extensive experience in the meeting rooms of Brussels.

Emil Joseph Kirchner. *Decision-making in the European Community: The Council Presidency and European Integration* (Manchester: Manchester University Press, 1992).

An assessment of the role of the presidency of the Council of Ministers in the process of European integration.

In addition, several journal articles and book chapters provide useful details, including Wolfgang Wessels, "The EC Council: The Community's Decisionmaking Center," in Robert O. Keohane and Stanley Hoffmann (Eds.), *The New European Community: Decisionmaking and Institutional Change* (Boulder: Westview Press, 1991); and Fiona Hayes-Renshaw, Christian Lequesne, and Pedro Mayor Lopez, "The Permanent Representations of the Member States of the European Communities," *Journal of Common Market Studies* 28:2 (December 1989), 119–137.

Notes

1. Wolfgang Wessels, "The EC Council: The Community's Decisionmaking Center," in Robert O. Keohane and Stanley Hoffmann (Eds.), *The New European Community: Decisionmaking and Institutional Change* (Boulder: Westview Press, 1991), 137.

2. Neill Nugent, *The Government and Politics of the European Union* (Durham, N.C.: Duke University Press, 1994), 124–125.

3. Ibid., 24.

4. Geoffrey Edwards, "National Sovereignty vs Integration? The Council of Ministers," in Jeremy Richardson (Ed), *European Union: Power and Policy-Making* (London and New York: Routledge, 1996).

5. Alan Clark, *Diaries* (London: Farrar, Straus and Giroux, 1993).

6. Fiona Hayes-Renshaw, Christian Lequesne, and Pedro Mayor Lopez, "The Permanent Representations of the Member States of the European Communities," *Journal of Common Market Studies* 28:2 (December 1989), 119–137.

7. For more details on the work of COREPER, see Fiona Hayes-Renshaw and Helen Wallace, *The Council of Ministers* (New York: St. Martin's Press, 1997), 72–84.

8. Hayes-Renshaw, Lequesne, and Mayor Lopez, "The Permanent Representations of the Member States of the European Communities."

9. Guy de Bassompierre, *Changing the Guard in Brussels: An Insider's View of the EC Presidency* (New York: Praeger, 1988), 48.

10. Christopher Brewin and Richard McAllister, "Annual Review of the Activities of the European Community in 1990," *Journal of Common Market Studies* 29:4 (June 1991), 385–430.

11. *The European*, December 28–30, 1990.

12. For a more detailed explanation of the process, see Hayes-Renshaw, Lequesne, and Lopez, "Permanent Representations."

13. Helen Wallace, "The Council and the Commission After the Single European Act," in Leon Hurwitz and Christian Lequesne (Eds.), *The State of the European Community: Policies, Institutions, and Debates in the Transition Years* (Boulder, CO: Lynne Rienner, 1991), 25.

14. Wessels, "The EC Council," 147.

15. De Bassompierre, *Changing the Guard in Brussels*, 35.

16. B. Guy Peters, "Bureaucratic Politics and the Institutions of the European Community," in Alberta Sbragia (Ed.), *Euro-Politics: Institutions and Policymaking in the "New" European Community* (Washington, D.C.: Brookings Institution, 1992), 79.

17. Cited in Jean Monnet, *Memoirs* (Garden City, N.Y.: Doubleday, 1978).

8

The European Parliament

At first glance, the European Parliament (EP) looks and sounds much like the legislature of the EU: It is the only directly elected institution in the EU system, and it has many of the trappings of a legislature, including party groupings and committees. However, it lacks three of the defining powers of a legislature: It cannot introduce laws, enact laws, or raise revenues. It can ask the Commission to propose a new law or policy, has almost equal powers with the Council of Ministers to amend legislative proposals and approve the EU budget, must approve and can fire the Commission, and can veto applications from aspirant EU members. However, the Commission still holds the power of initiation, and the Council has most of the real power of decisionmaking. In short, Parliament either shares powers with or negates the powers of other EU institutions.

Most of the EP's handicaps can be traced to the unwillingness of EU member-state governments to give up powers over decisionmaking in the Council of Ministers as well as to the emphasis in the Treaty of Rome on Parliament's "advisory" and "supervisory" powers. Parliament also has a credibility problem: Few EU citizens know (or much care) what it does or have the psychological ties to the EP that they have to their national legislatures. Furthermore, parties compete in European elections on national platforms and have not yet developed a strong European identity. In some ways, the EP suffers a double bind: Few voters are interested in it because of its limited powers, but its powers are limited largely because so few voters care. To make matters worse, media coverage of Parliament tends to focus on the trivial at the expense of the significant; the intricacies of the budgetary process make less thrilling headlines than easy charges that European legislators are overpaid, underworked, and occasionally corrupt.

In fairness, Parliament is a much more substantial body than most Europeans realize. With increasing confidence, it has used arguments about democratic accountability to win more responsibilities and to be taken more seriously. The EP has become less a body that reacts to Commission proposals and Council votes and has increasingly launched its own initiatives and forced the other institutions to pay more attention to its opinions. Parliament has had a say over the budget since the 1970s, it has won more powers to amend legislation and to check the activities of the other institutions, it has been a valuable source of ideas and new policy proposals, and it has acted as both the conscience of the EU and the guardian of its democratic ideals.[1] The introduction of direct elections in 1979 gave Parliament a moral advantage over the other institutions, and it has a critical role in building bridges across the chasm that still separates EU citizens from EU institutions.

Evolution

The European Parliament began life in 1952 as the Common Assembly of the European Coal and Steel Community (ECSC). The Assembly met in Strasbourg and consisted of seventy-eight members appointed by the national legislatures of the six ECSC members, although Article 12 of the Treaty of Paris held out the possibility that members could eventually be directly elected. The Assembly had the power to force the High Authority of the ECSC to resign through a vote of censure, but it never used this power and ended up as little more than an advisory forum for the discussion of High Authority proposals.[2] The Treaties of Rome did not create separate assemblies for the EEC and Euratom but instead transformed the ECSC Common Assembly into the joint European Parliamentary Assembly. Its powers were expanded to give it joint responsibility with the Council of Ministers over the budget, but its suggestions for amendments to European Economic Community (EEC) law and policy were nonbinding. In 1962, the Assembly was renamed the European Parliament.

The new Parliament still consisted of members appointed by national legislatures from among their own numbers, an arrangement that had two important effects. First, only pro-European legislators put their names forward for appointment to the European Parliament. Second, since Members of the European Parliament (MEPs) were also members of national legislatures, they placed national interests above European interests, mainly because their jobs at home depended on the support of voters. As a result, the European Parliament was seen as a junior member of the EC system, and it has since had to work to change its image and to win more power and credibility.

Article 138 of the EEC Treaty also mentioned the possibility of direct elections, and although Parliament pursued that goal, the Council of Ministers blocked its proposals throughout the 1960s and early 1970s. At stake were concerns about the tendency toward supranationalism and the

TABLE 8.1   Growth of the European Parliament

Year	Membership	
1952	78	Common Assembly of the ECSC
1958	142	Parliamentary Assembly of the European Communities
1973	198	Fifty-six seats added for Britain, Ireland, and Denmark
1976	410	Membership increased in anticipation of first direct elections
1981	434	Twenty-four seats added for Greece
1987	518	Eighty-four seats added for Spain and Portugal
1994	567	Adjustments made to account for the reunification of Germany
1995	626	Fifty-nine seats added for Austria, Finland, and Sweden
1998		Under Treaty of Amsterdam, growth in the number of seats as a result of future enlargement capped at 700.

determination of the Council (and of national leaders such as Charles de Gaulle) to keep a firm grip on decisionmaking powers. The 1976 European Council finally agreed on the need for direct elections, which were held for the first time in 1979. This was a watershed; now that they were directly elected and met in open session, MEPs could claim they were the elected representatives of the citizens of the EU and that they should be allowed to represent the interests of the voters.

EP membership had expanded to 410 members by the 1979 elections (see Table 8.1) and has since expanded to account for new members. More seats were added for Greece in 1981 and for Spain and Portugal in 1987. A major reconfiguration was made for the 1994 elections to take account of the reunification of Germany, and the most recent enlargement in January 1995 pushed the number of seats to 626. Under the Treaty of Amsterdam, the number of seats has been capped at 700, regardless of how many new members join the EU.

Structure

The European Parliament is the only directly elected international assembly in the world. It consists of a single chamber, and its 626 members are directly elected by universal suffrage for fixed, renewable five-year terms.

One of Parliament's major handicaps is that it must divide its time among three different cities (see Box 8.1). The parliamentary chamber is situated in Strasbourg, France. This is where members have most of their plenary sessions, but they meet there for just three or four days each month (except in August). Plenaries usually achieve little, can become bogged down in procedure, can last until late in the day, and may be followed by

BOX 8.1
Parliament's Multisite Dilemma

The low credibility suffered by the European Parliament is not helped by its division among three different sites, which not only forces a tiring and time-consuming travel schedule on MEPs but also encourages many to skip the Strasbourg plenary sessions because they are the least important. The division also inflates the parliamentary budget; about $70 million (10 percent of the total budget) is spent moving MEPs, staff, and files back and forth. The absurdity of this arrangement reflects poorly on Parliament and on MEPs, despite the fact that many are in favor of holding plenaries in Brussels.

The ECSC Treaty included the stipulation (Article 77) that the seat of the institutions would have to be worked out by the common accord of the member state governments. Luxembourg fought several court cases in the 1980s to prevent parts of the Secretariat being moved to Brussels, while France has stubbornly refused to give up the parliamentary chamber. Both countries may find themselves fighting an increasingly lonely battle if Belgium has its way. Brussels may be shabbier and more expensive than either Strasbourg or Luxembourg, but it is steadily emerging as the true administrative center of the EU. It is already home to the Commission and the Council of Ministers, EP committee meetings have become much more frequent, and plans are underway to make Brussels a major European hub for air travel.

With national governments bickering over the issue of a site, the Court of Justice took matters into its own hands with a December 1991 ruling that Parliament could move its administrative staff from Luxembourg to Brussels. Belgium went a step further in January 1992, when work was begun on a new, four-million-square-foot complex of office buildings in central Brussels——which just happens to contain a 750-seat chamber ideally suited to hold parliamentary plenaries. Conveniently, the Justus Lipsius Building (officially opened in 1995) is also home to the Council of Ministers.

The European Council decided in December 1992 that the EP Secretariat would remain in Luxembourg permanently, that the "seat" of the EP would remain in Strasbourg, that plenaries would be held in Strasbourg, but that "additional" plenaries could meet in Brussels. The EP responded by arguing that the decision was contrary to the right of a parliament to determine its own working methods and to carry out its tasks in the most effective manner, and signed a lease on the new Brussels complex, where additional plenaries have been held since September 1993. At the same time, a new and larger building was built in Strasbourg to house the EP. However, as the powers and the workload of Parliament increase and the commute becomes more onerous, fewer MEPs are likely to attend Strasbourg plenaries, and the focus of their activities will inevitably shift to Brussels.

evening meetings of the party groups or EP committees. The result is that attendance is low; the sight of many empty seats and the occasional dozing legislator do little to help the credibility of Parliament.

The administrative Secretariat is in Luxembourg. That is where most of the Parliament's 4,100 support staff work, over one-third on translation and interpretation. Few MEPs need to visit or spend time here, so the Secretariat is relatively isolated.

Parliamentary committees meet in Brussels for two weeks every month (except in August). This is where most of the real bargaining and revising take place, and since "additional" plenaries can be held in Brussels, and a third week is set aside for meetings of the party groups, committee meetings are relatively well attended, and MEPs tend to spend most of their time in Brussels.

The President

Much like the Speaker of the U.S. House of Representatives, the president of the EP presides over debates during plenary sessions, passes proposals to committees, and represents Parliament in its relations with other institutions. The president must be an MEP and is elected by other MEPs for two-and-a-half-year renewable terms (half the span of a parliamentary term) (see Table 8.2). The president would probably be from the majority party bloc if there was one, but because no one party has ever had a majority, the office is filled as a result of interparty bargaining. In 1989, the two largest party groups— the socialists and the conservative European People's Party (EPP)—struck a bargain whereby a Spanish socialist, Enrique Barón Crespo, was appointed president for one term on the understanding that he would be replaced by someone from the EPP. In 1992, Crespo duly stepped aside for a German Christian Democrat, who was succeeded in 1994 by a German social democrat, who was succeeded in 1997 by a Spanish conservative.

To help deal with the many different party groups in Parliament, the president has fourteen vice presidents. The president and the vice presidents make up the Bureau of the EP, which functions much like a governing council. The president also meets with the heads of all of the political groups in Parliament in the Conference of Presidents, which decides the agenda for plenary sessions and manages the committee system.

Committees

Much like most national legislatures, the European Parliament has a series of twenty standing committees (and a changing number of ad hoc committees) that meet in Brussels to consider legislation relevant to their areas. The number of committees, and the importance of their work, has grown as the

TABLE 8.2   Presidents of the European Parliament

Beginning of Term	Name	Member State	Party Group
Common Assembly of the ECSC			
Sept. 1952	Paul-Henri Spaak	Belgium	Socialist
May 1954	Alcide de Gasperi[a]	Italy	Christian Democrat
Nov. 1954	Giuseppe Pella	Italy	Christian Democrat
Nov. 1956	Hans Furler	Germany	Christian Democrat
European Parliament			
March 1958	Robert Schuman	France	Christian Democrat
March 1960	Hans Furler	Germany	Christian Democrat
March 1962	Gaetano Martino	Italy	Liberal Democrat
March 1964	Jean Duvieusart	Belgium	Christian Democrat
Sept. 1965	Victor Leemans	Belgium	Christian Democrat
March 1966	Alain Poher	France	Christian Democrat
March 1969	Mario Scelba	Italy	Christian Democrat
March 1971	Walter Behrendt	Germany	Socialist
March 1973	Cornelis Berkhouwer	Netherlands	Liberal Democrat
March 1975	Georges Spénale	France	Socialist
March 1977	Emilio Colombo	Italy	European People's Party
July 1979	Simone Veil	France	Liberal Democrat
Jan. 1982	Pieter Dankert	Netherlands	Socialist
July 1984	Pierre Pflimlin	France	European People's Party
Jan. 1987	Sir Henry Plumb	Britain	Conservative
July 1989	Enrique Barón Crespo	Spain	Socialist
Jan. 1992	Egon Klepsch	Germany	EPP
July 1994	Klaus Hänsch	Germany	Socialist
Jan. 1997	José Maria Gil-Robles	Spain	EPP

[a]Died in office August 1954.

powers of the EP have grown. As is the case in most national legislatures, the committees have their own hierarchy, which reflects the differing levels of parliamentary influence over different policy areas; among the most powerful are those that deal with the environment and the budget. Seats on committees are divided on the basis of a balance of party groups, the seniority of MEPs, and national interests. For example, member states such as Ireland and Denmark have a particular interest in agriculture and less interest in foreign and defense issues.

European Elections

The European Parliament is elected for fixed five-year terms, and all members stand for reelection at the same time. The number of seats is divided very roughly on the basis of population, with Germany having ninety-nine

TABLE 8.3 Distribution of European Parliamentary Seats by Population

	Population (million) 1997	Population Per Seat	Number of Seats	Number of Seats if Distributed by Population
Germany	82.20	830,000	99	138
France	58.50	672,000	87	98
United Kingdom	58.20	669,000	87	98
Italy	57.20	657,000	87	96
Spain	39.70	620,000	64	65
EU average		596,000		
Netherlands	15.70	506,000	31	26
Greece	10.50	420,000	25	18
Belgium	10.20	408,000	25	17
Portugal	9.80	392,000	25	16
Sweden	8.80	400,000	22	15
Austria	8.20	390,000	21	14
Denmark	5.20	325,000	16	9
Finland	5.10	319,000	16	9
Ireland	3.60	240,000	15	6
Luxembourg	0.40	66,000	6	1
Total	373.30		626	626

Source: Calculated on the basis of population figures from UN Population Fund, *The State of the World* (1997).

seats and Luxembourg just six. Given the math used in the calculations, the larger countries are underrepresented, and the smaller countries are over-represented (see Table 8.3).

Every country uses multimember districts and variations on the theme of proportional representation (PR). Most member states treat their entire ter-ritory as a single electoral district, while Belgium, Ireland, and Italy have four or five "Euro-constituencies" and Germany treats its states as separate constituencies. PR involves distributing seats among parties according to the share of the vote each receives. France, for example, has eighty-seven seats, so if French Party A wins 50 percent of the vote, it will be given 50 percent of the French seats (forty-four), and if Party B wins 40 percent of the vote, it will be given 40 percent of the seats (thirty-five), and so on. Until 1992, the United Kingdom (except for Northern Ireland) used the same winner-take-all, single-member district system it used at home—it fi-nally made the switch to PR in 1999.

The single-member system has the advantage of tying individual MEPs to a particular district and making them responsible to a distinct group of vot-ers. Under PR, by contrast, voters are represented by a group of MEPs from

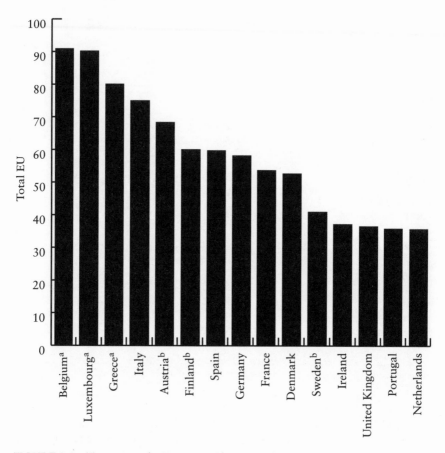

FIGURE 8.1   Turnout at the European Election, 1994

ª voting compulsory
ᵇ 1995

different parties, and constituents may never get to know or develop ties with a particular MEP. PR has the advantage, however, of more accurately reflecting the proportion of the vote given to different parties. At the same time, it spreads the distribution of seats so thinly that no one party has enough seats to form a majority. Although that situation encourages legislators from different parties to work together and reach compromises, it also makes it more difficult to get anything done.

The logistics of European elections are impressive. There were about 270 million eligible voters in 1994, almost half as many again as the number in the United States. Voters must be eighteen years of age and must be citizens of one of the EU member states. At one time, member states restricted voting to their own citizens, but since Maastricht, EU citizens have been allowed to vote in their country of residence, and even to run for the EP

TABLE 8.4   Distribution of Seats in the European Parliament, 1998

	GUE	PES	ERA	ELDR	UPE	EDN	V	EPP	Ind	Total
Austria	–	6	–	1	–	–	1	7	6	21
Belgium	–	6	1	6	–	–	2	7	3	25
Denmark	–	4	–	5	–	4	–	3	–	16
Finland	2	4	–	5	–	–	1	4	–	16
France	7	16	12	1	16	12	–	12	11	87
Germany	–	40	–	–	–	–	12	47	–	99
Greece	3	11	–	–	2	–	–	9	–	25
Ireland	–	1	–	1	7	–	2	4	–	15
Italy	5	18	2	6	27	–	4	14	11	87
Luxembourg	–	2	–	1	–	–	1	2	–	6
Netherlands	–	7	–	10	1	2	2	9	–	31
Portugal	3	10	–	–	3	–	–	9	–	25
Spain	9	22	1	2	–	–	–	30	–	64
Sweden	3	7	–	3	–	–	4	5	–	22
UK	–	63	2	2	–	–	–	19	1	87
EU	32	217	18	43	56	18	29	181	32	626

GUE   Confederal Group of the European United Left
PES   Party of European Socialists
ERA   European Radical Alliance
ELDR   European Liberal Democratic and Reform Group
UPE   Union for Europe
EDN   Europe of the Nations
V   Greens
EPP   European People's Party
Ind   Nonattached

wherever they live, regardless of citizenship. They must make a declaration to that effect to the electoral authority of the member state in which they are living; they must meet local qualifications if they want to vote and qualifications in their home state if they want to run. Member states have different rules on the minimum age for candidates, which ranges from eighteen to twenty-five, and also have different rules on how candidates qualify; some do not allow independent candidates, some require candidates to pay deposits, others require them to collect signatures, and so on.[3]

Turnout varies from one member state to another but is generally higher than voter turnout for elections in the United States; just over 56 percent of Europeans voted in 1994, compared to 49 percent in the 1996 U.S. presidential election (and an average of 35 percent in midterm elections). Belgium and Luxembourg usually have the best turnout (90 percent or more), while in Britain, Portugal, and the Netherlands, barely one in three of those eligible voted in 1994. There has been a tendency for turnout to fall in some of the poorer EU states (Portugal, Ireland, and Spain), to hold steady or decline slightly in the original six founder states

(Italy excepted), and—ironically—to grow slightly in the two most skeptical members, Britain and Denmark. Turnout at European elections is generally lower than that at national elections in the member states, and average turnout has fallen steadily from a high of over 67 percent in 1979. There are several possible reasons.

- There is the sheer novelty of European elections, which have been a feature of the electoral calendar only since 1979.
- Few European voters really know what Parliament does or what issues are at stake, and turnover among MEPs has been so high that none has developed the kind of transnational reputation that would encourage voters to turn out. As a result, EU voters have developed few psychological ties to the European Parliament, which still seems anonymous and distant to most.
- No change of government is at stake, as there would be in a national election, so voters feel there is less to be lost or gained. The leadership of the Commission bears no relation to the makeup of Parliament.
- Party groups in the European Parliament are still learning how to coordinate their election campaigns across all of the member states, and campaigns are still national rather than European. The Greens were the only group to run an EU-wide campaign in 1989, campaigning on their opposition to the single market, disarmament, and more devolution of powers to the local level.
- The media and national governments still tend to downplay the significance of European elections.
- Some voters have little interest in the EU or may be skeptical or hostile to the entire concept, making them disinclined to take part in European elections.

Another factor influencing turnout is that most voters still feel European elections are a poll on their national governments rather than an opportunity to influence EU policies, about which many voters are still confused and uncertain. In 1994, for example, disgruntled Spanish voters used the European election to take seats away from the governing Socialist Party of Felipe Gonzalez, British voters used it to state their disenchantment with the governing Conservative Party of John Major (the opposition Labour Party ended up with over three times as many seats), and Italian voters used the election to make a statement about their general disgust with the discredited leadership of the now defunct Christian Democrats. As the influence of the European Union spreads, as more voters understand the stakes of European elections, and as the powers of the European Parliament grow, turnout may improve.

The Party System

MEPs do not sit in national blocs but come together in cross-national ideological groups with roughly similar goals and values. Following the arrival of MEPs from Austria, Finland, and Sweden in 1995, over seventy parties were represented in Parliament. Many of them consisted of as few as one or two members; they could achieve nothing by themselves, so they worked to build alliances with other parties. Some groups are marriages of convenience, bringing together MEPs with different policies; over time, however, the groups have built more focus, and they cover a wide array of ideologies and policies, from left to right, from pro-European to anti-European.[4] A minimum of twenty-nine MEPs is needed to form a group if they all come from one member state, twenty-three if they come from two member states, eighteen if they come from three states, and fourteen if they come from four or more states.

No one party group has ever had enough seats to form a majority, so multipartisanship has been the order of business. The balance of power is also affected by changes in the number and makeup of party groups. Through all those changes, three groups have developed a particular consistency: the Socialists (on the left), the Liberals (on the center-right), and the European People's Party (on the right). Moving from left to right on the ideological spectrum, the party groups in January 1999 were as follows:

European United Left. The GUE is all that remains from the game of musical chairs played on the left of the chamber since the mid-1980s. Eurocommunists formed a Communist Group in 1973, but the collapse of the Soviet Union in 1989 encouraged Italian and Spanish communists to form their own European United Left; more hardline communists from France, Greece, and Portugal formed Left Unity. By 1994, only GUE remained, made up mainly of Spanish, French, and Italian communists.

Party of European Socialists. The Party of European Socialists (PES) has consistently been the largest group in Parliament, adding to the concerns of conservative Euroskeptics about the interventionist tendencies of the EU. PES has shades of opinion ranging from former communists on the left to more moderate social democrats toward the center. It has members from every EU country, with the British Labour Party forming the single biggest national bloc. PES has a potential ally in the small *European Radical Alliance* (ERA), which consists mainly of French left-wingers.

European Liberal Democratic and Reform Party. The ELDR contains members from every EU member state except Germany, Greece, and Portugal, but the group is difficult to pinpoint in ideological terms. Most of its members fall in or around the center, and the group has suffered over the years from defections to the EPP.

Union for Europe. Consisting mainly of Italian and French conservatives, the UPE is a center-right group created when French Gaullists defected from the ELDR in 1965. It has been reluctant to link up with its most natural ally, the EPP. During the 1994 elections, French center-right defectors created a new, anti-Maastricht *Europe of the Nations* Group (EDN).

European People's Party. The EPP is the major group on the right and has consistently been the second-largest bloc in Parliament. The group was once dominated by German and Italian Christian Democrats, but it changed its name to the EPP in 1976 and finally allowed the European Democrats (British and Danish conservatives) to join in 1992 on the condition that they accept the principles of the EPP, including federalism and a social Europe. The group is right of center and contains representatives from every EU member state, with the delegations from Germany, Spain, and Britain being the largest.

The Greens. Usually associated with environmental issues, the Greens in fact pursue a much wider variety of interests related to social justice, and they refuse to be placed on the traditional ideological spectrum. Once part of the Rainbow Group, the Greens formed their own group after the 1989 elections increased their numbers. German Greens form the biggest single national bloc.

In addition to the formal party groups, about 5 percent of MEPs sat as independents in 1998, describing themselves as nonattached. The number of nonattached legislators is usually high immediately after an election, but it begins to fall as they slowly join party groups. Cutting across the party groups are smaller intergroups tied to specific issues, such as joint stands on a foreign policy issue or a new initiative on European integration. One of the most famous of these intergroups was the Crocodile Club led by Italian Altiero Spinelli (a former European commissioner), which was behind a 1984 draft treaty on European Union that eventually provided one of the sparks that led to the 1991 Maastricht Treaty.

Candidates for elections are chosen by their national parties, but they have an independent mandate and cannot always be bound by those parties.[5] Parliament was once seen as a haven for also-rans, but the quality of candidates competing in European elections is improving, although many MEPs are still people who have failed to win office in national elections or who have been temporarily sidelined in (or have retired from) national politics.

Among the MEPs during the early 1980s were former German chancellor Willy Brandt, former French president Valéry Giscard d'Estaing, former Italian prime minister Emilio Colombo, and former Belgian prime minister Leo Tindemans. Parliament also contained several future members of the European Commission, including Jacques Delors, Jacques Santer, Ray MacSharry, Christiane Scrivener, Carlo Ripa de Meana, Karel van Miert, and Martin Bangemann.

Since the first direct elections in 1979, MEPs have taken their jobs more seriously and are kept much busier working on issues that have growing relevance and importance to the work of the EU. Until 1987, average attendance at plenaries was about 42 percent; since then it has grown to about 58 percent. It was once usual for MEPs to hold a dual mandate (sitting in both the EP and their home legislatures), but this is now very rare, and some member states (such as Spain and Belgium) have outlawed the dual mandate. This trend has not only weakened the links between national legislatures and the EP but has also given the EP greater independence and helped improve the credibility of MEPs.

Relatively speaking, women are well represented in the EP; the percentage has grown steadily from 16 percent in 1979 to 19 percent in 1989 to nearly 27 percent in 1996.[6] This is above the average for liberal democracies (16 percent) and well above the figures for the United States (13 percent) and most EU member states (several of which are in single digits).[7]

How Parliament Works

Conventional democratic legislatures have a virtual monopoly over the introduction, discussion, and adoption of new laws (adoption normally being subject to signature by the executive or the head of state). Unfortunately, the concern of member states with preserving their powers over decision-making in the Council of Ministers has left the European Parliament with a messy collection of formal and informal powers. To complicate matters further still, these powers have grown during the years in favor of the EP, so that it now has a bewildering array of substantial and insubstantial tools at its disposal. Very broadly, its powers fall into three main groups: those over legislation, over the budget, and over the other EU institutions.

Powers over Legislation

The European Commission has a monopoly over the development of new proposals for law, which only reach the EP after undergoing a thorough and complex process of review and amendment. The EP has informal channels of influence open to it at this stage; for example, it can send rep-

BOX 8.2
The Consultation, Cooperation, and Codecision Procedures

The tension between intergovernmentalism and supranationalism in the EU has produced a legislative process of mind-numbing complexity, involving the Commission, the Council, and the EP (Articles 189a–c):

Consultation (one reading)

Step 1   The Commission proposes a new piece of legislation.

Step 2   It is referred to national parliaments for comment.

Step 3   The Council adopts a "common position" by qualified majority.

Step 4   Parliament has three months to respond, but with or without a response from Parliament, the Council can adopt the proposal. It then becomes law. However:

Cooperation (two readings)

Step 5   On economic and monetary legislation, Parliament has the power to consider the Council's common position, and within three months it may:
- Approve the common position by an absolute majority of votes cast or fail to act; in either case, the proposal becomes law;
- Reject the common position by an absolute majority of MEPs, in which case the Council can convene a Conciliation Committee (made up of an equal number of EP and Council representatives) in order to try and reach agreement on a joint text; if a majority of MEPs still rejects the proposal, it lapses;
- Propose amendments by an absolute majority of MEPs; these are then sent back to the Commission and the Council for an opinion. However:

Codecision (three readings)

Step 6   On almost all other kinds of legislation, Council has three months to consider Parliament's amendments and can accept them by qualified majority or by unanimity (if the Commission has taken a negative position). If the Council cannot muster enough votes, a Conciliation Committee can be formed with Parliament.

Step 7   The Conciliation Committee meets to try and reach agreement, with Council representatives voting by qualified majority and EP representatives voting by absolute majority. They have six weeks. If they can reach agreement, the text goes back to the full Council and Parliament.

(continues)

(continued)

Step 8   Council and Parliament each have six additional weeks to adopt the new text, by a qualified majority and an absolute majority, respectively. If either vote fails, the proposal dies.

Step 9   If the Conciliation Committee fails to agree, Council (after another six weeks) can go back to its original common position and adopt the proposal by a qualified majority.

Step 10   Parliament has six weeks to overturn the Council decision by an absolute majority of MEPs, in which case the proposal dies. If they fail, the proposal becomes law.

resentatives to the early development meetings held by the Commission, to encourage the Commission to address. Beyond this, however, it must wait until it receives a proposal from the Commission before it can really get down to work. At that point, it enters a process of give-and-take with the Council of Ministers that has taken on absurdly complex proportions (see Box 8.2).

The *consultation procedure* allows Parliament to give a nonbinding opinion to the Council of Ministers before it adopts a new law in selected areas (such as agricultural price reviews). The Council can then ask the Commission to amend the draft, but the Commission has no obligation to respond. Although this does not seem like much of a power, no limit is placed on how long Parliament can take to give an opinion, thus giving it the power of delay—a traditional attribute of opposition parties in many national legislatures. This power was given new significance with a Court of Justice decision in 1980 (the isoglucose case) that annulled a law adopted by the Council on the grounds that Parliament had not yet given an opinion; Parliament has since been able to threaten delays as a means of having the Council take its opinion seriously.[8]

The Single European Act increased the powers of Parliament, introducing a *cooperation procedure* under which Parliament had the right to a second reading for certain laws adopted by the Council of Ministers—notably those relating to regional policy, the environment, and the European Social Fund. This meant Parliament was now involved more directly in the legislative process and no longer had a purely consultative role.[9] Once the Council adopted a law, Parliament had three months either to accept the Council's decision (in which case it became law) or to reject the decision by an absolute majority of MEPs (in which case the Council had three months to overrule the rejection unanimously). If Parliament failed to act within three months, the law came into force by default.

Maastricht strengthened the powers of Parliament even more by again amending Article 149 to introduce a *codecision procedure,* under which Parliament was given the right to a *third* reading on certain kinds of legislation, notably laws relating to the single market, consumer protection, and the environment. This effectively gave the EP equal powers with the Council of Ministers on decisionmaking.

Finally, under the *assent procedure*, Parliament has veto powers over the Council on allowing new members to join the EU and giving other countries associate status; the conclusion of international agreements; penalties the Council may choose to impose on a member state for serious and persistent violations of fundamental rights; any efforts to introduce a uniform electoral system for European elections; and the powers and tasks of the European Central Bank. Maastricht also extended Parliament's powers over foreign policy issues by obliging the presidency of the European Council to consult with the EP on the development of a common foreign and security policy.

The Amsterdam Treaty all but abolished the cooperation procedure (which is now used only on issues relating to economic and monetary union) and made the codecision procedure more or less the norm; almost every piece of EU legislation must now go through three readings in Parliament. Furthermore, national legislatures have been given a greater role in EU affairs; six weeks must be allowed to pass before Commission proposals are put on the agenda of the Council of Ministers, thereby allowing national legislatures to read them over and make recommendations.

The cumulative effect of all these changes has been to force the Council of Ministers to take Parliament's opinions even more seriously and to make the two institutions colegislatures in a sense. In other words, the EU now has a bicameral legislature in all but name. The changes have also encouraged party groups in Parliament to work more closely together, and they have made the EP a new target for lobbyists trying to influence the shape of new legislation. While lobbyists once concentrated most of their attention on the Commission, they now increasingly see Parliament as an influential arena, and more and more interest groups, corporations, and foreign governments are opening offices in Brussels and Strasbourg and hiring professional lobbying consultants.[10] The exact number of lobbyists is unknown, but there are thought to be at least 700 EU-level interest groups, about 63 percent of which represent business interests, 21 percent public interests, and about 10 percent the professions. [11]

Powers over the Budget

Parliament has joint powers with the Council of Ministers over fixing the EU budget, so that between them the two institutions constitute the "budgetary authority" of the EU. Parliament meets with the Council biannually to adopt a draft and then to discuss amendments. It can ask for changes to the budget, ask for new appropriations for areas not covered (but it cannot make decisions on how to raise money), and ultimately—with a two-thirds majority—completely reject the budget (see Chapter 11). It did this in 1979, and again in 1984, but has not done so again since, mainly because the treaties are ambiguous about what would happen next, and partly because a rejection would complicate matters for the EP's own internal budget.[12] A draft budget is normally introduced by the Commission in April each year and—following meetings between the Council and the Commission—is adopted in July, then sent to the EP for two readings. Only when Parliament has adopted the budget (usually in December) and it has been signed by the president of the EP does it come into force.

Powers over Other Institutions

Parliament has several direct powers over other EU institutions, including the right to debate the annual legislative program of the Commission, a practice that was introduced by Jacques Delors during the mid-1980s and has since been used by the Commission to emphasize its accountability to Parliament.[13] It can also take the Commission or the Council to the Court of Justice over alleged infringements of the treaties and has had the power since 1994 to approve the appointment of the president and all of the commissioners, although it cannot vote on individual commissioners. The extension of the term of the College of Commissioners from four years to five (to coincide with the term of the EP) has significantly altered the relationship between the two institutions. Commissioners are not elected, and the makeup of the College is not tied to the balance of party power in the EP (in the way that the membership of governments in parliamentary systems is a reflection of party numbers in the legislature). However, the right of the EP to vote on the proposed membership of the College is a step closer to the day when there will be ideological and policy alignment between the two, and membership of the College will be directly affected by the balance of party power in the EP.

The most potentially disruptive of Parliament's powers is its ability—under certain conditions and with a two-thirds majority—to force the resignation of the entire College of Commissioners through a vote of censure. Much like a nuclear weapon, though, this power is mainly a deterrent. Several censure motions have been proposed, but they have all been defeated or withdrawn, and a motion would likely all be defeated or withdrawn. The closest the EP has come to removing the College was during the vote in January 1999 over charges of fraud and corruption; 232 MEPs voted in favor of removing the College, but this was far less that the required two-thirds majority of 416. Nonetheless, the size of the negative vote apparently shocked the Commission and led to the creation of the committee of enquiry whose report ultimately brought down the

College. The event will almost certainly go down as a watershed in the relationship between the EP and the Commission.

Parliament has also taken the initiative over the years to win new powers for itself over the work of EU institutions. For example, it introduced its own question time in 1973 and thus can demand oral or written replies to questions from commissioners, helping to make them more accountable. It initiated the 1992 reconfiguration of the number of seats in Parliament, and it led the campaign for the creation of the Court of Auditors in 1993. It can generate public debate on EU policies and can set up committees of inquiry, as it did during 1996 to look into the crisis set off by mad cow disease in Britain. Finally, Maastricht created the new office of ombudsman, through which a citizen or legal resident of a member state who feels that any of the EU institutions other than the Court of Justice has been guilty of "maladministration" can ask for their complaint to be reviewed. The ombudsman is appointed for a five-year term that runs concurrently with the term of the EP, and it has received a growing number of complaints in recent years, most of them directed against the Commission.

Summary and Conclusions

The European Parliament is the only directly elected and accountable institution in the EU system, and it has steadily accumulated greater powers over legislation and over the other EU institutions. However, even though it has helped close the democratic deficit and has become a colegislature with the Council of Ministers, much still needs to be done before it can become a true legislature.

First, the EP needs to win more powers to check and balance those of the Commission and the Council of Ministers. At the very least, it needs the power to approve appointments to key positions such as the presidency of the European Central Bank.

Second, turnout at European elections needs to improve so that Parliament can strengthen its claims to represent European voters. This is unlikely to happen, however, until the EP has won the kind of powers over the European legislative process that convinces voters that their lives will be affected by the outcome of EP elections.

Third, the party structure needs to be tightened for party groups to develop more consistency. Most importantly, parties need to improve their coordination and to run campaigns that are more truly European and based on common European issues.

Finally, Parliament needs to settle on a single site for all its work. The more time that MEPs and their staff must spend traveling back and forth between Brussels and Strasbourg, the less time they will have to get on with the job of legislating.

The pressures for institutional reform persist and are unlikely to stop until the Commission loses its monopoly over the introduction of legislation, until the Council of Ministers is converted into a directly elected body along the lines of the U.S. and Canadian Senates (thereby creating a new bicameral legislature), and until there is a much-needed simplification of the legislative process.

Further Reading

Martin Westlake. *A Modern Guide to the European Parliament* (London and New York: Pinter and St. Martin's Press, 1994).

A critical and analytical guide to the European Parliament that examines its structure, functions, and powers.

Juliet Lodge (Ed.). *Euro-Elections 1994* (London and New York: Pinter and St. Martin's Press, 1994).

An edited collection of studies of different aspects of the 1994 European Parliament elections, with a focus on the fallout from the SEA and Maastricht.

Francis Jacobs, Richard Corbett, and Michael Shackelton. *The European Parliament,* 3d ed. (New York: Stockton, 1995).

Written by three staff members of the EP, this describes the powers and workings of Parliament and discusses potential future changes in those powers.

Simon Hix and Christopher Lord. *Political Parties in the European Union* (New York: St. Martin's Press, 1997).

The only systematic and book-length study of the role of political parties in the work of the European Union.

Richard Corbett. *The European Parliament's Role in Closer EU Integration* (New York: St. Martin's Press, 1998).

A study of the theory and practice of the EP's contribution to European integration, written by a socialist MEP.

Notes

1. Juliet Lodge, "EC Policymaking: Institutional Dynamics," in Juliet Lodge (Ed.), *The European Community and the Challenge of the Future,* 2d ed. (New York: St. Martin's Press, 1993).

2. John Gillingham, *Coal, Steel, and the Rebirth of Europe, 1945–55* (New York: Cambridge University Press, 1991), 282.

3. Martin Westlake, *A Modern Guide to the European Parliament* (London and New York: Pinter and St. Martin's Press, 1994), 84–85.

4. For details, see Simon Hix and Christopher Lord, *Political Parties in the European Union* (New York: St. Martin's Press, 1997), chapter 2.

5. Ibid., 85–90.

6. T. T. Mackie and F.W.S. Craig, *Europe Votes 2* (Chichester: Parliamentary Research Services, 1985), 242; T. T. Mackie (Ed.), *Europe Votes 3* (Brookfield, Vt.: Dartmouth, 1990), 5–16; Hix and Lord, 83.

7. Inter-Parliamentary Union (IPU), *Distribution of Seats Between Men and Women in National Parliaments* (Geneva: IPU, 1993).

8. Westlake, *A Modern Guide to the European Parliament*, 136.

9. Fitzmaurice, "Analysis of the European Community's Cooperation Procedure."

10. Axel Krause, *Inside the New Europe* (New York: HarperCollins, 1991), 6–11.

11. Mark Aspinwall and Justin Greenwood, "Conceptualising Collective Action in the European Union: An Introduction," in Justin Greenwood and Mark Aspinwall (Eds.), *Collective Action in the European Union* (New York: Routledge, 1998), 1–4.

12. Westlake, *A Modern Guide to the European Parliament*, 130.

13. Clive Archer and Fiona Butler, *The European Community: Structure and Process*, 2d ed. (London: Pinter, 1996), 47.

9

The Court of Justice

The European Court of Justice has been one of the most important champions of European integration but has pursued that cause largely out of the public eye. As media and political interest has focused on the Commission and the Council of Ministers, the Court has quietly gone about the business of interpreting EU law, working far away from the political fray in its Luxembourg headquarters, its judges remaining the least well-known of all the leading actors in the EU system.

Its contribution has been critical, however, because without a body of law that can be uniformly interpreted and applied throughout the EU, the Union would have no authority, and its decisions and policies would be arbitrary and largely meaningless. By working to build such a body of law, the Court of Justice—perhaps the most purely supranational of the major EU institutions—has been a key player in promoting integration. It made its most fundamental contribution in 1963 and 1964 (discussed later in this chapter) when it declared that the Treaty of Rome was not only a treaty but was a constitutional instrument that imposed direct and common obligations on member states and took precedence over national law.[1]

Unlike the U.S. Supreme Court, which bases its rulings on judicial review of the Constitution, the Court of Justice has no constitution beyond the accumulated treaties and laws agreed to by the member states. Taken together the treaties amount to something like a constitution for the European Union, but they need the kind of clarification that only the Court can provide. Just as the U.S. Supreme Court helped clarify its own powers with decisions such as *Marbury v. Madison* (the 1803 decision establishing the power of judicial review) and helped push the federal government into new policy areas with decisions such as *Brown v. Board of Education* (the watershed 1954 decision on desegregation), the Court of Justice has done much the same with decisions such as *Flaminio Costa v. ENEL* (1964; establishing the primacy of EU law) and the *Cassis de Dijon* case of 1979 (which greatly simplified completion of the single market).

The Court has the power to rule on the constitutionality, so to speak, of all EU law, to rule on conformity with the treaties of any international agreement considered by the EU, to give rulings to national courts in cases in which there are questions about EU law, and to rule in disputes involving EU institutions, member states, individuals, and corporations. Recent Court rulings have helped increase the powers of Parliament, strengthened the rights of EU citizens, promoted the free movement of workers, reduced gender discrimination, and helped the Commission break down barriers to competition.

Evolution

The Court was established in 1952 as the Court of Justice of the ECSC, which was to be a watchdog for the Treaty of Paris and to rule on the legality of decisions made by the ECSC High Authority in response to complaints submitted by either the member states or the national coal and steel industries; the Treaty of Paris was its primary source of authority. It made 137 decisions during its brief existence, many of which are still relevant to EU law today.[2]

The Treaties of Rome created separate courts for the EEC and the European Atomic Energy Community (Euratom), but a subsidiary agreement signed the same day gave jurisdiction over the treaties to a common seven-member Court. Members were appointed by the Council of Ministers on the recommendation of the member states. The new Court heard cases involving disputes between Community institutions and member states, and its verdicts were final. As the work of the Community expanded, as its membership grew during the 1970s and 1980s, and as the Court issued more and more judgments against Community institutions and member states, its power, reach, and significance grew.

Although decisionmaking in the EU essentially revolves around the axis of the Commission and the Council of Ministers, the Court has made decisions that have had far-reaching consequences for the process of European integration, and it is often argued that the Court has done more than the Commission or the Council for the cause of European integration.[3] Three of its most famous cases illustrate its contribution.

First, EU law is directly and uniformly applied in all of the member states as a consequence of the 1963 decision *Van Gend en Loos* (Case 26/62), one of the most important ever handed down by the Court. A Dutch transport company had brought an action against Dutch customs for increasing the duty it had to pay on a product imported from Germany. Its lawyers argued that this went against Article 12 of the EEC Treaty, which—in the interest of building the common market—prohibited new duties or increases in existing duties. The Dutch government argued that the Court had no power to decide whether the provisions of the EEC Treaty prevailed over Dutch law and that resolution fell exclusively within the jurisdiction of national courts. The Court disagreed, ruling that the treaties were more than international agreements and that EC law was "legally complete . . . and produces direct effects and creates individual rights which national courts must protect."[4]

Second, the principle of the primacy of EU law was established with the 1964 decision *Flaminio Costa v. ENEL* (Case 6/64). Costa was an Italian who had owned shares in Edison Volta, an electricity supply company. When the company was nationalized in 1962 and made part of the new National Electricity Board (ENEL), Costa refused to pay his electric bill (which was about $1.50) because he claimed he had been hurt by nationalization, and he argued that nationalization was contrary to the spirit of the Treaty of Rome. The local court in Milan asked the Court of Justice for a preliminary ruling, which elicited complaints from both the Italian government and from ENEL that there were no grounds for taking the case to the European Court. The government further argued that a national court could not take a dispute over domestic law to the European Court.

The Court of Justice disagreed, arguing that by creating "a Community of unlimited duration, having its own institutions, its own personality, its own legal capacity . . . and real powers stemming from limitation of sovereignty or a transfer of powers from the States to the Community, the Member States have limited their sovereign rights, albeit within limited fields, and have thus created a body of law which binds both their nationals and themselves." It also argued that "the executive force of Community law cannot vary from one State to another in deference to subsequent domestic laws, without jeopardizing the attainment of the objectives of the Treaty of Rome."[5]

Third, the issue of the supremacy of EEC law was confirmed—and the jurisdiction of the Community extended—with a dispute that broke in 1967 over the issue of human rights. The EEC Treaty said nothing about human rights, a reflection once again of how little authority the member states were prepared to give up to the EEC and how focused they had been on economic integration. In October 1967, the German Constitutional Court argued that the EEC had no democratic basis because it lacked protection for human rights and that the Community could not deprive German citizens of the rights they had under German law.[6] The Court of Justice refuted this in *Nold v. Commission* (Case 4/73), in which it established that "fundamental rights form an integral part of the general principles of law."[7]

Structure

The Court of Justice is based in a squat, glass and black steel building in the Centre Européen, a cluster of EU institutions situated on the Kirchberg Plateau above the city of Luxembourg. The land was bought by the Luxembourg government in 1961 as a site for the EC institutions, presumably in the hope that they would all eventually be moved there. The Palais de Justice was opened in 1973 and was extended in 1988 and 1992, and it now makes up part of a modest but not insubstantial complex that includes the Secretariat of the European Parliament, buildings for the Commission and the Council of Ministers, the seat of the Court of Auditors, and the headquarters of the European Investment Bank.

The Court has four main elements: the judges, the president of the Court, the advocates general, and the Court of First Instance.

The Judges

The Court of Justice has fifteen judges, each appointed for a six-year renewable term of office. About half come up for renewal every three years, so terms are staggered. Although most judges are renewed at least once, the Court has more turnover than the U.S. Supreme Court, in which appointments are for life. Life appointments have the benefit of encouraging independence and exploiting experience, but they cause appointments to become relatively highly charged political issues and reduce the influx of new thinking into the work of the Court. New appointments to the European Court, by contrast, are both relatively frequent and nonpolitical. The Euro-

TABLE 9.1   Presidents of the European Court of Justice

Term	Name	Country of Origin
1958–1961	A. M. Donner	Netherlands
1961–1964	A. M. Donner	Netherlands
1964–1967	Charles Hammes	Luxembourg
1967–1970	Robert Lecourt	France
1970–1973	Robert Lecourt	France
1973–1976	Robert Lecourt	France
1976–1979	Hans Kutscher	Germany
1979–1980	Hans Kutscher	Germany
1980–1984	J. Mertens de Wilmars	Belgium
1985–1988	McKenzie Stuart	Britain
1988–1991	Ole Due	Denmark
1991–1994	Ole Due	Denmark
1994–1997	G. C. Rodríguez Iglesias	Spain
1997–	G. C. Rodríguez Iglesias	Spain

TABLE 9.2   Judges of the European Court of Justice, January 1999
(by year of appointment)

	Member State of Origin	Year of Birth	Year of Appointment
G. C. Rodríguez Iglesias (president)	Spain	1946	1986
José Carlos de Almeida	Portugal	1936	1986
G. Federico Mancini	Italy	1927	1988
Paul Kapteyn	Netherlands	1928	1990
John Murray	Ireland	1943	1991
David Edward	United Kingdom	1934	1992
Jean-Pierre Puissochet	France	1936	1994
Günter Hirsch	Germany	1943	1994
Claus Gulmann	Denmark	1942	1994
Peter Jann	Austria	1935	1995
Melchior Wathelet	Belgium	1949	1995
Leif Sevón	Finland	1941	1995
Hans Ragnemalm	Sweden	1940	1995
Romain Schintgen	Luxembourg	1939	1996
Krateros Ioannou	Greece	1935	1997

Source: "Europa" home page, URL: <http://curia.eu.int/en/pres/cvcjen.htm>

pean Court has had over fifty judges since it was created, almost three times as many as the U.S. Supreme Court for the same period. The average age of European judges in late 1998 was sixty (compared to sixty-four for U.S. judges), and eight of the fifteen judges had served four years or less on the Court, while U.S. judges had been in their posts for an average of twelve years.

Theoretically, the European judges are appointed by common accord of the member-state governments, so there is no national quota and no "Spanish seat" or "Austrian seat" on the Court. Judges do not even have to be EU citizens; as Court President Lord McKenzie Stuart quipped in 1988, it could be made up "entirely of Russians."[8] In practice, however, because every member state has the right to make one appointment, all fifteen judges are national appointees. Parliament has argued more than once that it should be involved in the appointment process—even proposing during the 1980s that half of the judges be appointed by Parliament and half by the Council of Ministers and that the de facto national quota be abandoned. The persistence of the quota emphasizes the fact that national interests are still a factor in EU decisionmaking.

In addition to being acceptable to all of the other member states, judges must be scrupulously independent and must avoid promoting the national interests of their home states. Upon their appointment, they must take a short oath: "I swear that I will perform my duties impartially and conscien-

BOX 9.1
Liquor, Beer, and the Single Market

Of all the cases heard and rulings made by the Court regarding the single market, few were more fundamental to the market's completion than those establishing the principle of mutual recognition, under which a product made and sold legally in one member state cannot be barred from another member state.

The roots of the issue go back to a 1979 case arising out of a refusal by West Germany to allow imports of a French black currant liquor, Cassis de Dijon, on the grounds that its wine-spirit content (15–20 percent) was below the minimum set by the West German government for fruit liqueurs (25 percent).[1] The importer charged that this amounted to a "quantitative restriction on imports," which is prohibited under Article 30 of the Treaty of Rome. The Court of Justice agreed, ruling that alcoholic beverages lawfully produced and marketed in one member state could not be prohibited from sale in another on the grounds that they had a lower alcohol content. Although this established the principle of mutual recognition, it did not prevent challenges from occurring.

The issue came up again in the 1984 case *Commission v. Germany* over the question of beer imports into Germany.[2] The Germans have long taken pride in their beer, which, thanks to the Reinheitsgebot (a purity law passed in 1516 by the Duke of Bavaria), is allowed to contain only malted barley, hops, yeast, and water. Germans drink more beer than anyone else in world (an average of thirty-eight gallons per person per year, compared to twenty-four gallons per person per year in the United States) and long refused to import foreign beer on the grounds that most such beer contained "additives" such as rice, maize, sorghum, flavoring, and coloring. The Commission took Germany to court on the grounds that a 1952 German law effectively prevented any beer being imported and sold in Germany that did not meet the Reinheitsgebot, thereby infringing upon Article 30 of the Treaty of Rome.

Germany argued that since the average German male relies on beer for a quarter of his daily nutritional intake, allowing imports of "impure" foreign beer would pose a risk to public health. The Court disagreed and ruled in 1987 that Germany could not use the public health argument to ban beer imports and had to accept foreign beer imports as long as brewers printed a list of ingredients on the labels. The sky did not fall on Germany; even though the German market is now open, beer drinkers remain loyal to domestic brews, which still account for 98 percent of German beer sales.

The Court decision greatly simplified decisions on issues of trade between member states, and the precedent was used to open up European domestic markets to all kinds of food and drink imports.

Notes

1. *Rewe-Zentral AG v. Bundesmonopolverwaltung fur Branntwein* (Case 120/78), in Court of Justice of the European Communities, *Reports of Cases Before the Court*, 1979.

2. *Commission of the European Communities v. Federal Republic of Germany* (Case 178/84), in Court of Justice of the European Communities, *Reports of Cases Before the Court*, 1987–3.

tiously; I swear that I will preserve the secrecy of the deliberations of the Court." They must also be legally competent, or as Article 32b of the Treaty of Paris so thoughtfully puts it, they must "possess the qualifications required for appointment to the highest judicial offices in their respective countries or . . . be jurisconsults of recognized competence." Appointees to the U.S. Supreme Court do not have to be lawyers, although in practice most are. Some European judges have come to the Court with experience as government ministers, some have held elective office, and others have had careers as lawyers and academics—but, since the Treaty of Rome, they have all been lawyers.[9]

European judges enjoy immunity from having suits brought against them while they are on the Court, and even after they have left they cannot be sued for decisions they made. They are not allowed to hold administrative or political office while on the Court. They can resign, but they can only be removed by the other judges and the advocates general (not by member states or other EU institutions), and then only by unanimous agreement that they are no longer doing their job adequately.[10] So far, all of the judges have been men.

To speed up its work, the Court is divided into chambers of three or five judges, which used to hear only cases that did not need to be brought before the full Court. Most staff cases, for example, used to go to chambers before the existence of the Court of First Instance. Because the workload of the Court has increased, though, any case can now be assigned to a chamber, including preliminary rulings and actions brought by or against member states (unless a member state or an institution specifically asks for a hearing before the full Court). To further help with the workload, each judge and advocate general has his or her own team of assistants and legal secretaries, known as a *cabinet* (English: chamber). These groups are roughly equivalent to the cabinets of European commissioners and are responsible for helping with research and keeping records.

Unlike all of the other EU institutions, in which English is slowly becoming the working language, the Court mainly uses French, although a case can be heard in any of twelve languages (the eleven official languages plus Irish) at the request of the plaintiff or the defendant. The Court has about 950 staff members, most of whom are bureaucrats or translators.

The President

While the Chief Justice in the United States is nominated by the president and must be confirmed by the U.S. Senate, the president of the European Court of Justice is elected by the judges from among their own number by majority vote to serve a three-year renewable term. The president presides over meetings of the Court and is responsible for technical issues such as assigning cases to chambers, appointing judge-rapporteurs, and deciding the dates for hearings. Presidents also have considerable influence over the political direction of the Court, much like the chief justice of the U.S. Supreme Court. The president in January 1999 was Gil Carlos Rodríguez Iglesias, a fifty-two-year-old lawyer and professor of public international law from Spain. He was appointed to the Court when Spain joined the Community in 1986, was elected President in 1994, and was reelected for a second term in 1997.

The Advocates General

In a system based on the French legal model, the Court has nine advocates general who look at each of the cases as they come in, study the arguments, and deliver preliminary opinions in court before the judges decide on what action should be taken and which EU law applies. The judges are not obliged to agree with these opinions or even to refer to them, but they provide the main point of reference from which to reach a decision. Although in theory advocates general are also appointed by common accord, in practice one is appointed by each of the five biggest member states, and the rest are appointed by the smaller states; one is appointed first advocate general on a one-year rotation. Most so far have been men; the first woman—Simone Rozès of France—was appointed in 1981.

The Court of First Instance

The Court of Justice has become much busier over time. In the 1960s, it heard about fifty cases per year and made fifteen to twenty judgments; today it hears 400–450 cases per year (about twice the volume of cases coming before the U.S. Supreme Court) and makes well over three hundred judgments (see Table 9.3). It was particularly busy after 1987, hearing cases and making preliminary rulings on issues relating to the single market in the lead-up to 1992.

As the volume of work grew during the 1970s and 1980s, there were more and more delays, with the Court taking up to two years to reach a decision. To help clear the logjam, agreement was reached under the Single European Act to create a subsidiary Court of First Instance. One judge is appointed to the court from each of the member states for a total of fifteen, and the court uses the same basic procedures as the Court of Justice (although it has no advocates general and does not have its own staff). Judge Bo Vesterdorf of Denmark, a member of the court since 1989, was elected president in 1998.

The court began work in November 1989 and issued its first ruling in February 1990. It is the first point of decision on some of the less complicated cases involving aspects of competition, actions brought against the

TABLE 9.3   Activities of the Court of Justice and the Court of First Instance

	Court of Justice			Court of First Instance	
	Preliminary Hearings	Total Cases Brought	Judgments	Total Cases Brought	Judgments
1990	140	380	225	52	59
1991	182	340	227	92	52
1992	162	438	256	115	94
1993	203	486	272	589	76
1994	206	347	215	450	150
1995	242	409	225	260	165
1996	256	420	297	237	161
1997	234	444	341	636	149

Source: Commission of the European Communities, *General Report on the Activities of the European Communities* (Brussels/Luxembourg: Commission of the European Communities, various years).

Commission under the ECSC Treaty, and disputes between EU institutions and their staff. If the cases are lost at this level, the parties involved have the right to appeal to the Court of Justice, in much the same way as parties losing a case in a federal district court or circuit court of appeal in the United States can appeal to the Supreme Court. The court saw a particular rush of new cases in 1997 (636, up from 237 the previous year), mainly because of customs agents claiming damages resulting from the completion of the single market.[11]

Sources of European Union Law

Since the EU does not have a constitution, the Court of Justice must rely on several different sources for its authority. Dominik Lasok distinguishes between primary and secondary sources.[12] The primary sources are the "constitutional treaties" of the EU, including the Treaties of Paris and Rome, the 1965 Merger Treaty, treaties of accession signed by new members, the Single European Act, Maastricht, Amsterdam, various other key EU agreements, and all related annexes and amendments. Some of these (such as the Paris and Rome Treaties) were self-executing in the sense that they automatically became law in the member states once they were ratified, although the Court has often had to confirm just what self-execution actually means. Others (notably the Single European Act) required changes in national laws before they came into effect. The Court has played a particularly valuable role in promoting these changes.

BOX 9.2
The Court of Auditors

Although independent of the Court of Justice, and—under the terms of Maastricht—given the status of a full Community institution, the Court of Auditors is an important part of the legal-administrative cluster of institutions headquartered in Luxembourg. Situated beside the Court of Justice building, it was founded in 1977 to replace the separate auditing bodies for the EEC/Euratom and for the ECSC. It is the EU's financial watchdog, charged with auditing EU accounts.

The Court is headed by fifteen auditors, one appointed from each member state for a six-year renewable term. Nominations come from the national governments and must be approved unanimously by the Council of Ministers following nonbinding approval by Parliament (which the EP would like to see become binding approval). The auditors then elect one of their group to serve as president for a three-year renewable term. The members of the Court must be members of an external audit body in their own country or have other appropriate qualifications, but they are expected to act in the interests of the EU and to be completely independent. About four hundred staff back up the work of the Court.

The Court's brief is to carry out annual audits of the accounts of all EU institutions to ensure that revenue has been raised and expenditure incurred in a lawful and regular manner and to monitor the Union's financial management. Its most important job relates to the EU budget, which it audits on the basis both of accounts supplied by the Commission by June each year and its own independent research. The Court reports back to the Commission, the Council of Ministers, and Parliament by the end of November.

Parliament is supposed to approve the Court's report by the following April but can use the report to force changes in the Commission's spending and accounting habits.

The Court has issued often scathing criticisms of waste, mismanagement, and fraud in the EU's financial affairs. It has found everything from excessive expense claims by European commissioners to massive fraud in funds made available under the Common Agricultural Policy. It has been particularly critical in recent years of the inadequacy of steps taken by the Commission to keep an eye on how structural funds are used and managed. Although the nature of its work would seem to make it unpopular with the Commission, in fact the two bodies have a close working relationship. The Court also has a symbiotic relationship with Parliament; each has helped promote the powers and the profile of the other.

The Court also bases its decisions on secondary sources, so described because they come out of the primary sources. These consist of all the individual binding laws adopted by the EU (regulations, directives, and decisions—see Chapter 6), relevant international law (most of which is weak and vague but which the Court still often uses to create precedent), and—when EU or international law is unclear—its own interpretation. Judgments by the Court have helped give EU law more focus and strength, thus making up for the weaknesses that have often arisen out of the compromises made to reach agreement on various laws. The Court not only gives technical interpretations but often goes a step farther, filling in gaps and clarifying confusions—occasionally creating entirely new laws in the process.

As the European Union evolves, pressures will almost certainly grow for agreement on a constitution that brings together all of the principles established by the treaties and case law. Although this is unlikely to happen until consensus is reached on the balance of power between EU institutions and member states, Federico Mancini, a judge on the Court of Justice, believes the direction in which EU case law has moved since 1957 "coincides with the making of a constitution for Europe." He notes that the EU was created by a treaty (unlike the United States, which is founded on a constitution), that the EEC Treaty did not safeguard the fundamental rights of individuals or recognize a right to European citizenship, and that the main work of the Court has been to "constitutionalize" the EEC Treaty and "to fashion a constitutional framework for a quasi-federal structure in Europe." In this it has been helped by the Commission, as the guardian of the treaties, and by national courts, which have been indirectly responsible for some of the Court's biggest decisions and have lent credibility by adhering to those decisions.[13]

How the Court Works

The European Commission is often described as the "guardian of the treaties," but it is the European Court that is charged under each of the founding treaties with ensuring "that in the interpretation and application of this treaty the law is observed." The Court is the supreme legal body of the EU; its decisions are final, and it is the final court of appeal on all EU laws. As such, the Court has played a vital role in determining the character of the EU and in extending the reach of EU law. For example, when the Community slipped into a hiatus in the late 1970s and early 1980s, the Court kept alive the idea of the Community as something more than a customs union.[14] It has been particularly involved in cases relating to the internal market, and the *Cassis de Dijon* decision is credited by some with allowing the SEA initiative to restore the progress of the EU.[15]

The overall goal of the Court is to help build a body of common law for the EU that is equally, fairly, and uniformly applied throughout the member states. It does this by interpreting EU treaties and laws and in some cases taking responsibility for directly applying those laws. EU law takes precedence over the national laws of member states when the two come into conflict, but only in areas in which the EU is active and the member states have given up powers to the EU. The Court, for example, does not have powers over criminal and family law; it has made most of its decisions on the kinds of economic issues in which the EU has been most actively involved and has had much less to do with policy areas in which the EU has been less active, such as education and health.

Court proceedings usually begin with a written application made to the Court, which is filed by a lawyer with the Court registrar and published in its *Official Journal*. This describes the dispute and explains the grounds on which the application is based. The president then assigns the case to a chamber and appoints a judge-rapporteur from among the judges to draw up a preliminary report on the case; meanwhile, the first advocate general appoints an advocate general to the case. The defendant is notified and has one month to lodge a statement of defense; the plaintiff then has a month to reply and the defendant a month to re-reply to the plaintiff. The advocate general then examines the case in detail and delivers a submission at an administrative meeting of the Court. The parties involved can appear, expert reports can be commissioned, and witnesses can be called to give testimony.

The case is then argued by the parties involved at a public hearing before a chamber of three or five judges or before the full Court (a quorum is eight judges; all fifteen judges will usually be present only for the most important cases). The judges sit in order of seniority, wearing gowns of deep crimson; the lawyers appearing before them wear whatever garb is appropriate in their national courts. Several weeks after the hearing, the opinion of the advocate general is delivered, and the judges meet in the Deliberation Room, with its sweeping—and presumably inspiring—views over the city of Luxembourg. Having reached a conclusion, they deliver their judgment in open court.

The entire process can take as long as a year for preliminary rulings, and most other cases may take as long as two years. Court decisions are technically supposed to be unanimous, but votes are usually taken on a simple majority, as in the U.S. Supreme Court. Unlike the U.S. Supreme Court, however, all the decisions of the European Court are secret, so it is never publicly known who—if anyone—dissented. Once a judgment has been made, details of the case are published in the *Report of Cases Before the Court* (also known as the *European Court Reports*).

The Court has no direct powers to enforce its judgments; implementation is left up mainly to national courts or the governments of the member states, with the Commission keeping a close watch. Maastricht gave the Court of Justice new powers by allowing it to impose fines, but the question of how the fines would be collected was left open. It will also take some time before the implications of this new power become clear.

The work of the Court falls under two main headings.

Preliminary Rulings

These rulings make up the most important part of the Court's work and account for 50–60 percent of the cases it considers. Under Article 177 of the

EEC Treaty, a national court can (and sometimes must) ask the European Court for a ruling on the interpretation or validity of an EU law that arises in a national court case. The issue of validity is particularly critical, because chaos would reign if national courts could declare EU laws invalid.[16] Members of EU institutions can ask for preliminary rulings, but most are made on behalf of a national court and are binding on the court in the case concerned. (The word "preliminary" is misleading, because the rulings are usually requested and given *during* cases, not before they open.)

Van Gend en Loos and *Flaminio Costa v. ENEL* are the classic examples of preliminary rulings, but another ruling that had crucial implications for individual rights came in 1989. During a vacation in France, a British citizen named Ian Cowan was mugged outside a subway station in Paris. Under French law, he could have claimed state compensation for damages, but the French courts held that he was not entitled to damages because he was neither a French national nor a resident. Cowan argued that this amounted to discrimination, and the Court of Justice was asked for a ruling. In *Cowan v. Le Tresor Public* (Case 186/87), the Court argued that because Cowan was a tourist and was receiving a service he could invoke Article 7 of the EEC Treaty, which prohibits discrimination between nationals of member states on the grounds of nationality.[17]

Direct Actions

These are cases in which an individual, corporation, member state, or EU institution brings proceedings directly before the Court of Justice (rather than a national court), usually with an EU institution or a member state as the defendant. They can take several forms.

Actions for Failure to Fulfill an Obligation.   These are cases in which a member state has failed to meet its obligations under EU law; it can be brought either by the Commission or by a member state. The defending member state is given two months to make restitution, so most of these cases are settled before they go to the Court. If a state fails to comply once an action has been brought, the case goes to the Court, which investigates the problem and decides on the measures to be taken; these can involve a fine or suspension of EU payments to the state (under the Regional Development Fund, for example).

The Commission has regularly taken member states to the Court, claiming they have not met their obligations under the Single European Act. Although individuals cannot bring such cases, interest groups have reported a member state to the Commission for failing to enforce an EU law, and the Commission then takes the member state to the Court. Private companies are also often involved, especially in issues involving competition and trade policy. Even

U.S. and Japanese companies can take a case to the Court if they think a member state is discriminating against them or their products.

No member state has ever refused to accept a Court ruling on a major issue, although states often take their time implementing rulings. For example, in the famous Lamb War of 1978–1980, France was slow to accept a 1979 ruling that it must open its markets to imports of British lamb and mutton, under Articles 12 and 30 of the EEC Treaty. When France continued to refuse to comply, the Commission began a second action (*Commission v. France*, Case 24/80) under Article 171, which obliges a member state to comply with a judgment of the Court, and a third case under Article 169 regarding illegal charges on imports. Britain returned the compliment in 1983 by taking its time accepting imports of French long-life milk (milk that is specially treated and packed to extend its life).

Actions for Annulment. These actions are aimed at ensuring that EU laws (even nonbinding opinions and recommendations) conform to the treaties, and they are brought in an attempt to cancel those that do not conform. The defendant is almost always the Commission or the Council, because proceedings are usually brought against an act one of them has adopted.[18] One exception was Luxembourg's inconclusive attempt in 1981 to challenge a European Parliament resolution that all future plenary sessions of Parliament should be held in Strasbourg (Case 230/81). It has become increasingly common since the mid-1980s for member states to use such actions as a means of annulling new laws on which they were outvoted in the Council of Ministers.[19]

The EEC Treaty gave the power to bring actions for annulment only to member states, the Council of Ministers, and the Commission. Parliament was excluded because at the time its opinions had no binding value. However, as Parliament's powers grew, so did the political significance of its inability to challenge the legality of EU law. The Court has helped redress the balance by slowly building the number of circumstances in which Parliament can challenge the law. In addition to being allowed to bring actions for failure to act (see the next section), since 1990 Parliament has been able to bring actions for annulment when the security of its interests are at stake.[20] Actions can be brought on grounds of lack of competence, a treaty infringement, or misuse of powers.

Actions for Failure to Act. These actions relate to the failure of an EU institution to act in accordance with the terms of the treaties, and they can be instituted by other institutions, member states, or individuals who are directly and personally involved. For example, the European Parliament brought such an action against the Council of Ministers in 1983 (Case 13/83), charging that the Council had failed to agree to a Common Transport Policy as required under the EEC Treaty. The Court ruled in 1985 that although there was an obligation no timetable had been agreed to, so it was up to the member states to decide how to proceed.[21]

Actions for Damages. These are cases in which damages are claimed by third parties against EU institutions and their employees. A claim could be made that the institution was acting illegally, or an individual could claim his or her business was being hurt by a piece of EU law. Most of these cases are heard by the Court of First Instance.

Actions by Staff. These cases involve litigation brought by staff members against EU institutions as their employers, and they are the only cases in which a private individual can go directly to the Court. For example, someone who works for the European Parliament might ask the Court for a ruling on the application of a staff regulation, an instance of gender discrimination, a biased staff report, or a decision to hold a civil service exam on a religious holiday in their home country. Staff actions account for about one-third of the Court's workload, but most are dealt with by the Court of First Instance.

Appeals. The Court of Justice may hear appeals on points of law regarding judgments made by the Court of First Instance.

The Court also has the power of opinion in cases in which a decision is needed on the compatibility of draft international agreements with the treaties. The Commission, the Council of Ministers, and member states can ask for a Court opinion, and if the Court gives an unfavorable ruling, the draft agreement must be changed accordingly before the EU can sign it. Finally, the Court can be called in to arbitrate both on contracts concluded by or on behalf of the EU (conditional proceedings) and in disputes between member states over issues relating to the treaties.

Summary and Conclusions

Although it is much smaller than the other EU institutions and is physically distant from the political battles fought in Brussels and Strasbourg, the European Court of Justice has played a critical role in the process of European integration by helping to give the treaties both strength and stability. Its fifteen judges are charged with interpreting the treaties and adjudicating in disputes over their meaning, as well as in disputes involving EU institutions and member states.

The Court has made many significant rulings with important constitutional implications, defining the reach and meaning of the founding treaties in particular. Although struggles continue to be waged over the relative powers of the Commission, the Council of Ministers, and the European Council, the Court of Justice has steadily established its authority and acted as an anchor for the underlying principles of European integration. In this respect, there are many parallels with the U.S. Supreme Court and its role in clarifying the meaning of the U.S. Constitution and the relative powers of the presidency, Congress, and the individual states.

One critical element missing from the work of the European Court of Justice is a written constitution for the EU. As the reach of the EU spreads, the pressure to combine the treaties into a single constitution will almost inevitably grow, placing the Court of Justice at the heart of deliberations about the future course of the EU.

Further Reading

Much has been written about the Court of Justice, but a good deal of this work has been by lawyers, with their uniquely detailed, legalistic style, and it provides little political analysis. Among the more accessible general studies of the organization, jurisdiction, and procedure of the Court are the following:

L. Neville Brown and Tom Kennedy. *The Court of Justice of the European Communities*, 4th ed. (London: Sweet and Maxwell, 1994).

Trevor C. Hartley. *The Foundations of European Community Law*, 3d ed. (Oxford: Clarendon Press, 1994).

Bernard Rudden and Derrick Wyatt (Eds). *Basic Community Laws*, 6th ed. (New York: Oxford University Press, 1996).

Dominik Lasok. *Law and Institutions of the European Communities*, 7th ed. (London: Lexis Law Publishing, 1998).

For more detail on the nature of EU law, see Jo Shaw, *Law of the European Union* (Basingstoke: Macmillan, 1996); and for a discussion of a constitution for Europe by a judge on the Court of Justice, see G. Federico Mancini, "The Making of a Constitution for Europe," in Robert O. Keohane and Stanley Hoffmann (Eds.), *The New European Community: Decisionmaking and Institutional Change* (Boulder: Westview Press, 1991).

Notes

1. The European Court of Justice is often confused with two other European-based international courts: the Strasbourg-based European Court of Human Rights (which comes under the jurisdiction of the Council of Europe and promotes human rights issues in Europe) and the International Court of Justice (which is part of the UN system, is based in The Hague, and arbitrates on issues relating to UN activities).

2. D. Lasok, *Law and Institutions of the European Communities,* 7th ed. (London: Lexis Law Publishing, 1998), 15.

3. For example, see Jean Paul Jacqué and Joseph Weiler, *On the Road to European Union—A New Judicial Architecture* (Florence: European University Institute, 1990).

4. *Van Gend en Loos v. Nederlandse Administratie Belastingen* (Case 26/62), in Court of Justice of the European Communities, *Reports of Cases Before the Court,* 1963.

5. *Flaminio Costa v. ENEL* (Case 6/64), in Court of Justice of the European Communities, *Reports of Cases Before the Court,* 1964.

6. G. Federico Mancini, "The Making of a Constitution for Europe," in Robert O. Keohane and Stanley Hoffmann (Eds.), *The New European Community: Decisionmaking and Institutional Change* (Boulder: Westview Press, 1991), 187.

7. *Nold, Kohlen- und Baustoffgrosshandlung* (Case 4/73), in Court of Justice of the European Communities, *Reports of Cases Before the Court,* 1974.

8. L. Neville Brown and Tom Kennedy, *The Court of Justice of the European Communities,* 4th ed. (London: Sweet and Maxwell, 1994), 45.

9. Renaud Dehousse, *The European Court of Justice* (New York: St. Martin's Press, 1998), 8.

10. K. P. E. Lasok, *The European Court of Justice: Practice and Procedure* (London: Butterworths, 1984), 7–8.

11. "European Court of Justice," home page (1998), URL: <http://curia.eu.int/>.

12. Lasok, *Law and Institutions,* chapter 4.

13. Mancini, "The Making of a Constitution for Europe," 177–179.

14. Martin Shapiro, "The European Court of Justice," in Alberta Sbragia (Ed.), *Euro-Politics: Institutions and Policymaking in the 'New' European Community* (Washington, D.C.: Brookings Institution, 1992).

15. Nicholas Colchester and David Buchan, *Europower: The Essential Guide to Europe's Economic Transformation* (London: Economist Books, 1990).

16. Brown and Kennedy, *Court of Justice,* 173–176.

17. *Cowan v. Le Tresor Public* (Case 186/87), in Court of Justice of the European Communities, *Reports of Cases Before the Court,* 1989.

18. Lasok, *European Court of Justice,* 323.

19. Neill Nugent, *The Government and Politics of the European Union,* 3d ed. (Durham, N.C.: Duke University Press, 1994), 182.

20. Alain Van Hamme, "The European Court of Justice: Recent Developments," in Leon Hurwitz and Christian Lequesne (Eds.), *The State of the European Community: Policies, Institutions, and Debates in the Transition Years* (Boulder, CO: Lynne Rienner, 1991), 50.

21. *European Parliament v. Council* (Case 13/83), in Court of Justice of the European Communities, *Reports of Cases Before the Court,* 1985.

10

The European Council and Other Institutions

The European Council is the newest, the most ambiguous, and arguably the most influential of the EU's five major institutions (although it is more a process or a forum than an institution).[1] Simply defined, it is the meeting place for the heads of government of EU member states, their foreign ministers, and the president of the Commission. This small group convenes periodically at short summit meetings and provides strategic policy direction for the EU. The Council is something like a steering committee or a board of directors for the EU; it sketches the broad picture and leaves it to the other institutions (particularly the Commission and the Council of Ministers) to fill in the details.

The Council was created in 1974 in response to a growing feeling among EC leaders that the Community needed stronger leadership to clear blockages in decisionmaking and to give it a sense of direction. Nothing was said in the treaties of Paris or Rome about an institution like the European Council, and its existence was only finally given legal recognition with the Single European Act (SEA), and Maastricht noted that the Council would "provide the Union with the necessary impetus for its development and shall define the general political guidelines thereof." The Council is almost purely intergovernmental in nature, and its role and powers reflect once again the unwillingness of the member states to give up power to the EU.

At the same time, though, the Council has been an important motor for integration and has launched major new initiatives (such as the European Monetary System in 1978, the SEA, and the Maastricht and Amsterdam Treaties), has issued major declarations on international crises, reached key decisions on EC institutional changes (such as the 1974 decision to begin direct elections to the European Parliament [EP]), and has given new momentum to EU foreign policy. It has been argued that without these regular summits, the EC would not have survived the Eurosclerosis of the 1970s, launched the single market program during the 1980s, or adjusted to the changes in the international environment during the 1990s.[2] However, the Council has also had its failures, including its inability to speed up agricultural and budgetary reform and to reach agreement on common EU responses to the 1990–1991 Gulf War, the Bosnian conflict, and the crisis in Kosovo in 1998–1999.

Evolution

The idea of formal high-level meetings among the leaders of the EC traces its roots to Charles de Gaulle's ideas about political union. In July 1960, he broached the idea of a European political union that would include periodic summit meetings of heads of state or government and foreign ministers.[3] Although his motives were distrusted by many of his EEC partners, the idea survived, and the first formal summits were held during 1961 (Paris in February and Bonn in July). At the Paris meeting, a committee was created to look into European Political Cooperation. Headed by Christian Fouchet, the French ambassador to Denmark, the group produced a draft treaty for a "union of states," which included a specific recommendation for a council of heads of government or foreign ministers that would meet every four months and take decisions on the basis of unanimity. Because at heart the Fouchet plan was an attempt to build an EEC dominated by France, the proposal met with little support outside that country.[4]

No more summits were held until 1967 and 1969, by which time it was becoming increasingly obvious to many that the EC had no sense of direction. The abandonment of the Bretton Woods system in 1971 provided proof of Europe's inability to respond quickly and effectively to major external crises, as did the Community's halfhearted response to the resolution of the 1973 energy crisis, which prompted French Foreign Minister Michel Jobert to declare that Europe was a "nonentity."[5] Decisionmaking had become blocked by struggles over national interests in the Council of Ministers; what was needed, Jean Monnet argued at the time, was "a supreme body to steer Europe through the difficult transition from national to collective sovereignty"; he even suggested calling it the "Provisional European Government."[6]

Agreement was reached at a summit in Copenhagen in December 1973 to encourage more frequent meetings among heads of government. The EC was by now in the depths of Eurosclerosis, and the urgency of taking action was brought to a head by changes of leadership in Britain, Germany, and France. In Britain, pro-European prime minister Edward Heath lost the

February 1974 election to Harold Wilson, who demanded a renegotiation of the terms of Britain's membership. In West Germany, Willy Brandt was replaced as chancellor in May by Helmut Schmidt, and German foreign policy switched from a focus on *Ostpolitik* (accommodation with the East) to a focus on the EC. Meanwhile, the pro-European Valéry Giscard d'Estaing was elected president of France in May. Schmidt and Giscard were both economists who had worked together as finance ministers during the early 1970s, and both appreciated the complexity of the kinds of economic issues that were jostling for attention.

This combination of crises and changes in leadership formed the background to the December 1974 summit of heads of government in Paris, where it was decided to formalize the links among them. Giscard and Schmidt argued for the need to bring leaders together regularly to provide policy direction and clear logjams. A declaration was issued committing heads of government to meet at least three times annually and emphasizing the need for "an overall approach" to the challenges of integration and the need "to ensure progress and overall consistency in the activities of the Communities and in the work on political co-operation."

The wording of the declaration was kept deliberately vague; it said nothing about the precise powers of the new body or its relationship to the other institutions and gave it no legal standing. The new body even lacked a name until Giscard's announcement at a press conference at the close of the meeting that "the European summit is dead, long live the European Council."[7] Legal recognition was finally given by the Single European Act. Although this did little more than confirm the membership of the Council and reduce the number of annual meetings from three to two, by the second half of the 1980s Council summits had become a regular part of the Community timetable.

Structure

The 1974 Paris Declaration was careful not to allow the creation of the European Council to disturb or complicate the existing EC decisionmaking system. For example, concerns among the Benelux states that the summits would weaken the supranationalist elements of the EC were offset in part by an agreement on direct elections to the European Parliament.[8] Suggestions that a new secretariat be created for the Council were outweighed by desires not to create yet another bureaucracy or weaken the work of existing institutions. The Council has been institutionalized to the extent that it exists and follows increasingly routine patterns of functioning, but it is the only branch of the EU without a secretariat or a large, salaried body of staff.

The Council has multiple personalities. It can be seen as the decision-maker of last resort, as a collective presidency in which sovereignty is pooled, as a body that parallels other EU institutions by dealing with issues outside their competence, or as a true "council" that can engineer broad package deals.[9] There are three keys to understanding the way it works and fits into the EU system:

1. Flexibility. The lack of rules, regulations, and attendant bureaucrats gives the Council a level of freedom and independence enjoyed by very few governing bodies.
2. Informality. European Council summits are built on months of advance preparation, but agendas are kept general, summits try to keep away from formal votes, and meetings are kept as small and informal as possible.
3. Delegation. Any signs that the Council is becoming bogged down in the routine day-to-day business of the EU have regularly been resisted.[10] The Council focuses on the big picture, leaves the other institutions to work out the details, and acts something like a "court of appeal" if attempts to reach agreement at a lower level fail.[11]

The first meeting of the European Council was held in Dublin in March 1975 under the lumbering title "the Heads of Government Meeting as the Council of the Community and in Political Cooperation." It met more or less triannually throughout the 1970s and 1980s, but a decision was taken at the December 1985 summit to hold just two regular summits each year, in June and December, with additional extraordinary meetings as needed (see Appendix 4).

Meetings are hosted by the country holding the presidency of the Council of Ministers and take place either in the capital of that country or in a regional city or town, such as Cardiff, Milan, Strasbourg, or—in December 1991—Maastricht in the Netherlands, where the Treaty on European Union was agreed. The Greeks have used their summits to mix business and pleasure, convening them on the islands of Rhodes (1988) and Corfu (1994). The Council brings together the president and senior vice president of the Commission, the heads of government (and the French head of state), and small retinues of staff and advisers. Organization is left largely to the presidency, which in effect means the prime minister and the foreign minister of the country holding the presidency. Some heads of government take a hands-on approach to determining the agenda, while others are more low-key. The major goal of each summit meeting is to agree to a set of Conclusions of the Presidency. An advanced draft of this document usually awaits the leaders at the beginning of the summit, and it provides the focus for their discussions (see Box 10.1).

BOX 10.1
European Summits

Summits usually run over a period of two days, although emergency summits will normally last no more than a day. They begin with informal discussions over breakfast and move into the nuts and bolts at plenary sessions during the morning and afternoon. The first plenary normally includes an address by the president of the European Parliament. Formal dinners in the evening were once followed routinely by a "fireside chat" among the heads of government and the president of the Commission, but they may opt for another plenary session. Overnight, officials from the presidency and the Secretariat of the Council of Ministers will work on the draft set of Conclusions, which are discussed at a second plenary on the morning of Day Two, and—if necessary—at a third in the afternoon. The summit then normally ends with a press conference and the publication of the Conclusions.

During summit plenaries, the prime ministers of the member states (and the president of France) sit around a table with their respective foreign ministers and two officials from the Commission, including the president. To keep the meeting intimate and manageable, very few other people are allowed into the meeting chamber: no more than one adviser per country, interpreters, two officials from the country holding the presidency, one from the Council of Ministers Secretariat, and three from the Commission—about sixty people in all. Every delegation has a nearby suite it can use as a base, but national delegations are limited to seventeen members each.

European Council decisions are usually taken on the basis of unanimity or at least of consensus, but an occasional lack of unanimity may force a formal vote, and some member states may want to attach conditions or reservations to the Conclusions. In addition to the formal plenary sessions, summits usually break out into several subsidiary meetings, including those of foreign ministers and regular bilateral meetings of prime ministers over breakfast or coffee.

The summits are always major media events and are surrounded by extensive security. In addition to the substantive political discussions that take place, enormous symbolism is also attached to the outcomes of the summits, which are assessed according to the extent to which they represent breakthroughs or show EU leaders to be bogged down in disagreement. Failure and success reflect not only on the presidency but on the entire process of European integration. The headline-making nature of the summits is sufficient to focus the minds of participants and to encourage them to agree. A "family picture" is also taken of the fifteen leaders and the president of the Commission, symbolizing the process of European integration. The smiles on their faces would look very shallow if major disagreements had not been resolved.

How the Council Works

Preparation is the key to the success of European summits.[12] Officially, the Council has no set agenda, but some direction is needed, so senior officials from the country holding the presidency usually work with the Council of

Ministers to identify agenda items, which are channeled through the Antici Group to the Committee of Permanent Representatives (see Chapter 7). Preparation begins as soon as a member state takes over the presidency in January or July. The monthly meetings of the foreign ministers under the General Affairs Council try to resolve potential disagreements, and as the date for the summit approaches, the prime minister and foreign minister of the state holding the presidency become increasingly involved. The more agreements they can broker in advance, the less likely it is that the summit will end in failure.[13]

About ten days before the summit, the foreign ministers meet to finalize the agenda and to iron out any remaining problems and disputes. The items on the agenda depend on circumstances: National delegations normally have issues they want to raise, there has to be some continuity from previous summits, and leaders often have to deal with a breaking problem or an emergency that requires a decision, such as aid to Russia or progress on world trade talks. Some issues (especially economic issues) are routinely discussed at every summit. The Commission may also promote issues it would like to see discussed, and an active presidency might use the summit to bring items of national or regional interest to the attention of the heads of government. Calls are occasionally made for the launch of a major policy initiative, such as the decision taken at the 1989 Strasbourg summit to call an intergovernmental conference on economic and monetary union. Some summits are routine and result in general agreement among leaders; in others, deep differences in opinion arise, with some member states perhaps refusing to agree to a common set of conclusions.

The exact role of the European Council has been kept deliberately ambiguous by its members. An attempt to define that role was made at the Stuttgart European Council in 1983 and its agreement on the Solemn Declaration on European Union, drawn up to preempt the draft treaty on European Union being worked on by Parliament. "A good rule of thumb in European matters," mused Guy de Bassompierre, "is that the more solemn the declaration, the more empty it is of true content."[14] Combining the 1974 Paris Declaration and the 1983 Stuttgart Declaration produces a list of goals for Council summits that can be summed up as follows:

- To exchange views and reach a consensus;
- To give political impetus to the development of the EU;
- To begin cooperation in new policy areas;
- To provide general political guidelines for the EU and the development of a common foreign policy;
- To guarantee policy consistency; and
- To reach common positions on foreign policy issues.[15]

TABLE 10.1   Leaders of EU Member States, January 1999

State	Leader	Party	Ideology[a]
Greece	Costas Simitis	Socialist	L
Italy	Massimo D'Alema	Coalition	L
Netherlands	Wim Kok	Labour	L
Portugal	Antonio Guterres	Socialist	L
Austria	Viktor Klima	Social Democrat	CL
Denmark	Poul Nyrup Rasmussen	Social Democrat	CL
Finland	Paavo Lipponen	Social Democrat	CL
Germany	Gerhard Schröder	Social Democrat	CL
Sweden	Goran Persson	Social Democrat	CL
United Kingdom	Tony Blair	Labour	CL
Belgium	Jean-Luc Dehaene	Christian Democrat[b]	C
Luxembourg	Jean-Claude Juncker	Christian Democrat[b]	C
Ireland	Bertie Ahern	Fianna Fail	CR
France	Jacques Chirac	Gaullist[c]	R
Spain	Jose Maria Aznar	People's Party	R

[a]L = left, CL = center left, CR = center right, R = right.
[b]in coalition with Social Democrats
[c]National Assembly majority held by socialists under Lionel Jospin

More specifically, the Council makes the key decisions on the overall direction of political integration and the single currency, internal economic matters, foreign policy issues, budget disputes, treaty revisions, new member applications, and institutional reforms (such as enlargement of the European Parliament). The summits achieve all this through a combination of brainstorming, intensive bilateral and multilateral discussions, and bargaining. The mechanics of decisionmaking depend on a combination of the quality of organization and preparation, the leadership skills of the presidency, and the ideological and personal agendas of the individual leaders (see Table 10.1). The interpersonal dynamics of the participants are also important.

1. The political significance of the Franco-German axis has always been critical, and it has been given additional influence by the strong personal relations that have usually existed between the leaders of the two states (Brandt and Pompidou, Schmidt and Giscard, and Kohl and Mitterrand).
2. Leaders who have been in office for a long time (such as a Felipe Gonzalez or a Helmut Kohl) or who have a solid base of political support at home (such as a Tony Blair) will be in very different nego-

tiating positions from those who have not. In late 1994, for example, John Major suffered from low popularity and a rebellion by anti-EU members of his party, Silvio Berlusconi faced corruption charges as his government in Italy teetered on the brink of collapse, and the socialist François Mitterrand had to cohabit with a legislature dominated by conservatives as his final term drew to a close with no obvious successor in sight. These political problems unavoidably affected the judgment and performance of the leaders.

3. Some leaders are respected and have strong credibility, while others do not. For example, Helmut Kohl became a towering presence on the EU stage; as other leaders fell by the wayside, Kohl lasted sixteen years in office (1982–1998) and, by the mid-1990s, had become something of an elder statesman of European integration (helped, of course, by the dominating economic power of Germany). Margaret Thatcher may have irritated and harangued her colleagues, but her political skills, grasp of detail, and leadership abilities were unquestioned.

In addition to the regular biannual summits, occasional special meetings of the Council can also be convened to deal with a breaking issue or a persistent problem. Examples include the November 1989 summit in Paris to discuss rapidly changing events in Eastern Europe, the October 1992 summit in Birmingham to discuss the crisis in the Exchange Rate Mechanism (ERM), the July 1994 summit convened to choose a successor to Jacques Delors, and the March 1999 summit to negotiate reforms to the EU budget.

Because the European Council obviously has much more power over decisionmaking than any other EU institution, it has tended to take power away from the other institutions. It can, in effect, set the agenda for the Commission, override decisions reached by the Council of Ministers, and largely ignore Parliament. Any hopes the Commission might have held for developing an independent sphere of action and power have largely disappeared with the rise of the European Council. Certainty regarding the current and potential future role of the Council is clouded by its ambiguities, and opinion remains divided over whether it is an integrative or a disintegrative body.[16]

Other EU Institutions

As the reach of the EU has broadened and deepened, the work of its more specialized institutions—and the pressure for the creation of new institutions—have grown. Some have been there from the beginning, while others have been set up more recently in response to new needs.

Economic and Social Committee

Based in Brussels, the Economic and Social Committee (ESC) is an advisory body that was set up under the Treaty of Rome to give employers, workers, and other sectional interests a forum in which they could meet, talk, and issue opinions to the Commission, the Council of Ministers, and more—recently—the European Parliament. The idea flowed out of the Consultative Committee set up by the ECSC and copied the parallel bodies that existed in five of the six founder members of the EEC (West Germany being the exception). It was created in part because few people thought the European Parliament would represent sectional interests, and it has since been described as a "functional complement" of the EP.[17]

The ESC has 222 members, drawn from the member states roughly in proportion to population size (see Table 10.2). They are proposed by national governments and appointed by the Council of Ministers for renewable four-year terms. There are three groups of members: Group I comes from industry, services, small businesses, chambers of commerce, banking, insurance, and similar areas; Group II is made up of representatives from labor unions; and Group III represents more varied interests, such as agriculture, small businesses, consumer and environmental groups, and the professions.

A president is elected by the ESC for a two-year term and chairs two-day meetings of the Committee in Brussels about nine or ten times each year. The three groups hold separate meetings to discuss issues of common interest, breaking down into smaller sections to deal with specific issues, such as agriculture, social issues, transport, energy, regional development, and the environment. Although questions have long been raised about its value, consultation of the ESC by the Commission is mandatory in several areas, including agriculture, the movement of workers, social policy, regional policy, and the environment.

The basic weakness of the ESC is that neither the Commission nor the Council of Ministers is obliged to act on its opinions or views. "Consultation" is an ambiguous concept, and although the Commission can "take note" of an ESC opinion and the Council of Ministers can recognize a "useful" opinion, this amounts to little. The influence of the ESC is further minimized by the fact that its members are unpaid part-time appointees (they can claim expenses for attending meetings) and are not officially recognized as representatives of the bodies to which they belong; further, EU proposals are often sent to the ESC only after they have reached an advanced stage of agreement by the Council of Ministers. The best that can be said of the ESC is that it is another forum for the representation of sectional interests, but as the European Parliament becomes stronger and the number of lobbyists in Brussels grows, the value of the Committee in its present form becomes more questionable.

TABLE 10.2   Membership of the ESC and the CoR

Germany	24	Portugal	12
United Kingdom	24	Austria	12
France	24	Sweden	12
Italy	24	Denmark	9
Spain	21	Finland	9
Belgium	12	Ireland	9
Greece	12	Luxembourg	6
Netherlands	12		
		Total	222

Committee of the Regions

Disparities in wealth and income across Western Europe have always posed a handicap to the process of integration; there can never be balanced free trade, a true single market, or even meaningful economic and political union as long as some parts of the EU are richer or poorer than others. The setting up of the European Regional Development Fund in 1975 was one approach to the problem, as was the creation in 1985 of an ad hoc Assembly of European Regions and the creation by the Commission in 1988 of a Consultative Council of Regional and Local Authorities. The need for a stronger response led to the creation under the terms of Maastricht of the new Committee of the Regions (CoR).

Based in Brussels, the CoR met for the first time in January 1994 and began a new four-year term in January 1998. It has the same membership structure as the ESC: 222 members chosen by the member states and appointed by the Council of Ministers for four-year renewable terms. Although Maastricht does not specify what qualifications Committee members should have beyond saying they should be "representatives of regional and local bodies," most are elected local government officials, including mayors and members of state, regional, district, provincial, and county councils. It meets in plenary session five times per year and has the same advisory role as the ESC. It promotes subsidiarity and must be consulted by the Commission and the Council of Ministers on issues relating to economic and social cohesion, trans-European networks (see chapter 12), public health, education, and culture, and provides the EU with a local and regional perspective on policy. However, it suffers from the same structural problems as the ESC.

European Central Bank (ECB)

First proposed in 1988, the framework of the Bank was described in the Maastricht Treaty, and its precursor was founded in 1994 as the European

Monetary Institute (EMI), charged with strengthening central bank cooperation and coordination of monetary policy in preparation for the creation of the single European currency. The European Central Bank was formally established on June 1, 1998, and the EMI was liquidated. Based in Frankfurt, its main job is to work with the national banks of the member states in the European System of Central Banks (ESCB) to ensure monetary stability by setting interest rates and managing foreign reserves for the countries participating in the euro. All fifteen national banks are in the ESCB, but those outside the euro-zone are not allowed to take part in decisionmaking on the single monetary policy.

The Bank has a governing body consisting of the central bank governors from each state in the euro-zone and a full-time six-member executive board. The president and the executive board are appointed by "common accord" of the member state governments, serve nonrenewable terms of eight years, and can only be removed by their peers or by an order from the European Court of Justice. The Bank also has links to nonparticipating countries through a general council composed of the central bank governors of the member states.

Concerned about the need to convince the skeptical German public that the euro would be as strong as the deutschmark, Helmut Kohl insisted that the ECB should be an almost direct copy of the famously independent German Bundesbank. In fact, it is even more independent; neither national nor EU leaders are allowed to influence the Bank, its board, or its constituent national central banks, and the only body that can play any kind of watchdog role over the Bank is the monetary subcommittee of the European Parliament, but it so far lacks the resources to be able to hold the Bank or its president particularly accountable. This makes it very different from the U.S. Federal Reserve, whose chairman is regularly brought to account for Federal Reserve policies before the banking committee of the U.S. Senate.

The Bank got off to a shaky start, thanks to yet another of the rather silly nationalistic squabbles that occasionally tie down the work of EU institutions. Most governments were in favor of seeing Wim Duisenberg, the Dutch president of the EMI, confirmed as the first president of the ECB. The French government disagreed, preferring the governor of the Bank of France, Jean-Claude Trichet, at the helm. After a twelve-hour argument at the May 1998 summit convened to launch the euro, a messy compromise was reached whereby Duisenberg would serve half a term (1998–2002), then would "voluntarily" step down in favor of Trichet.

European Bank for Reconstruction and Development

Based in London, the European Bank for Reconstruction and Development (EBRD) is not actually part of the EU, but it was founded in 1990 on

BOX 10.2
Specialized Agencies of the European Union

In addition to the institutions discussed in the body of the text, several more specialized agencies have been created by the EU to deal with specific aspects of its work. Listed by their year of creation, they include the following:

European Centre for the Development of Vocational Training (CEDEFOP). (Based in Thessaloniki, Greece; established 1975). Promotes vocational training in the EU, mainly through information exchange, courses, seminars, and pilot projects.

European Foundation for the Improvement of Living and Working Conditions. (Dublin; 1975). Develops ideas on the improvement of working conditions in the EU.

European Training Foundation. (Turin, Italy; 1990). Promotes vocational training in Eastern Europe, the former USSR, and non-EU Mediterranean states, working closely with the Tempus program (see Chapter 13).

Office for Harmonization in the Internal Market. (Alicante, Spain; 1994). Responsible for the registration and administration of EU trademarks.

European Monitoring Centre for Drugs and Drug Addiction. (Lisbon, Portugal; 1994). Provides EU institutions and member states with information on drugs and drug addiction that can be used in antidrug campaigns.

Translation Centre. (Luxembourg; 1994). Helps most of these specialized agencies with their translation needs.

European Agency for Health and Safety at Work. (Bilbao, Spain; 1995). Provides EU institutions and member states with information in support of improvements in worker health and safety.

Community Plant Variety Rights Office. (Brussels; 1995). Independent of the EU, this office is responsible for implementing EU plant variety rights.

EU initiative, derives 51 percent of its capital from the EU, deals in euros, and will inevitably have a growing influence on EU decisions. Much like the International Bank for Reconstruction and Development (the World Bank), the EBRD was founded to provide loans, encourage capital investment, and promote trade, but its specific focus is in helping the countries of Eastern Europe make the transition to free-market economies. Suggested by François Mitterrand in October 1989 and endorsed by the European Council in December of that year, the EBRD began operations in March 1991. East and West European states are members, as are the United States and Russia. While the World Bank lends mainly to governments, the EBRD (at the insistence of the United States) makes 60 percent of its loans to the private sector. Hörst Kohler of Germany was appointed president in 1998.

European Investment Bank

Based in Luxembourg, the European Investment Bank (EIB) is an autonomous institution that was set up in 1958 under the terms of the Treaty of Rome to encourage "balanced and steady development" within the EEC by providing long-term finance for capital projects. It must give preference to projects that help the poorer regions of the EU, support the creation of communications networks, promote environmental protection and energy conservation, and support the modernization and improved competitiveness of EU industry; it can also make loans to non-EU members. The EIB's major focus in recent years has been on projects that help promote the single market through the development of trans-European road, rail, and communications networks;[18] its single biggest project was the Eurotunnel between Britain and France, which opened in 1994. It has also supported the Airbus project and France's high-speed train system (see Chapter 11) and has financed projects aimed at helping Eastern European countries prepare for EU membership.

The EIB has a staff of about 750 and is managed by a board of governors consisting of the finance ministers of the member states, a twenty-five-member board of directors appointed by the board of governors (one representative from the European Commission, three each from France, Germany, Italy, and Britain, two from Spain, and one each from the remaining member states) who serve five-year renewable terms, and a six-person management committee appointed for six-year renewable terms by the board of governors. In 1998 the president was Sir Brian Unwin of Britain.

The EIB's funds come from borrowing on worldwide capital markets and from subscriptions by EU member states. Its loans have risen steadily in recent years, from 7 billion ecu ($8.4 billion) in 1991 to 19.6 billion ecu ($23.5 billion) in 1993 to 26.2 billion ecu ($31.4 billion) in 1997. Most of its loans go either to the EU's poorest regions (Italy and Spain have been the major beneficiaries) or outside the EU. The bank deals only in large loans of over 10 million ecu ($12 million), it rarely lends over half of the total investment cost of a project, and it often cofinances projects with other banks.

European Environment Agency

The EC began developing environmental policies in 1972 (see Chapter 14) and instituted a series of five-year environmental action programs in 1973. With new powers over environmental policy given to the Commission by the SEA, the need for a new system of administration became more pressing, which led to a May 1990 decision to create the European Environment

Agency (EEA). Further progress became bogged down because France refused to agree to a site for the EEA until assurance was given that plenary meetings of Parliament would not be moved from Strasbourg; the stalemate finally ended in 1993 with the decision to locate the EEA in Copenhagen.

The EEA has a staff of about fifty, and its main job is to provide information; this makes it very different from the U.S. Environmental Protection Agency, which has a staff of 18,000 and is responsible for ensuring that states implement most of the major pieces of federal environmental law. EU member states opposed the idea of creating an inspectorate that could become involved in national environmental monitoring.[19] The EEA runs a European Information and Observation Network to collect information from the member states and neighboring non-EU states. This information is then used to help develop EU and national environmental protection policies and to measure the results of those policies. The EEA has begun publishing a series of triennial reports on the state of the European environment (the first came in 1995, the second in 1998) and is working with other international organizations, such as the Organization for Economic Cooperation and Development, the Council of Europe, and the UN Environment Program.

European Police Office

With the SEA opening up the borders between member states, and Maastricht making justice and home affairs one of the three pillars of the European Union, some direction had to be given to the development of police cooperation. Hence the creation of Europol, which is charged with setting up an EU-wide system of information exchange targeted at combating terrorism, drug trafficking, vehicle smuggling, clandestine immigration networks, illegal nuclear material trafficking, money laundering, and other serious forms of international crime. Set up in 1993 as the European Drug Unit, it operated in limbo thanks to a refusal by the British government to agree to questions over Europol's job being interpreted by the European Court of Justice. It demurred when it was given an opt-out on Court rulings, the Europol Convention was signed at the European Council in Florence in June 1996, and it became fully operational in October 1998.

Based in The Hague, Europol is not a law enforcement body in the pattern of the FBI in the United States but is rather a criminal intelligence organization. Its job is to coordinate operations in its selected fields of responsibility among the national police forces of the EU, playing a supporting role to them. Since there is no common penal code or police law in the EU, it is unlikely that there will be a common European police force any time soon. [20]

European Agency for
the Evaluation of Medicinal Products

Roughly parallel to the U.S. Food and Drug Administration (FDA), but without FDA-style centralization, the European Agency for the Evaluation of Medicinal Products (EMEA) was set up in 1995 with EU funding in an attempt to harmonize (but not replace) the work of existing national drug regulatory bodies. The hope is that this plan will not only reduce the $350 million annual cost drug companies incur by having to win separate approvals from each member state but that it will also eliminate the protectionist tendencies of states unwilling to approve new drugs that might compete with those already produced by domestic drug companies. The EU is currently the source of about one-third of the new drugs brought onto the world market each year.

Based in London, the EMEA was born after more than seven years of negotiations among EU governments and replaced the Committee for Proprietary Medicinal Products set up in 1977. It is focusing initially on new drugs (rather than trying to establish standards for existing drugs). It has a staff of two hundred and decentralizes its decisionmaking structure by working through a computer-linked network of about 3,000 experts throughout the EU. Its decisions must be ratified by the Commission, and member states are then given a maximum of ninety days to lodge objections. It hopes to reach its decisions within a maximum of three hundred days (which compares well with the average of five hundred days taken by the U.S. FDA). EMEA's first administrator was Fernand Sauer of France.

Summary and Conclusions

By bringing together the leaders of the fifteen EU member states on a regular basis, the European Council provides the kind of macrolevel leadership and direction that was patently missing from the European Community during the 1960s and early 1970s. It deliberately keeps away from the details of European integration, instead providing the impetus for "high policy" issues, such as economic union, political union, and a common foreign policy.

Opinion is divided on whether the European Council contributes to—or detracts from—European integration. On the one hand, it has encouraged integration by helping to steer the EU through major crises, encouraging consensus among EU leaders that might never have been achieved otherwise and agreeing to some of the biggest integrative initiatives since the mid-1970s. On the other hand, the Council has taken away from the powers of the Commission and the European Parliament, has helped promote intergovernmentalism by keeping decisionmaking powers in the hands of the member states, and has long failed to make much progress on critical issues such as budgetary reform.

At the opposite end of the scale, the growing workload of the EU has spurred the creation of specialized agencies charged with encouraging microlevel cooperation on everything from monetary policy to the environment and promoting vocational training, worker health and safety, and the fights against drugs and crime. All these agencies have a deliberately decentralized focus, encouraging coordination rather than integration but opening the door to federalism a little wider. In their own ways, both the European Council and the specialized agencies are promoting the kind of cooperation neofunctionalists would portray as a process of bridge-building across the chasm that divides states.

Further Reading

Jan Werts. *The European Council* (Amsterdam: North-Holland, 1992).
A look at the history and organization of the Council, with details on how it works and how it relates to other EU institutions. Ends with a survey of the results of Council meetings between 1975 and 1991.
Mary Troy Johnston. *The European Council: Gatekeeper of the European Community* (Boulder: Westview Press, 1994).
One of the most recent of several studies of the European Council, which focuses particularly on the extent to which the EC has become institutionalized and on its impact on integration.
Martin Westlake. *The European Council* (New York: Stockton, 1995).
A study of the structure and workings of the Council and of how it fits with the other EU institutions.
Simon Bulmer and Wolfgang Wessels. *The European Council: Decisionmaking in European Politics*, 2d ed. (New York: St. Martin's Press, forthcoming).
One of the earliest full-length studies of the Council and its work, now in its second edition.

Notes

1. Strictly speaking, the European Council overlaps at almost every turn with the Council of Ministers, and many scholars feel the two should be studied as one. However, differences in the briefs, agendas, and powers of the two institutions make it more informative to approach them separately.

2. Desmond Dinan, *Ever Closer Union? An Introduction to the European Community* (Boulder: Lynne Rienner, 1994), 230.

3. Annette Morgan, *From Summit to Council: Evolution in the EEC* (London: Chatham House, 1976), 9.

4. Mary Troy Johnston, *The European Council: Gatekeeper of the European Community* (Boulder: Westview Press, 1994), 2–4.

5. Philippe Moreau Defarges, "Twelve Years of European Council History (1974–1986): The Crystallizing Forum," in Jean-Marc Hoscheit and Wolfgang Wessels (Eds.), *The European Council 1974–1986: Evaluation and Prospects* (Maastricht: European Institute of Public Administration, 1988), 38–39.

6. Jean Monnet, *Memoirs* (Garden City, N.Y.: Doubleday, 1978), 502–503.

7. Morgan, *From Summit to Council*, 5.

8. Johnston, *The European Council*, 14.

9. Wolfgang Wessels, "The European Council: A Denaturing of the Community or Indispensable Decision-Making Body?" in Hoscheit and Wessels, *The European Council 1974–1986*, 9–11.

10. See, for example, Ad Hoc Committee for Institutional Affairs, *Report to the European Council* (the Dooge Report) (March 1985), Bull. EC 3–1985.

11. Guy de Bassompierre, *Changing the Guard in Brussels: An Insider's View of the EC Presidency* (Westport, Conn.: Praeger, 1988), 78.

12. See ibid., 80–87, for more detail on the organization and outcomes of the European Council.

13. See Johnston, *The European Council*, 27–31.

14. De Bassompierre, *Changing the Guard*, 78.

15. Paris Declaration 1974, in European Parliament, Committee on Institutional Affairs, *Selection of Texts Concerning Institutional Matters of the Community from 1950 to 1982* (Luxembourg: European Parliament, 1982); Statement of the European Council London 1977, in Commission of the EC, *Bulletin 7* (1977); and Solemn Declaration of Stuttgart 1983, in Commission of the EC, *Bulletin 6* (1983).

16. See Johnston, *The European Council*, 41–48.

17. Neill Nugent, *The Government and Politics of the European Union*, 3d ed. (Durham, N.C.: Duke University Press, 1994), 241.

18. Peter Doyle, Interview with Sir Brian Unwin, president of the EIB, *Europe* 334 (March 1994), 12–14.

19. Ken Collins and David Earnshaw, "The Implementation and Enforcement of European Community Environment Legislation," in David Judge (Ed.), *A Green Dimension for the European Community* (London: Frank Cass, 1993), 238–239.

20. *European Voice*, October 1–7, 1998, 18.

Part Three

Policies

11

Policy Processes
and the Budget

Public policy consists of the positions that governments adopt and the actions they take—deliberately or opportunistically—in response to the problems and needs of the societies they govern. When parties or candidates run for office, they put forward a list of ideas and proposals for dealing with the needs and demands of their constituents. Once elected, ideally they govern on the basis of those ideas (or variants), which together constitute their policies. Discussions of policy often include words such as "goals," "programs," "platforms," "objectives," "values," and "needs." The options governments and elected officials choose (and those they ignore) collectively define their policies, which are usually expressed as laws, orders, regulations, public statements, and actions. Put another way, if elections and public opinion are the inputs of politics in a democracy, then public policies are the outputs.

Debates have long raged about how policy is made and implemented at the national level in democracies, even though most have relatively predictable, stable, and institutionalized systems of government. Taken to the level of the European Union, those debates become more complicated. Not only is its governing structure very different from those found in conventional states but the EU is still evolving, and the balance of power among its institutions and member states is constantly changing, complicating the job of defining and identifying the key sources of power and of describing (or at least predicting) how that power is used. It is Jeremy Richardson's conclusion that the complexity of the policy process in the EU defies explanation by any one of the conventional models of that process.[1]

Much of the problem stems from the EU's lack of a constitution and the many ambiguities built into its major treaties. Maastricht, for example, tried to define the powers of the EU by focusing on subsidiarity and saying that the EU should act only if "the objectives of the proposed action cannot be sufficiently achieved by the Member States and can therefore, by reason of the scale or effects of proposed action, be better achieved by the Community" (Article 3b). But how can the member states or the EU institutions be absolutely certain about what can and what cannot be better undertaken at one level or the other?

Although the sources and parameters of EU powers are ambiguous, there is little question that its authority has deepened and broadened. From a time when the EU dealt only with coal and steel policy, the member states have transferred so many powers that the EU now touches (to varying degrees) on most aspects of economic, foreign, social, agricultural, and environmental policy. However, despite this "Europeanization" of the policy process, and despite concerns about loss of sovereignty and complaints about the mythical monolith of "Brussels," the EU still has no direct powers of enforcement and implementation and has a very small budget. Against that background, this chapter will look at how EU policy is made and implemented and will discuss one of the key influences on EU policy authority—the budget.

The European Union Policy Cycle

There are many different ways of approaching the study of public policy, but the most common method is to describe it in terms of a cycle. Reduced to its key elements, the EU policy cycle—and the key players in that cycle— can be expressed as follows.

Problem Recognition and Agenda Setting

Before a policy choice can be made, the existence of a problem must be recognized. In other words, something must have been identified and accepted as a legitimate concern of government, meriting a response. Different people see problems differently at different times and will argue over whether they are even problems at all. Their assessments and decisions are influenced by prevailing economic, social, and ideological values (problems routinely go in and out of fashion) and by the extent of government authority.

Issues move up and down the agenda according to changing levels of public and political interest. Precisely how and why this happens in the European Union is debatable and raises questions about the extent to which agenda setting is a reactive or a proactive phenomenon. In some respects, it is reactive in the sense that spillover and external events cause issues (particularly foreign policy issues) to be brought to the policy agenda. In other respects it is proactive because particular heads of government or Commission presidents (for example) have pushed issues onto the agenda through the political acts of will discussed in Chapter 1 or by other means.[2]

One important difference between agenda setting at the national and at the European level lies in the relative roles of public accountability (see Box 11.1). Elected leaders at the national level often push issues onto the policy agenda in response to public opinion, ostensibly because they want to represent the public will but also because they want to be reelected. In that sense, agenda setting is voter-driven. In the EU, however, the only directly elected policymakers are Members of the European Parliament, and they have limited influence on the overall policy process. Most policymaking power currently rests with the Commission and the Council of Ministers, neither of which is directly elected or accountable to an EU-wide constituency and thus is less subject to voter influence.

A second important difference lies in the complexity and fragmentation of EU institutions and the absence of effective policy coordination that is provided by political parties in national democratic systems. Guy Peters argues that the fragmentation (notably within the Commission) can be both a barrier and an opportunity for the agenda-setter—it complicates the task but also offers multiple avenues of political influence. However, the lack of policy coordination and the impact of the different national policy styles of commissioners on the work of the Commission interferes with the development of a common purpose and stable policy agendas.[3]

A third important difference between national and EU agenda setting lies in the extent to which easily identified solutions exist. At the national or subnational level, it is easier (but by no means easy) to identify problems and their causes and so to push the issue onto the policy agenda and formulate a response. At the EU level, the sheer complexity and variety of the needs and priorities of the fifteen member states make it much more difficult to be certain about the existence or the causes of problems or the potential effects of policy alternatives. This makes it more difficult to make the case for placing an issue on the agenda.

The European Council outlines the broad policy goals of the EU and often sparks new policy initiatives, but the pressures and influences that lead to those initiatives can come from many different sources: public opinion, treaty obligations, judgments of the Court of Justice, personal initiatives of individual leaders, internal and external pressures (such as the need to respond to security problems such as those in the Balkans, or the shock of the Danish rejection of Maastricht in 1992), and changes in the outside world (such as economic problems in Asia and Russia in 1998).

Agenda setting in the EU is based in part on the extent to which national governments are prepared to allow the EU to have authority in different fields; on the extent to which economic, political, or technical pressures demand an EU response; and on the compromises reached in the process of

BOX 11.1
The Pressures for Agenda Setting

Most studies of public policy argue that agenda setting is determined in one of three ways. The pluralist approach argues that policymaking in government is divided into separate arenas influenced by different groups and that government is ultimately the sum of all the competing interests in a society. The elitist approach argues that decisionmaking is dominated by a power elite consisting of individuals with the means to exert influence, be it money, status, charisma, or some other commodity. The state-centric approach argues that the major source of policies is the environment in which policymakers find themselves, and that government itself, rather than external social interests, is the locus of agenda setting.

The way the agenda is set in the EU—as in every level of government—arguably reflects elements of all three of these approaches.

It is pluralist to the extent that groups play a role in determining EU priorities. The most fundamental of those "groups" are the member states themselves, but pluralists usually think in terms of more specific interest groups. The ECSC was at heart a coalition of the coal and steel industries of its six member states; farmers have exerted enormous influence through their defense of the Common Agricultural Policy; the EU has paid more attention to environmental policy in part because environmental interest groups have successfully lobbied the Commission and Parliament, and have occasionally used the EU to bypass their own national governments.

It is elitist to the extent that priorities have long been set by the leaders of the member states, the Council of Ministers, and by the unelected and largely unaccountable European Commissioners. The democratic deficit is derived largely from the fact that so few individuals in the EU power structure are elected and that so many of their meetings take place out of public view. The rise of interest group lobbying and the growing powers of the European Parliament are helping to make the process more open and democratic.

It is state-centric (or rather superstate-centric) to the extent that the setting of the EU agenda has been determined in large part by the nature of integration. EU leaders made a conscious decision to sign the Single European Act, for example, which meant the EU had to become involved in a wide variety of new policy areas and deepened its authority in policy areas in which it was already involved. Despite the fact that EU institutions have been constrained by the limits placed on their powers and their briefs by national governments, the member states have found themselves (willingly or unwillingly) giving up more sovereignty, and thus they find their own national agendas set increasingly by the pressures and needs of European integration.

resolving the often conflicting demands and needs of the member states. The EU is guided through this by the treaties, which lay down the basic goals of the EU. The treaties act as something like a constitution for the EU, but constitutions usually describe what governments *can* do rather than what they *should* do. Not only are the EU treaties often prescriptive, but the founding treaties were drawn up at a time when many Europeans were doubtful about integration. Much has happened since then that has changed both the original intention of those treaties and the direction in which the EU has moved.

Policy Formulation

Once a problem or a need has been recognized, a response must be formulated. This means a plan or a program must be developed to deal with the problem, which may include agreeing on new laws and new budgetary allocations. Logic suggests that some kind of methodical and rational policy analysis should be conducted in which the causes and dimensions of the problem are studied and all of the options and their relative costs and benefits are considered before taking action, but this rarely happens. In practice, the sheer number of dependent and independent variables causes most policy to be designed and applied incrementally, intuitively, as a result of political opportunism, or in response to emergencies or changes in public opinion.

Several obstacles exist to the rational formulation of policy. First, people are unpredictable and inconsistent. It is often difficult to know what drives human nature or what makes people act the way they do. What may seem logical, moral, or reasonable to one person may seem illogical, immoral, or unreasonable to another. In an entity as complex as the European Union, few common values and little common ground will be found among Greek office workers, Viennese storekeepers, German chief executives, Irish farmers, and unemployed Finns.

Second, policymakers may not always have enough information to give them a clear understanding of a problem or its causes. Even if they have such information, they are unlikely to agree on its interpretation. What, for example, causes poverty? Are people poor because they lack the will, the ambition, or the imagination to improve their lives; is it because of their social environment, because they are lazy or uneducated; or is it because political and economic barriers make it impossible for them to improve their lives? The EU has several structural funds that are designed to reduce economic disparities by helping poorer regions of the EU (see Chapter 13), but the causes of poverty in rural Italy may be different from those in urban Ireland or eastern Germany.

Third, the causes of and responses to problems are always affected by personal, social, and ideological biases. A conservative French president will see policy issues in a different light than a Dutch socialist and a Swedish social democrat, not only because of their different ideological values but also because of their different worldviews and the often different needs of their constituencies.

Fourth, it is often difficult or impossible to be sure about the outcomes of a policy or of how that policy will work in practice. Even with the best intentions and the finest research and planning, policies often have unintended or unanticipated results.

Finally, the distribution of power in any system of government is often ambiguous, in part because constitutions are subject to different interpretations but also because the process of government is determined largely by *implied* powers; by the personal values, biases, and abilities of officeholders; and by the varied ways in which different officeholders use and manipulate the powers of the same office. For example, (as noted in Chapter 6), the role of the European Commission in the policy process has depended less on the terms of reference of its president than on the personality of the president.

The major focus of policy formulation in the EU is the Commission, which has the sole power to initiate new legislation, is responsible for protecting the treaties and ensuring that their spirit is expressed in specific laws and policies, and is charged with overseeing the EU budget. However, its proposals are routinely and often extensively changed as they go through the directorates-general, as a result of lobbying by interest groups or national governments, as a response to internal and external emergencies and crises, and as they are discussed by the Council of Ministers and the European Parliament. The Commission has been described as an "adolescent bureaucracy" in the sense that its relationship with interest groups is still fluid, and it tends to be more open to their inputs than are national bureaucracies,[4] but the term could also be used to describe its limited policymaking resources and the changeability of its powers.

Legitimation

Policies cannot work unless, at a minimum, they are based on legal authority and win public recognition. Leon Lindberg has argued that "the essence of a political community . . . is the existence of a legitimate system for the resolution of conflict, for the making of authoritative decisions for the group as a whole."[5] The less legitimacy such a community enjoys, the less it will be able to achieve by democratic means. In political systems founded on the rule of law (government on the basis of a mutually agreed upon set of rules and laws, to which all citizens are equally subject), there are usually few questions about the authority of government to make and implement policies. With the EU, however, authority and legitimacy have long been major bones of contention. As discussed in Part 1, the history of the EU has been driven by debates over the authority of EU institutions and fears about the loss of national sovereignty. Among the EU's fundamental handicaps have been the democratic deficit and the "authority gap"—the difference between what EU institutions would like to be able to do and what EU citizens and governments allow them to do.

That gap is wide, but it has slowly been closed, helped by direct elections to the European Parliament and by the passage of time. In the first case, despite its weaknesses and low voter turnout, Parliament is still the only institution in the EU system that is directly accountable to the citizens. Voting in fair, regular, and competitive elections is one of the foundations of political legitimacy, and direct elections have given EU voters a direct psychological tie to the EU, which has helped promote its credibility and legitimacy. In the second case, the legitimacy of the EU can be said to be growing simply because EU citizens are learning to live with the effects of European integration, and the EU is becoming more real, more permanent, and more acceptable as time goes on.

Implementation

Policies remain only words until they are implemented and enforced. This usually means agreeing on new laws and regulations, passing instructions on to bureaucrats, and informing the people affected by the new policy— arguably the most difficult step in the entire policy cycle. Implementation has been described as "a process of interaction between the setting of goals and the actions geared to achieving them."[6] To assume that once a government has made a decision it will automatically be enforced is delusory; policies can be reinterpreted and redefined even at the stage of implementation.[7] There may be a lack of political agreement; lack of funding; lack of workable or realistic goals; a failure to understand the causes of a problem; a redefinition of priorities as a result of changed circumstances or new data; lack of agreement on underlying goals and the best methods of implementation; conflicting interpretations; lack of public support; inefficiency or stagnation or conflicting interests within bureaucracies; and unanticipated structural problems or side effects.

Although the Council of Ministers has the final authority in making decisions, they are in fact made as the result of a complex interplay among the Council, the Commission, Parliament, and the member states, with the Court of Justice providing interpretation when necessary. Responsibility for overseeing implementation lies with the Commission, although implementation is carried out through the member states (actually, their bureaucracies). Limits on Commission resources and staff mean it must rely to some extent on reports from member states, individuals, and interest groups in helping to ensure implementation. The Court of Justice plays a crucial role in ensuring that laws are uniformly interpreted and applied and that disputes are resolved.

Implementation is being made easier by the creation of new specialized agencies, such as Europol and the European Central Bank, but it still depends on many different factors over which the EU has varied levels of control. These include the efficiency of the institutions responsible for implementation, the cooperation of the subjects of policy (people, corporations, public agencies, and governments), and the authority of the EU (which is tenuous in the sense that the EU has no direct powers of enforcement; European integration has been based from the beginning on the voluntary cooperation of the member states). The Commission is also subject to many of the problems and pitfalls commonly associated with bureaucracies, including limited accountability and an inclination toward self-justification; the tenure of bureaucrats ultimately depends on how much they have to do, and some are inclined to exaggerate their importance in the interests of guaranteeing continued power and budgetary allocations.

Evaluation

The final stage in the policy cycle is to determine whether a law or policy has worked. This is difficult unless specific goals were set and unless bureaucrats can be trusted to report accurately to the government on the results of policies. In many cases it is almost impossible to know which actions resulted in which consequences or whether the results are being accurately reported. Assuming that the outcomes of policies can be identified and measured (in whole or in part), adjustments can be made, or policies can be abandoned altogether. Evaluation in the EU is conducted by a combination of the Commission, the Council of Ministers, the European Council, the European Parliament, and reports from member states, interest groups, and individuals.

Policymaking in the EU

Writing about the policy process in the United States, Guy Peters argues that "American government has a number of structures but no real organization." He notes the lack of effective coordination and control, which he argues was intentional, given the concern of the framers of the Constitution about the potential for tyranny of a powerful central executive.[8] In many respects, the same can be said about policymaking in the EU. There is no true organization, in large part because of the ubiquitous concerns about loss of sovereignty. A simple description of the policy cycle in the EU would read as follows: The European Council sets the agenda, the Commission

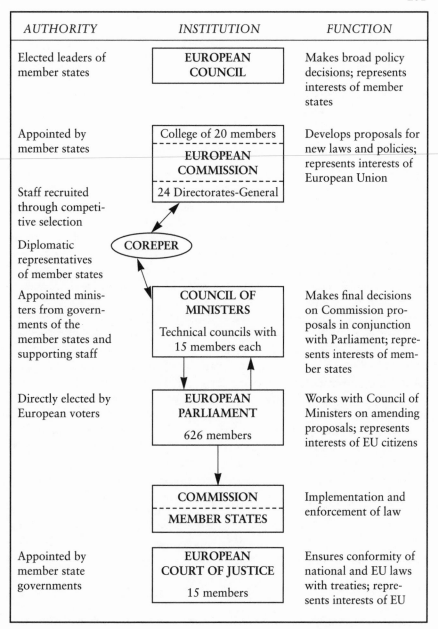

FIGURE 11.1   The European Union Policymaking Process

initiates the policy process, the European Parliament discusses and amends, the Council of Ministers makes the final decisions, the Commission oversees implementation through the member states, and the Court of Justice interprets and adjudicates. However, the absence of central control has created a policy process that is driven largely by compromise, opportunism, and unpredictable political pressures.

Compromise and Bargaining

Except in dictatorships, all politics is a matter of compromise. The fewest compromises are necessary in unitary systems of government with majoritarian political parties (such as Britain and Spain), where the focus of political power rests with a national government made up of a single political party and local government has little independent political power. In federal systems that have constitutional balances between national and local government (such as Canada, Germany, and the United States) or in countries governed by coalitions (such as Italy and Belgium), more compromises are needed. With a polity such as the European Union, where power is still not clearly defined, political relationships are still evolving, and the government is effectively a coalition of the representatives of fifteen member states, it could be argued that the entire policy process revolves around compromise. Nowhere is this more obvious than in the European Parliament, where over seventy political parties are represented and no one party group has a majority.

Robert Keohane and Stanley Hoffmann have argued that the negotiations involved in EU policymaking take place between governments and that successful spillover requires prior intergovernmental bargains.[9] One bargaining mechanism often used by the EU is the package deal, which links a series of usually unrelated but often controversial policy issues together to make sure everyone benefits, providing a sugarcoating for the pill. The creation of the Common Agricultural Policy was based around such a deal, with France winning concessions on agriculture in return for concessions given to German industry. The negotiations leading up to the Maastricht Treaty were also riddled with compromises and package deals, especially over the timetable for the development of a common currency.

Turf Battles

Politics, by definition, is about struggles for power and influence, but such struggles are magnified in the EU by the extent to which member states and institutions compete with each other, unconstrained by the presence of a constitution. Guy Peters describes three sets of interconnected "games" being played out in the EU: a national game among member states, which are trying to extract as much as possible from the EU while giving up as little as possible; a game played out among EU institutions, which are trying to win more power relative to each other; and a bureaucratic game in which the directorates-general in the Commission are developing their own organizational cultures and competing for policy space.[10]

Peters goes on to argue that policymaking has become fragmented as institutional and policy goals have parted company and different policy communities have emerged.[11] Keohane and Hoffmann argue that the EU has become a network of institutions that out of self-interest prefer to interact with each other rather than with outsiders.[12] There is little doubt that the constant give-and-take has brought many changes in the balance of power, posing a stark contrast between the EU and national systems of government in democracies, which usually have stable constitutions and relatively stable rules of procedure and decisionmaking.

The Democratic Deficit

Despite all the weaknesses, limitations, and inconsistencies found in the practice of democracy, most liberal democracies have high levels of public accountability, and public opinion plays a vital role in policymaking. The same is not true for the EU, where secrecy abounds. Public opinion has played an increasingly important role, notably with the growth of lobbying, direct elections to Parliament, the creation of the European ombudsman, and the Commission's efforts to promote transparency. However, the links between the governors and the governed are still poorly developed, and EU institutions have much less direct public accountability than do the institutions of most democracies, so policymaking remains largely an elitist, top-down phenomenon.

Incrementalism

Because of concerns over the loss of national sovereignty, the absence of a consensus about the wisdom of European integration, and the need for constant compromise, EU policymaking is generally slow and cautious. The EU has occasionally made relatively radical changes (as occurred after the passage of the Single European Act and the Maastricht Treaty, for example), but most EU policymaking is based on gradualism and incrementalism. Because there are so many counterweights and counterbalances in the policy process, member states and EU institutions can rarely take the initiative without conferring first with other member states or EU institutions.

The process sometimes slows to the point where critics of integration complain about Eurosclerosis, but this is probably unfair. The EC did hit the doldrums during the 1970s, and there have been many teething troubles (not surprisingly, given the sheer immensity of the task and the fact that the

EU is sailing in largely uncharted waters), but it has made policy decisions that have accelerated the process of integration, such as plans for the euro, convergence on foreign policy, and enlargement. None of these initiatives came out of the ether; all emerged incrementally from a combination of opportunity and need.

Spillover

Although this concept is usually identified with neofunctionalist theories of regional integration, it can be applied equally to policymaking at the national and subnational levels. The more a government feels it needs to be involved in the administration of society, the more policy spillover will occur. Privatization has cut the size of the public sector in most EU member states, but most still have large welfare systems and publicly owned and operated industries and services, which widen the set of government interests. Critics of the EU (like critics of the U.S. federal government) charge that it has tried to become involved in too many policy areas, but it has often had little choice; the creation of a new government program can reveal or create new problems, which in turn can lead to a demand for additional supporting programs. As Aaron Wildavsky put it, policy becomes its own cause.[13]

The EU Budget

The critical influence on policy cycles at any level of government is ultimately the budget. The amount of money a government has available—and how and where it decides to raise and spend that money—ultimately affects its policy choices and the true effectiveness of policy implementation. It is often less a question of how *much* is raised and spent than of *how* money is raised and spent. The budget is arguably at the heart of all politics in the sense that it shows where the true powers and priorities of governments lie.

Budgets are always controversial because of concerns about who pays and who benefits and because of questions about whether finite resources are being used to the best possible effect. The EU budget is no exception, but the controversy it attracts is surprising considering how small it is: nearly \$110 billion in 1998, or slightly less than 1.3 percent of the combined GNPs of the fifteen member states, and smaller than the budget of many of the bigger U.S. states or Canadian provinces. Less than 5 percent of the budget (about \$4 billion) is spent on administration. However, nearly half of the EU expenditure goes to agriculture, which says much about the way the EU has evolved.

The budget has several other revealing features and characteristics. First, unlike almost any national budget, the EU budget must be balanced. Article

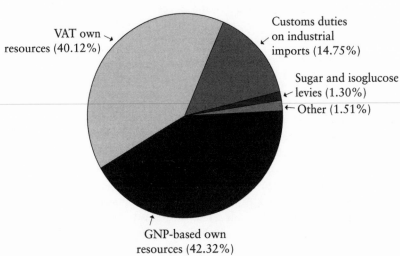

Revenues

VAT own
resources (40.12%)

Customs duties
on industrial
imports (14.75%)

Sugar and isoglucose
levies (1.30%)

Other (1.51%)

GNP-based own
resources (42.32%)

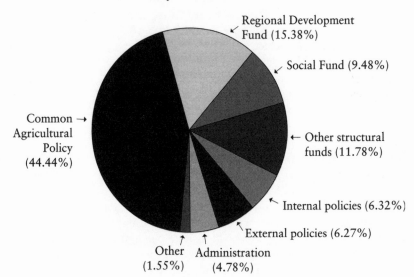

Expenditures

Regional Development
Fund (15.38%)

Social Fund (9.48%)

Common
Agricultural
Policy
(44.44%)

Other structural
funds (11.78%)

Internal policies (6.32%)

External policies (6.27%)

Other
(1.55%)

Administration
(4.78%)

FIGURE 11.2   The European Union Budget, 1998

Source: European Commission

199 of the Treaty of Rome holds that revenue and expenditure must be the same. Because the budget cannot go into the red, there is no EU debt, so the EU is spared the problems that normally accompany debts (such as interest payments). At the same time, it also means the EU has to find new sources of revenue to keep its books balanced.[14]

Second, the sources and the quantity of EU revenues have been at the heart of the conflicts that have emerged during the evolution of the EU. John Pinder has argued that the budget has been an arena for struggles about the distribution of gains from integration and a focus for conflict over the powers of institutions.[15]

Battles have raged over the balance between national contributions (which give member states leverage over the EU) and the EU's own sources of revenue. The fact that the budget is so small emphasizes just how much power over policy remains with the member states, who hold responsibility for the most expensive elements of policy activity (such as defense, education, health, and welfare). Unlike almost any other international organization, however, the EU has guaranteed sources of income over which its member states have no legal control.

Finally, decisionmaking on the budget is unusual in the sense that it follows a timetable that has specific deadlines, and the input and authority of the Council of Ministers and Parliament are more equally balanced than is the case with decisionmaking in almost any other part of the EU policy process. Both institutions consider the draft budget twice, and both have the power of amendment, which must be accepted by the other. In this area the Council of Ministers begins to look more like the upper chamber of a legislature and Parliament like the lower. The Commission, meanwhile, plays roughly the role of the White House in drawing up the U.S. federal budget.

Revenues

The EEC and the Atomic Energy Community—like most international organizations—were originally funded by national contributions, while the Coal and Steel Community had its own income, which was raised by a levy on producers. The contributions to the EEC were calculated very roughly on the basis of size; thus France, Germany, and Italy each contributed 28 percent, Belgium and the Netherlands 7.9 percent, and Luxembourg 0.2 percent. In an attempt to win more independence, the Commission in 1965 proposed that the revenue from tariffs placed on imports from outside the EC should go directly to the Community, thereby providing the EC with its own resources. At the same time, Parliament began pushing for more control over the budget as a means of gaining more influence over policy. Charles de Gaulle thought the Commission already had too much power, and it was these proposals (combined with France's opposition to reform of the Common Agricultural Policy) that led to the 1965 empty-chair crisis.

Pressure for budgetary reform persisted regardless, and changes between 1970 and 1975 led gradually to an increase in the proportion of revenues derived from the EC's own resources: customs duties, levies on agricultural imports, and a proportion (no more than 1 percent) of value-added tax (VAT). Two problems with this formula emerged. First, it took no account of the relative size of member-state economies. This became a particular problem for Britain, which paid much more into the EU coffers than it received. Second, the amounts involved were insufficient to meet the needs of the Community, which was not allowed to run a deficit or to borrow to meet shortfalls. The EC's freedom of action was reduced further by the fact that two-thirds of spending went to agricultural price supports, which grew as European farmers produced more crops (see Chapter 13). At the same time, revenue from customs duties fell because the Community's external tariffs were reduced, revenue from agricultural levies fell as the EC's self-sufficiency in food production grew, and income from VAT failed to grow quickly enough because consumption was falling as a percentage of EC GDP.[16] The problem was compounded by the unwillingness of some member states to raise the limit on the EC's own resources.

By the early 1980s, the Community was on the brink of insolvency, and it was obvious that either revenues had to be increased or expenditures had to be restructured or cut. The issue of budget reform was brought to a head by Margaret Thatcher's insistence on a recalculation of the British contribution. A complex deal was reached at the 1984 Fontainebleau European Council in which Britain was given a rebate and its contribution was cut, and the Community's own resources were increased with the setting of a new ceiling of 1.4 percent from VAT. More reforms agreed on at an extraordinary meeting of the European Council in Brussels during February 1988 resulted in the current system of revenue raising:

- The budget cannot exceed 1.27 percent of the combined GNP of the member states.
- About 42 percent of revenues in 1998 came from national contributions based on national GNP levels. Each member state pays a set amount in proportion to its GNP.
- Revenues from VAT accounted for 40 percent of revenues in 1998. Most of the revenues from VAT still go to the national governments, but a small percentage goes to the EU (it was 1.4 percent until 1994, then fell by annual increments of 0.08 percent to 1 percent by 1999).
- Just less than 15 percent of revenues in 1998 came from agricultural levies and customs duties on imports from nonmember states.

This formula produces a system in which the richer states make the biggest net contributions (see Box 11.2), while the poorer states have the biggest net receipts.

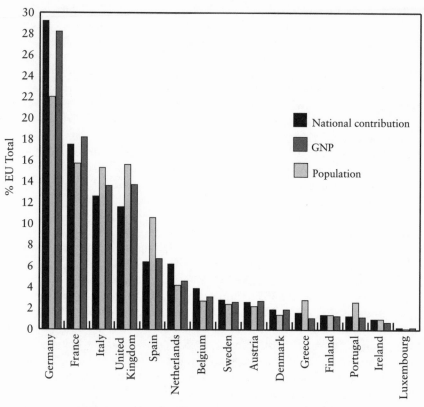

FIGURE 11.3   EU Revenues by Member State, 1996

Source: Contribution figures from Court of Auditors; population figures from UN Population Fund; GNP figures from World Bank.

Expenditures

As in almost any budget, EU expenses consist of a combination of compulsory payments over which it has little or no control (such as agricultural price supports) and noncompulsory payments over which it has more control (such as spending on regional or energy policy). About half of the EU's spending is obligatory. Total spending in 1998 was divided as follows.

- About 44 percent (or $48 billion) went to agricultural subsidies and supports to fisheries. These guarantee minimum prices to farmers for their produce, regardless of volume. The United States criticizes European farm spending; however, not only are many U.S. farmers subsidized but the proportion of EU spending that goes to agricul-

BOX 11.2
The Controversy over National Contributions

The arrangement by which national contributions to the EU budget are calculated has long been a matter of controversy, particularly among the states that make the largest contributions. The issue is not so much the amount that each country pays, which works out to be very roughly proportionate to population and national wealth (see Figure 11.3), but rather their net contribution when payments are weighed against receipts.

One of Margaret Thatcher's most famous conflicts with the Community revolved around her insistence that Britain was paying too much and that its contribution should be recalculated. Her predecessors as prime minister during the mid-1970s had argued that Britain was one of the poorer members of the EC yet bore an unfair share of the Community budget and received an inadequate amount in return. At her first European Council appearance in 1979 she bluntly told her Community partners: "I want my money back." Her campaign continued through the early 1980s, tied to her demands for a reform of the Common Agricultural Policy. After much acrimonious debate, contributions were finally recalculated in 1984 as part of preparations for the accessions of Spain and Portugal, which, as poor countries, were to be net recipients of Community funds. Britain subsequently received annual average rebates of 3 billion ecus ($3.6 billion).

More recently, Germany has been the leading discontent, arguing that the deal Britain received should be extended to all "overburdened" member states. Its criticisms have been sparked by the fact that it makes 60 percent of the net contributions to the EU budget. When the Commission published its Agenda 2000 proposals in 1997, aimed at preparing for eastward enlargement and reform of the Common Agricultural Policy and the regional funds, it stirred up a hornet's nest of debate about the future of the budget. As this book went to press, several of the countries that were net contributors—including Germany, the Netherlands, Sweden, and Austria—were pressing for a reexamination of the budget, suggesting that contributions be capped at 0.3 percent of national income. This caused particular nervousness among net recipients such as Spain and Greece, which were concerned that they would have to take on a greater burden of funding rebates.

ture has fallen substantially from its peak during the 1970s, when it accounted for nearly three-fourths of the budget.

- About 36 percent of spending (just over $40 billion) went to the structural funds: development spending on poorer regions of the EU, including spending under the European Social Fund aimed at helping offset the effects of unemployment, and investments in agriculture. The proportion of EU expenditures in this area has almost tripled since the mid-1970s.
- Nearly 7 percent went as aid to Eastern and Central Europe and to the poorer countries of Africa, Latin America, and Asia.
- About 5 percent went to administrative costs.

Under the budgetary system in 1998, Germany, the Netherlands, Britain, Italy, Sweden, and Austria (in that order) were net contributors, while the remaining states were net recipients of EU funds, with Ireland, Portugal, Greece, and Spain receiving the most.

Summary and Conclusions

The policy process of the European Union is complex, confusing, and constantly changing. The challenge of identifying the sources of, controllers of, and limits on power is heightened by the sheer novelty of the EU and by the lack of a constitution that could provide a guide through the maze. We can try to make analogies between policymaking units in the United States, Canada, and those in the EU, but there are limits to how far that exercise can go. The College of Commissioners is like the U.S. presidential cabinet, but not exactly. Parliament is like the House of Representatives or the House of Commons, but not exactly. The Council of Ministers is like the Senate, but not exactly. The difficulties go on.

As argued in Chapter 5, the key to grasping how the EU works is to appreciate that it is a work in progress. We know what it looked like during the 1960s and 1970s, and we still know what it looks like today, but it is unclear exactly how the dynamics of the relationships among the parts work, and it is debatable what it will look like in another generation or when it has finally reached some kind of equilibrium.

The EU has not yet developed coherence or decisiveness in the manner in which it makes policy. Keith Middlemass argues that there is a gap between the official and the real and that, in this constantly changing environment, the informal sphere of policymaking is as critical to an understanding of how decisions are reached in the EU as the formal.[17] Preceding chapters have looked at the major actors involved in the EU policy process; the chapters that follow look at the major policy interests of the EU and argue that those interests depend heavily upon the balance of informal opinion within the governments of the member states regarding the priorities of integration.

Further Reading

Jeremy Richardson (Ed.). *European Union: Power and Policy-Making* (London and New York: Routledge, 1996).

Helen Wallace and William Wallace (Eds.). *Policy-Making in the European Union*, 3d ed. (Oxford: Oxford University Press, 1996).

Two edited collections of studies of EU policy; the first focuses on the policy process, while the second includes chapters on specific policy areas.

Keith Middlemass. *Orchestrating Europe: The Informal Politics of European Union, 1973–1995* (London: Fontana, 1995).

A study of the informal elements in the EU policy process, placing the role of the EU institutions and key nongovernmental actors in the context of recent EU history.

Jill Preston (Ed.). *Spicers European Union Policy Briefings* (New York: Stockton, various years).

A series of detailed (but expensive) briefings on different EU policy areas, including guides to competition and trade, the environment, regional policy, the structural funds, and telecommunications.

Brigid Laffan. *The Finances of the European Union* (New York: St. Martin's Press, 1997).

A study of the complex budgetary system of the EU.

Notes

1. Jeremy Richardson, "Policy-Making in the EU: Interests, Ideas, and Garbage Cans of Primeval Soup," in Jeremy Richardson (Ed.), *European Union: Power and Policy-Making* (New York: Routledge, 1996), 20.

2. See Robert O. Keohane and Stanley Hoffmann, "Conclusions: Community Politics and Institutional Change," in William Wallace (Ed.), *The Dynamics of European Integration* (London: Royal Institute of International Affairs, 1990).

3. Guy Peters, "Agenda-Setting in the European Union," in Jeremy Richardson (Ed.), *European Union*, 65–68.

4. Sonia Mazey and Jeremy Richardson, "Pressure Groups and Lobbyists in the EC," in Juliet Lodge (Ed.), *The European Community and the Challenge of the Future* (New York: St. Martin's Press, 1993), 40–41.

5. Leon N. Lindberg, *The Political Dynamics of European Economic Integration* (Stanford: Stanford University Press, 1963), vii.

6. Jeffrey L. Pressman and Aaron Wildavsky, *Implementation*, 3d ed. (Berkeley: University of California Press, 1984), xxiii.

7. B. Guy Peters, "Bureaucratic Politics and the Institutions of the European Community," in Alberta Sbragia (Ed.), *Euro-Politics: Institutions and Policymaking in the "New" European Community* (Washington, D.C.: Brookings Institution, 1992), 103.

8. B. Guy Peters, *American Public Policy: Promise and Performance* (Chatham, N.J.: Chatham House, 1993), 17.

9. Robert O. Keohane and Stanley Hoffmann, "Institutional Change in Europe in the 1980s," in Robert O. Keohane and Stanley Hoffmann, *The New European Community: Decisionmaking and Institutional Change* (Boulder: Westview Press, 1991), 17.

10. Peters, "Bureaucratic Politics," 106–107.

11. Ibid., 115–121.

12. Keohane and Hoffmann, "Institutional Change," 13–14.

13. Aaron Wildavsky (Ed.), *Speaking Truth to Power* (Boston: Little, Brown, 1979), 62–85.

14. Michael Shackleton, *Financing the European Community* (New York: Council on Foreign Relations Press, 1990), 2.

15. John Pinder, *European Community: The Building of a Union*, 2d ed. (Oxford: Oxford University Press, 1995), 152.

16. Shackleton, *Financing the European Community*, 10–11.

17. Keith Middlemass, *Orchestrating Europe: The Informal Politics of European Union, 1973–1995* (London: Fontana, 1995).

12

Economic Policy

For most of its short life, the European Union has been driven mainly by the goal of economic integration. It began life during the early 1950s as a limited experiment in economic cooperation, was broadened during the 1960s to become a customs union, wrestled during the 1970s with attempts to build common economic policies and exchange rate stability, focused during the late 1980s on completing the single market, and is now working on the conversion to a single currency. The EU made progress in other policy areas (such as agriculture, the environment, and development aid to poorer countries), but only since the late 1980s has it really paid more attention to issues outside the economic sphere. The change in emphasis was symbolized during the 1980s by the way in which the "European Economic Community" slowly came to be known simply as the "European Community," and then, in 1993, by the way the European Community became one of the three "pillars" of the new European Union.

Elements of a common market were built during the first ten to fifteen years, the Common Agricultural Policy was in place by the late 1960s (in the sense that farmers were being paid guaranteed prices for their produce), and a customs union was completed with the agreement on a common external tariff in 1968. However, nontariff barriers persisted, including varying technical standards and quality controls, different health and safety standards, and different levels of indirect taxation. The gap between dream and reality widened during the mid-1970s as recession encouraged member states to think more about protecting their national markets than about building a new European market.

The mood changed during the 1980s with the sense that something needed to be done to reverse the EC's relative economic decline, to respond to the superiority of the United States and Japan in high-technology industries, and to exploit more fully the potential of its own market, which had almost as many consumers as the United States and Japan combined. Reducing duplication of

213

effort, encouraging joint research, and removing the final barriers that prevented European companies from doing business in all the member states would reduce costs and improve efficiency and competitiveness.

This change of thinking produced three landmark initiatives that were to transform the character of the European Union. Concerned about the slowness with which the barriers to the free movement of people, goods, money, and services were being removed, several countries signed the Schengen Agreement in 1985, which made arrangements for fast-track removal of internal border controls and came into force in 1995. At the same time, work was begun on the Single European Act (SEA), signed in 1986 with the goal of achieving a unified single market by December 1992. Finally, it was recognized that a true single market could not exist without agreement on a single currency; hence a plan on economic and monetary union was developed in 1989, was confirmed in 1993 when the Maastricht Treaty came into force, and led to eleven member states adopting the euro in January 1999.

The Single Market

The 1985 Cockfield White Paper provided the list of specific steps needed to complete the internal market.[1] As discussed in Chapter 4, this list became the basis of the Single European Act of 1986, which came into force in 1987. Its goal was to remove the remaining nontariff barriers to the free movement of people, goods, services, and capital within five years. Those barriers took three main forms: physical, fiscal, and technical.

Physical Barriers

Customs and border checks persisted at the EC's internal frontiers because national governments wanted to control the movement of people (especially illegal immigrants), collect taxes and excises on goods being moved from one state to another, and enforce different health standards. These barriers not only continued to remind Europeans of their differences, thereby posing a psychological block to integration, but they were also a significant economic constraint, a problem compounded by the fact that there was little consistency in these checks. Anyone driving among the Benelux states, for example, simply had to slow down when crossing the border, and customs officials would decide on the spot whether checks were needed. Meanwhile, train travelers could be vetted by customs and police officials, and air travelers went through rigorous security controls.

Barriers to the movement of goods were removed in stages. Despite agreement on the customs union in 1968, most goods were still subject to cross-border checks in the interests of enforcing trade quotas, controlling banned products, collecting taxes, and preventing the spread of plant and animal disease. These checks were costly and time-consuming. The first step in simplifying the process came in 1988 with a decision to move the administrative checks away from internal frontiers by agreeing on common laws as quickly as possible. A second step was taken with the consolidation of paperwork; between 1985 and 1988 over 130 different forms used by different customs authorities were replaced by a Single Administrative Document, which in turn was almost entirely abolished in January 1993.

Concerns that the removal of border checks would make it easier for drug traffickers and terrorists to move more freely encouraged governments to insist that the SEA should not affect the rights of member states to take whatever action they thought necessary to control terrorism, drugs, trade in arts and antiques, and immigration from outside the EU as long as such action did not interfere with trade. At the same time, the member states agreed to work toward police cooperation (to which end they created Europol in 1993) and toward common measures on visas, immigration, extradition, and political asylum. The goal is not so much to stop terrorists moving from one member state to another as it is to control them at the EU's external borders. This means border controls must be equally effective; in the past, terrorists have found it easier to enter states such as Greece and Portugal than states such as Britain and Germany.

A fast track for the removal of border controls was launched in 1985 by France, Germany, and the Benelux states. Named for the town in Luxembourg near which it was signed, the Schengen Agreement abolishes all border controls among its signatories, which now include all member states except Britain and Ireland; membership has even been extended to the Nordic passport union, thereby bringing in Iceland and Norway. The Schengen Agreement took longer to implement than originally planned, thanks mainly to problems with the setting up of the computerized Schengen Information System, which gives police and customs officials a database of undesirables whose entry into "Schengenland" they want to control. Full implementation has meant the end of checks at airports for flights among signatory states, the free circulation of non-EU citizens, common rules on asylum, the right of hot pursuit across frontiers, and moves toward a common policy on visas. The Schengen Agreement remained informal until the Treaty of Amsterdam brought it under the umbrella of the Union.

Fiscal Barriers

Indirect taxation caused distortions of competition and artificial price differences among the member states and thus was a barrier to the single market. All fifteen member states have a value-added tax, but rates during the 1980s were as low as 12 percent in Luxembourg and as high as 22 percent in Denmark. Excise duties also varied, reflecting different levels of national concern about human health; for example, smokers in France paid nearly twice as much tax on cigarettes as those in Spain, smokers in Ireland paid four times as much, and smokers in Denmark paid six times as much.

As goods moved from one state to another, they had to be controlled so governments could collect VAT and excise duties and prevent fraud and tax evasion. Consumers saw the effects most directly when they tried to take home alcohol, tobacco products, and other consumer items bought duty-free in another country. For example, British visitors to France could buy French wine much more cheaply than they could at home, but they were allowed to take back only limited quantities. Under the SEA, duty-free limits were gradually decreased, then were abolished altogether in January 1993. Agreement was reached in 1991 on a minimum rate of 15 percent VAT, with lower rates on basic necessities such as food, and in 1992 various minimum rates were agreed on excise duties. Agreement has since been reached on an EU-wide VAT system whereby tax is collected only in the country of origin, the ultimate goal being a single VAT rate or, at least, variations within a very narrow band. Controversially, duty-free sales were abolished for travelers among EU member states in July 1999; critics charged that the benefits for the single market were marginal.

Technical Barriers

The EEC had been able to do little to address the persistence of different technical regulations and standards among the member states, which seemed to pose an almost insurmountable barrier to the single market. Most of these regulations were based on different safety, health, environmental, and consumer protection standards, and many seemed petty and inconsequential: different definitions of chocolate that prevented British chocolate from being sold in many other member states, for example, and the insistence by Germans that no beer could be sold in Germany that did not meet local "purity laws." At one level, technical standards were in the interests of consumer safety; at another, they amounted to economic protectionism. The Community had tried to remove technical barriers by developing EC standards and encouraging member states to conform, but this was a time-consuming and tedious task that did little to discourage the common image of interfering Eurocrats.

Three breakthroughs helped to simplify the process:

1. The 1979 *Cassis de Dijon* decision (see Chapter 9) confirmed that all member states had to accept products from other states that met domestic technical standards. With trade in foodstuffs, for exam-

ple, the implication was that a member state could not block imports from another member state on the basis of local health regulations.

2. The 1983 mutual information directive required member states to tell the Commission and the other member states if they planned to implement any new domestic technical regulations and to allow the others three months to respond if they felt these regulations would create new barriers to trade.

3. The Cockfield White Paper included a "new approach" to technical regulation: Instead of having the Commission try to work out agreements on every rule and regulation, the Council of Ministers would agree on laws that had general objectives, and detailed specifications could then be drawn up by existing private standards institutes, such as the European Standardization Committee.

These three arrangements helped the EC clear many bureaucratic and political hurdles. Progress has been made on regulations for road vehicles, for example, where nearly fifty directives have been agreed to regarding everything from the brilliance of headlights to the depth of tire treads to limits on exhaust emissions. There is also more agreement on food content, and since 1990 all EU member states have had to print details about nutritional content on packages, following the U.S. model.

There has been less progress in other areas, however. The pharmaceuticals industry (which has $30 billion in sales per year) is still fragmented, although the work of the European Agency for the Evaluation of Medical Products is helping promote improved coordination. Free trade also continues to be handicapped by technical differences the marketplace is powerless to overcome. For example, everyone in the EU drives on the right except the British and Irish, who drive on the left. Similarly, television systems are different throughout the EU, obliging manufacturers to make eight different kinds of television sets. Most member states use the German PAL system of TV broadcasting, but the French use their own system, called SECAM. (Both of these are different from the U.S. standard, NTSC.) Similarly, the design of electrical plugs and sockets differs from one member state to another, forcing travelers to take an adapter with them wherever they go.

Differences in professional qualifications constitute another technical barrier. The EU has had to reach agreement on the standardization and recognition of such qualifications, which has not been easy. Although the basic training for most health workers (doctors, nurses, dentists, and so on) was harmonized relatively early, and they were given the right to work in any EC member state, it took seventeen years to harmonize the requirements for architects and sixteen years for pharmacists. Progress was made in 1988 with agreement on the general systems directive, under which member states agree to trust that for some jobs professional standards in other member states are adequate.[2] The list of mutually recognized professions is growing and now includes accountants, librarians, architects, engineers, and—since 1998—lawyers. The Commission has published a comparative guide to national qualifications for over two hundred occupations, helping employers work out equivalencies across the member states.

Effects of the Single European Act

In contrast to the often controversial decisions taken during the course of European integration, agreement on the SEA was widely welcomed. In addition to accelerating economic integration, it has also had a number of more tangible effects on the lives of Europeans.

Rights of Residence

Since January 1993, any resident of an EU member state has been allowed to live and work in any other EU member state, open a bank account, take out a mortgage, transfer unlimited amounts of capital, and vote in local and European elections. A few restrictions remain, but they are relatively trivial. For example, students are given annual residence permits, and they must be enrolled in college and be able to support themselves. Retirees and people of independent means are given five-year renewable residence permits; pensions are not yet entirely mobile, although work has been under way to make it possible for workers to move their pensions with them.

Joint Ventures and Corporate Mergers

European corporations have a long history of transnational mergers, which have produced such giants as Unilever and Royal Dutch Shell (both Anglo-Dutch) and Asea Brown Boveri (Sweden and Switzerland). Despite this, from 1950 to the early 1980s European companies steadily lost markets at home and abroad to competition, first from the United States and then from Japan. (Americans worried about the inroads being made in the U.S. market by foreign auto manufacturers sometimes overlook the other side of the coin; for example, Ford and General Motors together account for nearly one-fourth of the Western European auto market.) With the revival of competitiveness being pushed to the top of the EC agenda, the Commission became actively involved in trying to overcome market fragmentation and the emphasis placed by national governments on promoting the interests of often state-owned "national champions." To the delight of the authors of pithy acronyms, the EC also launched new programs aimed at encouraging research in information technology (ESPRIT), advanced communications (RACE), industrial technologies (BRITE), and weapons manufacture (EUREKA).[3]

Among the more notable joint ventures have been those between Thompson of France and Philips of the Netherlands (high-definition television), Pirelli of Italy and Dunlop of Britain (tires), and BMW and Rolls-Royce (aeroengines), as well as among the fourteen member states of the European Space Agency (ESA), set up in 1973 in an attempt to establish European autonomy in space.[4] Twelve European countries have also cooperated in the development of Arianespace, a space-launch consortium owned by governments and state-owned companies (France has a stake of just over 50 percent). Since the first launch in its series of Ariane rockets in 1979 from Kourou, French Guiana, Arianespace has won over half of the global market for launching commercial satellites,[5] eating into a market long dominated by the United States.

The single market has also helped encourage the growth of new pan-European businesses seeking to profit from the opportunities it offers and looking for the resources to allow them to compete more effectively with the United States and Japan. An unprecedented surge of takeovers and mergers has occurred since the mid-1980s, notably in the chemicals, pharmaceuticals, and electronics industries. During 1984–1985 there were 208 mergers and acquisitions in the EC; in 1989–1990 there were 622, and— for the first time—the number of intra-EC mergers overtook the number of national mergers.[6] In 1996, the value of cross-border mergers reached a record value of $253 billion; the European mergers and acquisitions market is now about two-thirds the size of that of the United States and is likely to overtake the U.S. market during the next few years. Recent notable examples include the 1992 purchase by Air France of a 37.5 percent stake in the Belgian airline Sabena, the 1996 merger between Ciba-Geigy and Sandoz to create Novartis, the world's second largest drug group, and the takeover by BMW of the British car manufacturer Rover Group in 1994, and by Volkswagen of Rolls-Royce in 1998.

Access to the larger European market has also provided a broader base for the development of European multinational corporations, which have become increasingly aggressive in pursuing mergers, takeovers, and joint ventures outside the EU. Many of these corporations have long had a presence outside Europe; names such as Shell, Fiat, Philips, Rolex, Armani, Volkswagen, and BP come readily to mind. However, the possibilities of an even greater presence in the global economy for European corporations are illustrated by the development of British Airways as one of the world's most profitable airlines and the 1998 merger between Daimler-Benz of Germany and Chrysler in the United States.

At the same time, care has been taken to ensure that the bigger corporations do not develop monopolies and overwhelm smaller businesses, so the

EU has developed a controversial competition policy to avoid abuses such as price fixing and to watch out for "abuses of dominant position" by bigger companies.[7] The 1989 merger regulation allows the European Commission to scrutinize all large mergers (even those involving companies based outside the EU that might have an effect on EU business), and the Commission also keeps an eye on the effect of state subsidies on competition in trade.[8]

A Common Transport System

Markets are only as close as the ties that bind them, and one of the priorities of economic policy in the EU has been to build a system of Trans-European Networks (TENs) aimed at integrating fifteen different transport, energy supply, and telecommunications systems, thereby pulling the EU together and promoting mobility. Until 1987, the lack of harmonization in the transport sector was one of the great failures of the common market— almost nothing of substance had been done to deal with problems such as an airline industry split along national lines or time-consuming cross-border checks on trucks that led to a black market in fake permits and licenses, national highway systems that did not connect with each other, and telephone lines incapable of carrying advanced electronic communications. Three phenomena have begun to make a difference.

First, there has been a dramatic increase in tourism. Not only is Europe the biggest tourist destination in the world, capturing nearly 60 percent of the world tourist trade,[9] but Europeans are now traveling to each other's countries in much greater numbers, which has helped to break down prejudices, made Europeans more familiar with each other, and encouraged greater cooperation in the area of transportation by increasing the demand for cheap and easy access. Tourism now accounts for about 6 percent of the GDP of the EU.

Second, the rail industry has been revitalized as a cost-efficient and environmentally friendly alternative to road and air transport. The EU hopes to develop a 22,000-mile high-speed train (HST) network connecting Europe's major cities; the building of the $15 billion Eurotunnel under the channel between Britain and France and the construction of a bridge between Sjaelland and Fyn in Denmark have been important steps. France has led the way in new technology with its high-speed TGV (which needs special new track), and Germany has developed its intercity express (ICE) network (which can use existing track). With trains traveling between 125 and 190 mph (some with coaches finished to luxurious standards), the HST system has already cut travel times considerably. The development of TENs is now one of the priorities of the EU, and the Commission has proposed a program aimed at spending a projected 400 billion euros ($480 billion) by 2010 on 44,000 miles of railroad track (including 14,000 miles of new and

BOX 12.1
European Cooperation and the Aerospace Industry

The possibilities and potential benefits of multinational cooperation among Europeans—and the nature of European economic integration itself—are illustrated by the example of the aerospace industry. Western Europe was once a major producer of civilian and military aircraft, home to some of the greatest names in the aircraft industry, including Vickers, Hawker Siddeley, Messerschmitt, and Dassault. However, rationalization, competition, and other economic pressures led to mergers and closures, and many of the old manufacturers became part of large new national corporations. Meanwhile, the United States and the USSR were producing most of the world's military aircraft, and the civilian airliner market was dominated by U.S. makers Boeing, McDonnell-Douglas, and Lockheed.

The Europeans have begun to offer renewed competition in recent years by launching transnational cooperative ventures. The best known of these is Airbus Industrie, a European consortium created in 1970 that is now the only significant non-American manufacturer of civilian aircraft in the world. The Airbus consortium is made up of Aérospatiale of France and Daimler-Chrysler Aerospace (Dasa) of Germany (which each have a 37.9 percent stake), British Aerospace (20 percent), and CASA of Spain (4.2 percent). It produces a line of seven different airliners, which between them have captured 30 percent of the global market for passenger aircraft with over one hundred seats.[1]

Discussions are currently under way that may lead to a merger of Aérospatiale, Dasa, and British Aerospace and the creation of what is already being called the European Aerospace and Defence Company. The idea has been prompted by the argument that economies of scale give American corporations such as Boeing and Lockheed an advantage over the big three European industries, whose national markets are too small to sustain them.

Meanwhile, Europeans have also made significant strides in the market for military aircraft. Individual member states still make competitive products, such as France's Mirage jet fighters and Britain's Harrier jump jets, but they are finding it makes better commercial sense to pool resources. One of the most successful of Europe's collaborations to date has been the profitable Tornado fighter-bomber (a British-German-Italian collaboration), which played a critical role during the 1999 Kosovo crisis. Another project that has been in the pipeline since 1985 is the Typhoon (formerly Eurofighter, a British-German-Italian-Spanish joint venture). The Europeans have also been dipping their toes in the market for military transport aircraft, currently dominated by the United States with planes such as the Lockheed Hercules.

Note

1. World Wide Web, Airbus Industrie Homepage (1998), <http://www.airbus.com/>.

upgraded track for HSTs) and 9,300 miles of new roads, mainly on the outer edges of the EU.

Finally, the long tradition of protectionism in the European airline market is being broken down.[10] Until the 1980s, most European countries had state-owned national carriers—such as Air France, Lufthansa in Germany, and Alitalia—that played an influential role in making air transport policy and maintained national monopolies over most of the international routes they flew. The result was that air transport was highly regulated and was very expensive to consumers. For example, following the deregulation of U.S. airlines in 1978, it was cheaper to fly from London to Madrid by way of New York than to fly direct. The privatization of British Airways in 1987 helped prompt new EU laws and regulations that opened up the European air transport market. Big carriers have since taken over smaller ones, national carriers have created international alliances, there has been a growth in the number of cut-price operators, and European consumers now have greater choice and can fly more cheaply than before.

Information and Telecommunications

The mass media play an important role in shaping and determining the extent to which people feel they belong to a community with common interests. The emphasis on localism in the United States, for example, has created media dominated by local newspapers, television, and radio; except for network TV news, public broadcasting, *USA Today,* and weeklies such as *Time* and *Newsweek,* the United States has few national media, which is partly why many Americans are less interested in national and foreign news than they are in local news. By contrast, smaller European countries are dominated by national radio, television, and newspapers—but they remain national rather than European.

The building of European media as a contribution to the creation of a European identity has moved slowly up the EU agenda, but so far it has achieved little. An attempt was made during the mid-1980s to launch a daily European newspaper, the *European,* but it was published in Britain and was in English. The five-nation Europa-TV consortium, which hoped to transmit multilingual TV broadcasts to 5 million homes in the EC, collapsed in 1986 after amassing huge debts.[11] More recently, Euronews was created in 1993 as a multilingual European response to CNN. Based in Lyon, France, it broadcasts twenty-four hours per day to cable and satellite viewers and shares some newsgathering operations with CNN, yet it faces stiff competition from nationally based services in Britain, Germany, and France, as well as American channels such as NBC and CNN. It is owned jointly by eighteen European broadcasters, with Britain's Independent Television News holding a 49 percent stake.

The European Commission developed a green paper entitled "Television Without Borders" in 1984, and the Cockfield White Paper talked of the need to develop a single market in TV broadcasting, which the Commission saw as an important element of the broader single-market project. The Commission subsequently tried to become involved in regulating satellite broadcasting, but the technology was developing faster than it could respond; its involvement was also criticized by several member states who argued that it had no competence in this area.

A major concern for the Commission has been controlling the cultural inroads made by Anglo-American broadcasting and trying to protect the European cinema and electronics industries from U.S. and Japanese competition. A directive was adopted on television broadcasting in 1989, aimed at making sure broadcasters—"where practicable"—used a majority of European programming. Siegfried Magiera has argued that this goes against the European tradition of encouraging cultural interaction with other parts of the world and also against freedom of expression and information.[12] The attempt to impose quotas faces other problems as well: U.S. films and TV shows are more popular on the continent than is much locally produced material, and Europeans do not tend to much like each other's programming (the French, the Germans, and the British, for example, have very different senses of humor); there is also the twin assault of U.S. programming provided by CNN and MTV and Anglo-American programming provided by British satellite companies such as Sky Television and British Satellite Broadcasting.

Toward a Single Currency

Few aspects of European integration have been so controversial as the idea of a single currency, yet few barriers to the creation of a true single market are so fundamental as the existence of fifteen different currencies with fluctuating exchange rates. The latest—and perhaps riskiest—step in the process of European integration was taken in January 1999, when eleven EU member states locked in their exchange rates as a prelude to the final switch in July 2002 to a single European currency—the euro. The issue of the single currency cuts to the heart of sovereignty and independence, because a state that gives up control over its national currency effectively gives up control over all significant domestic economic policy choices, such as the freedom to be able to adjust interest rates (See Box 12.2). The creation of a single currency is also seen by its detractors as a significant additional step toward the creation of a unified system of government. Whether or not it will lead to a United States of Europe is a debatable point, but it certainly promises to completely change the way that Europeans do business with each other.

BOX 12.2
Pros and Cons of a Single Currency

The development of the single currency is the single most controversial project so far undertaken in the cause of European integration. Its implications are not fully understood, and Europeans have mixed feelings over the idea: According to Eurobarometer polls, only 51 percent was in favor in 1997, with the most enthusiasm (57–78 percent in favor) coming from France, Italy, the Benelux states, and the poorer states, the least enthusiasm (45–59 percent opposed) coming from Germany, Britain, and Scandinavia.

Possible advantages of the euro include the following:

1. Travelers will no longer need to change currencies, which will save them time and money and will help make Europeans feel more connected to one another.
2. The euro will be more stable against speculation, helping reduce currency instability and helping exporters project future markets with greater confidence.
3. Businesses will not have to pay hedging costs to insure themselves against the possibility of currency fluctuations.
4. Backed by the size and strength of the European marketplace, the euro should become a world-class currency in the same league as the U.S. dollar and the Japanese yen, giving the EU more influence over global economic policy.

Among the concerns about the single currency:

1. There is the threat of the unknown. Never before has a group of sovereign states with a long history of independence tried combining currencies.
2. Unless Europeans learn each other's languages and move freely in search of jobs, the euro may perpetuate the pockets of poverty and wealth that already exist across the EU, thereby interfering with the development of a true single market.
3. Different countries have different economic cycles, and separate currencies allow them to devalue, borrow, and adjust interest rates in response to changed economic circumstances; such flexibility will no longer be available.
4. The one-off cost of switching to the euro will be expensive; new coins and banknotes will have to be produced (and old ones destroyed), machines that take or dispense coins and banknotes will need to be redesigned, computer software will need changing, and banks will need to prepare for the switch.
5. There are concerns over loss of sovereignty.

Economic union implies agreement on economic policies (which in practice means the establishment of a single market), while *monetary union* means the agreement of fixed exchange rates and a single currency. Whether economic union is a necessary precondition for monetary union, or vice versa, has long been a bone of contention, but attempts to achieve fixed (or at least stable) exchange rates failed during the early 1970s, contributing to the shift of focus toward establishment of the single market.

Stable exchange rates were identified by European leaders as early as the 1950s as being central to the building of a common market, but the post-war system of fixed exchange rates took care of most of their concerns. It was only when this system began to crumble during the late 1960s, and finally collapsed with the U.S. decision in 1971 to break the link between gold and the U.S. dollar, that European leaders paid more attention to the idea of monetary union. The first attempt to plan the transition to a single currency came out of the Werner Committee during 1969–1970 but was derailed by international currency turbulence in the wake of the energy crises of the 1970s.

The European Monetary System (EMS) followed in 1979 (see Chapter 4), with the goals of creating a zone of exchange rate stability and of keeping inflation under control. Economic and financial policies were coordinated through an Exchange Rate Mechanism (ERM), designed to reduce the fluctuations of EC currencies relative to each other. The ERM was centered on the European Currency Unit (ecu). Several member states experienced difficulties keeping their currencies stable relative to the ecu, but the EMS contributed to exchange rate stability in Europe during the 1980s and to the longest period of sustained economic expansion since the war. The Delors Plan in 1989 focused new attention on monetary union, and despite its near-collapse during 1992–1993, when Britain and Italy left the ERM and several other countries had to devalue their currencies, the Maastricht Treaty affirmed the basic principles behind the plan. EU member states wanting to take part in the single currency had to meet four "convergence criteria" that were considered essential prerequisites:

1. A national budget deficit of 3 percent or less of GDP (the average deficit in the member states fell from 6.1 percent of GDP in 1993 to 2.4 percent in 1997);
2. A public debt of less than 60 percent of GDP;
3. A consumer inflation rate within 1.5 percent of the average in the three countries with the lowest rates; and
4. A long-term interest rate within 2 percent of the average in the three countries with the lowest rates.

At the Madrid European Council in December 1995, EU leaders decided to call the new currency the euro and agreed to introduce it in three steps. The first step came in May 1998, when it was determined which countries were ready: All member states had met the budget deficit goal, but Greece had not been able to reduce its interest rates sufficiently, Germany and Ireland had not met the inflation reduction target, and only seven member states had met the debt target.[13] However, the Maastricht Treaty included a clause that allowed countries to qualify if their debt-to-GDP ratio was "sufficiently diminishing and approaching the reference value at a satisfactory pace." In the event, despite the fact that the national debt in Belgium and Italy was nearly twice the target, all but Britain, Denmark (both of which had met all four criteria), Greece, and Sweden were given the green light. This raised questions in the minds of Euroskeptics about the seriousness with which member states were approaching the convergence criteria, the wisdom of which had already been questioned by many economists.[14] Questions were raised in particular about the extent to which efforts by governments to meet the criteria had contributed to economic problems in several EU states (notably Germany), and therefore about the strength of the foundations upon which the euro was built.

Pressing on regardless, the second step came on January 1, 1999, when participating countries fixed the exchange rates of their national currencies against the euro and the new European Central Bank began overseeing the single monetary policy. All its dealings with commercial banks and all its foreign exchange activities are now transacted in euros, which is quoted against the yen and the U.S. dollar. The next step is due to be taken on January 1, 2002, when—if all goes to plan—euro coins and notes will become available. Europeans will then be given six months to make the final transition from national currencies to the euro and to turn in all their old bank notes and coins; national currencies will cease to be legal tender by July 1, 2002, at the latest.

One of the principle motives behind European integration has been the argument that Europe must create the conditions in which it can meet external economic threats without being undermined by internal divisions. For many, the single currency—if it succeeds—will represent the crowning achievement of exactly fifty years' worth of effort (1952–2002) aimed at removing the barriers to trade among Europeans and the construction of a single market that will allow Europe to compete on the global stage from a position of strength. It has been argued that European monetary integration has been driven in large part by external forces and the pressures of an international monetary system dominated by the U.S. dollar.[15] Although its effects on the domestic economies of Europe are debatable, there is little question that the successful adoption of the euro will make the EU a substantial new actor in that international system.

Summary and Conclusions

From the beginning, economic integration was seen by many of the founders of the EEC as a means toward the end of political union. The goal of economic integration, for its part, was to be achieved by bringing down the barriers to trade and, more specifically, to the free movement of people, money, goods, and services. The process has roughly followed the stages outlined in Box 1.1: development of a free trade area, agreement on a customs union, formation of a common (or single) market, and movement toward economic union as a prelude to possible political union.

The first of these steps was more or less in place by 1968. Progress was made on the second step, but nontariff barriers continued to stand in the way of a truly unified market and overlapped with concerns about European competitiveness and Eurosclerosis to prompt a conscious decision among the governments of EC member states to again "relaunch" Europe with the Single European Act in 1987. The European Union is now one of the two biggest markets in the world, and—after a number of false starts—is now on the brink of replacing the national currencies of its member states with a single currency, which should rank alongside the U.S. dollar and the Japanese yen as one of the primary currencies in the world. This will effectively complete the economic union of Western Europe, but whether or not it will lead to political union remains to be seen.

Further Reading

Loukas Tsoukalis. *The New European Economy Revisited: The Politics and Economics of Integration,* 3d ed. (Oxford: Oxford University Press, 1997).

A general introduction to the political economy of the European Union that explains how economic integration has happened and with what results.

Frank McDonald and Stephen Dearden (Eds.). *European Economic Integration,* 3d ed. (New York: Addison-Wesley, 1998).

Written as a college textbook, this is a useful introduction to EU economic integration, with separate chapters on related policy areas from agriculture to the environment.

David Thornton. *Airbus Industrie* (New York: St. Martin's Press, 1995).

A case study of one of the most notable examples of European industrial and commercial cooperation that looks at the development, structure, and performance of the Airbus project.

Kenneth A. Armstrong and Simon J. Bulmer. *The Governance of the Single European Market* (New York: Manchester University Press, 1998).

An assessment of the manner in which the single market functions, with case studies on issues such as air transport, waste shipment, and workplace safety.

Larry Neal and Daniel Barbezat. *The Economics of the European Union and the Economics of Europe* (New York: Oxford University Press, 1998).

Combines a study of different aspects of EU policies (such as the single market and the Common Agricultural Policy) with chapters on the national economies of the member states.

Notes

1. Commission of the European Communities, *Completing the Internal Market* (the Cockfield Report), COM(85)310 (Brussels: Commission of the European Communities, 1985).

2. See Louis H. Orzak, "The General Systems Directive and the Liberal Profession," in Leon Hurwitz and Christian Lequesne (Eds.), *The State of the European Community* (Boulder: Lynne Rienner, 1991).

3. Loukas Tsoukalis, *The New European Economy Revisited: The Politics and Economics of Integration,* 3d ed. (Oxford: Oxford University Press, 1997), 53–56. Acronyms: ESPRIT (European Strategic Programme for Research and Development in Information Technology), RACE (Research in Advanced Communications for Europe), BRITE (Basic Research in Industrial Technologies for Europe), (EUREKA) (European Research Coordinating Agency).

4. The fourteen members of the ESA in 1998 were Switzerland, Norway, and all of the EU member states except Greece, Luxembourg, and Portugal. The largest shares of the ESA budget came from France (21.5 percent), Germany (17.2 percent), Italy (11.3 percent), and Britain (4.9 percent).

5. Axel Krause, *Inside the New Europe* (New York: HarperCollins, 1991), 118.

6. European Commission figures quoted in Tsoukalis, *The New European Economy Revisited,* 110.

7. Michelle Cini and Lee McGowan, *Competition Policy in the European Union,* (London: Macmillan Press, 1998).

8. David Allen, "Competition Policy: Policing the Single Market," in Helen Wallace and William Wallace (Eds.), *Policy-Making in the European Union* (Oxford: Oxford University Press, 1996).

9. World Trade Organization, *Compendium of Tourist Statistics 1989–1994* (Madrid: World Trade Organization, 1996).

10. For details, see Kenneth Armstrong and Simon Bulmer, *The Governance of the Single European Market* (Manchester: Manchester Universitry Press, 1998, chapter 7.

11. Richard Owen and Michael Dynes: *The Times Guide to the Single European Market* (London: Times Books, 1992), 222.

12. Siegfried Magiera, "A Citizen's Europe: Personal, Political, and Cultural Rights," in Hurwitz and Lequesne, *The State of the European Community.*

13. *The Economist,* 11 April 1998.

14. *The Economist,* 5 August 1995.

15. Peter H. Loedel, "Enhancing Europe's International Monetary Power: The Drive Toward a Single Currency," in Pierre-Henri Laurent and Marc Maresceau (Eds). *The State of the European Union, Vol. 4: Deepening and Widening* (Boulder, CO: Lynne Rienner, 1998).

13

Agricultural and Regional Policy

One of the priorities of the European Union has been to ensure that the benefits of freer trade are equally distributed among the member states, regardless of region or economic sector. To that end, it has developed policies on agriculture, fisheries, and regional development aimed at redistributing wealth and opportunity and at providing subsidies to generate growth in less developed areas. The result—as far as agriculture is concerned—has been controversial. Farming employs just 5 percent of the European workforce and accounts for just 3 percent of the combined GDP of the member states, yet it is the most expensive of the policy areas in which the EU has been involved. The EU has more powers over agriculture than over any other policy area, and it has passed more legislation on agriculture than on any other single policy area. Agricultural policy also differs from other EU policy areas in two more important respects.

First, while barriers are being taken down and markets opened up in almost every area of EU economic activity, agriculture has been heavily interventionist; the EU has taken a hands-on approach to keeping agricultural prices high, thereby drawing criticism not only from the member states but also from the EU's major trading partners, such as the United States. Second, unlike most other EU policy areas, agricultural policy was built in to the Treaty of Rome, where the commitment to a common agricultural policy was spelled out more clearly than was the case for any other policy area (although the details were only agreed to during the 1960s).

The goal of improving the standard of living of Europe's agricultural communities overlaps with another important aspect of EU activities: regional policy. This focuses on the reduction of disparities in wealth among the different parts of the EU and the promotion of social and economic cohesion. Most economists agree that the free market almost unavoidably contains or promotes social and economic inequalities that have so far defied all attempts to remove them, and cohesion may be more an ideal than an achievable objective. Even so, the EU has developed several structural funds aimed at shifting resources from the wealthier parts of the EU to the poorer regions, investing in decaying industrial areas and poorer rural areas, promoting employment and equal opportunities, and improving living and working conditions. These funds include spending under the European Regional Development Fund (ERDF) and the Cohesion Fund (covered in this chapter), and spending under the European Social Fund (discussed in Chapter 14).

Agricultural Policy

At the time the Treaties of Rome were being negotiated, agriculture sat high on the agendas of European policymakers. Not only were the disruptions of the war and the memories of postwar food shortages and rationing still fresh in their minds, but agriculture still accounted for about 12 percent of the GNP of the Six and for the employment of about one-fifth of the workforce.[1] Agricultural policy had several unique political and economic implications.

First, agriculture was a key element in the tradeoff between Germany and France when the EEC was first discussed.[2] France was concerned that the common market would benefit German industry while providing the French economy with relatively few benefits. France had a large and efficient agricultural sector during the mid-1950s, accounting for 12 percent of GNP and employing nearly 25 percent of the French workforce—more than was the case in Germany (where agriculture accounted for 8 percent of GNP and 15 percent of the workforce).[3] Concerns that the common market would not provide enough benefits to its farmers encouraged the French government to insist on a protectionist system.

Second, agricultural prices are more subject to fluctuation than are prices on most other goods, and since Europeans spend about a quarter of their incomes on food, those fluctuations can have serious knock-on effects throughout the economy. Price increases can contribute to inflation, while price decreases can force farmers to go deeper into debt, perhaps leading to bankruptcies and unemployment. The problem of maintaining minimum incomes has been exacerbated by mechanization, which has led to fewer Europeans working in farming. Thus it was argued that subsidies would help encourage people to stay in the rural areas and discourage them from moving to towns and cities and perhaps adding to unemployment problems.

Third, self-sufficiency in food has been a primary factor in determining the direction of agricultural policy. World War II made Europeans aware of how much they depended on imported food and how prone those imports were to disruption in the event of war and other crises. Before the war, for example, Britain imported about 70 percent of its food needs, including wheat from the United States and Canada, beef from Argentina, and sugar-cane from the Caribbean. The war made it clear that this reliance on imports was a security problem, so a massive program of agricultural intensification was launched in Britain after the war, with the result that Britain now imports only about 35 percent of its food needs. The pattern has been similar across the EU, which has experienced a large decline in agricultural imports from outside the EU and a growth in trade among the member states. Although reliance on imports is no longer the factor it once was, the drive to self-sufficiency had a key formative influence on agricultural policy whose effects have not yet gone away.

Finally, although the farm vote in Europe is generally much smaller than it was during the mid-1960s, it is not insubstantial. Across the EU as a whole, the number of people employed in agriculture has fallen from about 25 percent in 1958 to about 5 percent today (compared to 2.6 percent in the United States), but there are wide variations across countries: from 2–3 percent in Britain, Belgium, and Germany to 6–7 percent in Austria and Italy, 8 percent in Spain, 12–14 percent in Ireland and Portugal, and nearly 19 percent in Greece.[4]

Furthermore, farmers in the richer EU states have traditionally had strong unions working for them. In addition to national unions, over 150 EU-wide agricultural organizations have been formed, many of which directly lobby the EU. Among the most powerful of these is the Committee of Professional Agricultural Organizations (COPA), which represents farmers generally on a wide range of issues. Other organizations represent more specialized interests. Not only are farmers a powerful lobby in the EU, but many other people live in rural areas, and there are many rurally based services. Farmers and the residents of small towns and villages add up to a sizable proportion of the population and the vote. No political party can afford to ignore that vote, especially because there is little organized resistance to the agricultural or rural lobbies at either the national or the EU level.

No discussion of EU agricultural policy would be complete without mentioning the special case of France. Farmers account for barely one in thirty-five French workers (or less than 0.4 percent of the total EU population), yet they have enormous influence over the French government, which lobbies on their behalf in the halls and corridors of Brussels. This situation helps to underpin the centrality of agricultural spending in the EU budget, causes spillover effects into other EU policy areas, and helps sour EU relations with the United States. Why does the farm lobby have so much influence in French domestic politics?

Not only does over 20 percent of all EU agricultural production come from France, but it is the world's second largest exporter of food after the

United States. The role of the farm lobby must also be seen in the context of the French national psyche. Even though three of every four French citizens live in towns or cities, the rural ideal still has a strong nostalgic hold on the sentiments of many, as does the idea that France is still a great power. Italian journalist Luigi Barzini once argued that "foreigners have to remind themselves that they are not dealing with a country that really exists . . . but with a country that most Frenchmen dream still exists. The gap between the two is a large one, but the French indefatigably try to ignore it or forget it."[5] Even urban voters are prepared to defend the rural ideal, to which any attempts to reform European agricultural policy are seen as a threat.

The Common Agricultural Policy

The foundation of agricultural policy in the EU is the misnamed Common Agricultural Policy (CAP). The underlying principles of CAP—which were worked out at a landmark conference convened in Stresa, Italy, in July 1958—are the promotion of a common market in agricultural produce, of "Community preference" (a polite term for protectionism aimed at giving priority to EU produce over imported produce), and of joint financing (the costs of CAP are to be shared equitably across all the member states). The goals set out in the Treaty of Rome (Articles 38–47) included increased agricultural productivity, a "fair standard of living" for the farming community, stable markets, regular supplies, and "reasonable" prices for consumers. What this means in practice is that CAP guarantees farmers throughout the EU the same minimum price for their produce, regardless of volume and of prevailing levels of supply and demand, and all the member states share the financial burden for making this possible.

The specifics of how CAP would work were agreed to in discussions with the Council of Ministers during the early 1960s. What they agreed to was not so much a common agricultural policy as a common agricultural price support system, which works as follows: Annual prices for all agricultural products are fixed at the meeting of agriculture ministers each spring (usually April or May). On the basis of discussions and negotiations that usually have been going on since the previous September among the Commission, the Agriculture Council, interest groups, and national governments, the ministers set three kinds of prices:[6]

- Target prices, or the prices they hope farmers will receive on the open market to receive a fair return on their investments.
- Threshold prices, or the prices to which EU imports will be raised to ensure that target prices are not undercut.

- Guaranteed (or intervention) prices, or the prices the Commission will pay as a last resort to take produce off the market if it is not meeting the target price. The EU will buy produce from farmers and place it in storage, thereby reducing the supply and pushing up demand and prices. If prices go above the target price, the EU will sell some of its stored produce until the price has leveled out again, although in practice it has never had to do this because the target prices have always been set high enough to encourage farmers to produce more than the market needs.

This arrangement became increasingly expensive over time as technological developments helped European farmers produce more food from less land, exceeding the demands of consumers for commodities such as butter, cereals, beef, and sugar. The EU has been forced to buy the surplus, some of which is stored in warehouses strung across the EU. The rest is sold outside the EU, given as food aid to poorer countries, or "denatured" (that is, destroyed or converted into another product; for example, excess wine might be turned into spirits, which take up less space, or even into heating fuel). The EU has tried to discourage production by subsidizing exports (thereby upsetting other agricultural producers such as the United States) and by paying farmers not to produce food (which has encouraged new golf courses to sprout up in various parts of the EU as farmers have converted their land to other uses). The real problem with CAP is the artificially high levels at which prices have been set.

The costs of CAP are borne by the European Agricultural Guidance and Guarantee Fund (EAGGF), which was created in 1962 and has since been consistently the single biggest item in the EU budget (although agricultural spending has fallen from about 85 percent of the budget in 1970 to slightly less than 50 percent in 1998). The bulk of funds (nearly $46 billion in 1998) are spent in the Guarantee Section, which finances markets and prices by buying and storing surplus produce and encourages agricultural exports. Most of the money goes to producers of dairy products (the EU accounts for 60 percent of global dairy production) and to producers of cereals, oils and fats, beef, veal, and sugar. The Guidance Section is one of the four elements that make up the EU's structural funds (discussed later in this chapter), and it is used to improve agriculture by investing in new equipment and technology and helping those working in agriculture with pensions, illness benefits, and other support.

In terms of increasing productivity, stabilizing markets, securing supplies, and protecting European farmers from the fluctuations in world market prices, CAP has been a huge success. The EU is the world's largest exporter of sugar, eggs, poultry, and dairy products and accounts for nearly 20 percent of world food exports, compared to the U.S. share of 13 percent. Encouraged by guaranteed prices, European farmers have produced as much as possible from their land, with the result that production has gone up in virtually every area; the EU now produces far more butter, cereals, beef, and sugar than it needs. The EU is self-sufficient in almost every product it can grow or produce in its climate, including wheat, barley, wine, meat, vegetables, and dairy products. These successes have come partly through intensification and partly from the increased use of fertilizers; EU farmers use nearly 2.5 times as much fertilizer per acre of land as U.S. farmers.

At the same time, member states have tended to specialize in various products, so duplication has been reduced. For example, most of the permanent cropland is now found in the southern states, and most livestock is raised in the northern states. CAP has also helped make farmers wealthier and their livelihoods more predictable and stable; even though overall unemployment in the EU has grown, farm employment and incomes have generally remained steady.

Unfortunately, CAP has also created problems. First, EU farmers produce much more than the market can bear. By the early 1970s, the purchase and storage of excess production had prompted the media to begin referring to butter mountains and wine lakes, to which the more gullible visitors to Brussels began asking for directions. In a sense they did exist, because all surplus production was stockpiled throughout the EU, and there were warehouses literally filled with surplus cereal, powdered milk, beef, olive oil, raisins, figs, and even manure. By the late 1990s, the stockpiles had largely disappeared, but there were warnings that rising world prices could lead to their reappearance unless the EU reformed the agricultural price structure.

Second, stories of fraud and the abuse of CAP funds abound. The Commission does not have enough staff to ensure that requests for payments are fair, and differences between EU prices and world prices have meant high refunds that provide an irresistible temptation for less honest farmers. The Court of Auditors has regularly criticized the problem of fraud.[7]

Third, CAP has not closed the income gap between rich and poor farmers in the EU. While mechanization and intensification have brought new profits to farmers in the north, those in Ireland, Greece, and Portugal remain relatively poor. To make matters worse, spending on productive northern farmers erodes the support that could be going to less productive southern farmers, thereby undermining attempts to encourage them to stay on the land.[8]

Fourth, environmentalists have been unhappy about the way CAP has encouraged the increased use of chemical fertilizers and herbicides and has also encouraged farmers to cut down hedges and trees and to "reclaim" wetlands in the interests of making their farms bigger and more efficient. CAP has also upset consumers forced to pay inflated prices for food despite production that is often surplus to needs; the contradiction between high prices and increased production has been a major source of public skepticism about the wisdom and benefits of European integration.

As if all this is not bad enough, CAP has distorted market prices, soured EU relations with its major trading partners, and perpetuated the idea of a protectionist European Union that cannot seem to get its priorities and values straight.

Reforming Agricultural Policy

Several attempts have been made to reform EU agricultural policy dating back to the 1960s, but with only variable success. The earliest discussions included the suggestion that small farmers be encouraged to leave the land and that farms be amalgamated into bigger and more efficient units. This was vehemently opposed by small farmers in France and Germany, and reform slipped down the agenda as currency problems pushed economic and monetary issues up the agenda. Margaret Thatcher brought new pressures for change during the early 1980s, although she was concerned less with reforming CAP than with renegotiating British contributions to the EC budget. Her campaign to win a British rebate drew new attention to the absurdities of agricultural overproduction, and by the late 1980s there was a general agreement that reform was needed. One proposal agreed to at the February 1988 summit of the European Council was to establish maximum guaranteed quantities (MGQs), or quotas beyond which support payments to farmers would be reduced.

Pressure for reform was increased by the growing international criticism leveled at CAP as the EC negotiated tariff reductions under the Uruguay Round of GATT (which finally concluded in late 1993) and by the trade embargo imposed by the EC on Iraq during 1990–1991 (which caused a drop in export prices). In 1991, Agriculture Commissioner Ray MacSharry took up the banner of reform, warning of the rising volume of stored agricultural produce, which included 20 million tonnes of cereals, nearly 1 million tonnes of dairy products, and 750,000 tonnes of beef (a figure that was growing by 15,000 to 20,000 tonnes per week).[9] MacSharry proposed moving away from guaranteed prices; reducing subsidies on grain by 29 percent, those on beef by 15 percent, and those on butter by 5 percent; and encouraging farmers to take land out of production (the set-aside system, whereby farmers would be compensated for subsidy reductions only if they took 15 percent of their land out of production).[10] All of this predictably earned MacSharry the sobriquet "Mack the Knife."

Despite the opposition of many farmers and their unions, the proposals were finally approved by the Agriculture Council in May 1992 after eighteen

---

BOX 13.1
Mad Cows and European Politics

The usual controversies over EU agricultural policy were diverted between 1996 and 1998 by a squabble between Britain and the rest of Europe over the problem of mad cow disease. The issue caused the most serious disruption in EU decisionmaking since the empty-chair crisis of 1965 and strained relations between Britain and its EU partners, notably Germany.

Bovine spongiform encephalopathy (BSE, or mad cow disease) was first noticed in Britain during 1984–1985, when the attention of a farmer in southeast England was drawn to the attention of strange behavior among some of his cows. The disease causes microscopic holes in the brains of cows, making the cows stagger and lose balance, leading eventually to death. By 1988, it was determined that the disease had been spread by animal feed, so feed derived from protein was banned, and the government decided to slaughter all BSE-affected cattle. Community restrictions on the export of British beef began during 1989–1990, but BSE did not really became a headline issue until March 1996, when the British government announced a possible link between BSE and a new variant of a brain disease in humans, known as Creutzfeldt-Jakob disease (CJD). The Community almost immediately announced a worldwide export ban on all British beef.

The British government responded in May by announcing a policy of noncooperation with its EU partners until the ban was lifted; among other things, British ministers were able to block every vote in the Council of Ministers for which unanimity was required. It is debatable whether or not this was a genuine attempt to put pressure on the Commission or was simply a ploy by the John Major government to deal with deep divisions within his party over its policy on the EU. At the same time, Britain applied to the European Court of Justice to have the ban overturned. With the agreement by the European Council in June of a phased lifting of the ban, conditional upon Britain speeding up the eradication of BSE and making changes to livestock feeding and management policies, the policy of noncooperation was dropped. It was not until November 1998 that the ban was finally lifted (in the face of continued German opposition); exports were resumed in March 1999.

Until 1996, British beef was worth over $1 billion in annual exports, and there were estimates in late 1998 that the crisis had cost Britain $6 billion in lost income, in measures taken to impound and incinerate meat and bonemeal, and in measures taken to isolate and remove the problem. The noncooperation policy of the Major government in 1996 also caused considerable ill feeling among Britain's EU partners. At the same time, the crisis probably brought home to many Britons just how much their country now relied on the rest of the EU as a market for agricultural produce.

---

months of talks. Although they initially made CAP more expensive and led to warnings from the Court of Auditors that they heightened opportunities for fraudulent claims from farmers, the changes promised to lead to a medium-term reduction in surpluses, lower food prices for consumers, and—over the longer term—better use of the money spent on CAP. The reforms were seen as sufficiently radical to merit a distinction between the "old" CAP and the "new" CAP, but it was also recognized that more changes would be needed as the impact of the MacSharry reforms began to take effect.

In recent years, food surpluses have diminished, farm incomes have risen, and the rise in world cereal prices has helped negate the effects for farmers of CAP price cuts. Proposals were introduced in 1998 by Agriculture Commissioner Franz Fischler that involved a shift away from compensating farmers when prices fall below a certain level and toward subsidizing them for certain kinds of production. He proposed price cuts on cereals, beef, and milk, the end of set-aside schemes, more environmental management conditions to be attached to payments to farmers, and more investment in rural development generally. Such changes would continue to build on EU agricultural reforms as pressures grow on the EU as a result of global trade negotiations under the auspices of the World Trade Organization. For now, agriculture has slipped down the list of media and public concerns in the EU, but this does not mean that it has gone away, and it will move back up the agenda as membership of the EU expands eastward.

The Common Fisheries Policy

Since 1983, the EU has also had a Common Fisheries Policy (CFP), the main goal of which has been to resolve conflicts over territorial fishing rights and to prevent overfishing by setting catch quotas. Even though fishing employs just 0.2 percent of the EU workforce, the state of the fishing industry is a key part of life in coastal communities all around the EU, and so the issue has important economic implications for some of Europe's poorer regions.

Disputes over fishing grounds in European waters have occasionally led to bitter confrontation between EU partners and their neighbors. There were, for example, the infamous cod wars of the 1960s between Britain and Iceland over access to fisheries in the North Atlantic. Similarly, in 1984 French patrol boats fired on Spanish trawlers operating inside the Community's two-hundred–mile limit, and over two dozen Spanish trawlers were intercepted off the coast of Ireland. Spain's fishing fleet was bigger than that of the entire EC fleet at the time, and fishing rights were a major issue in Spain's negotiations to join the EC. Spanish fishing boats became an issue in domestic British politics in 1994 when Euroskeptics in the governing Conservative Party used, among other things, the Spanish presence in traditional British waters to complain about the effects of British membership in the EU.

Attempts to resolve competing claims to fishing grounds and to develop an equitable management plan for Community fisheries were bitter and controversial, but they finally resulted in an agreement in 1983, which was modified in 1992. The CFP regulates fisheries in four main ways. First, it has opened all the waters within the EU's two-hundred–mile limit to all EU fishing boats but gives member states the right to restrict access to fishing grounds within twelve miles of their shores. One of the problems with this arrangement was that it was difficult to police, so, since 1995, all EU fishing boats have had to be licensed, and the Commission has been given greater powers to monitor fishing activities, using satellites and its own (few) inspectors on the ground.

Second, the CFP prevents overfishing by imposing national quotas (or Total Allowable Catches, or TACs) on the take of Atlantic and North Sea fish and by regulating fishing areas and equipment. For example, limits have been set on the mesh size of fishing nets, and minimum weights have been established for catch sizes so as to prevent catches of young fish. TACs are set at the end of every year by the Council of Ministers on the basis of scientific advice, and the quotas are distributed among the member states, which can allocate them nationally or exchange them with other member states.

Third, the CFP set up a market organization to oversee prices, quality, marketing, and external trade. Finally, it guides negotiations with other countries on access to waters outside those controlled by member states and on the conservation of fisheries.

Regional Policy

The European Union is far from homogeneous; not only are there significant economic and social disparities within most of its member states but there are disparities from one state to another. The standard measure for comparing differences among countries is to use per capita GDP adjusted for purchasing power parity (PPP, or the purchasing power of each member-state currency). On that basis, and expressing the average for the EU as 100, the differences in per capita GDP in 1995 ranged from 135 in Luxembourg to 48 in Greece. Disparities among regions within the member states were even greater, ranging from 195 in Hamburg, Germany, to 43 in Ipeiros, Greece.[11]

Generally speaking, the wealthiest parts of the EU are in the north-central area, particularly in and around the "golden triangle" (or the "hot banana") between London, Dortmund, Paris, and Milan, while the poorest parts are the eastern, southern, and western peripheries, from Greece across southern Italy to Spain, Portugal, Ireland, and western Scotland. The EU's marginal areas are relatively poor for different reasons; some are depressed agricultural areas with little industry and high unemployment, some are declining industrial areas with outdated plants, some are geographically isolated from the prosperity and opportunity offered by bigger markets, and

BOX 13.2
The Structural Funds

The structural funds are the primary means by which aid is provided to the poorer regions of the EU, and they have steadily become an increasingly important part of EU policy and a larger part of the European budget. Together, the major funds accounted in 1998 for over one-third of EU spending (just over $40 billion). There are now five structural funds:

The Guidance section of the EAGGF is the part of the Common Agricultural Policy that helps reform farm structures and promote the development of rural areas, including measures to encourage diversification away from agriculture.

The European Social Fund is designed to promote employment and worker mobility, combat long-term unemployment, and help workers adapt to technological changes (see Chapter 14). Money from the fund is intended to complement spending by national governments, and particular attention is paid to the needs of migrant workers, women, and the disabled.

The European Regional Development Fund directs funds mainly to underdeveloped areas and inner cities. It is the biggest of the structural funds, and spending has grown rapidly—up from $11 billion in 1994 to nearly $17 billion during the period 1994–1998 alone.

The Cohesion Fund was set up under the terms of Maastricht to compensate poorer states (in practice, Greece, Portugal, Spain, and Ireland) for the costs of tightening environmental regulations and to provide financial assistance for transportation projects.

Often overlooked in discussions about the structural funds, the Financial Instrument for Fisheries Guidance sets aside about $3 billion each year to help modernize fishing fleets and to invest in aquaculture and the development of coastal waters, port facilities, processing, and marketing.

most suffer relatively low levels of education and health care and have underdeveloped infrastructure, especially roads and utilities.

In the interests of promoting economic efficiency and social equality, EU priorities have included trying to prevent the persistence of a two-speed Europe and encouraging greater economic and social cohesion by bringing the poorer member states closer to the level of their wealthier partners. Harvey Armstrong outlines four arguments in favor of the EU approach: In theory, at least, it ensures that spending is concentrated in the areas of greatest need and ensures coordination of the spending of the different member states; the member states have a vested interest in the welfare of their EU partners, and without the EU approach economic and social disparities could be a barrier to integration.[12] At the same time, there is an important psychological element: Payments made by the EU to the poorer sections of the member states can help the citizens of those states to see some of the benefits of EU membership.

Individual EU member states have tried to deal with their own internal problems in different ways. Britain, for example, has designated special Development Areas and has given industry incentives to invest in those areas and to relocate factories. Italy created the Fund for the South to help provide infrastructure and encourage investment in the Mezzogiorno—everywhere south of Rome, including areas so riddled with corruption and so heavily controlled by organized crime that they are effectively independent subgovernments. All the major industrialized states have also tried to address the problem of urban decline in different ways.

The European Coal and Steel Community made provision for grants to depressed areas for industrial conversion and retraining, but the idea of helping depressed regions went against the free market principles of allowing people and money to follow the opportunities. The Guidance segment of CAP included a welfare element in the sense that funds could be used to upgrade farms and farming equipment, improve farming methods, and provide benefits to farmers. Broader regional disparities were not addressed until 1969, however, when the Commission proposed a common regional policy—including the creation of a regional development fund—but the idea met with little enthusiasm in Germany and France, which were already concerned, respectively, about the costs of CAP and the surrender of more powers to the EC.

Little more was done until the first round of enlargement during the early 1970s, when a complex pattern of political and economic interests came together to make the idea of a regional policy more palatable. The accession of Britain and Ireland widened the economic disparities of the Community, Germany and France wanted to see Britain settle in to the Community, and the 1973 Thomson Report on regional issues (sponsored by the Commission) argued that regional imbalances were a barrier to a balanced expansion in economic activity, that they threatened to undermine plans for EMU, and that they could even pose a threat to the common market.[13] Agreement was thus reached on the European Regional Development Fund, launched in 1975.

Funds were originally distributed by a system of national quotas that were worked out during the negotiations leading up to the creation of the ERDF. The biggest net beneficiaries were Britain, Ireland, France, and Italy, although the balance changed when Greece, Spain, and Portugal joined. The ERDF was not to be used in place of preexisting national development spending but was to provide matching grants of—at most—50 percent, supplemented by loans from the European Investment Bank. Requests had to come from the member states, and funds could be spent only on industrial and service-sector projects aimed at creating new jobs or protecting existing ones, on infrastructure related to industry, and in unusual areas such as remote and mountainous regions.

Reforms during the late 1970s led to the introduction of a small "non-quota" element in the ERDF (5 percent of the total could be determined by the Commission on the basis of need) and to suggestions that the richer countries should give up their quotas altogether on the grounds that they could afford their own internal development costs. From being a passive recipient of requests for aid, the EC took on a more active approach to addressing the problem of regional disparities. Reforms during 1984 led to a tighter definition of the parts of the EU most in need of help, and further reforms during 1988 led to spending on regional development growing to 32 percent of the Community budget in 1993 and to nearly 37 percent of the EU budget in 1998. The EU's regional policy today has the following goals:[14]

- It provides help for the poorest regions, described as Objective 1 regions and defined as those in which per capita GDP is less than 75 percent of the EU average. The biggest recipients are Spain, Portugal, Greece, Italy, and Germany (for investment in the former East Germany), while Denmark and the Benelux countries receive the least. Objective 1 projects are funded mainly out of the ERDF and the Cohesion Fund and now account for about 60 percent of all structural fund spending.
- It provides help for Objective 2 areas, defined as those suffering from high unemployment and job losses and industrial decline; these are mainly in the older industrial regions of north-central Europe and parts of Italy and Spain. These projects are funded primarily out of the ERDF.
- Objectives 3 and 4 are programs aimed at dealing with long-term unemployment and creating jobs for young people. They are funded mainly out of the European Social Fund; Britain, France, Germany, Spain, and Italy are the biggest recipients.
- Objective 5 focuses on helping agricultural and rural areas and is funded mainly out of the EAGGF, while Objective 6 was added after the 1995 enlargement to deal with the problems of the thinly populated parts of Northern Europe.
- In addition, a host of specialized programs have specific objectives, some of which overlap with social policy and all of which have once again provided a field day for the authors of clever acronyms; these include RECHAR (converting coal-mining areas), REGIS (help for overseas regions of the EU), INTERREG (helping border regions prepare for completion of the single market), and PRISMA (aid for infrastructure and business services in poorer regions).

One of the problems with the way in which the structural funds have been set up is that the definitions of "regions" and "priority areas" have been left up to the member states. Each state has a different kind of administrative unit, ranging from the states of Austria and Germany (which have a range of powers independent of those of their respective federal governments) to the *départements* of France and the counties of Britain (which have few independent powers and are governed in very different ways). This means member states have different ideas about how to justify regional spending, which has tended to be justified less on the basis of real "need" (however that is defined) than on the basis of the relative political and economic influence member states bring to bear on regional policy negotiations; the structural funds have always carried the danger of promoting pork-barrel politics in the European Union.

David Coombes and Nicholas Rees argue that politics enters the equation in at least two ways.[15] First, member states have been reluctant to give the EU powers over industrial development, employment, and social security because doing so would reduce their control over domestic economic policy. Second, member states have been unwilling to transfer powers without the promise of net gains to themselves. They have looked for some kind of compensation and put national interests above European interests. The structural funds have routinely been seen as a way of compensating for the uneven distribution of spending under CAP—in that sense, they have become a form of institutionalized bribery.

Another political complication is added by the rise of the nationalist factor in EU politics. As Western European states have integrated at the macrolevel, there have been growing demands for self-determination at the microlevel by cultural regions.[16] The bitter struggles between Catholics and Protestants in Northern Ireland are well-known, as are the movements for devolution in Scotland and Wales. At the same time, there are similar pressures from (among others) Bretons and Corsicans in France, Basques on the Spanish-French border, Catalans in Spain, and Walloons in Belgium. These have long been the domestic affairs of the national governments involved, but European integration, ironically, has given national minorities an opportunity to bypass their governments and to lobby at the European level for a higher priority status, greater self-determination, or both.

Summary and Conclusions

For years, what critics of the European Community most disliked about European integration was related mainly to its implications for agriculture. The popular image of the EC was inextricably linked with charges of spending and regulation gone mad, of militant French farmers blocking any attempts to undermine their privileged position and bring EC spending under control, and of outrageous food surpluses at a time when many people in the world were starving. The images were not entirely wrong, but they tended to give short shrift to some of the benefits of EC agricultural policy, including increases in production, greater efficiency, and economic boosts to a rural sector that in many parts of the Community had long experienced hardship and occasional poverty.

One of the consequences of the CAP has been to help shift economic resources and political power from the richer to the poorer parts of Europe, a trend that has overlapped with the consequences of EU regional policy. For the EU, regional development has long meant an attempt to help the poorer regions catch up with their richer neighbors, with the utopian goal of encouraging economic and social "cohesion," and an equitable distribution of the benefits of regional integration. The EU has tended to equate development with growth, but whether quantity and quality go hand in hand has long been debatable. It is also debatable whether the free market can ever entirely eliminate inequalities of opportunity, which is why agricultural and regional policies in the EU have been organized around a kind of grand welfare system based on the redistribution of wealth as a means to encourage equal opportunity. How long it will take to bring the different parts of the EU to the same economic level (assuming it is even possible) remains to be seen. The goals of agricultural and regional policy will be further complicated over the next few years as the EU considers membership for Eastern European states that are poorer and have larger agricultural sectors.

Further Reading

Wyn Grant. *The Common Agricultural Policy* (New York: St. Martin's Press, 1997).
Despite all the fuss and expense surrounding CAP, this is the only recent full-length study that explores how decisions on CAP are taken, and with what effect.
John Marsh and Bryn Green (Eds.). *The Changing Role of the Common Agricultural Policy: The Future of Farming in Europe* (London: Belhaven, 1991).
Joanne Scott. *Development Dilemmas in the European Community: Rethinking Regional Development Policy* (Buckingham: Open University Press, 1995).
Provides a study of the evolution and consequences of regional development policy in the EU.

Notes

1. European Commission, *The Agricultural Situation in the Community, 1993 Report* (Luxembourg: Office for Official Publications, 1994), table 3.5.1.3.
2. Wyn Grant, *The Common Agricultural Policy* (New York: St. Martin's Press, 1997), 71–72.

3. H. von der Groeben, *The European Community, the Formative Years: The Struggle to Establish the Common Market and the Political Union (1958–1966)* (Brussels: European Commission, 1987), 71–72.

4. Food and Agriculture Organization (FAO) of the United Nations, *FAO Production Yearbook 1996* (New York: FAO, 1997), table 3.

5. Luigi Barzini, *The Europeans* (London: Penguin, 1983), 124.

6. Neill Nugent, *The Government and Politics of the European Union*, 3d ed. (Durham: Duke University Press, 1994), 369.

7. Michael Shackleton, *Financing the European Community* (New York: Council on Foreign Relations Press, 1990), 38–40.

8. Anne Daltrop, *Politics and the European Community* (London: Longman, 1987), 175–176.

9. Debates of the European Parliament, OJ 3–407, July 11, 1991, 282.

10. David P. Lewis, *The Road to Europe: History, Institutions and Prospects of European Integration 1945–1993* (New York: Peter Lang, 1993), 337.

11. *Eurostat*, April 1998.

12. Harvey Armstrong, "Community Regional Policy," in Juliet Lodge (Ed.), *The European Community and the Challenge of the Future* (New York: St. Martin's Press, 1993).

13. Commission of the European Communities, *Report on the Regional Problems of the Enlarged Community* (the Thomson Report), COM(73)550 (Brussels: Commission of the European Communities, 1979).

14. David Allen, "Cohesion and Structural Adjustment," in Helen Wallace and William Wallace (Eds.), *Policy-Making in the European Union*, 3d ed. (Oxford: Oxford University Press, 1996).

15. David Coombes and Nicholas Rees, "Regional and Social Policy," in Leon Hurwitz and Christian Lequesne (Eds.), *The State of the European Community* (Boulder: Lynne Rienner, 1991), 209–211.

16. James G. Kellas, "European Integration and the Regions," *Parliamentary Affairs* 44:2 (April 1991), 226–239.

14

Environmental and Social Policy

The process of European integration was long motivated by quantity. The EEC Treaty may have mentioned the need for "an accelerated raising of the standard of living," but efficiency, economic expansion, and profit were at the heart of the common market program, and qualitative issues were a relatively minor motivating force during the early years of the Community.

By the early 1970s, however, the emphasis had begun to change. Western public opinion became increasingly critical of what was widely seen as uncaring affluence,[1] and there was a shift in favor of promoting issues related to quality of life. The change was exemplified by the rise of the feminist, antiwar, and environmental movements on both sides of the Atlantic. The EC could not avoid becoming caught up in the change, and by the early 1970s it was increasingly involved in promoting both qualitative improvements in the lives of the citizens of its member states and an equitable distribution of the benefits of integration. The 1973 enlargement accelerated that process by widening the gap between the richest and poorest areas of the Community. The pressure grew as states with stronger laws on environmental protection and workers' rights became concerned about the flight of industry and jobs to countries with looser standards (anticipating concerns that were later raised in the United States and Canada when Mexico was brought in to the North American Free Trade Agreement).

Environmental and social issues have subsequently been high on the EU agenda. Improvements in environmental quality were driven at first by concerns over the extent to which different standards distorted competition and complicated progress toward the building of a common market. A series of Environmental Action Programmes (EAPs) provided more policy consistency and direction, and the Single European Act (SEA) gave the environment legal status as a policy concern of the Community. Maastricht and Amsterdam placed further emphasis on sustainable development and environmental protection as an essential part of "harmonious and balanced" economic growth, and institutional changes gave public opinion (through the European Parliament) a greater voice in making environmental policy and introduced qualified majority voting on most environmental law and policy.

Meanwhile, full economic integration also demanded social cohesion, something that was being addressed by agricultural and regional policy but that went well beyond the scope of either. The EU began more actively addressing such issues as employment, working conditions, social security, labor relations, education, training, housing, and health. A series of Social Action Programmes (SAPs) was developed, aimed at improving living and working conditions in the EC, and a new and controversial focus on social issues came with the Social Charter of 1989, which pushed the EU farther toward protecting the rights of workers—an area that proved to be an ideological and political minefield.

Environmental Policy

Environmental problems do not respect national frontiers. Since the mid-1970s, growing scientific and political awareness of this reality has led to a new emphasis on international responses to such problems as air pollution and the management of shared rivers. However, national governments have been slow to take unilateral action for fear of losing comparative economic advantage and have been unwilling to give significant powers to international organizations, such as the United Nations Environment Programme, and to commit to ambitious goals under the terms of international environmental treaties.

Regional integration offers a solution to both dilemmas. As states become more dependent on trade and foreign investment, and more inclined to reduce the barriers to trade, so they will be more inclined to eliminate any differences in environmental standards that may cause trade distortions, particularly if they know that neighbors are moving in the same direction. International negotiations and treaties are useful in this regard, but regional integration is a much more compelling influence, because participating states know they are involved in a joint endeavor with shared costs and benefits.

There was no mention of the environment in the Treaty of Rome, and although the EEC agreed on several pieces of environmental law during the 1960s, they came from the drive to build a common market and were incidental to the Community's overriding economic goals.[2] Only during the 1970s did the EEC begin to develop a broader environmental policy. It did this against a background of new public and political interest in the environment, arising out of a combination of improved scientific understanding, several headline-making environmental disasters, new affluence among Western middle classes, and growing concern about quality-of-life issues.[3]

Changes in public and political opinion during the 1960s culminated in the landmark United Nations Conference on the Human Environment in Stockholm, which drew widespread political and public attention to the problems of the environment for the first time, prompting the creation of national environmental ministries and a growth in the volume of national environmental law. In October 1972, just three months after Stockholm, the EEC heads of government meeting in Paris agreed to the need for an environmental policy, as a result of which the Commission adopted its first Environmental Action Programme in late 1973. Subsequent EAPs came into force in 1977, 1982, 1987, and 1993.

The first two EAPs were based on taking preventive action and on working against allowing divergent national policies to become barriers to building a common market, a problem noted by the Court of Justice in 1980 when it argued that competition could be "appreciably distorted" without harmonization of environmental regulations.[4] States with weaker pollution laws, for example, had less of a financial and regulatory burden than those with stronger laws and might attract corporations wanting to build new factories with a minimum of built-in environmental safeguards. The third EAP marked a sea change, with a switch to a focus on environmental management as the basis of economic and social development. For the first time, environmental factors were consciously factored in to other policy areas—notably agriculture, industry, energy, and transport—and were no longer subordinate to the goal of building a common market.[5]

All of these changes took place without amendments to the EEC Treaty, so Community environmental policy lacked a clear legal basis and was technically unauthorized by the member states.[6] Additional complications came with the expansion of Community membership during the 1980s to include Greece, Spain, and Portugal, whose industries were relatively underdeveloped and pollutive and whose environmental standards were relatively weak. The problems these changes posed were finally addressed by the SEA, which gave a legal basis to Community environmental policy and made environmental protection a component of all EC policies. Maastricht provided further clarification by making "sustainable and non-inflationary growth respecting the environment" a fundamental goal of the EU, introducing qualified majority voting in the Council of Ministers on most environmental issues and making environmental laws subject to codecisions by the European Parliament. Amsterdam built on these changes by listing sustainable development (economic development that takes place within the carrying capacity of the environment) as one of the general goals of European integration.

Additional boosts to EU action have come from public opinion; Eurobarometer polls have found that over two-thirds of Europeans believe that decisions on the environment should be taken at the EU level rather than at the national level and that pollution is an "urgent and immediate problem." Meanwhile, green parties have won support in most member states; by 1995 green members sat in the national legislatures of Austria, Belgium, Finland, Germany, Greece, Ireland, Italy, Luxembourg, Portugal, and Sweden.

By the end of 1998, the EU had adopted five EAPs, run several continent-wide research programs and created a data-processing European Environment Agency (EEA), established several programs to finance environmental management projects, published multiple green and white papers on environmental issues, and adopted over seven hundred laws covering everything from environmental impact assessment to controls on lead in fuel, sulfur dioxide and suspended particulates, lead in air, pollutants from industrial and large combustion plants, nitrogen dioxide, and vehicle exhaust emissions; it even adopted over forty laws on noise pollution. Environmental policy in the EU is now arguably driven more by the needs and effects of regional integration than by the priorities of the individual member states.

However, EU environmental law remains patchy, it is regularly criticized by industry and environmentalists alike for lacking coherence, and much work remains to be done (see Box 14.1). The adoption of laws and the publication of policy statements are important, but a number of problems have emerged in recent years that need to be addressed if the EU is to ensure that its efforts are directed as effectively as possible.

The Implementation Deficit

Although there has been progress on environmental policymaking, the record regarding implementation is less positive. The reasons are many and varied. Nigel Haigh notes the complications arising out of the sheer number of pieces of EU law, the difficulties of assessment arising out of the many different goals and time frames of environmental law, the many different national, regional, and local authorities that may be involved in implementation, the large number of projects subject to broad-ranging laws such as the 1985 directive on environmental impact assessment, and ambiguities in reporting requirements.[7]

Another problem arises from the differences in the regulatory programs and systems of member states. For example, Greece and Spain have had problems with implementation mainly because local government in both states is relatively poorly organized and underequipped. Germany and the Netherlands also have weak records on implementation, but this is because both have sophisticated systems of domestic environmental law and thus lack the motivation fully to adapt their own measures to EC requirements.

BOX 14.1
The State of the European Environment

Concerns about the quality of the data upon which Community policy was based led to the creation in 1994 of the European Environment Agency. A data-gathering body rather than a regulatory agency, the EEA has been charged with—among other things—compiling triennial reports on the state of the European environment. The first of these was published in 1995,[1] the second in 1998,[2] and together they painted a picture of mixed progress:

Europe's water and air is cleaner, there is more public awareness of the threats posed by chemicals to food and water, fish stocks are better managed, the EU is quieter, and differences in environmental standards pose less of a handicap than before to trade among the member states.

In the case of poorer states such as Greece, Spain, and Portugal, who possessed little in the way of preexisting laws and policies, almost all their environmental activities have been driven by the obligations of EU membership.

Even though levels of sulfur dioxide, lead, and particulates have declined in the EU, many European cities still have dirty air, mainly because of heavy (and growing) concentrations of road vehicles. The volume of road traffic in Western Europe is expected to almost double by 2010 from 1990 levels.

Energy consumption in the EU continues to grow, as does the production of the greenhouse gases implicated in global warming.

Intensive agriculture continues to exert pressure on natural habitats, helping threaten 45 percent of Europe's reptiles and 42 percent of its mammals with extinction, introducing nitrogen and phosphorus into surface waters, and emitting acidifying ammonia into the atmosphere. Meanwhile, groundwater concentrations of some pesticides frequently exceed maximum admissible levels.

There has been little progress in the development of waste disposal policies, and total waste production continues to grow, although the proportion going into landfills has fallen as the use of incinerators has grown.

Freshwater is overexploited and is polluted by sewage, pesticides, and industrial waste; overfishing and pollution continue to be problems in many coastal zones and marine water.

Notes

1. David Stanners and Philippe Bourdeau, *Europe's Environment: The Dobris Assessment* (Luxembourg: Office of Official Publications of the European Communities, 1995).

2. European Environment Agency, *Europe's Environment: The Second Assessment* (Copenhagen: EEA, 1998).

Meanwhile, Denmark has a good record on implementation, helped by high levels of public and official environmental awareness, effective monitoring systems, and the involvement of the Danish parliament in negotiating new environmental law.[8]

It has been argued that the Commission—through the EEA—should be given the power to carry out inspections and ensure compliance, but this would raise fundamental questions about sovereignty and the "interference" of the Commission in the domestic affairs of the member states. Additionally, effective inspections would demand a huge new staff; even the U.S. Environmental Protection Agency—with a staff of 18,000 and a 1999 budget of $8 billion—is hard-pressed to keep up with everything it is expected to do. For the foreseeable future, the Commission will have to continue to rely on whistle-blowing by interest groups and on cases being brought before national courts and the European Court of Justice.

The Complexities of Policy Integration

Given the broad-ranging nature of environmental problems, and the growing complexity of EU decisionmaking processes, the time taken to develop new environmental laws and policies has lengthened from an average of two to three years to as long as six to seven years. This allows more interests to have their say, and—theoretically—helps ensure that the implications of EU actions are thoroughly considered, but it also makes it difficult for the EU to respond quickly to worsening problems. The challenge faced by the Commission is heightened by the ambitious goals that the leaders of the member states have set for the EU. Most notably, the SEA introduced the principle that "environmental protection requirements shall be a component of the Community's other policies." This was strengthened by Article 6 of the Amsterdam Treaty, which requires that they "must be integrated into the definition and implementation" of Community policies. In few other EU policy areas does this principle apply, and its effect has been to oblige the Commission to ensure that legislative proposals are widely distributed and discussed before being sent to the Council and Parliament. This has meant often lengthy interactions involving all the major EU institutions, national bureaucrats, representatives of non-EU governments where necessary, and representatives of industry and interest groups.

To complicate matters, as Jan Jans points out, it is unclear what is meant by "environmental protection requirements"; questions have been raised as to whether or not the principle implies that environmental policy has priority over all other EU policy areas; and nothing is said in the treaties about how conflicts between environmental protection and the goals of other policy areas should be resolved.[9] It also raises the legal question of whether or not the legitimacy of an action of the Council or the Commission in the fields of transport or agriculture, for example, could be challenged on the basis that it infringed or did not fully take into account the environmental implications.

Unbalanced Interests

The Commission has become adept at identifying and working with outside parties with an interest in developing environmental law. However, those interests are unbalanced, and industry has considerably more influence over the legislative process than do environmental interest groups. Corporate interests and Brussels-based industrial federations such as the European Chemical Industry Council represent communities with specific interests, are well organized and funded, employ experts who can respond persuasively to the often detailed technical content of Commission proposals, and have a vested interest in the negotiations, given that they are centrally involved in the implementation of subsequent legislation.

By contrast, environmental groups have limited resources and represent a constituency that is broad and sometimes difficult to define. Several have opened offices in Brussels—notably Friends of the Earth, Greenpeace, and the World Wildlife Fund—and their representatives are invited to attend Commission advisory committee meetings, but they rarely have the time and the expert staffs, with the result that EU environmental law and policy often reflect the priorities of corporate Europe more than they do the environmental lobby and European consumers. In order to improve the balance, the Commission has tried to help groups, for example, by funding the European Environmental Bureau, an umbrella body founded in 1974 to represent the interests of local, national, and regional nongovernmental organizations in Brussels. With Commission prompting, the European Consultative Forum on the Environment and Sustainable Development (the European Green Forum) was created in 1993, providing representatives of environmental groups, industry, business, local authorities, trade unions, and academia with a channel through which they could advise the Commission on policy development.

The Changing Balance of Member States

There has always been a multispeed approach to environmental protection in the EU, with some member states (notably the Netherlands and Germany) being in favor of tighter regulation and others (notably Britain) not. The political balance shifted in favor of a more aggressive approach with the accession in 1995 of Austria, Finland, and Sweden, but it will shift in favor of a less aggressive approach when poorer Central and Eastern European states join the EU. It is already clear that countries such as Poland,

Hungary, and the Czech Republic have much to do to meet the environmental policy conditions required for entry. Not only do they lack national strategies and have poor records on monitoring and enforcing national laws, but there are signs that the environment has been slipping down their policy agendas as governments have put more effort into economic growth.

Despite the problems, the EU experience has shown that regional cooperation among countries promises a more rapid and effective resolution of transnational environmental problems than does any other approach, at least among countries with similar political systems and levels of economic development. Isolated national approaches may be handicapped by fears of a loss of competitive advantage; bilateral and multilateral approaches have worked only when they have been limited to selected issues of mutual concern, such as the management of shared rivers, lakes, and oceans; broader global approaches are handicapped by the increased likelihood of disagreement and deadlock and the lack of competent authorities with the powers to promote and enforce regulation. Given the extent to which the causes and effects of environmental problems do not respect national frontiers, the EU model may provide the *only* effective response to such problems.

Social Policy

Cohesion in the EU has meant investments not only in agriculture, industry, and services but also in social issues such as workers' rights, women's rights, and improved working and living conditions. Social policies are a logical outcome of the long histories of welfare promotion in individual Western European states and an important part of the drive toward building a single market by ensuring equal opportunities and working conditions. At the same time, they are controversial and have led to some of the most bruising ideological battles the EU has witnessed since its foundation. Generally speaking, national labor unions are in favor, as are the Commission and Parliament (dominated as it is by social democratic parties), while business interests and conservative political parties are opposed, arguing that social policy threatens to make European companies less competitive in the global market.[10]

Relatively little attention was initially paid to social issues. Even though worker mobility and the expansion of a skilled labor force were important parts of the idea of building a common market, the Treaty of Rome was ultimately based on the naive assumption that the benefits of the common market would improve life for all European workers. This was true to the extent that it helped increase wages, but market forces failed to deal with gender and age discrimination, disparities in wage levels, different levels of unemployment, and safety and health in the workplace. Although the

Treaty made it the Community's business to deal with such issues as equal pay for equal work, working conditions, and social security for migrant workers, and Article 123 set the goal of creating the European Social Fund (ESF) to help promote worker mobility, social issues moved down the Community agenda as it concentrated on completing the common market and resolving battles over agricultural policy, and the movement of workers was heavily restricted.

The widening of the gap in economic conditions brought on by enlargement in 1973 pushed social issues back up the agenda, and the first in a series of four-year Social Action Programmes was launched in 1974, aimed at developing a plan of action to achieve full employment, improved living and working conditions, and gender equality. A combination of recession and ideological resistance from several European leaders ensured that the words failed to be translated into deeds, but the EEC did establish the ESF in 1974, aimed at helping to combat long-term unemployment and creating jobs and training schemes for young people. ESF spending grew rapidly during the 1980s; the major recipients were Ireland, Portugal, Spain, and Finland (see Figure 14.1). By 1998, the ESF accounted for over 9 percent of the EU budget (8.6 billion euros, or $10.3 billion).

The Single European Act again underlined the importance of social policy by raising questions about the mobility of workers (one of the goals of the SEA was to make it possible for Europeans to live and work wherever they liked in the Community) and bringing up concerns about "social dumping" (money, services, and businesses moving to those parts of the EU with the lowest wages and social security costs). The Commission began promoting social policy more actively, trying to focus the attention of national governments on the "social dimension" of the single market. However, economic recession ensured that the SEA initially lacked a social dimension, which encouraged Jacques Delors—a moderate socialist—to launch an attempt in 1988 to draw more attention to the social consequences of the single market.

The idea of a charter of basic social rights had been introduced by the Belgian presidency of the Council of Ministers in 1987, modeled on Belgium's new national charter. The concept was taken up by Delors in 1989 and was helped by the determination of the socialist government of François Mitterrand to promote social policy during the French presidency of the EC. Germany was also in favor—even though it was led by the moderate-conservative government of Helmut Kohl—as were states with socialist governments, such as Spain and Greece. By contrast, the Conservative Margaret Thatcher was enthusiastically opposed; she considered it "quite inappropriate" for laws on working regulations and welfare benefits to be set at the Community level and saw the Charter of the Fundamental Social Rights of Workers (the Social Charter) as "a socialist charter—devised by

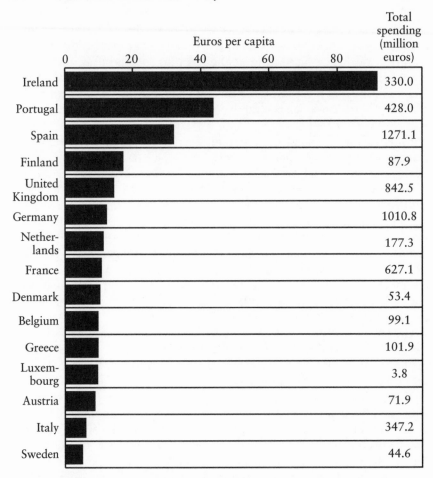

FIGURE 14.1 Spending Under the European Social Fund, 1996

Source: Calculated from figures in the Annual Report of the Court of Auditors (1997).

socialists in the Commission and favored predominantly by socialist member states."[11] In the event, the Social Charter was adopted at the 1989 Strasbourg summit by eleven of the twelve member states—all but Britain.

The Social Charter brought together all of the social policy goals that had been mentioned throughout the life of the Community, including freedom of movement, improved living and working conditions, vocational training, gender equality, and protection for children, the elderly, and the handicapped, but it was heavy on feel-good goals and light on specifics. An action program listed forty-seven separate measures that needed to be taken to achieve the goals of the Social Charter, but the challenge of reaching unanimity on social legislation in the Council of Ministers meant very little progress was made on turning principles into law. Britain was regularly painted as the major opponent of the Social Charter, but there was heated debate involving several member states over issues such as working hours, maternity leave, and employment benefits for part-time workers.

There were plans to incorporate the Social Charter into Maastricht, but the British government under Prime Minister John Major again refused to go along, so a compromise was reached whereby it was attached to Maastricht as a social protocol and Britain was excluded from voting in the Council on social issues while the other eleven member states formed their own ad hoc Social Community. This all changed in 1997 when the newly elected government under Tony Blair committed Britain to the goals of the social protocol, and it was incorporated into the treaties by the Treaty of Amsterdam.

Despite all the rhetoric about social issues, the focus of most attention since 1991 has been on just one problem: the failure of the EU to ease unemployment, the persistence of which was once described as equivalent to the persistence of poverty in the United States.[12] The single market has not been able to generate enough jobs for Europeans, and while unemployment in late 1998 hovered around 8 percent in Canada, 5 percent in the United States, and 4 percent in Japan, EU states had figures ranging from 4 to 6 percent in the Netherlands, Britain, and Sweden to 11 to 12 percent in Germany, France, and Italy to a high of nearly 19 percent in Spain.[13]

Why the rates are so high is debatable, but at least part of the problem has been the relative weakness of labor unions and the relative ease with which workers can be laid off. Another factor is the size of the black market, which is all but institutionalized in southern Italy, where it overlaps with the destructive power of organized crime. The EU has launched a host of retraining programs and is shifting resources to the poorer parts of the EU through various regional and social programs, but with mixed results. Robert Geyer and Beverly Springer argue that EU employment policy has had "high visibility but little focus" and that the search for solutions is hampered by a lack of support among member states, traditionally responsible for employment policy. They also note that the EU faces the problem of trying to create jobs through increased competitiveness while preserving the traditional rights of employees.

The Amsterdam Treaty introduced a new employment chapter that called on the member states to "work towards developing a coordinated strategy for employment," but it only requires the Commission and the member states to report to each other, leaving most of the responsibility for employment policy with the member states. In November 1997 the European Council met, with unemployment being the sole item on its agenda, and agreed to common guidelines on employment policy, including fresh starts for the young and the long-term unemployed and simplifying rules for

BOX 14.2
Women in the European Union

The position of women in politics and the workforce in the EU is not that different (overall) from their relative position in the United States and Canada, but the situation varies from one member state to another, giving added significance to EU social policy and the goal of building economic and social cohesion. Very generally, women are in a better situation in progressive northern states such as Denmark, Finland, and Sweden and relatively worse off in poorer southern states such as Portugal, Greece, and Spain.

Women make up about one-third of the workforce in the EU. Career options are still relatively limited; proportionately more women are employed in part-time jobs, and women are more likely to work in traditionally feminized jobs—such as nursing and teaching—than in management; women are also more likely to work in the less well-paid and more labor-intensive sectors of industry.[1] Like their North American counterparts, European women are also paid less than men for comparable work—about 80 cents in the euro. On the credit side of the ledger, about 75 percent of working women are employed in the expanding service sector, every EU member state is legally obliged to provide maternity leave, several member states offer paternity leave, and the public provision of child care is improving.

Although the rights of working women were mentioned in the Treaty of Rome (Article 119, for example, establishes the principle of equal pay for men and women), it was not until the EC began to more actively examine social policy during the 1970s that women's issues began to be addressed. The 1974 SAP included the goal of achieving gender equality in access to employment and vocational training, and equal rights at work were promoted by new EC laws such as the 1975 Equal Pay Directive and the 1976 Equal Treatment Directive. Even though direct and indirect gender discrimination are illegal under EU law, women still face the same kind of invisible barriers and glass ceilings in the EU as they do in North America.

The Single European Act and Maastricht were both concerned more with broad institutional reform than with human rights, and they did little in specific terms to address gender imbalances. Beverly Springer has argued that the single market may actually pose a threat both to the jobs that women hold and the laws that protect them. Little was done in the planning stages to anticipate how the changes would affect women, and not all of the proposals made under the SAPs or related Commission white papers have the force of law; thus compliance is voluntary.[2]

The elitism and gender biases of the EU are exemplified by the obvious imbalances in the staffing of the major EU institutions. The first woman appointed to the Commission was Vasso Papandreou of Greece in 1991 (although five of the twenty commissioners during 1995–1999 were women); there are many more men in the more senior positions within the Commission and Council of Ministers, many more women in secretarial and clerical positions; there has never been a woman on the Court of Justice, and only two women—Margaret Thatcher and former French prime minister Edith Cresson—have ever taken part in meetings of the European Council.

Notes

1. Beverly Springer, *The Social Dimension of 1992: Europe Faces a New EC* (Westport, Conn: Prager, 1992), 66.
2. Ibid., 72–73.

small and medium-sized enterprises. Although millions of new jobs have been created in the EU over the last decade, nearly half are temporary or part-time jobs, and many of them are in the service sector; because many of these jobs are being filled by men and women new to the job market, they have done little to help ease long-term unemployment.

Building Worker Mobility

It had been understood as early as the signing of the Treaty of Rome that an open labor market was an essential part of the creation of a true single market, and although Article 8a gave every citizen of the Community the right to "move and reside freely" within the territory of the member states, Article 48 made this subject "to limitations justified on grounds of public policy, public security or public health." The movement of workers was initially seen mainly in economic terms, so the emphasis was placed on removing the barriers for those EU citizens who were economically active. Migration was at first limited because of employment opportunities within their home states (governments were protecting against the possibility of a shortage of skilled workers) but was subsequently limited because of the lack of opportunities in the target states.[14]

More recently, there has been a new emphasis on allowing free movement to all EU nationals, whether or not they are economically active. Hence, changes arising out of the SEA made it possible for any EU citizens to move and live anywhere in the EU provided they were covered by health insurance and had enough income to avoid becoming a burden, so to speak, on the welfare system of the country in which they were living. The concerns of national governments have been twofold: to control the effects of economic pressures that encourage workers to leave the poorer parts of the EU for the richer parts, thereby destabilizing the employment situation and living off welfare in those richer parts; and to control the movement of non-EU citizens, notably nationals of Turkey and North Africa. At the heart of the debate about free movement has been a concern about differences in welfare laws, which is why harmonization of social policies has been given high priority and why there has been a particular focus on dealing with the needs of younger and older people.

There is no question that Europeans have become much more mobile in the last ten to fifteen years, and the numbers of nonnationals living in member states has grown: There were 5 million immigrants in 1950, 10 million in 1970, and probably close to 15 million today (although the growing openness of borders makes it difficult to be precise). Meanwhile, there are an estimated 550,000 Europeans who have been posted temporarily to another member state by their employers. Although the flow of immigration was initially from the south to the north, and consisted largely of workers from Mediterranean states seeking employment and then bringing their families with them, immigration flows in recent years have become much more complex, and there has been an increase in the movement of professionals and managers.[15] In other words, there has been a tendency away from economically motivated migration toward voluntary migration by people wanting to move to a different environment for a variety of reasons.

Language differences pose a barrier to the free movement of workers, so—particularly since Maastricht—member states have taken more steps to encourage educational exchanges and training in second and even third languages. These steps include the following:

- ERASMUS, a program to encourage student and faculty exchanges among colleges and universities and to make it easier for students to transfer credits. (Since 1991, degrees and diplomas awarded by any institution of higher education in the EU after three years of study are automatically recognized in all the member states.) Over 50,000 students have taken advantage of ERASMUS since it was launched in 1987.
- LINGUA is a program that encourages training in second and third languages;
- TEMPUS is a program to link universities in the United States and Western and Eastern Europe by promoting joint research projects;
- COMETT is a program that encourages universities and industry to work together on training projects; and
- PETRA is a program aimed at modernizing vocational training.

The EU now has eleven official languages: Danish, Dutch, English, Finnish, French, German, Greek, Italian, Portuguese, Spanish, and Swedish. Almost all EU business is conducted in English and French, although Germany is eager to ensure that German is not forgotten. One of the consequences of an eastward expansion of the EU will be an increase in the number of Europeans who speak German, which will alter the linguistic balance of power. Almost all secondary school pupils in the EU learn at least one foreign language, but the record varies from one state to another. The British have the worst record, but they have been spoiled by the steady growth of English as the international language of commerce and entertainment and by the fact that a growing number of continental Europeans speak English; over 90 percent of secondary school pupils in Germany, Spain, the Netherlands, and Denmark learn English as a second language. Meanwhile, only 33 percent of Italian pupils and 23 percent of German pupils are learning French.[16]

259

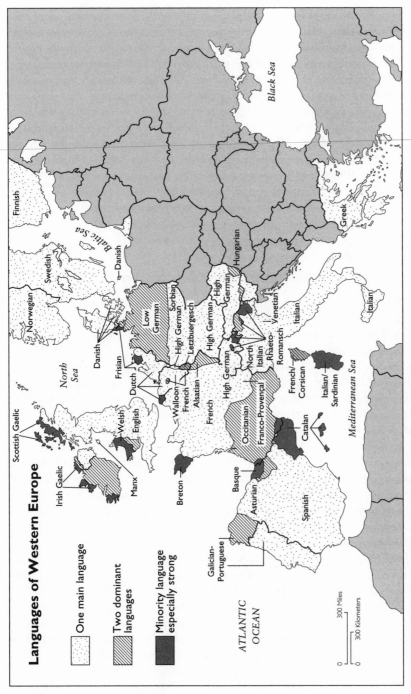

Source: Based on map in Viktor Keegan and Martin Kettle (Eds.), *The New Europe* (London: Fourth Estate, 1993), p. 92.

The issue of language cuts to the very core of cultural pride and particularly upsets the French, who have done everything they can to stop the perfidious spread of "franglais"—the common use of English words in French, such as *le jumbo jet* (officially *le gros porteur*) and *le fast food* (officially *pret-à-manger*). In an attempt to prevent any one language from winning out over the others, suggestions have been made for all Europeans to learn Esperanto—an artificial language developed in 1887—or even for Latin to be revived. Despite the number of EU employees who work as translators, the publication of every EU document in all eleven official languages, and the attempts by France to stave off the inroads made by English and Anglo-American culture, it seems almost inevitable that English—with the help of U.S. and Japanese business—will continue its steady trend toward becoming the common language of Europe, presenting the French, so to speak, with a fait accompli.

Summary and Conclusions

At the heart of the process of European integration has been a continuing debate about the kinds of policy issues that are best dealt with jointly and those that are best left to the member states. In the case of the environment, there is little question that international cooperation is both desirable and inevitable. Problems such as air and water pollution ignore national boundaries, and there are repeated examples from around the world of one state being a producer of pollution and other states downwind or downriver being the recipients. As construction proceeds on the global economy, a new dimension is added by the barriers posed to trade by different environmental standards. There will always be strong ideological disagreements about the extent to which the state should manage natural resources and regulate industry, but there is a strong internal logic to international cooperation on environmental management. A consensus is emerging that holds that the EU has been a progressive force in environmental protection and that European environmental problems are better dealt with at the EU level than at the national and local levels.

Much less agreement is found on the role of the EU in social policy. There is little question that among the foundations of a workable single market are equal pay, equal working conditions, and the provision of the kind of education and training that can help promote worker mobility. However, social policy treads on sensitive ideological and cultural toes; conservatives and socialists will never agree on the best way to build a level social playing field; and programs that may be seen as progressive by one member state may be seen as a threat to cultural identity by another. During the late 1990s, Western Europe seemed to take a shift to the left as one country after another elected left-leaning governments, thereby increasing the likelihood of more agreement across the member states on social issues.

Further Reading

David Judge (Ed.). *A Green Dimension for the European Community: Political Is sues and Processes* (London: Frank Cass, 1993).
J. Duncan Liefferink, Philip Lowe, and Arthur Mol (Eds.). *European Integration and Environmental Policy* (London: Belhaven, 1993).
Two collections of edited essays on the evolution, nature, and consequences of EU environmental policy.
John McCormick. *The European Union and the Environment* (New York: St. Martin's Press, forthcoming).
The only full-length monograph on EU environmental policy, with chapters on the policy process and on specific policy areas, including air and water pollution.
Michael Gold. *The Social Dimension: Employment Policy in the European Community* (London: Macmillan, 1993).
A study of employment policy in the EU and its implications for social policy.
Beverly Springer. *The Social Dimension of 1992: Europe Faces a New EC* (Westport, Conn.: Praeger, 1992).
A look at social policy in the EU, with an emphasis on the underlying goals and possible consequences of the Single European Act.

Notes

1. Ronald Inglehart, *The Silent Revolution: Changing Values and Political Styles Among Western Publics* (Princeton: Princeton University Press, 1977).
2. Philipp M. Hildebrand, "The European Community's Environmental Policy, 1957 to '1992': From Incidental Measures to an International Regime?" in David Judge (Ed.), *A Green Dimension for the European Community: Political Issues and Processes* (London: Frank Cass, 1993).
3. See chapter 3 in John McCormick, *The Global Environmental Movement*, 2d ed. (London: John Wiley, 1995).
4. *Commission v. Italy* (Case 91/79), in Court of Justice of the European Communities, *Reports of Cases Before the Court*, 1980.
5. Hildebrand, "The European Community's Environmental Policy."
6. Eckard Rehbinder and Richard Steward (Eds.), *Environmental Protection Policy, Vol 2—Integration Through Law: Europe and the American Federal Experience* (Firenze, Italy: European University Institute, 1985), 19.
7. Nigel Haigh, "Effective Environment Protection—Challenges for the Implementation of EC Law." Background paper presented to Joint Public Hearing on Implementation and Enforcement of EC Environmental Law, European Parliament, Brussels, May 1996.
8. Ken Collins and David Earnshaw, "The Implementation and Enforcement of European Community Environment Legislation," in David Judge, *A Green Dimension for the European Community*.

9. Jan Jans, "Objectives and Principles of EC Environmental Law," in Gerd Winter (Ed), *European Environment Law: A Comparative Perspective* (Aldershot: Dartmouth Publishing, 1996).

10. Robert Geyer and Beverly Springer, "EU Social Policy After Maastricht: The Works Directive and the British Opt-Out," in Pierre-Henri Laurent and Marc Maresceau (Eds), *The State of the European Union Vol. 4: Deepening and Widening* (Boulder, CO: Lynne Rienner, 1998), 208.

11. Margaret Thatcher, *The Downing Street Years* (New York: HarperCollins, 1993), 750.

12. Ralf Dahrendorf, *The Modern Social Conflict* (London: Weidenfeld and Nicholson, 1988), 149.

13. *The Economist,* various issues, late 1998.

14. Ian Barnes and Pamela M. Barnes, *The Enlarged European Union* (London: Longman, 1995), 108.

15. Federico Romero, "Cross-Border Population Movements," in William Wallace (Ed.), *The Dynamics of European Integration* (London: Pinter, 1992).

16. Eurostat figures, quoted in *The Economist,* January 14, 1995.

15

Foreign and Security Policy

The crisis that emerged in the Yugoslav province of Kosovo during the first half of 1998 dragged European foreign policy into the harsh light of day and—as had been the case so many times before—found it wanting. European leaders were quick to condemn the actions taken by Yugoslav leader Slobodan Milosevic to put down an insurrection led by ethnic Albanians living in the province, but they did not back up words with significant action. As Serbian forces battled the Kosovo Liberation Army (KLA), leading to the deaths of dozens and the expulsion of as many as 200,000 Kosovars from their homes, EU foreign ministers dithered. Lacking European armed forces that could be sent in to Yugoslavia to back up their verbal disapproval, equivocating over whether to encourage talks between the Serbs and the KLA or to back the demands of the KLA for full independence, and undecided over which international forum to use to put pressure on the Milosevic government, the EU watched as the most active initiatives for peace were taken by the United States.

For many, the EU response was another illustration of how little progress it was making on the development of a common foreign policy. As more was expected from the Europeans, so their inability to agree on critical security problems had become more visible. The divisions had been most notable during the Gulf crisis of 1990–1991, when Iraq invaded Kuwait; even though European leaders condemned the invasion, the levels of support they gave to the U.S.-led counterinvasion varied dramatically, from the substantial commitment made in arms and personnel by Britain and France, to Belgium's refusal to sell ammunition to Britain, to the insistence by Ireland that it maintain its neutrality.[1] The divisions became clear again in responses to crises in the Balkans during the 1990s (see Box 15.1), as well as

BOX 15.1
The EU and the Balkans

The outbreak of a civil war on Europe's back porch in 1991 provided a demanding test of the EU's foreign policy capacity. Critics charge that it failed the test, but the crisis forced an accelerated development of EU foreign policy, and—in all fairness—the EU was neither politically nor militarily prepared for a crisis of such proportions. Ironically, the fact that the EU was so roundly criticized by the United States for the weakness of its response suggested just how much had come to be expected of the EU as a political entity.

The creation of Yugoslavia was one of the outcomes of World War I and brought together several independent states whose internal ethnic, religious, and nationalist tensions were kept in check after World War II only by the power of the Tito regime (1944–1980). The end of the cold war brought those tensions into the open, resulting in the June 1991 declaration of independence by Slovenia and Croatia. When Bosnia too seemed about to declare its independence, Bosnian Serbs attacked in April 1992. In May 1993, fighting broke out in Bosnia between Croats and Muslims over historically Croat-controlled territory.

The initial EC position was to try to keep Yugoslavia intact, but under German pressure it recognized Slovenia and Croatia in January 1992, thereby undermining its credibility with the Serbs. The EC then tried without success to broker cease-fires, sent unarmed monitors to attempt to keep the warring factions apart, imposed sanctions on Serbia, supported an embargo on arms sales to Bosnian Muslims in hopes of reducing hostilities, and contributed most of the UN peacekeeping forces deployed in the area.

Although the Balkans are on Europe's doorstep, they represent a political quagmire into which the EU has been reluctant to venture. Despite the obvious attempts by Serbs to expand Serbia and to eradicate Bosnia's Muslims, and then to brutally put down an insurrection in 1998 among ethnic Albanians in the province of Kosovo, the EU has been concerned about becoming directly involved in hostilities and about the implications of Russia's traditional ties with the Serbs. At the same time, however, the EU has faced political pressure to address the flagrant disregard for human rights in the region. The key problem has been the EU's inability to back words with coordinated military action, which is why—when it finally responded to the problem in Kosovo in March 1999—it did so under the auspices of NATO.

---

in the refusal of all but Britain to support renewed U.S. threats against Iraq during 1998.

Yet even though the various international security crises of the 1990s may have found the EU unprepared and lacking both political unanimity and military preparedness, in other respects the EU *has* made progress on external policies, and in fact it has become an increasingly assertive influence on international affairs. As Christopher Hill puts it, setbacks have produced renewed efforts at policy cooperation, which has followed a pattern of peaks and troughs along a gradual upward gradient, and "consensus has become more habit-forming."[2] It may not yet be a military power,

but the economic power of the EU is no longer in any doubt: It is an economic superpower in a league of its own. It accounts for 28 percent of global GNP and 36 percent of global trade, its fifteen member states constitute the biggest and richest market in the world, and the EU has become a force to be reckoned with in international trade negotiations.

Foreign Policy Cooperation: From EPC to CFSP

Foreign policy was a latecomer to the agenda of European integration. It was not mentioned in the Treaties of Rome, and the Communities focused during the 1950s and 1960s on internal economic matters, although the logic of spillover implied that it would be difficult for the member states to long avoid developing common external economic and security policies. There were several stillborn attempts to build common foreign and security policies in the early years, including the European Defence Community, the European Political Community, and Charles de Gaulle's plans for regular meetings of leaders of the Six to coordinate foreign policy. In 1970, agreement was reached on European Political Cooperation (EPC; cooperation on foreign policy), but this was to occur on a purely intergovernmental basis, revolving around biannual—and eventually monthly—meetings of the foreign ministers. No new institutions were to be created, although the European Council was launched in 1974, in part to bring leaders together to coordinate policies.

EPC was originally concerned more with *how* foreign policy should be agreed on than with *what* that policy should be,[3] and it was not given formal recognition until the passage of the Single European Act, which charged under Title III that member states would "endeavour jointly to formulate and implement a European foreign policy." However, EPC remained a loose and voluntary arrangement, no laws were passed on foreign policy, each of the member states could still act independently, and most of the key decisions on foreign policy had to be arrived at unanimously. Overall leadership was provided by the European Council, with continuity ensured by regular meetings of senior officials from all the foreign ministries. A small secretariat was also set up in Brussels to help the country holding the presidency, which tended to provide most of the momentum. Larger and more active states such as Britain and France had few problems providing that momentum, but foreign policy coordination put a strain on smaller and neutral countries such as Luxembourg and Ireland. (In order to help smaller countries, the rotation for the presidency of the Council of Ministers was changed with effect from 1998: Instead of running alphabetically, it now alternates big countries with small ones, thereby more effectively balancing leadership.)

The Maastricht Treaty noted that one of the goals of the EU was "to assert its identity on the international scene, in particular through the implementation of a common foreign and security policy which shall include the eventual framing of a common defence policy." Hence the Common Foreign and Security Policy (CFSP) became one of three "pillars" that now make up the European Union, and defense was finally pushed more squarely onto the EU agenda. Although decisionmaking is still loosely structured, the CFSP gives more direction to foreign policy, committing the member states (under Maastricht) to defining and implementing a common policy that includes "all questions related to the security of the Union, including the eventual framing of a common defence policy, which might in time lead to a common defence." The goals of the CFSP are very loosely defined, with vague talk about defending "common values" and "fundamental interests," but the CFSP is based around systematic cooperation among the member states, with the European Council agreeing on common positions when necessary.

Although all these developments have been part of a gradual movement toward greater coordination, the development of a European foreign policy still faces at least three major handicaps.

First, the member states have different agendas and different priorities. The most fundamental division is that between Atlanticists such as Britain, the Netherlands, and Portugal, who argue in favor of a close security association with the United States through NATO, and Europeanists such as France and sometimes Germany, who look more toward European independence. Meanwhile, both Britain and France have special interests in their former colonies, Germany has given priority to building links with Eastern Europe, and Ireland, Sweden, and Finland want to maintain their neutrality. There are very few issues (other than trade) that engage the common interest of all EU member states, and even where such issues exist, the fifteen states vary enormously in their abilities to respond.

Second, the EU lacks focus and leadership. Not only does the presidency of the Council of Ministers change every six months, but there has been no one in the EU institutions who could act as a focal point for discussions with other countries, which are obliged to switch their attention from one member state to another and establish contacts with ministers and bureaucrats in fifteen capitals. As former U.S. Secretary of State Henry Kissinger once quipped, "When I want to speak to Europe, whom do I call?" His concern was at least partly addressed by institutional changes made under the Treaty of Amsterdam. The Policy Planning and Early Warning Unit (PPEWU) was set up in Brussels to help the EU anticipate foreign crises. It consists of twenty members: one each from the member states, the Western European Union (WEU), and the European Commission, and three from the Council of Ministers. At the same time, the practice of distributing external relations portfolios in the Commission among four different Commissioners and the president was replaced with the creation of a new foreign policy position with the rank of vice president.

Finally, and most importantly, no matter what institutional changes it agrees to, the EU will always work with one arm tied behind its back until it can back up its words with the threat of military force. Together, the fifteen member states amount to a formidable force; they have over 2 million troops, 22,000 tanks, 21,000 artillery pieces, and 6,300 combat aircraft, which among them make up 85–95 percent of NATO capability in Europe. However, the development of security arrangements in Western Europe since World War II has created a confusing mélange of commitments by dif-

FIGURE 15.1   Overlapping Security Alliances in Europe

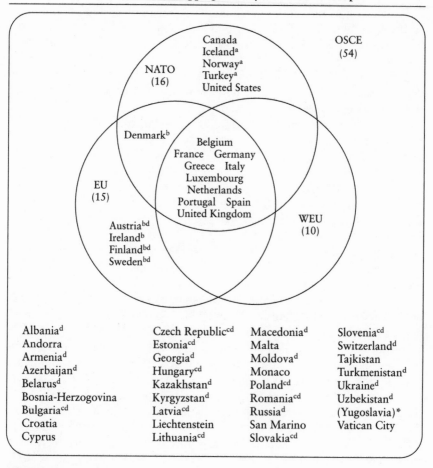

[a]WEU associate member.
[b]WEU observer.
[c]WEU associate partner.
[d]Member of the NATO Partnership for Peace program.
*Suspended from membership of OSCE in 1992.

ferent groups of countries to different organizations, and at different levels (see Figure 15.1).

Preeminent among these is NATO, set up in 1949 in response to concerns about the Soviet threat; but NATO is dominated by the United States and has had to redefine its mission since the end of the cold war. Its future depends upon, first, the extent to which the United States continues feeling obliged to respond to security threats in Europe and, second, the extent to which France and other Europeanists continue to welcome the U.S. role in European defense.

Then there is the Organization for Security and Cooperation in Europe (OSCE), born out of a reorganization in 1994 of the Conference on Security and Cooperation in Europe (CSCE). The OSCE is the only truly pan-European security organization, but it has so far restricted itself to conflict prevention and postconflict rehabilitation, rather than to preparation for defense. With members from North America, Western Europe, and the former Soviet Union, it is even less likely to reach agreement on the definition of security threats than is NATO.

The most likely prospects for the development of a joint European defense capability may lie with the Western European Union, a long-moribund organization given new life by Maastricht. Founded by the Treaty of Brussels in 1954 in the wake of the collapse of the European Defence Community, the WEU originally consisted of the six members of the ECSC and Britain; it was an attempt to help Germany contribute to the defense of Western Europe without taking part in the kind of European Army envisioned by the EDC. With the United States playing a key role in Europe's postwar defense, however, the WEU was quickly overshadowed by NATO. As one diplomat put it, the WEU became "a place where you found jobs for retired Italian admirals."[4] Following the failure of a plan to give EPC a security dimension, the WEU was revived in 1984 and passed its first modest test in 1987 when it coordinated minesweeping by its members in the Persian Gulf during the Iran-Iraq War.

With a secretariat in Brussels (to which it was moved from London in 1993) and a ministerial Council and consultative Assembly in Paris, the WEU hosts biannual meetings of the foreign and defense ministers of its ten member states: Belgium, France, Germany, Greece, Italy, Luxembourg, the Netherlands, Portugal, Spain, and the United Kingdom (Austria, Denmark, Finland, Ireland, and Sweden are observers). As a possible foundation for the development of a real European defense capability, the WEU has several advantages: It already exists; it could be used by the Europeans to develop their own defense policies independent of the United States; it can operate outside its member states (unlike NATO, which—until Kosovo—was limited to the territory of its member states); and not all EU member states are members of the WEU, so countries such as Ireland, Finland, and Sweden can be members of the EU while preserving their neutrality.

However, questions remain about the relationship between the WEU and NATO, about what the WEU should be, and whether it should remain independent of the EU, be integrated into the EU,[5] or even whether it should be abolished completely and its military component integrated into NATO. Much will depend on the outcome of a fifty-year review of the WEU that began in 1998 as one of the requirements of the Treaty of Brussels. For now, its work is limited mainly to jobs agreed to under the terms of a June 1992 declaration by the WEU Council of Ministers in Petersberg, near Bonn: Under the terms of the declaration, military units of member states acting under the authority of the WEU can be used for humanitarian, rescue, peacekeeping, and other crisis management tasks. Thus, for example, it helped set up a unified Croat-Muslim police force in the Bosnian city of Mostar during 1994–1996 and helped restructure and train the Albanian police force during 1997. It possesses little in the way of human resources, although this is changing: Among other things, the 20,000-member Rapid Deployment Force (EUROFOR) has been created with a view to strengthening the WEU's humanitarian and peacekeeping capabilities.

Although the leaders of the member states have disagreed over the development of European defense policy, the French and the Germans took the lead in May 1992 with the creation of Eurocorps, which grew out of an experimental Franco-German brigade set up in 1990. Headquartered in Strasbourg, the 50,000-member Eurocorps has been operational since November 1995 and has been joined by contingents from Belgium, Spain, and Luxembourg. It was conceived as a step toward the development of a European army that was to give substance to the CFSP, give the EU an independent defense capability, and provide some insurance for Europe in the event the United States decided to withdraw militarily from Europe. Germany insists that Eurocorps would complement NATO and that it would be placed under NATO's "operational command" in the event of a threat to Western European security, but Britain, the Netherlands, and the United States suspect that France's objective is to displace the U.S. dominance of NATO.

External Economic Relations

If many questions remain about the EU's military power and global political influence, there is little question as to its economic power. The common external tariff is in place, the single market is all but complete, the Commission has new powers to represent the governments of all the member states in negotiations on world trade, and it is now well understood by everyone that the EU is the most powerful actor in those negotiations. A successful conversion to the euro will likely add to the economic weight of Europe by giving it a currency that can stand alongside the U.S. dollar and the Japanese yen in terms of credibility and influence.

With just 6.4 percent of the world's population, the European Union now accounts for 28 percent of the world's gross national product, 36 percent of its imports, and nearly 37 percent of its exports. Given such eye-opening statistics as these, the external economic policies of the EU have understandably moved to the top of the agendas of its major trading part-

TABLE 15.1 The EU in the Global Economy

	Population 1997 (million)	Share of World Population %	GNP 1995 ($US bill)	Share World GNP %	Per Capita GNP ($US)
Germany	82.2	1.4	2252	8.0	27,400
France	58.5	1.0	1451	5.1	24,800
United Kingdom	58.2	1.0	1095	3.9	18,800
Italy	57.2	1.0	1088	3.9	19,000
Spain	39.7	0.7	532	1.9	13,400
Netherlands	15.7	0.3	371	1.3	23,600
Belgium	10.2	0.2	250	0.9	24,500
Austria	8.2	0.1	216	0.8	26,300
Sweden	8.8	0.1	210	0.7	23,900
Denmark	5.2	0.1	156	0.6	30,000
Finland	5.1	0.1	105	0.4	20,600
Portugal	9.8	0.2	97	0.3	9,900
Greece	10.5	0.2	86	0.3	8,200
Ireland	3.6	0.06	53	0.2	14,700
Luxembourg	0.4	0.006	17	0.06	42,500
EU	*373.3*	*6.4*	*7979*	*28.3*	*21,400*
United States	272.0	4.7	7100	25.2	26,100
Canada	30.3	0.5	574	2.0	23,400
Mexico	97.6	1.7	305	1.1	7,700
NAFTA	*399.9*	*6.8*	*7979*	*28.3*	*19,952*
Japan	126.0	2.2	4963	17.6	39,400
Russia	147.7	2.5	745	1.2	5,300
China	1221.6	20.1	332	2.6	2,800
WORLD	*5848.7*	*100.0*	*28182.8*	*100.0*	*–*

Source: Population figures from UN Population Fund, *The State of the World* (1997); GNP figures from World Bank, *World Bank Atlas 1996* (1997).

ners, not all of whom have liked what they have seen. Article 110 of the EEC Treaty outlined a Common Commercial Policy (CCP) based on the principle that the Community would contribute "to the harmonious development of world trade, the progressive abolition of restrictions on international trade, and the lowering of customs barriers." The CCP was not finally put in place until the completion of the single market; meanwhile, the EC's position on global trade negotiations and its focus on internal eco-

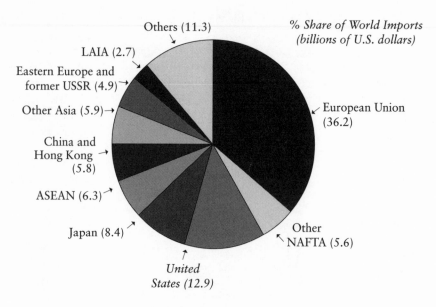

Others (11.3)

LAIA (2.7)

Eastern Europe and
former USSR (4.9)

Other Asia (5.9)

China and
Hong Kong
(5.8)

ASEAN (6.3)

Japan (8.4)

*United
States (12.9)*

*% Share of World Imports
(billions of U.S. dollars)*

European Union
(36.2)

Other
NAFTA (5.6)

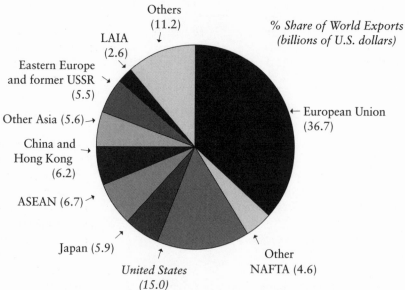

Others
(11.2)

LAIA
(2.6)

Eastern Europe
and former USSR
(5.5)

Other Asia (5.6)

China and
Hong Kong
(6.2)

ASEAN (6.7)

Japan (5.9)

*United States
(15.0)*

*% Share of World Exports
(billions of U.S. dollars)*

European Union
(36.7)

Other
NAFTA (4.6)

FIGURE 15.2   The EU Share of World Trade, 1996

ASEAN = Association of Southeast Asian Nations, consisting of Brunei, Indonesia, Laos, Malaysia, Nepal, the Philippines, Singapore, Thailand, and Vietnam

LAIA = Latin American Integration Association, consisting of Argentina, Bolivia, Brazil, Chile, Colombia, Ecuador, Paraguay, Peru, Uruguay, and Venezuela. Figures for Mexico included in those for NAFTA

Source: Calculated from figures in International Monetary Fund, *Direction of Trade Statistics* (Washington, D.C.: International Monetary Fund, March 1998), 2–5.

nomic issues led to talk about "Fortress Europe," particularly by U.S. political and corporate leaders concerned over both the implications of the single market and the EC's unwillingness to cut agricultural subsidies.

The concerns have been particularly visible during international trade negotiations held under the auspices of the World Trade Organization (WTO), which replaced the General Agreement on Tariffs and Trade (GATT, founded in 1948) in 1995. GATT oversaw several rounds of negotiations, the lengthiest and most contentious of which was the Uruguay Round, which was launched in 1986 by 105 countries and concluded in 1993. The Community had been involved in several earlier rounds of GATT negotiations, but the Uruguay Round was particularly controversial because it was expanded to include agricultural trade, thereby posing a direct challenge to the most protectionist Community policy area.

Led by the United States, the Community's major trading partners insisted on cuts of 90 percent in export subsidies and of 75 percent in other farm support over a period of ten years, charging that such support gave EC farmers an unfair advantage. The EC initially agreed to only a 30 percent cut in farm subsidies and refused to reform the Common Agricultural Policy (CAP). After teetering several times on the brink of collapse, negotiations finally achieved a breakthrough in 1992, thanks in part to CAP reforms agreed to by the EC, including production and price reductions and a move away from subsidies to farmers based on production (see Chapter 13). The Millennium Round of negotiations is due to be launched during late 1999–early 2000, and the United States is keen to see agriculture at the top of the agenda again. However, the new role of the European Commission as a negotiator on behalf of all the member states will give the EU significantly more influence than it had under the Uruguay Round.

Intra-European trade has grown enormously as a result of integration, but the record of EU trade with other parts of the world has been mixed. The United States remains the EU's largest single trade partner, accounting for 19.7 percent of exports and 19.4 percent of imports, but the balance may change as the United States looks increasingly toward building economic ties with the Pacific Rim. The program for African, Caribbean, and Pacific states (the ACP states—discussed later in this chapter) has invested in building trade with developing countries, but it has had mixed results, and among them the seventy-one ACP states account for barely 4 percent of EU trade. India, China, Japan, and Australasia, meanwhile, are more likely to continue building links among themselves; Japan is the second largest single source of imports to the EU but takes only 5 percent of EU exports. The greatest medium-term possibilities lie in Eastern Europe (with over 127 million consumers and enormous productive potential), while longer-term possibilities lie with Russia and the other former Soviet republics (with about 220 million consumers, massive productive potential, and a wealth of largely untapped natural resources). Building ties with the East and both strengthening and expanding its own internal market are likely to remain the EU's major trade priorities for the foreseeable future.

Relations with the United States

The EU's relationship with the United States has fluctuated as the interests of the two sides have joined and parted. The United States was originally supportive of the idea of European integration, seeing it as a way to build European security as a bulwark against the Soviets and as a means to help West Germany rebuild. Relations cooled during the early 1960s with Konrad Adenauer's dislike of John F. Kennedy and Charles de Gaulle's neuroses regarding Anglo-American relations. They continued to cool as the Europeans disagreed with the United States over Vietnam and as German Chancellor Willy Brandt began to make diplomatic overtures to Eastern Europe. Anti-Americanism grew despite the money, personnel, and resources the United States was still committing to the defense of Western Europe.

The collapse of the Bretton Woods system in 1971 marked the beginning of U.S. withdrawal from responsibility for global leadership; the unilateral decision by the Nixon administration to pull the United States off the gold standard also emphasized to many Europeans U.S. unwillingness to take Europe's position into account. EC economies were rapidly catching up with that of the United States, and the EC was trading less with the United States and more with Eastern Europe. The revival of the European antinuclear movement during the 1980s further strained U.S.-EC relations.

The changing balance was exemplified by the steady withdrawal of the U.S. military forces from Western Europe with the end of the cold war and by the increasing differences of opinion on policy between the two sides; the EC was slow to criticize the 1979 Soviet invasion of Afghanistan, for example, and West Germany was the only EC member to support the U.S.-led boycott of the 1980 Moscow Olympics. Europeans have also been more critical than the United States of Israeli policy in the occupied territories, the U.S. was disappointed by the lukewarm response of some EC members to the Gulf crises during 1990–1991 and again in 1998, and the two sides have disagreed over policy in the Balkans and over how much to cut farm subsidies (their disagreements during the final stages of the Uruguay Round of GATT negotiations were symptomatic of the growing economic power of the EC relative to that of the United States).[6]

None of these differences is a surprise, because adjustments such as these would inevitably result from a reassertion of European economic and military influence, the relative decline of U.S. influence, and the recalculation of the balance of power in the vacuum left by the collapse of the USSR. Con-

BOX 15.2
Cuba, the Europeans, and the Americans

Although the political and economic relationship between the United States and the European Union is normally strong, the two sides have not always agreed, as illustrated by the ongoing dispute over European agricultural subsidies. Particular criticism has been directed at the EU by the United States over the matter of the banana trade; the EU favors bananas from its former Caribbean colonies over those from Latin America, which are distributed mainly by U.S. corporations. The U.S. threatened to impose 100 percent duties on a wide selection of imports from the EU unless the EU opened its market to Latin American bananas. With WTO prompting, the EU conceded in April 1999.

However, the biggest controversy during recent years was a political dispute grounded in U.S. policy on Cuba, Libya, Iran, and other so-called pariah states. It began in March 1996, when President Clinton signed into law the Cuban Liberty and Democratic Solidarity Act, otherwise known—after its two principal sponsors—as the Helms-Burton Act. It was ostensibly a response to the Cuban government's downing of two civilian aircraft associated with the movement against Cuban leader Fidel Castro, and its objective was to increase the economic pressure for political change in Cuba by discouraging foreign investment in land and property expropriated by the Castro regime. Had it applied only to the United States, the matter might have ended there, but it made provision for foreign companies investing in Cuba to be sued in U.S. courts and for executives from those companies to be barred from entry into the United States.

Helms-Burton was heavily criticized by the major trading partners of the United States, notably Canada and Japan, and was met with outrage in the EU, which threatened sanctions against U.S. firms and citizens. The passage of Helms-Burton was widely seen as a domestic political ploy by Bill Clinton as he prepared to run for a second term and worked to court the influential Cuban-Hispanic vote in large southern states such as Florida and Texas. It added fuel to the flames of a preexisting transatlantic dispute over another U.S. law requiring that sanctions be imposed on foreign firms investing in the oil industries of Iran and Libya. A disputes panel was set up within the World Trade Organization to investigate, and regular meetings took place between U.S. trade representatives and the European Commission. The problem was finally resolved in May 1998 when the United States agreed to a progressive lifting of the sanctions imposed on European companies and to waive the ban on European executives entering the United States.

tacts between the United States and the EC were regularized during 1989–1990 following the signing in November 1990 of their Transatlantic Declaration, committing the two sides to regular high-level contacts at a time when the United States was becoming concerned over Europe's growing volatility. In 1995, the New Transatlantic Agenda and Joint EU-U.S. Action Plan were adopted, whereby the two sides agreed to move from consultation to joint action aimed at promoting peace and democracy around the world, contributing to the expansion of world trade, and improving transatlantic ties. Biannual meetings now take place between the presidents of the United States, the Commission, and the European Council, between the U.S. secretary of state and EU foreign ministers, and between the Commission and members of the U.S. Cabinet.

The two sides have had their policy differences (see Box 15.2), and President Clinton made a number of overtures to Pacific Rim states during the mid-1990s, but the interests of the United States and Western Europe continue to overlap at almost every turn. The EU remains a major U.S. ally, the largest market for U.S. exports, the largest destination of U.S. foreign investment, and the largest source of foreign direct investment in the United States. However, as economic issues replace military security as the key element in the transatlantic relationship, and as the power of the EU grows and the United States looks increasingly to Latin America and Asia, the United States will need to redefine the balance between prosperity and security and bring economic issues to bear in its relationship with Europe.[7]

Relations with Eastern Europe

EU relations with Central and Eastern European countries (CEECs in Eurospeak) have strengthened so rapidly during the past few years that the EU is now the major source of Western aid for the Eastern bloc, and several CEECs have applied for membership in the EU. The Europeans moved very quickly in response to changes in Eastern Europe, agreeing to a joint policy at the December 1988 Rhodes European Council. Within three months of taking office in January 1989, U.S. President George Bush was describing Western Europe as an economic magnet that could pull Eastern Europe toward a new commonwealth of free nations, and the United States began to encourage the EC to take responsibility for coordinating Western economic aid to the East. This was formalized at the 1989 G7 meeting, and a program was launched in December 1989 to help with economic restructuring in Poland and Hungary (the program is known as PHARE for *Pologne-Hongrie: Actions pour la Reconversion Economique*; in French, *phare* also means "lighthouse"). PHARE has since been extended to other Eastern European states and to the Baltic states, channeling 5.3 billion ecus to the east during the period 1990–1995.

Trade and cooperation agreements have been signed with almost all of the Eastern European states, several billion dollars in loans have been made available by the European Investment Bank, the EU has sent food aid east, and several functional programs have been launched to help Eastern European social reform (including help in upgrading university departments under the Tempus program). Another step was taken in 1990 with the creation of the European Bank for Reconstruction and Development, which has channeled public money from the EU, the United States, and Japan to help develop the private sector in the East. The Commission now coordinates the aid efforts of the G–24 countries: the EU, what remains of the European Free Trade Association, as well as the United States, Canada, Japan, Australia, New Zealand, and Turkey. The EU's leading role in this program has not only helped build EU foreign policy but has also made the EU a major independent actor in the economic and political future of Eastern Europe.

With the end of the cold war, a growing number of requests was made from the East for associate or full EU membership, and irresistible moral pressure was directed toward the EU to open its doors to eastern expansion. Germany and German chancellor Helmut Kohl were particularly active in promoting this idea, in part because of the country's historical links with the East; the Conservative government in Britain also supported eastern expansion, but it did so mainly to slow down the process of integration. Europe Agreements— a step beyond associate membership—came into force with Hungary and Poland in 1994, with the Czech Republic, Slovakia, Bulgaria, and Romania in 1995, and with the three Baltic states in 1998. In order to help them prepare for membership, "preaccession" strategies have also been agreed with ten CEECs and Cyprus, which will include the spending of 21 billion euros in aid during the period 2000–2006. The Treaty of Amsterdam finally paved the way for eastward expansion, which was confirmed during 1998 when enlargement negotiations began with Hungary, Poland, the Czech Republic, Slovenia, Estonia, and Cyprus. (Slovakia was left out because of concerns over its record on human rights and its slow progress on democratization.)

In 1997, the EU launched Agenda 2000, a working program for the EU until 2006 that lists all the measures that the Commission believes will need to be agreed upon in order to bring ten CEECs into the EU without risking institutional paralysis and substantially increasing costs for existing members. The measures include reform of the structural funds to make sure that they are spent in the regions of greatest need, reducing subsidies under the CAP, and a new focus for PHARE on training local specialists in fields such as law and administration. The Commission also used Agenda 2000 to make a new appeal for institutional reform, including a reweighting of votes in the Council of Ministers, a limit of one Commissioner per member state, and the convening of a new intergovernmental conference by 2002 at the latest to overhaul the EU decisionmaking process in preparation for enlargement.

Development Cooperation

Since most larger European states at one time or another had colonial empires, they have historically had close cultural, economic, and political links with the South: Latin America, southern Asia, and Africa. The result is that these regions play a prominent part in the EU's foreign policy considerations, most notably in its development-aid program. EU policy toward the South is based partly on concerns about quality-of-life issues, such as poverty and hunger, but altruism is also a factor. The South accounts for 34 percent of EU exports (half again as much as the United States and Japan combined), over one-fifth of exports from the South go to the EU, and the EU continues to rely on the South for key raw materials imports such as oil, rubber, copper, and uranium. The EU in 1997 provided about $4.8 billion in development aid, adding to the over $26 billion in bilateral flows of aid from each of the member states.

The EU aid program takes several forms. In addition to allowing all Southern states to export industrial products to the EU tariff- and duty-free (subject to some limits on volume), the EU provides food and emergency aid and sponsors development projects undertaken by nongovernmental organizations. The EU has also negotiated a series of cooperative agreements with selected former colonies (mainly the non-Asian former colonies of Britain and France). They began with the 1963 and 1969 Yaoundé Conventions (named for the capital of Cameroon where they were signed), which gave eighteen former colonies of the original six EEC member states preferential access to Community markets. The eighteen states in turn allowed the Community limited duty-free or quota-free access to their markets. The process was expanded by the series of Lomé Conventions (named for the capital of Togo), the first three (each lasting five years) being signed in 1975, 1979, and 1984; Lomé IV was signed in 1989 to cover the period 1990–2000 and to do the following:

1. Provide financial aid to 71 ACP states (see Figure 15.3) under the European Development Fund, mainly grants for development projects as well as low-interest loans. The amount available under the fund increased from 7.5 billion ecus ($9.0 billion) under Lomé III to just over 14.6 billion ecus ($17.5 billion) for the last five years of Lomé IV (1995–2000).
2. Allow ACP states to export almost anything to the EU duty-free, with the exception of agricultural products covered by the CAP.
3. Provide an insurance fund, called Stabex, for ACP exports. The goal is to offset declines in the value of fifty specified ACP agricultural exports. If prices fall below a certain level, Stabex will make up the deficit. If they go above that level, ACP countries invest the profits in the fund for future use.

Opinions are mixed on the efficacy of the ACP program. On the one hand, the EU has become the biggest source of official development assistance in the world, with its member states collectively accounting for 45–50 percent of the total in 1998[8] (compared to 20 percent from the United

FIGURE 15.3   The ACP states

AFRICA (47)	Madagascar	Bahamas
Angola	Malawi	Barbados
Benin	Mali	Barbuda
Botswana	Mauritania	Belize
Burkina Faso	Mauritius	Dominica
Burundi	Mozambique	Dominican Republic
Cameroon	Namibia	Grenada
Cape Verde	Niger	Guyana
Central African Republic	Nigeria	Haiti
Chad	Rwanda	Jamaica
Comoros	Sao Tome and Principe	St. Christopher and Nevis
Congo	Senegal	St. Lucia
Congo (Democratic	Seychelles	St. Vincent and
Republic)	Sierra Leone	Grenadines
Djibouti	Somalia	Suriname
Equatorial Guinea	South Africa	Trinidad and Tobago
Ethiopia	Sudan	
Gabon	Swaziland	*PACIFIC (8)*
Gambia	Tanzania	Fiji
Ghana	Togo	Kiribati
Guinea	Uganda	Papua New Guinea
Guinea Bissau	Zambia	Solomon Islands
Ivory Coast	Zimbabwe	Tonga
Kenya		Tuvalu
Lesotho	*CARIBBEAN (16)*	Vanuatu
Liberia	Antigua	Western Samoa

States and 18 percent from Japan), it has built closer commercial ties between the EU and the ACP states, and there has been an overall increase in ACP exports to Europe. However, oil accounts for a large part of the total export volume, Stabex does not help countries that do not produce the specified commodities, the European Development Fund becomes relatively small when it is divided up seventy-one ways, and the ACP program excludes larger Southern states (such as India and China) that have negotiated separate agreements with the EU. Additionally, too little attention has been paid to the environmental implications of the focus on cash crops for export, and the program has neither helped address the ACP debt crisis nor really changed the relationship between the EU and the ACP states.[9]

Lomé IV included an attempt to push EU policy in new directions by adding a structural adjustment element to ACP aid; in other words, it now encourages economic diversification in the ACP states rather than simply providing project aid. This has made the EU more like the International Monetary Fund or the World Bank as a significant financial actor in international economic relations,[10] but whether this will improve prospects for the South remains to be seen. Negotiations opened in September 1998 between the EU and the ACP states and aimed at replacing the Lomé Convention with a more flexible structure based around a series of interregional free trade agreements between groups of ACP countries and the EU. The goal is to bring them into force from 2005 and to allow an additional ten to fifteen years for full application.

Summary and Conclusions

The process of European integration has become increasingly extroverted with time. From an era in which it focused mainly on internal economic integration, the EU has had to look increasingly outward and toward building common positions on foreign security and economic policies. The process has steadily gained more consistency and regularity, and the CFSP now makes up one of the three "pillars" that constitute the European Union. However, the EU finds itself trying to build a wider base of common foreign, security, and trade policies at a time of great change in the world.

One of the sparks that led to the creation of the EU was the relatively definable security threat posed by the Soviet Union, but that threat has since been replaced by less easily definable economic issues and by dilemmas over how to approach more localized security problems such as the crises in the Balkans. The EU is developing the seeds of a common army in the form of Eurocorps, but only five of the fifteen member states have so far become involved. Some prefer to maintain their neutrality, while others have different sets of priorities, conflicting opinions regarding the U.S. role in European defense, and varied positions on the future status of NATO, the OSCE, and the WEU. The EU has two of the five permanent seats on the UN Security Council (through Britain and France), it has a nuclear capability (again through Britain and France), and the armed forces of its fifteen members add up to substantial firepower, but the achievement of a common European defense policy has so far proved elusive.

Even though the EU is not yet a global military power, it has become the preeminent global economic power. Not only is it the source of over one-third of global exports and the market for over one-third of global imports; it has agreed to a Common Commercial Policy, and the Commission represents the member states in negotiations under the auspices of the World Trade Organization. If the promise of the single European currency, the euro, is fulfilled, the EU is likely to find itself taking on the mantle of global economic leadership during the twenty-first century, making the need to build a common defense capability all the more urgent.

Further Reading

Michael Smith and Stephen Woolcock. *Redefining the US-EC Relationship* (New York: Council on Foreign Relations Press, 1993).

A brief assessment of the causes and possible consequences of changes in relations between the EU and the United States that compares their relative responses to security issues and the global economy.

Richard G. Whitman. *From Civilian Power to Superpower? The International Identity of the European Union* (New York: St. Martin's Press, 1998).

A study of EU foreign policy which argues that the EU has become a significant actor in global politics without transforming itself into a nation-state.

G. Wyn Rees. *The Western European Union at the Crossroads: Between Transatlantic Solidarity and European Integration* (Boulder: Westview Press, 1998).

The first full-length study of the WEU, assessing both its development and its current role in European defense.

Carolyn Rhodes (Ed). *The European Union in the World Community* (Boulder: Lynne Rienner, 1998).

An edited collection that looks at the EU as an actor in international affairs, focusing on security, trade issues, and relationships with particular regions of the world.

Notes

1. For details, see Stephanie B. Anderson, "Problems and Possibilities: The Development of the CFSP From Maastricht to the 1996 IGC," in Pierre-Henri Laurent and Marc Maresceau (Eds), *The State of the European Union Vol. 4: Deepening and Widening* (Boulder: Lynne Rienner, 1998).

2. Christopher Hill, "EPC's Performance in Crises," in Reinhardt Rummel (Ed.), *Toward Political Union: Planning a Common Foreign and Security Policy in the European Community* (Boulder, CO: Westview Press, 1992), 135-136.

3. Clive Archer and Fiona Butler, *The European Community: Structure and Process* (New York: St. Martin's Press, 1992), 173.

4. *The Economist*, February 2, 1991.

5. Joseph I. Coffey, "WEU After the Second Maastricht," in Laurent and Maresceau, *State of the European Union.*

6. Michael Smith and Stephen Woolcock, *Redefining the US-EC Relationship* (New York: Council on Foreign Relations Press, 1993), 2.

7. Ibid., 7.

8. "Europa," home page, 1998, URL: <http://europa.eu. int/pol/dev/en/info.htm>.

9. For a discussion of the problems with the ACP program, see Archer and Butler, *The European Community*, Chapter 8.

10. Carol Cosgrove and Pierre-Henri Laurent, "The Unique Relationship: The European Community and the ACP," in John Redmond (Ed.), *The External Relations of the European Community* (New York: St. Martin's Press, 1992).

Conclusions:
Into the
Twenty-First Century

The European Union was born out of the rubble of the most devastating war the world has ever known. It took its first tentative steps during an era that was divided by potentially fatal ideological tensions and that saw the end of colonialism and the construction of a global economy. Against a background of momentous change, Europeans embarked on an experiment in regional integration that obliged them to redefine both their place in the world and their attitudes toward one another. The experiment stumbled occasionally, made a few significant breakthroughs, sometimes seemed about to fulfill the prophecies of the skeptics, and at other times left them eating their words. The result was the creation of the European Union.

Fifty years on, much remains to be done, and there is no certainty about what the EU will become. As the new millennium opens, Europeans find themselves faced with difficult choices that may give the EU more definition but may also detract from its past achievements. Many of those decisions are being forced on the EU by the need to adapt itself to eastward expansion and the growth of membership from fifteen countries to twenty or more. An organization designed around its six founding members must do some substantial rethinking in order to catch up with the changes that have come since the Single European Act. At least seven major issues will be on the agenda as the new millennium progresses.

First, institutions will need to be reformed and the democratic deficit closed. The EU has bred five major institutions and a cluster of subsidiary bodies to deal with specific issues. None of these institutions has been static; their powers and character have changed as the process of integration has evolved, as the demands made on them have grown, and as the relationships among them have been reshaped. More change is to come as "the government of Europe" is given clearer definition:

- Particularly in response to the crisis of March 1999, there will be pressure to make the Commission more transparent and accountable by democratizing the process by which commissioners and the president are chosen; there will also be pressure to rethink the distribution of positions as more new member states join the EU.
- There will be a need to reconsider the place of the Council of Ministers and to make its deliberations more open, democratic, and representative; there will be pressure to rethink the Council's system of voting as the EU expands; the role of the presidency of the EU will also change as membership of the EU grows.
- The powers of the European Parliament will likely grow in light of increasing demands for accountability, the Parliament will become more like a true legislature, national political parties will, it is hoped, become more adept at running European election campaigns, and the search for majority parties in the Parliament will continue; at the same time, the national quotas of seats will need to be recalculated.
- The influence of the Court of Justice will grow in tandem with the breadth and depth of European law.
- The tension between supranationalism and intergovernmentalism will encourage a redefinition of both the role of the European Council and the relationship among the five major institutions.

One of the most glaring deficiencies of the European Union is the gap between popular will and the goals of the elites who have made most of the key decisions relating to European integration. As the EU becomes more real to more Europeans and its decisions more strongly affect their lives, popular pressure for more direct input into EU decisionmaking will surely grow. Among the institutions that are ripest for reform are the Council of Ministers and the Commission.

Second, adjustments will need to be made in light of eastward enlargement. There are twenty-four potential new members: three in Western Europe (Norway, Iceland, and Switzerland), three in the Mediterranean (Malta, Cyprus, and Turkey), twelve in Eastern Europe (including the five states of the former Yugoslavia), and six in the former Soviet Union. About half of these states have realistic short- to medium-term possibilities for membership. The next enlargement will focus on Poland, the Czech Republic, Hungary, Slovenia, Estonia, and Cyprus; this will change the economic, political, cultural, and geographic balance of the Union and make more urgent the need to reform the EU's institutions and decisionmaking processes.

Third, the EU must address the problem of unemployment, one of the most glaring failures of both domestic and European economic policy. Allied to this failure is the disparity in the levels of unemployment among the EU member states, which are highest on the southern and western margins and in the old industrial areas and lowest in the increasingly affluent center. Amsterdam moved employment policy farther up the EU agenda, but the EU must still achieve sustained economic growth and create millions of new jobs, ensure that most of those jobs are created in the areas hardest hit by recession, and continue promoting the kinds of education and training needed to help maintain Europe's competitiveness in the global market.

Fourth, to give it a solid base from which to compete as an actor in the global market, the EU will need to continue to emphasize the building of European corporate, transportation, and communications networks. This will mean anticipating more corporate mergers, liberalizing telecommunications, building a European data-transmission network, and creating a European energy generation and supply system.

Fifth, the construction of a true economic union remains high on the agenda of priorities. Despite much skepticism about the chances of success, eleven member states have committed themselves to the single currency and have taken a leap into the unknown. At one level, a single currency makes good sense, as it means the final completion of the single market; at another level, it has already caused some member states problems as they have lost freedom of movement to deal with inflation, budget deficits, exchange rates, and national deficits, and it may yet cause more difficulties in the lead-up to 2002.

Sixth, the EU must begin to take care of its own security needs. As it becomes more assertive and confident, its relationship with the United States and its place within NATO will change so as to reduce dependence on the U.S. security blanket and compel the building of a fourth "pillar": common defense policies and a common defense force. The seeds of a security union have already been planted, and crises in the Middle East and the Balkans have emphasized both the policy fault lines in the European military capacity and the urgency of creating the ability to respond to future emergencies. However, a security union will not be developed without a resolution of several key problems:

- Policy differences among the EU member states, notably the neutrality of some, the independent nature of others, and the different spheres of influence and interest of the most powerful member states (Britain and the Commonwealth, France and its former colonies, Germany and Eastern Europe).
- Agreement on the role Germany will play. How long will it take for other Europeans to be comfortable with the prospect of German

troops on their soil or of German troops being sent into neighboring trouble spots such as the Balkans?

- Agreement on the relative contributions of the different member states. Will the bigger powers such as Britain, France, and Italy agree to bear the largest share of the burden?
- Agreement on the relationship between the EU and other preexisting security arrangements, notably NATO and the OSCE.
- Agreement on a new balance in the tripartite relationship among the EU, the United States, and Russia. What effect will Europe's failure to always agree with U.S. foreign and defense policy have on the transatlantic relationship?

Finally, there is the controversial issue of political union. In a sense, everything that has happened since the Schuman Declaration has been a preamble to this. Such a union is now virtually inevitable; the only questions concern the time it will take, the membership, and the structure of the union. It may be federal, confederal, or consociational, or it may be an entirely new form of association tailored to meet the needs of what is, after all, a unique situation. It may be a true political union with all members moving together at the same speed, or it may be a multispeed Europe with members moving toward the same ultimate goal but at a different pace. Some want Europe à la carte—with governments picking and choosing the policies they want to adopt—while others want an equal commitment by every member state.

Whatever form it takes, European political union *will* happen for at least four reasons: The EU experiment has brought peace and prosperity, Europeans have too much in common to allow their differences to act as an insurmountable barrier, Europeans are tied with knots and bonds that are far too complex to be easily unraveled, and European integration has developed an irresistible speed and momentum. The train left the station long ago, and even though the ride may be bumpy, the destination unclear, the design of the engine uncertain, and the relationship among the engineer, the guards, and the passengers still evolving, it is too late for anyone to leave the train.

List of Acronyms

ACP	African, Caribbean, and Pacific states
BEU	Benelux Economic Union
CAP	Common Agricultural Policy
CEECs	Central and Eastern European Countries
CFSP	Common Foreign and Security Policy
CoR	Committee of the Regions
COREPER	Committee of Permanent Representatives
DG	directorate-general
EAGGF	European Agriculture Guidance and Guarantee Fund
EBRD	European Bank for Reconstruction and Development
EC	European Community
ECB	European Central Bank
ECSC	European Coal and Steel Community
ecu	European Currency Unit
EDC	European Defence Community
EEA	European Economic Area/European Environment Agency
EEC	European Economic Community
EFTA	European Free Trade Association
EIB	European Investment Bank
EMEA	European Agency for the Evaluation of Medicinal Products
EMI	European Monetary Institute
EMS	European Monetary System
EMU	economic and monetary union
EP	European Parliament
EPC	European Political Cooperation
EPP	European People's Party
ERDF	European Regional Development Fund
ERM	Exchange Rate Mechanism
ESC	Economic and Social Committee
ESF	European Social Fund
EU	European Union
GAC	General Affairs Council
GATT	General Agreement on Tariffs and Trade
GDP	gross domestic product
GNP	gross national product
IGC	intergovernmental conference

IGO	intergovernmental organization
IMF	International Monetary Fund
INGO	international nongovernmental organization
IO	international organization
MEP	Member of the European Parliament
NAFTA	North American Free Trade Agreement
NATO	North Atlantic Treaty Organization
OECD	Organization for Economic Cooperation and Development
OEEC	Organization for European Economic Cooperation
OSCE	Organization for Security and Cooperation in Europe
PR	proportional representation
QMV	qualified majority vote
SAP	Social Action Programme
SEA	Single European Act
TEN	Trans-European Network
VAT	value-added tax
WEU	Western European Union
WTO	World Trade Organization

Chronology of
European Integration

1944	July	Representatives from forty-four countries meet at Bretton Woods, New Hampshire, to plan the postwar global economy
1945	May	Germany surrenders; European war ends
	June	Creation of United Nations
1946	March	Churchill makes his "iron curtain" speech at Fulton, Missouri
1947	March	Announcement of the Truman Doctrine
	June	U.S. Secretary of State George Marshall offers Europe aid for economic recovery
	September	Sixteen countries join the European Recovery Program
	October	General Agreement on Tariffs and Trade signed in Geneva; enters into force January 1948
1948	January	Benelux customs union created
	March	Mutual defense treaty (Treaty of Brussels) signed in Brussels by Britain, France, and the Benelux states
	April	Organization for European Economic Cooperation founded
	May	Congress of Europe held in The Hague
	June	Soviets impose blockade of West Berlin, sparking a year-long airlift of supplies from the West
1949	April	North Atlantic Treaty signed in Washington, D.C.
	May	Council of Europe founded; formalization of division of Germany
1950	May	Schuman Plan published
	October	Publication of plan outlining the European Defence Community
1951	April	Treaty of Paris signed, creating the European Coal and Steel Community
1952	March	Nordic Council founded
	May	The six ECSC members sign a draft treaty creating the European Defence Community
	August	ECSC comes into operation
1953	November	Plans announced for a European Political Community
1954	April	French defeat in Indochina
	August	Plans for European Defence Community and European Political Community collapse

	October	Paris Agreement signed, creating the Western European Union
1955	May	Western European Union comes into operation, headquartered in London
	June	Meeting of ECSC foreign ministers in Messina agrees to take the next step in European integration
1956	October	Soviet invasion of Hungary
	October–December	Suez crisis
1957	March	Treaties of Rome signed, creating Euratom and the European Economic Community
1958	January	Euratom and EEC come into operation
	February	Treaty creating the Benelux Economic Union signed in The Hague
	July	Conference in Stresa, Italy, works out details of Common Agricultural Policy
1960	January	Seven countries sign European Free Trade Association Convention in Stockholm, which comes into force in May
	November	Benelux Economic Union comes into force
	December	OEEC reorganized to become Organization for Economic Co-operation and Development
1961	February	First summit of EEC heads of government
	July	Greece becomes associate member of EEC
	August	Britain, Ireland, and Denmark apply for EEC membership; construction begins on Berlin Wall
1962	April	Norway applies for EEC membership
1963	January	De Gaulle vetoes British membership in the Community; France and Germany sign Treaty of Friendship and Co-operation
1965	April	Merger Treaty signed, establishing a single Commission and Council for the three European Communities
	July	France begins boycott of Community institutions (the "empty chair" crisis)
1966	January	Agreement on Luxembourg Compromise
	May	Britain, Ireland, and Denmark apply for EEC membership for the second time
	July	Norway applies for EEC membership for the second time; Merger Treaty comes into force
1967	December	De Gaulle vetoes British membership in the Community for the second time
1968	July	Agreement on a common external tariff completes the creation of an EEC customs union; agreement on Common Agricultural Policy
1970	June	Membership negotiations opened with Britain, Denmark, Ireland, and Norway; concluded in January 1972
1971	August	Richard Nixon takes the United States off the gold standard, signaling the end of the Bretton Woods system of fixed exchange rates

1972	April	Launch of the European exchange rate stabilization system (the "snake")
	September	National referendum in Norway goes against membership in the Community
1973	January	Britain, Denmark, and Ireland join the Community, bringing membership to nine
1974	January	Creation of the European Social Fund
1975	January	Creation of the European Regional Development Fund
	March	First meeting of the European Council in Dublin
	June	Greece applies for Community membership; negotiations open in July 1976
1977	March	Portugal applies for Community membership; negotiations open in October 1978
	July	Spain applies for Community membership; negotiations open in February 1979
1979	March	European Monetary System comes into operation
	June	First direct elections to the European Parliament
1981	January	Greece joins the Community, bringing membership to ten
1984	January	Free trade area established between EFTA and the Community
	June	Second direct elections to the European Parliament
1985	January	Jacques Delors begins his first term as president of the European Commission
1986	January	Spain and Portugal join the Community, bringing membership to twelve
	February	Single European Act signed in Luxembourg
1987	June	Turkey applies to join the Community
	July	Single European Act comes into force
1989	April	Publication of Delors Report on Economic and Monetary Union
	June	Third direct elections to the European Parliament
	July	Austria applies for Community membership
	December	Adoption of the Social Charter by eleven EC member states; rejection of Turkey membership application
1990	June	Schengen Agreement signed by France, Germany, and the Benelux states
	July	Cyprus and Malta apply for Community membership
	October	German reunification brings the former East Germany into the Community
	December	Opening of intergovernmental conferences on economic and monetary union and on political union
1991	December	Treaty on European Union agreed to in Maastricht, signed in February 1992; Europe Agreements signed with Poland, Hungary, and Czechoslovakia
1992	May	France and Germany announce the creation of a 35,000-member Eurocorps
	June	Danish voters reject the terms of Maastricht in a national referendum

1993	January	Creation of the single market
	May	Danish voters accept the terms of Maastricht in a second national referendum; Secretariat of WEU moved from London to Brussels
	November	Treaty on European Union comes into force; the European Community becomes one of three "pillars" of a new European Union
1994	January	Creation of the European Economic Area and the European Monetary Institute
	March	Poland and Hungary become associate members of the EU
	May	Opening of the Channel tunnel linking Britain and France
	June	Fourth direct elections to the European Parliament; public referendum in Austria favors EU membership
	October	Public referendum in Finland favors EU membership
	November	Public referendum in Sweden favors EU membership, but referendum in Norway rejects membership
1995	January	Austria, Finland, and Sweden join the European Union, bringing membership to fifteen
	March	Schengen Agreement comes into force
	June	Europol Convention signed
1997	October	Treaty of Amsterdam signed
1998	March	Decision to open negotiations on EU membership with the Czech Republic, Cyprus, Estonia, Hungary, Poland, and Slovenia
	June	Establishment of the European Central Bank
1999	January	Adoption of single currency by eleven EU member states
	March	President Jacques Santer and College of Commissioners resign following publication of a report alleging fraud, nepotism, and cronyism in the Commission.
	May	Treaty of Amsterdam comes into force
	June	Fifth direct elections to the European Parliament

Glossary

This Glossary contains brief definitions of key terms relating to the European Union and the process of European integration.

Acquis communitaire. A collective term for all the laws and regulations adopted by the EU.

Assent procedure. The legislative process that ensures that no new members are allowed to join the EU without the support of an absolute majority of members of the European Parliament.

Association agreements. Agreements signed between the EU and non-EU states under which those states are given associate membership in the EU, which allows them preferential access to the EU market without being directly involved in EU government or policymaking. See also **Europe Agreements.**

Benelux. A collective term for Belgium, the Netherlands, and Luxembourg.

Bretton Woods system. A plan worked out at a 1944 meeting in Bretton Woods, New Hampshire, among representatives of forty-four countries. Based on U.S. leadership, it was aimed at establishing international management of the global economy, stable exchange rates, low tariffs, and aid to war-damaged economies.

Codecision procedure. The legislative process whereby the Council of Ministers cannot make a final decision on new laws without giving the European Parliament the opportunity for a third reading. Its increased use in recent years has almost made the two bodies "colegislatures."

Cohesion. The goal of ensuring that the development of the European Union closes the social and economic differences between the poorer and richer regions of the Union.

Common Agricultural Policy. An agricultural price support system incorporated in the EEC Treaty that originally supported guaranteed prices to Community farmers for their produce but that has since shifted toward providing compensation for taking land out of production.

Common Foreign and Security Policy. The process introduced by Maastricht under which the EU works toward agreeing on common foreign and defense policy positions.

Common market. See **Single market.**

Confederalism. An administrative system whereby independent political units come together for mutual convenience and cooperate on issues of mutual interest while retaining sovereignty and control over their own affairs.

Consociationalism. A system of administration often proposed for small or deeply divided societies that is based on government by a grand coalition, proportional representation for the groups involved, the power of veto for those groups, and the delegation of authority.

Consultation procedure. An arrangement under which the Council of Ministers cannot make a final decision on a new law without giving the European Parliament the opportunity to issue an opinion.

Convergence. The progressive movement of the policies of EU member states toward a common position.

Convergence criteria. The four requirements that EU member states had to meet before being allowed to join the euro. They included controls on national deficits, public debt, consumer inflation, and interest rates.

Cooperation procedure. The legislative process whereby the Council of Ministers cannot make a final decision on new laws without giving the European Parliament the opportunity for a second reading. All but abolished by the Treaty of Amsterdam, under which its use is restricted to economic and monetary issues.

Customs union. An arrangement whereby a group of states agree on a common external tariff on all goods entering the union from outside.

Deepening. The argument that the EU should focus on consolidating integration among existing members before allowing new members to join. Although this seems to contradict arguments in favor of enlargement (see **Widening**), the two are now seen less as alternatives and more as two sides of the same coin.

Democratic deficit. The gap between the powers of EU institutions and the ability of EU citizens to influence those institutions. In other words, the argument that there is too little of a democratic nature in the way the members of EU institutions (other than the European Parliament) are appointed and too little direct accountability and sense of public responsibility among those institutions.

Economic and monetary union. The process by which the EU worked toward the goals of establishing fixed exchange rates and common monetary policies in preparing for the adoption of a single currency.

Eurocrat. A nickname for EU bureaucrats, particularly those who work in the European Commission.

Europe Agreements. Agreements signed between the EU and selected Eastern European states that allow for gradual movement toward free trade and are seen as a first step toward eventual EU membership for those states.

European currency unit. A unit of account calculated on the basis of a basket of EU currencies that provided an anchor for the **Exchange Rate Mechanism**. Replaced in 1999 with the euro.

Eurosclerosis. A term used to describe the apparent lack of growth or progress in European integration during the early 1970s and that has since been used to describe any indications that the members of the European Union are failing to agree.

Exchange Rate Mechanism. An arrangement under the European Monetary System by which EU member states agreed to take whatever action was needed to keep the value of their currencies relatively stable against those of the other EU member states. Seen as a key step in the process of building a single European currency.

Federalism. An administrative arrangement whereby central and local levels of government coexist, with independent powers over particular policy areas.

Free trade. An arrangement whereby the barriers to trade between or among states are either reduced or removed.

Functionalism. A theory that argues that states can promote cooperation by working together in selected functional areas (such as the management of coal and steel) and that the ties they build will compel them to cooperate in other areas as well.

Government. The exercise of influence and authority over a group of people, either through law or coercion. Also used to describe the body of people and institutions that exercise that power.

Gross national product. The total value of all goods and services produced by a state, including the value of its overseas operations (gross domestic product is a measure that excludes the latter). The basic measure of the absolute wealth of a state.

Harmonization. The goal of standardizing national legislation in EU member states in the interest of promoting competition and free trade. Involves removing legal and fiscal barriers to competition and free trade.

Intergovernmentalism. The phenomenon by which decisions are reached by cooperation among governments. Usually applied to the Council of Ministers and the European Council. Contrast with **Supranationalism**.

Internal market. See **Single market**.

Luxembourg Compromise. An arrangement worked out in 1966 following a crisis set off by Charles de Gaulle's concerns about the accumulation of powers by the European Commission. The "compromise" allowed member states to veto proposals when they believed their national interests were at stake.

Mutual recognition. Agreement that if a product or service can be lawfully produced and marketed in one EU member state, it should be allowed to be marketed in any other member state.

Neofunctionalism. A variation on the theme of functionalism, which argues that certain prerequisites are needed before functional cooperation can lead to integration and that integration takes place through a process of **spillover**: Cooperation in one area creates pressures that lead to integration in others.

Realism. A theory often described as the "traditional" approach to the study of international relations and that dominated the study of that field from the 1940s to the 1960s. It argues that states are the major actors in the world system, that world politics is driven by a struggle for power among states, and that states place national interests, security, and autonomy at the top of their agendas.

Schuman Plan. The plan developed by Jean Monnet and Robert Schuman to coordinate the coal and steel industries of Europe. Announced to the public on May 9, 1950, it led to the creation of the European Coal and Steel Community.

Single market. An area within which there is free movement of goods, services, capital, and people. Also known as a common market or internal market. The term can be applied to a single state (such as the United States) or to a group of states that have removed the necessary barriers.

Sovereignty. The right to own and control. In relation to states, the term is usually used to connote jurisdiction over a territory, but it can also refer to the rights of one person or group relative to those of another (for example, the sovereignty of the people over government).

Spillover. An element of neofunctional theory that suggests that if states integrate in one area, the economic, technical, social, and political pressures for them to integrate in other areas will increase.

State. A community of individuals living within recognized frontiers, adhering to a common body of law, and coming under the jurisdiction of a common government. Also used to describe collectively the officials, laws, and powers of that government.

Structural funds. Funds made available by the EU to promote regional development and economic and social **cohesion**. The structural funds include the European Regional Development Fund, the European Social Fund, the guidance element of the European Agricultural Guidance and Guarantee Fund, and the Cohesion Fund.

Subsidiarity. A guiding principle whereby the EU agrees to take action only in those policy areas that are best dealt with at the EU level rather than at the national or local level.

Supranationalism. A condition whereby decisions are made by a process or an institution that is independent of national governments or as a result of accommodations among national governments; those decisions are binding on the subject governments. Often used to describe the work and tendencies of the European Commission but also of the process of European integration. Contrast with **Intergovernmentalism**.

Transparency. The process by which the documents, decisions, and decisionmaking processes of the EU are made more accessible and understandable to EU citizens.

Value-added tax. A form of sales tax used in most European states and applied to any product whose form has been changed through manufacturing, thereby adding value (for example, steel used to construct a car).

Widening. The argument that EU membership should be extended to other European states. Sometimes also used to describe the expansion of EU powers and/or policy interests.

Appendix I:
Key Institutions Related
to the EU and Europe

Committee of Permanent Representatives (Brussels). A group consisting of the permanent representatives of the EU member states to the Council of Ministers. COREPER meets weekly to vet and discuss proposals for new policies and laws submitted by the European Commission and to reduce the workload of the Council of Ministers.

Committee of the Regions (Brussels). An advisory body that provides representatives of local government units in the EU with a forum in which they can meet, talk, and give opinions on laws and policies to the European Commission and the Council of Ministers. Consists of 222 members nominated by the EU member states for four-year renewable terms.

*Council of Europe (Strasbourg). Founded in 1949 by ten Western European states to promote political cooperation and to complement the economic goals of the Organization for European Economic Cooperation. It remained intergovernmental, however, and has been limited to dealing with issues relating to culture, education, and human rights. Since 1989, it has become a pan-European organization, and its membership has expanded from twenty-three to forty.

Council of Ministers (Brussels). The primary decisionmaking arm of the EU, consisting of the relevant national government ministers of the member states. In consultation with the European Commission and the European Parliament, it makes the final decisions on adopting or rejecting new laws and policies.

Court of Auditors (Luxembourg). Founded in 1977, this is the financial watchdog of the EU, charged with auditing EU accounts and ensuring budgetary responsibility. Headed by fifteen auditors appointed for six-year renewable terms by the governments of the member states.

Court of First Instance (Luxembourg). A subsidiary of the European Court of Justice, created in 1989 to help ease the growing workload of the higher court. Headed by fifteen judges appointed for six-year renewable terms by the governments of the member states.

Economic and Social Committee (Brussels). An advisory body that provides employers, workers, and other sectional interests with a forum in which they can meet, talk, and give opinions on laws and policies to the European Commission, the Council of Ministers, and the European Parliament. Consists of 222 members nominated by the EU member states for four-year renewable terms.

European Atomic Energy Community (Brussels, Luxembourg, and Strasbourg). One of the three original European Communities, created in 1958 as a result of the Treaty of Rome. Charged with promoting the integration of the national atomic energy industries of its member states.

*European Bank for Reconstruction and Development (London). An independent development bank created in 1990, with the majority of its capital coming from the EU. Charged with providing loans, encouraging capital investment, and promoting trade, with a focus on Eastern Europe and the former Soviet Union.

European Central Bank (Frankfurt). Replacing the European Monetary Institute in 1998, the ECB is charged with helping to coordinate the monetary policies of the EU member states and overseeing the conversion to the euro.

European Coal and Steel Community (Luxembourg and Strasbourg). The first of the three original European Communities, created in 1952 as a result of the 1951 Treaty of Paris. Charged with promoting integration of the national coal and steel industries of its member states.

European Commission (mainly Brussels). The primary bureaucratic and executive arm of the EU. With 21,000 staff, it is charged with initiating new laws and policies and overseeing implementation by the member states. Headed by twenty commissioners appointed for five-year renewable terms by the governments of the member states.

European Council (no permanent secretariat). A forum in which the heads of government of the EU member states (or the head of state in the case of France) meet at least twice annually to discuss new policy initiatives and the general direction of the EU.

European Court of Justice (Luxembourg). The primary judicial arm of the EU, charged with interpreting the major treaties and resolving disputes between or among member states, EU institutions, corporations, citizens, and other interested parties. Headed by fifteen judges appointed for six-year renewable terms by the governments of the member states.

European Economic Community (Brussels, Luxembourg, and Strasbourg). One of the three original European Communities, created in 1958 as a result of the Treaty of Rome. Charged with building a common market among its member states and promoting the harmonization of their economic policies. It largely superseded the ECSC and Euratom and became one of the three "pillars" of the European Union.

*European Free Trade Association (Geneva). An alternative free trade area created in 1960 at the urging of Britain, which did not support the implied federalism of the EEC. It originally had seven members, and three more countries eventually joined. All members but Iceland, Liechtenstein, Norway, and Switzerland have since joined the EU.

European Investment Bank (Luxembourg). An autonomous institution set up in 1958 under the Treaty of Rome to promote development in the poorer areas of the EEC through the provision of loans and guarantees. Governed by the finance ministers of the EU member states, it now also provides loans outside the EU.

European Parliament (Strasbourg, Brussels, and Luxembourg). The primary representative arm of the EU, one that is slowly winning more of the lawmaking powers usually associated with a legislature. Charged with discussing and suggesting amendments to EU law before a final decision is made by the Council of Ministers. Consists of 626 members elected for renewable five-year terms by EU voters.

General Agreement on Tariffs and Trade. See World Trade Organization.

Nordic Council (Stockholm and Oslo). Set up in 1952 to promote cooperation and integration among the Nordic states; Denmark, Iceland, Norway, and Sweden were founder-members, and Finland joined in 1955.

North Atlantic Treaty Organization (Brussels). A security organization founded in 1949, consisting of the United States, Canada, thirteen Western European states, and Turkey. Charged with promoting the mutual security of its members from external attack, it commits each of its members to take "such action as it deems necessary" to restore and maintain security in the event of an attack on any one member.

Organization for Economic Cooperation and Development (Paris). An international organization that promotes consultation and coordination on sustainable economic growth, collects and analyzes economic data, and arbitrates negotiations on multilateral agreements. Membership was once restricted to the industrialized countries of Western Europe and North America but has since expanded. Its twenty-nine members now include all fifteen EU member states, the United States, Canada, Japan, Mexico, and Poland.

Organization for European Economic Cooperation. Founded by sixteen Western European states in 1948 to oversee the administration of funds made available under the Marshall Plan. Envisaged by the United States as the possible seed of a European economic and political union, it remained purely intergovernmental and was superseded in 1961 by the Organization for Economic Cooperation and Development.

Organization for Security and Cooperation in Europe (Vienna). A pan-European security body that was created in 1994 to replace the Conference on Security and Cooperation in Europe, set up during the early 1970s to promote pan-European cooperation on trade and on civil and human rights. The OSCE now has fifty-four members (including the United States, Canada, Russia, and every European state except Yugoslavia) and is a self-described "primary instrument for early warning, conflict prevention, crisis management and post-conflict rehabilitation in Europe."

Western European Union (Brussels). A security organization founded in 1954 by Britain and the six members of the ECSC. Moribund for most of its life, it took on new vitality with the end of the cold war, although its precise mission—and its relationship with the EU—remains unclear. It has ten full members and eighteen associate members, observers, and associate partners.

World Trade Organization (Geneva). Founded in 1995 to replace the General Agreement on Tariffs and Trade and to continue promoting the reduction and removal of barriers to global trade. GATT was created in 1947 and oversaw several rounds of multilateral negotiations aimed at reducing tariff and nontariff barriers to trade. More a framework for discussions than an institution, it was given greater institutional solidity with the creation of the WTO.

Appendix II:
Other Experiments in Regional Integration

The European Union is the best-known and the most highly evolved example of regional integration among states to date, but it was neither the first nor is it the only such example. This appendix briefly describes some of the more notable past and current experiments in integration in other parts of the world (NAFTA excluded; see Chapter 1).

Latin America and the Caribbean

Latin American Integration Association (LAIA). All eleven independent states in Latin America except Guyana and Suriname are members of LAIA, which was founded in 1980 with headquarters in Montevideo, Uruguay. It replaced the Latin American Free Trade Association (LAFTA), which was founded in 1960 with a twelve-year timetable for eliminating all trade barriers among its members. LAFTA began by negotiating trade liberalization product by product, reaching agreement in 1967 on across-the-board tariff reductions. However, its plans were undermined by political upheavals in several member states and by their varied levels of economic development.

LAIA abandoned the goal of a free trade area in favor of bilateral preference agreements that would account for the differences in the levels of economic development of its members. To help achieve this goal, its members were divided into three groups: most developed (Argentina, Brazil, Mexico), intermediate (Chile, Colombia, Peru, Uruguay, Venezuela), and least developed (Bolivia, Ecuador, Paraguay). Cuba has been an observer member since 1986.

The Andean Group. Also known as the Andean Common Market, this group was founded in 1969 as a subgroup of LAFTA with headquarters in Lima, Peru. It originally had six members (Bolivia, Chile, Colombia, Ecuador, Peru, and Venezuela), but Chile left in 1976. Mexico has been a working partner since 1972. The Andean Group promotes mutual development through accelerated economic integration, coordinated regional industrial development, regulation of foreign investment, and a common external tariff. Disputes are resolved by an Andean Judicial Tribunal set up in 1980, with one judge from each country serving a six-year term.

Southern Cone Common Market (Mercosur). Mercosur was founded in 1991 by four LAIA members: Argentina, Brazil, Paraguay, and Uruguay. Its goal is to abolish tariffs on 85 percent of internal trade and to agree to a common external tariff. Bolivia, Colombia, Ecuador, Peru, and Venezuela have expressed an interest in joining.

Central American Common Market (CACM). CACM was founded in 1961 with headquarters in Guatemala City, Guatemala. Its original goals were to complete a common market by 1965, to attract industrial capital, and to encourage economic diversification. Although it has helped to reduce trade barriers among its five members (Costa Rica, El Salvador, Guatemala, Honduras, and Nicaragua) and has agreed on a common external tariff for many goods, its progress has been undermined by political disagreements and military conflicts in several of its members. It agreed in 1991 to establish a common external tariff by 1993, but that was delayed. In 1993, all of its members except Costa Rica agreed to create a Central American Trade Zone aimed at reducing tariffs on internal trade.

Caribbean Community and Common Market (CARICOM). Founded in 1973 with headquarters in Georgetown, Guyana, CARICOM superseded the Caribbean Free Trade Area (CARIFTA), founded in 1968 by five former British colonies. It has fourteen member states: Antigua and Barbuda, the Bahamas, Barbados, Belize, Dominica, Grenada, Guyana, Jamaica, Saint Kitts and Nevis, Saint Lucia, Saint Vincent and the Grenadines, Suriname, Trinidad and Tobago, and the British colony of Montserrat. The members have agreed to a customs union with a common external tariff.

CARICOM is helped by the logic of having its mainly small island states pool their resources, but its work began to unravel during the late 1970s because of concern among the poorer members that they were not receiving their fair share of the benefits. In 1981, seven CARICOM members formed their own subregional Organization of Eastern Caribbean States while remaining members of CARICOM. Various target dates for establishing a common external tariff have come and gone with agreement on only selected products.

South and Southeast Asia

Association of Southeast Asian Nations (ASEAN). Founded in 1967 to replace the Association of Southeast Asia (ASA), which was founded in 1961 by Malaya, the Philippines, and Thailand, ASEAN is headquartered in Jakarta, Indonesia. It was founded by Indonesia, Malaysia, the Philippines, Singapore, and Thailand; Brunei joined in 1984, Vietnam in 1995, and Laos and Burma in 1997. From an initial interest in security issues, ASEAN has moved steadily into the areas of economic cooperation and trade, with a view to eventually building a free trade area by 2007. It gained new momentum as a result of the changing balance of power in the region following the Vietnam War and played an important role in ending the Vietnam-Cambodia War. The rapid economic growth of several of its members has given ASEAN new purpose, confidence, and significance.

ASEAN heads of state meet at periodic summits. There are annual meetings of the foreign ministers of member states, and a standing committee conducts business between ministerial meetings. The Secretariat is helped by a secretary general, appointed from one of the member states in three-year rotations.

Asia Pacific Economic Cooperation (APEC). Promoted most actively since 1989 by the United States and Australia, APEC is less an institution than a forum for the discussion of regional economic cooperation among eighteen states on the Pacific Rim: Australia, Canada, Chile, China, Hong Kong, Indonesia, Japan, Malaysia, Mexico, New Zealand, Papua New Guinea, the Philippines, Singapore, South Korea, Taiwan, Thailand, Vietnam, and the United States.

South Asian Association for Regional Cooperation (SAARC). Founded during the early 1980s as a result of growing regional cooperation, SAARC now has seven members: India, Pakistan, Bangladesh, Nepal, Bhutan, Sri Lanka, and the Maldives. They work on "collective self-reliance" in nine specific areas, including agriculture, transport, and telecommunications, and since 1985 the leaders of the seven have met at annual summits rotating among the different countries, with the host country assuming the chairmanship for that year. SAARC has a population of 1.2 billion, or one-fifth of the world's population, but its member states have considerable divisions to overcome, notably tensions between India and Pakistan.

Sub-Saharan Africa

East African Community (defunct). Founded in 1967 with headquarters in Arusha, Tanzania, this organization promoted joint ventures among its three members (Kenya, Tanzania, and Uganda), such as East African Airways and East African Railways and Harbours, which were inherited from the British colonial era. Beginning with the advantage of a single currency already in place and a lingua franca (Swahili), the Community promoted tariff reduction and free trade, and its wealthiest member—Kenya—provided development assistance for Tanzania and Uganda.

The Community began to collapse as a result of the military coup that brought Idi Amin to power in Uganda in 1970, but it had already been weakened by the perception that Kenya was deriving most of the benefits and attracting most of the foreign investment. It broke up in 1977, but there are signs that its former members are now trying to rebuild it.

Economic Community of West African States (ECOWAS). Founded in 1975 with headquarters in Abuja, Nigeria, ECOWAS was set up to promote trade, economic cooperation, self-reliance, the harmonization of agricultural policies, and the free movement of people, services, and capital among its sixteen members: Benin, Burkina Faso, Cape Verde, Gambia, Ghana, Guinea, Guinea-Bissau, Ivory Coast, Liberia, Mali, Mauritania, Niger, Nigeria, Senegal, Sierra Leone, and Togo. Its development has been handicapped in recent years by severe political and economic instability in many of its member states, notably Nigeria, the dominant regional power, and Burkina Faso, Liberia, and Sierra Leone.

Southern African Development Community (SADC). Founded in 1980, the members of SADC were given common cause by trying to reduce their economic dependence on South Africa and to develop a common transport system that would allow its six landlocked members to bypass South African railroads and ports. Headquartered in Gabarone, Botswana, its leaders meet annually to coordinate activities. SADC plans, coordinates, and finances a variety of projects in the areas of agriculture, energy, mining, telecommunications, and regional trade.

It now has fourteen members: Angola, Botswana, Democratic Republic of the Congo, Lesotho, Malawi, Mauritius, Mozambique, Namibia, the Seychelles, South Africa, Swaziland, Tanzania, Zambia, and Zimbabwe. Its prospects for success have been greatly enhanced by the democratic transition in South Africa, which has an economy that is over three times bigger than those of the other SADC members combined. At their August 1995 summit in South Africa, SADC leaders declared their hope of creating a Southern African free trade area by the year 2000 and even eventually setting up a single currency for the region.

Middle East

With a common heritage, language, and religion and similar economic bases, the states of the Middle East would seem ripe for economic integration, but to date the region has made only modest progress, mainly because of political disagreements and instability. A Council of Arab Economic Unity was created in 1957; it met for the first time in 1964 and in 1965 founded the Arab Common Market. Headquartered in Amman, Jordan, membership of the Council is open to all twenty-one members of the Arab League, but only eleven have joined. The Gulf Cooperation Council was founded in 1981 with headquarters in Riyadh, Saudi Arabia, to promote freer trade and closer economic and defense ties among its six members: Bahrain, Kuwait, Oman, Qatar, Saudi Arabia, and the United Arab Emirates.

Appendix III:
Selected Sources of Information

If you are setting out to research the EU, shortage of information will be the least of your problems. Publishing on the EU has become a growth industry, particularly since the mid-1990s, and the flow of new books and journal articles matches both the changes in the powers and reach of the EU, and its growing impact on global politics, economics, and public opinion. The challenge for the researcher lies less in finding material than in making sense of it all and in keeping up with developments. Rather than provide a lengthy bibliography that would quickly go out of date, in this section I provide a very selective list of sources of information, which can be used as the foundation for a more expansive search.

Online Sources

Since the first edition of this book was published in 1996, the internet has changed out of all recognition and continues to evolve so rapidly that it would be a lost cause to list all the best sites here; not only do URLs change, but new sites are constantly created and old ones die. Instead, I would guide you to the following:

Europa <http://europa.eu.int/>. This is the official Web site of the EU, with multiple links to almost every kind of official EU information you could possibly want.
Delegation of the European Commission-US <http://www.eurunion.org/> and **Delegation of the European Commission-Canada** <http://www.eudelcan.org/>. These are the Web sites for the Commission offices in Washington, D.C., and Ottawa, which contain useful links and reading lists.

In addition, you might want to visit my home page at <http://www.iupui.edu/~jmc-cormi/>, where I have set up a short series of links; I hope to keep them updated and add new ones as I find them.

Periodicals and Journals

The Economist. A weekly British news magazine that has stories and statistics on world politics, including a section on Europe (and occasional special supplements on the EU). Contact The Economist, 111 West 57th Street, New York, NY 10019. Tel: (800) 456-6086, or visit the Web site at <http://www.economist.com/>.

The Economist also publishes two series of quarterly reports that are treasure houses of information but very expensive—hence you will probably need to look them up in your nearest research library: *Economist Intelligence Unit Country Reports* (which are published on almost every country in the world and include a series on the EU) and *European Policy Analyst*.

European Voice. A weekly newspaper published in Brussels by *The Economist*; the best single source of news and features on the latest developments in the EU. Contact European Voice, Rue Montoyerstraat 17–19, 1000 Bruxelles, Belgium. Tel: 02–540 9090, or visit the Web site at <http://www.european-voice.com.>.

Journal of Common Market Studies. The main academic journal devoted solely to the EU. Published quarterly, it contains scholarly articles and book reviews. Many other academic journals include articles on the EU; the most consistently useful include *West European Politics, International Organization,* and *Parliamentary Affairs.*

European Union Sources

There are literally dozens of these, an increasing number of which are now available online. Among the best are the following:

Europe. A monthly glossy magazine published by the EU in the United States, containing stories and features on the EU and its member states. Contact Delegation of the European Commission, 2300 M Street NW, Suite 700, Washington, DC 20037. Tel: (800) 627–7961.

Eurecom. A free four-page monthly bulletin of political, economic, and monetary news from the EU, published by the EU office in New York. Contact European Commission, 3 Dag Hammarskjold Plaza, 305 East 47th Street, New York, NY 10017. Tel: (212) 371–3804.

EU pamphlets. The EU publishes a series of short pamphlets on its history, institutions, and policies. Although they are exercises in public relations, many are packed with information, and some are surprisingly honest. All are available free from the Delegations of the European Commission in North America. For the United States, contact the Delegation at 2300 M Street NW, Washington, DC 20037. Tel: (202) 862–9500/1/2, fax: (202) 429–1766. For Canada, contact the Delegation at 111 Albert Street, Suite 330, Ottawa, Ontario K1P 1AS. Tel: (613) 238-6464, fax: (613) 238-1649.

Eurostat News. Published quarterly by the Statistical Office of the European Communities. Contains basic statistical information on the EU, much of which is presented as special issues.

Official Journal of the European Communities. Published daily, this is the authoritative source of information on all EU legislation, Commission proposals for new legislation, decisions and resolutions of the Council of Ministers, debates of the

European Parliament, new actions brought before the Court of Justice, opinions of the Economic and Social Committee, the annual report of the Court of Auditors, and the EU budget. An index is published monthly, with an annual cumulation.

General Report on the Activities of the European Union. The major annual report of the EU, with a record of developments in all of the key EU policy areas and key statistical information.

Bulletin of the European Union. Published monthly, this is the official record of events and policies for all EU institutions. Contains reports on the activities of the Commission and other EU institutions, along with special feature articles. Supplements contain key Commission documents, including proposed legislation.

Directorate-General Documentation. Every DG in the Commission publishes its own periodicals, reports, and surveys, which are too numerous to list here. One of the most useful of the regular publications is the series of biannual *Eurobarometer* opinion polls published by DGX (Information, Communication, and Culture). These polls have been carried out since 1973, mainly to provide EU institutions and the media with statistics on public attitudes toward European issues and European integration. EU Depository Libraries receive copies of every survey.

Eurostat. An acronym for the Statistical Office of the European Communities, Eurostat is based in Luxembourg and collects and collates many different kinds of statistical information from the EU member states. Much of this material is available on computer online services such as CRONOS, REGIO, and COMEXT; all of it is published in the form of yearbooks, surveys, studies, and reports.

Directory of Community Legislation in Force and Other Acts of the Community Institutions. Published annually, with biannual supplements. Lists directives, regulations, and other legislation, as well as internal and external agreements.

EU Information Centers in North America

Most major university and college libraries carry general information on the EU, but some also contain more specialized resources. A series of new "European Union Centers" was created in 1998 aimed at promoting the study of the EU through teaching programs, scholarly research, and outreach activities:

California	Cripps College, the Claremont Colleges, and the University of Southern California
Georgia	University System of Georgia and Georgia Institute of Technology
Illinois	University of Illinois, Urbana-Champaign
Massachusetts	Harvard University
Missouri	University of Missouri, Columbia
New York	New York Consortium for European Studies (New York University, Columbia University, City University of New York, and The New School for Social Research)

North Carolina	University of North Carolina, Chapel Hill and Duke University
Pennsylvania	University of Pittsburgh
Washington	University of Washington, Seattle
Wisconsin	University of Wisconsin, Madison

In addition, EU Depository Libraries are based in academic institutions and receive a wide range of EU publications.

United States

Arizona	University of Arizona, Tucson
Arkansas	University of Arkansas, Little Rock
California	Stanford University, Stanford
	University of California, Berkeley
	University of California, La Jolla
	University of California, Los Angeles
	University of California, San Diego
	University of Southern California, Los Angeles
Colorado	University of Colorado, Boulder
Connecticut	Yale University, New Haven
Florida	University of Florida, Gainesville
Georgia	Emory University, Atlanta
	University of Georgia, Athens (a European Documentation Center, or EDC)
Illinois	Illinois Institute of Technology, Chicago
	Northwestern University, Evanston
	University of Chicago
	University of Illinois, Champaign
Indiana	Indiana University, Bloomington
	University of Notre Dame, South Bend
Iowa	University of Iowa, Iowa City
Kansas	University of Kansas, Lawrence
Kentucky	University of Kentucky, Lexington
Louisiana	University of New Orleans
Maine	University of Maine, Portland
Massachusetts	Harvard Law School, Cambridge
Michigan	Michigan State University, East Lansing
	University of Michigan, Ann Arbor
Minnesota	University of Minnesota, Minneapolis
Missouri	Washington University, St. Louis
Nebraska	University of Nebraska, Lincoln
New Jersey	Princeton University, Princeton
New Mexico	University of New Mexico, Albuquerque
New York	Cornell University, Ithaca
	Council on Foreign Relations, New York City
	New York Public Library, New York City

	New York University Law Library, New York City
	State University of New York at Albany
	State University of New York at Buffalo
North Carolina	Duke University, Durham
Ohio	Miami University of Ohio, Oxford
	Ohio State University, Columbus
Oklahoma	University of Oklahoma, Norman
Oregon	University of Oregon, Eugene
Pennsylvania	Pennsylvania State University, University Park
	University of Pennsylvania, Philadelphia
	University of Pittsburgh
Puerto Rico	University of Puerto Rico, San Juan
South Carolina	University of South Carolina, Columbia
Texas	Texas Christian University, Fort Worth
	University of Texas, Austin
Utah	University of Utah, Salt Lake City
Virginia	George Mason University, Arlington
	University of Virginia, Charlottesville
Washington	University of Washington, Seattle
Washington, D.C.	American University (EDC)
	Library of Congress
Wisconsin	University of Wisconsin, Madison

Canada

Collections in Canada are found either in European Documentation Centers (EDCs), which receive a wide range of EU publications, or in European Reference Centers (ERCs), which have basic EU documentation only. All the following are ERCs unless otherwise indicated.

Alberta	University of Alberta, Edmonton
British Columbia	Simon Fraser University, Burnaby
	University of British Columbia, Vancouver
Manitoba	University of Manitoba, Winnipeg (EDC)
New Brunswick	University of Moncton, Moncton
	University of New Brunswick, Fredericton
Newfoundland	Memorial University of Newfoundland, St. John's
Nova Scotia	Acadia University, Wolfville
	Dalhousie University, Halifax (EDC)
	Brock University, St. Catherine's
	Carleton University, Ottawa (EDC)
	Queen's University, Kingston (EDC)
	Université Laurentienne, Sudbury
	University of Ottawa, Ottawa
	University of Toronto, Toronto (EDC)
	University of Waterloo, Waterloo

	Wilfrid Laurier University, Waterloo
	York University, North York
Prince Edward Island	University of Prince Edward Island, Charlottetown
Quebec	McGill University (EDC)
	Université de Montréal (EDC)
	Université Laval, Ste. Foy (EDC)
	University of Sherbrooke, Sherbrooke
Saskatchewan	University of Regina, Regina
	University of Saskatchewan, Saskatoon (EDC)

Appendix IV:
Summits of European Leaders, 1961–1999

Date	Presidency	Place	Key Agenda Items and Outcomes
Pre–European Council			
Feb. 1961	—	Paris	Appointment of Fouchet Committee on political union
July 1961	—	Bonn	Resolution to hold regular meetings of heads of government
May 1967	—	Rome	Tenth anniversary of Treaty of Rome
Dec. 1969	—	The Hague	Enlargement; new initiatives on monetary union and political cooperation
Oct. 1972	—	Paris	Agreement to complete EMU by 1980 and to work on regional and social policies
Dec. 1973	—	Copenhagen	Called in response to energy crisis
Sept. 1974	—	Paris	Informal meeting to discuss future of EC
Dec. 1974	—	Paris	Decision made to create European Council, hold direct elections to EP
Post–European Council			
1975			
March	Ireland	Dublin	First meeting of European Council; renegotiation of British membership
July	Italy	Brussels	Economic recession; relations with Arab world
December	Italy	Rome	Budget reform; direct elections to EP

311

1976

April	Luxembourg	Luxembourg	EMU and EP elections
July	Netherlands	Brussels	Terrorism; fisheries; appointment of Roy Jenkins as president of Commission; agreement on number and allocation of EP seats
November	Netherlands	The Hague	Trade with Japan

1977

March	UK	Rome	Twentieth anniversary of Treaty of Rome
June	UK	London	EPC; Middle East
December	Belgium	Brussels	Introduction of a European unit of account; budget contributions

1978

April	Denmark	Copenhagen	Fixed date for first EP elections; discussions of EMS
July	Germany	Bremen	Further development of EMS
December	Germany	Brussels	Launch of EMS; agreement to reform CAP

1979

March	France	Paris	Social policy; employment
June	France	Strasbourg	Energy crisis; first appearance of Margaret Thatcher; beginning of renegotiation of British budget contribution
November	Ireland	Dublin	British budget contribution; Iran and Cambodia

1980

April	Italy	Luxembourg	Convergence; British budget contribution
June	Italy	Venice	EPC; Middle East
December	Luxembourg	Luxembourg	EPC

1981

March	Netherlands	Maastricht	Fisheries; economic and social issues
June	Netherlands	Luxembourg	EPC; economic and social issues; first appearance of François Mitterrand
November	UK	London	CAP and dairy policy

1982

March	Belgium	Brussels	EPC; twenty-fifth anniversary of Treaty of Rome
June	Belgium	Brussels	EPC; Middle East
December	Denmark	Copenhagen	Early discussions on single market; first appearance of Helmut Kohl

1983

March	Germany	Brussels	Exchange rate realignment
June	Germany	Stuttgart	Budget reform; Solemn Declaration on European Union
December	Greece	Athens	Budget reform

1984

March	France	Brussels	Budget reform
June	France	Fontainebleau	British rebate and budget reforms agreed on
December	Ireland	Dublin	Internal market; membership of Spain and Portugal

1985

March	Italy	Brussels	Agreement on single market by December 1992
June	Italy	Milan	Agreed to call IGC on institutional reform
December	Luxembourg	Luxembourg	Terms of the Single European Act adopted; decision made to hold only two regular annual meetings of European Council

1986

June	Netherlands	The Hague	Chernobyl; South Africa; EPC; single market issues
December	UK	London	Terrorism; internal security; drugs; asylum

1987

March*	Belgium	Rome	Thirtieth anniversary of Treaty of Rome
June	Belgium	Brussels	Talks on Delors Plan for EMU
December	Denmark	Copenhagen	CAP reform; structural funds

1988

February*	Germany	Brussels	Emergency summit to agree on budget reforms
June	Germany	Hanover	Creation of Delors Committee on EMU
December	Greece	Rhodes	Progress report on SEA

1989

June	Spain	Madrid	EMU debated; first stage adopted
November*	France	Paris	Emergency summit to discuss events in Eastern Europe
December	France	Strasbourg	Endorsed German reunification; approved creation of EBRD; accepted Social Charter; agreed to establish IGC on EMU

1990

April*	Ireland	Dublin I	Agreed on commitment to political union; discussed German reunification
June	Ireland	Dublin II	Agreed to IGC on political union
October*	Italy	Rome I	Set timetable for EMU; decision made to create European central bank; final appearance of Margaret Thatcher
December	Italy	Rome II	Opening of IGCs on EMU and political union

1991

April*	Luxembourg	Luxembourg	Emergency summit to discuss fallout from Gulf War
June	Luxembourg	Luxembourg	Balkan crisis; discussion of draft Treaty on European Union
December	Netherlands	Maastricht	Agreement on Treaty on European Union and timetable for EMU

1992

June	Portugal	Lisbon	Budget; enlargement; Eastern Europe
October*	UK	Birmingham	ERM crisis; new impetus for Maastricht
December	UK	Edinburgh	Agreed on opt-out clauses for Denmark on Maastricht; program of meetings of institutions

1993

June	Denmark	Copenhagen	Progress on single market and GATT trade talks; agreed on enlargement to Eastern Europe
October*	Belgium	Brussels	Guidelines for implementation of Maastricht; Europol; location of seats of institutions
December	Belgium	Brussels	Implementation of Maastricht

1994

June	Greece	Corfu	Signature of Treaties of Accession on enlargement and treaty of cooperation with Russia; failed to agree on new Commission president
July*	Germany	Brussels	Agreement reached on Jacques Santer as Commission president
December	Germany	Essen	white Paper on growth, competitiveness, and unemployment; eastward enlargement

1995

June	France	Cannes	Agreement on creation of Europol; target date of January 1999 set for EMU; aid to Africa
December	Spain	Madrid	Single currency named euro; start date of January 1, 1999 confirmed, enlargement to Eastern Europe

1996

June	Italy	Florence	British beef, unemployment, signature of Europol Convention
December	Ireland	Dublin	Monetary union, the IGC

1997

June	Netherlands	Amsterdam	Signature of the Treaty of Amsterdam, Eastern enlargement, monetary union
November*	Luxembourg	Luxembourg	Employment
December	Luxembourg	Luxembourg	Enlargement

1998

June	UK	Cardiff	Declaration on Kosovo, reform of CAP and the EU budget
October*	Austria	Pörtschach	Development of the EU in light of Eastern enlargement and the launch of the euro
December	Austria	Vienna	As Pörtschach

1999

February*	Germany	Bonn	Agenda 2000; farm spending
March*	Germany	Berlin	Response to the crisis set off by the resignation of the College of Commissioners; negotiations on budgetary reforms.
June	Germany	Cologne	

*Extraordinary meetings (since 1986).